Learn Database Programming
Using SQL of Microsoft Access
Second Edition

Easy Transition

For MS Access 2003,
MS Access 2002 ...

For MS Windows XP,
MS Windows 2000 ...

To Other

SQL Platforms

Eghosa Ugboma
Florida Memorial University

BookSurge Publishing

To download the textbook's database, go to http://www.sqltextbook.com

This textbook has been carefully prepared by the author to meet the underlying goal for writing it – learning database programming using MS Access SQL. The database created for the book's hands-on demonstrations and activities has been tested numerous times during the course of writing the book and the database is deemed complete. The database is neither locked nor protected, and as such, the user can alter the data that are stored in it.

The book is written with good intent to assist the learner master the necessary concepts and skills to becoming an excellent database programmer. However, it should be noted that no book is complete in itself and for that reason, the author is not liable for typographical and grammar errors found in the book, and for invalid results generated from the database. In that regard, the author offers no warranty and he is not responsible for damages that occur in the use of the book and the database. The author reserves the right to make changes to the contents of both the book and the database when the needs arise without formal notice to the public.

Microsoft Windows, Windows XP, Windows 2000, Microsoft Access are all registered trademarks of Microsoft Corporation. Oracle is a registered trademark of Oracle Corporation. The author and the book's publisher are not affiliated in any way with either Microsoft Corporation or Oracle Corporation, and as such, they are distant independent bodies from the corporations.

Library of Congress Catalog Publication Data
Ugboma, Eghosa
Learn Database Programming Using SQL of Microsoft Access *Second Edition*: Easy Transition to Other SQL Platforms / Eghosa Ugboma
Includes Index
ISBN 1-4196-5358-X (pbk)
1. Database Management. 2. Database Programming. 3. Relational Database. 4. Structured Query Language. 5. SQL. 6. MS Access. I Title. II. Eghosa Ugboma

To order the book or additional copies, please contact us
BookSurge Publishing
www.booksurge.com
Toll free: 1-866-308-6235
orders@booksurge.com

Printed in the United States

To download the textbook's database, go to http://www.sqltextbook.com

Dedication

This book is dedicated to my wife Doris Villarmea and my four children, Erasto, Ememgini, Rischi, Euhan, to the memory of my deceased parents, and to all those who have assisted me to become what I am today.

Table of Contents

Table of Contents

Chapter Six
More on Single-Row Functions

Table of Contents

Chapter Seven
Multiple-Row Functions and Results Sets

Chapter Eight
Subqueries

Table of Contents

Chapter Eleven
Manipulating Data in Tables

Table of Contents

Chapter Fourteen
Using VBA Procedures to Establish Database Security

Preface

In recent years, Microsoft (MS) Access has become the most popular relational database management system used in the personal computer (PC) environment. The package works superbly as front-end software and can be used as back-end software for small groups of PC users.

Beginning with MS Access 97 and to date, MS Access software has incorporated many SQL commands and features and has been supporting SQL programming in its own way much as the language is supported by other SQL versions. MS Access supports SQL programming to a very competent level that makes the learner to be professionally ready in the arena of SQL programming. Today, learning and teaching SQL using MS Access is intriguing, knowledge-gathering, and developing the necessary skills, just as leaning and teaching the language using any other high-end SQL.

Textbook

The textbook covers SQL concepts, syntax, statements, and programming practices from basics to the advanced level using MS Access SQL, and the book is well suited for the learner who is seeking to be proficient in database programming using SQL. The textbook is easy to understand as each chapter and the examples listed in the chapter are presented in a consistence fashion.

All chapters in the book that discuss SQL programming statements are adequately supported with explanations and programming examples. In addition, the chapters also show how to accomplish the same results in Oracle platform whenever the solutions' methods are different. In other words, these chapters do not only teach how to program using MS Access SQL, they also teach how to program in Oracle SQL. With this unique approach, the learner understands the concepts and the hands-on aspects of SQL in both MS Access and Oracle platforms. These chapters provide enough information for the learner to have the required foundation in database programming using MS Access SQL and other SQL versions.

The majority of the alternative methods that are presented in the textbook and used to accomplish certain SQL operations also work perfectly in other versions of SQL, so users of other SQL platforms can, as well, benefit from using this textbook.

With this book, the learner (i) develops the necessary concepts needed to understand SQL, its commands, and its statements' syntax, (ii) experiences the powerful features of SQL that are contained in MS Access, and (iii) builds, through hands-on activities, the professional skills required to program in SQL environment.

In fact, the primary aim of the book is to teach the learner how to be both theoretically and practically competent in SQL programming.

Textbook Overview

Chapter one explains relational database model, the three main tools – normalization process, entity-relationship model, and planning sheet - used at the conceptual design level, MS Access SQL used to meet the requirement of a database physical design level, and the step-by-step approach for activating MS Access SQL window.

Chapter two focuses on the complete syntax of the SELECT statement, how to write a simple SELECT statement, and other basic operations, besides listing columns, that can be performed in the SELECT clause of the statement. The chapter shows also how to open a database in MS Access environment.

Chapter three discusses conditional retrievals using the WHERE clause, simple and compound conditions, uses of comparison and logical operators in conditional retrievals, and displaying data in an organized form (sorting) using both columns and columns' positions.

Chapter four addresses different types of joins, relational algebra, SET operators that include, among other operators, the DIVIDE operator and how it is achieved in MS Access SQL, TOP-N analysis and how it is used to display a specified number of records from tables.

Chapter five teaches single-row functions that include case-conversion functions, character manipulation functions, numeric functions, and how the functions are written in MS Access SQL statements.

Chapter six explains date and time single-row functions, converting data from one type to another, formatting functions, nesting single-row functions, and displaying data that are not contained in existing tables.

Chapter seven introduces multiple-row functions, the extent to which multiple-row functions can be nested, GROUP BY and HAVING clauses and aggregate data such as subtotals, grand totals, and cross tabulations for grouped records.

Chapter eight teaches different types of subqueries, their functions, how to construct them in SELECT statements, and the differences between correlated and uncorrelated subqueries.

Chapter nine explains how to create database tables using the CREATE TABLE statement and the special SELECT statement, and how to modify tables' structures using the ALTER TABLE statement.

Chapter ten discusses columns' constraints, how constraints are defined for columns using the column-level method and the table-level method, and how to remove constraints from columns.

Chapter eleven teaches Data Manipulation Language (DML) statements - INSERT INTO, UPDATE, and DELETE and their functions, IN clause, PARAMETERS declaration and PROCEDURE clause statements and how they are used to manipulate data in MS Access SQL, and how MS Access SQL uses the implicit COMMIT command to achieve transaction control statement operations.

Chapter twelve explains different types of views and indexes, how to create and modify them in MS Access databases, and how to delete them from MS Access databases.

Chapter thirteen addresses Visual Basic for Applications (VBA) procedures and how they are used to run several SQL statements at the same time in MS Access environment.

Chapter fourteen discusses Visual Basic for Applications (VBA) procedures, how to use the procedures to create MS Access databases' passwords and create users' and workgroups' accounts, how to assign permissions to users and workgroups, how to

Preface

revoke permissions from users and workgroups, and how to remove users' and workgroups' accounts from secured MS Access databases.

In addition, the textbook contains many MS Access Graphical User Interface (GUI) and VBA procedures graphics, database tables' examples, and entity-relationship diagrams as figures to illustrate how certain operations are achieved. These figures help the learner to visualize the concept that is being presented.

Read the following Subsections before using the Textbook

New Information
This second edition contains some major additional information. Chapter two includes a seventh clause - WITH OWNERACCESS OPTION clause - that is used in MS Access SQL SELECT statement to grant a user the permissions to perform certain operations on tables in a multiuser environment. Chapter four shows one more option for writing nested INNER JOIN...ON clauses and explains the positions of both open and close parentheses for both options. In chapter eleven, a new clause - the IN clause – is discussed. The clause is used to connect to an external database without physically opening the external database. Chapter thirteen contains an additional topic on how to group and summarize tables' data in VBA environment. Appendix D is included in this edition to show the structures of the tables used for the book's hands-on activities, the tables' relationships, and the Screen display for Windows 2000 operating system used to launch MS Access.

Audience
The intent of this book is to assist the learner to acquire the concepts and the skills needed to become a professional SQL programmer and to create and maintain databases, databases' objects, and databases' data through SQL. The textbook is also written to help students who are taking database SQL programming courses. The book can be used as a (i) database programming course textbook, (ii) SQL course textbook, (iii) reference textbook, (iv) self-taught textbook, or (v) supplement textbook.

Required Software
One of the many gains of this textbook is that the learner does not have to purchase expensive high-end database SQL programming software to starting learning and writing SQL statements. Today, MS Access software is found in virtually every desktop computers, laptop computers, and notebook computers that run on Windows operating systems. So learning database SQL using this textbook is almost instantaneous as the needed software package is readily available to the learner.

No additional software is required to be purchased for chapters thirteen and fourteen of the textbook. Visual Basic for Applications (VBA) language is incorporated into MS office suite - including MS Access and the language is available once MS Access is installed on a computer.

Merits
The following reasons are the merits why a SQL learner needs this textbook.

1. SQL is the main programming language for creating relational databases.

2. MS Access is commonly found in many desktop, laptop, and notebook computers, universities' and colleges' computer laboratories, universities' and

colleges' libraries, and communities' libraries, so the software is readily available.

3. MS Access software is very much less expensive than other high-end SQL software therefore the software can easily be afforded by the learner.

4. Today, MS Access contains tons of SQL commands and features, and as such, learning SQL with the software is highly productive.

5. MS Access is an excellent software tool for teaching and learning database SQL programming.

6. The user of this textbook will acquire the necessary concepts and skills needed to program in SQL.

7. The user of this textbook will find it very easy to crossover to high-end SQL platforms.

8. The textbook shows how to accomplish results in Oracle SQL whenever the solutions' methods of MS Access SQL are different from other SQL versions.

9. The textbook uses actual examples that are related to the topics discussed in the book, and as a result, the learner can use the examples as hands-on exercises. This is in addition to the hands-on activities' questions provided at the end of each SQL- or VBA-related chapter.

10. Many universities and colleges teach database programming courses using SQL, so using the textbook with less expensive SQL software, such as MS Access, to teach the courses will be a money-saving undertaking for these institutions.

Re-enforcement Tools
Each chapter of the textbook, in addition to the topics presented, contains

- objectives
- summary, syntax, and statements' table
- key terms
- review questions
- lots of in-chapter hands-on exercises and solutions
- hand-on activities' questions

Database Download, Comments, and Recommendations
The user of this book can download the database (**AcademicX**) created for this textbook for hands-on practices by going to the textbook's web site. The site is

http://www.sqltextbook.com
or
http://sqltextbook.com

Once on the web site, click the Database page tab to display the page. On the top-right corner of the page and below the text that begins with "*The AcademicX Database hyperlink...*" is the database hyperlink. The name of the link is _AcademicX Database_. Click the hyperlink to download the database.

During the download, a dialog box showing two different methods of downloading the database appears. Click the SAVE button of the dialog box. DO NOT click the OPEN button of the dialog box as the database is created for different versions of MS Access. By clicking the SAVE button the database is downloaded correctly without assuming any particular version of MS Access as the default database software.

Preface

After downloading the database to your computer, make a copy of the database either to the same folder as the downloaded version or to a different folder in your computer. When MS Access is launched, activate the copied version of the database. By making a copy of the database preserves the original version in case the copied version is corrupted or deleted by mistake.

Data contained in the tables of the practice database were chosen randomly and the tables' records were also created arbitrarily. However, any resemblance of the tables' records to actual records in the real world occurred by coincidence.

The user of the textbook can also send comments and recommendations on the book to the author by sending an e-mail to **eugboma@sqltextbook.com**.

Addendum

The tables for the practice database with the tables' contents are listed in Appendix A. The answers to the odd-numbered review questions for each chapter, except for the essay type questions, are provided in Appendix B and the solutions to the selected odd-numbered hands-on activities' questions, from chapter two to chapter fourteen, are provided in Appendix C. The even-numbered questions and the essay type questions of the chapters' review questions are offered as tests and challenges to the user of this textbook. The even-numbered and other odd-numbered hands-on activities' questions which solutions are not given in appendix C are projects' questions. The author offers challenging opportunities to the user of the textbook to supply the correct solutions' statements to the projects' questions. Appendix D shows the tables' structures, the tables' relationships, and the Screen display for Windows 2000 operating system used to launch MS Access.

Instructors

Instructors who adopt the book for classroom settings' instruction can also request the power point slides' presentations for all chapters by sending an e-mail to **eugboma@sqltextbook.com**.

Conventions

The textbook uses the following conventions.

- SQL keywords are in uppercases. Example: SELECT

- VBA keywords are in mixed cases. Example: Dim

- User-defined names are in italics. Example: *existingColumnName*

- Symbols [ ] indicate items are optional. Example: [WHERE *rowCondition*]

- Symbol | indicates OR operator – that is any of the items listed in the particular SQL clause or in the VBA statement can be used in the operation. Example: *existingColumnName | columnExpressioin*

- Symbols ... indicate more items can be listed in the particular SQL clause or in the VBA statement. Example: *existingTableName, ...*

Note: When an item is created or defined in a SQL or VBA syntax in the textbook, the expression "*... is the name of the ...*" is used. If the item is already existing, has been previously created, or has been previously defined, the expression "*... is the ...*" is used.

Chapter One

Reviewing Relational Database Model

Chapter Objectives

After completing this chapter, you should be able to

- Discuss the fundamentals of relational database model
- Define relational database, tables, records, fields, and characters
- List some benefits and drawbacks of relational database model
- Distinguish between conceptual design phase and physical design phase
- Understand normalization process and its basic normal forms
- Understand entity-relationship model and entity-relationship diagrams
- Understand planning sheet
- Discuss relational database management systems (RDBMSs)
- Understand the functions of structured query language (SQL)
- Activate MS Access SQL Window

Relational Database Model

Relational database model is the most popular model used today in designing databases. The model is based on a concept that data can be stored in a structure that consists of rows and columns and the data can be retrieved quickly and efficiently. The idea that such a model is more effective among previously used models (hierarchical, network) to store and manage data was conceived in 1970 by Dr. E.F. Codd of International Business Machine (IBM), hence relational database model was born. Today, the model has expanded beyond its original concept to include object-oriented features that allow its data structures to store and manipulate images and other object-oriented constructs. This model is implemented physically by using software called **Relational Database Management Systems** (RDBMSs).

Relational Database Management Systems (RDBMSs) are used to create relational databases' objects. The software is used also to make changes to objects' structures, populate objects with data, update objects' data, display data contained in objects, delete data from objects, and remove objects from databases. The most common and the most popular of the objects of relational database model is the table - also known as a relation. The table is usually the first to be planned, designed, and created. Other relational databases' objects are built using either the data contained in tables or the existence of the tables.

Relational Databases

A relational database is an integrated structure that contains organized collection of objects such as tables, views, and indexes, the objects' data, the description of the data, the associations among the objects, and the attributes that describe the characteristics of the objects. This integrated structure can be shared among several users. An example is a college database. The database might include faculty table, student table, non-academic staff table, expenditure table etc. All tables created under a college's umbrella constitute that college's database. Typically, a relational database is a collection of an organization's, such as a college, data tables. A table is a data file.

Reviewing Relational Database Model

Tables

An individual table, also called a relation, is a matrix that consists of rows and columns. The rows are sometimes referred to as records while the columns are sometimes called fields. Data are arranged horizontally (row-wise) to indicate records and they are arranged vertically (column-wise) to denote facts about records. Tables in a relational database are associated or related to each other by sharing common characteristics hence they are called relations. In fact, a table is a data file – a structure that contains data that can be manipulated by a user, but the name "table" or "relation" is used to describe such data file in a relational database arena. The name "table" depicts the structure's two-dimensional form - columns and rows, and the name "relation" depicts the relationship that is established between tables.

Examples of tables include student data file and faculty data file of a college's database. A student table contains data (records) of students in the college and a faculty table contains data (records) of faculty members employed by the college. In conclusion, a table is a collection of related records.

Records

A record also called a row or tuple is a collection or block of related columns that uniquely describes an entity. Here, an entity can be a person, an event, a location, an activity, or a thing. For instance, a series of related data describing a college instructor, based on the information he or she entered in the college's employment application form, is the instructor's record. A record is a collection of related columns. Figure 1.1 shows a sample table containing some records - faculty and the courses they are assigned to teach.

Figure 1.1
Table Name: facultyCourse

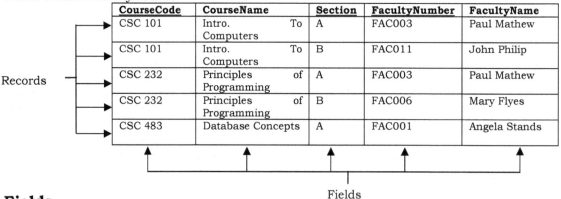

	CourseCode	CourseName	Section	FacultyNumber	FacultyName
Records	CSC 101	Intro. To Computers	A	FAC003	Paul Mathew
	CSC 101	Intro. To Computers	B	FAC011	John Philip
	CSC 232	Principles of Programming	A	FAC003	Paul Mathew
	CSC 232	Principles of Programming	B	FAC006	Mary Flyes
	CSC 483	Database Concepts	A	FAC001	Angela Stands

Fields

Fields

A field is a column or an attribute that describes one characteristic or one aspect of a table's data. Majority of tables in a relational database usually consists of several columns. Some examples of columns that might be part of a table designed to store students' records are **studentNumber** column, **lastName** column, **firstName** column, and **courseCode** column. Each column is made up of a collection of characters that represent a meaningful expression such as the expression **Zip Code**. Each column is used to (i) define the type of data that can be stored in a table, (ii) establish restrictions called constraints, and (iii) how much data, in terms of character positions (size), can be fitted into that column. Each column in a table is assigned a descriptive name – a column label or a column identifier - that helps describe the function of the column.

Characters

A character is any printable symbol. A character is the smallest, usable, meaningful piece (unit) of data that can be stored on a computer storage medium. Some examples of characters are **A**, **9**, **&**, **#**, *@*, and **?**. Characters are letters of the alphabet including upper and lower case letters (A through Z, a through z), numeric digits (0 through 9), and special symbols such as ^, %, $, :, \, and].

Selected Benefits of Relational Databases

Having a single pool (reservoir) of data: Relational database model reduces (sometimes eliminates) the multiple pools of data that were pervasive with the older systems. Data stored in multiple locations create environments where data are duplicated (data redundancy) and are not consistent (data inconsistency). These problems lead to lack of data integrity. With relational database, data are in a single pool thus minimizing the chance of data being duplicated and improving the database integrity.

Data can be shared among several users: Due to the fact that a single pool of data exists, several database users can access the same data reservoir to exploit data in different ways and generate different types of reports. A single data pool eliminates the task of accessing several locations for the needed data.

Reduce redundancy: Relational database minimizes the duplications of data that lead to a problem called data redundancy. Data redundancy is the replication or duplication of the same piece of data in several or different locations. Having data stored in one location reduces the risk of entering erroneous data. Data can be entered only once for a particular item if a database's data is stored in one location. This reduces time and effort in comparison to entering the same data into multiple locations.

Use planned (controlled) redundancy to establish relationships among data tables: Unlike older systems, the only replication of data that exists in relational database environment is a controlled duplication that is used to arrive at positive ends to meet database requirement. Controlled data redundancy is used to uniquely identify records in tables when the tables have composite primary keys (ensuring entity integrity) and to establish relationships between tables (ensuring referential integrity).

Increase the degree of data consistency: With data stored in a single location, entering erroneous data is reduced, data inconsistency is minimized, and the validity of database data is assured.

Establish better integrity constraints: It is very much easier to define and establish integrity constraints when data are kept in a single pool than when they are scattered in different locations. Such restrictions on data can easily be defined in a single location by a database administrator or a team of database administrators.

Better security features: When the same pieces of data are stored in several locations, the chances of obtaining sensitive data are increased and the critical data are at easy reach. For example, an unauthorized user who is unsuccessful to retrieve sensitive data from location A, might be lucky to retrieve the same piece of data from locations B or C. But with data kept in one location, security measures are tighter and vital data are better secured.

Data and structural independences: Relational database model provides data and structural independencies. Using this model, a change or a modification to a database structure, for example adding columns, does not necessarily mean that the database program used in an application and/or the data will be altered.

Selected Drawbacks of Relational Databases

Data pool failure might lead to total lost of the database: Due to the fact that relational database model reduces the number of data pools to a single pool, errors on the parts of users might lead to a dangerous situation where vital data are lost. In addition, natural disasters such as fires might also lead to the lost of the database. But such situation can be evaded by making backups of the database and storing them in different safe locations. The backups can be restored to the database system in case the original database is lost or corrupted.

Relational database software becoming more complex with added sophisticated features: Relational database management systems (RDMSs) instruction files have increased tremendously in recent year, both in sizes and in number. More features are constantly being added to the software requiring more time and effort in learning the software. To be able to use modern-day relational database management systems to their fullest capability, users need to understand the functions of most, if not all, of the software instruction files, and thus, requiring users to spend countless hours and efforts learning the software.

Larger memory spaces (RAM and Storage media) required: Due to the continuous increase in sizes and in number of the software instruction files, coupled with users' objects and data created using the software, larger memory and storage spaces are now needed to run the software.

Note: Regardless of what the drawbacks are, the benefits of relational database outweigh the disadvantages.

Relational Database Design

Relational database design is the process of mentally visualizing, planning, producing the structural layout, and implementing relational databases. Like other database models, relational databases are created in two phases namely, the conceptual design phase and the physical design phase.

Conceptual Design Phase

This is the first phase of database design process. This design phase involves the mental picture or the perception of how data are to be arranged in tables. In enough shell, the phase involves the conceptual discussion of planning and designing the blue prints of relational databases. This phase is also referred to as the information-level phase or the logical design phase.

To design a good relational database at this phase, three data-modeling tools are needed. The tools are normalization process, entity-relationship model, and planning sheet. Each tool has its own unique functions and their jobs are clearly stated within this design phase. At this phase, database design is independent of any database management system that will later be used to develop the database. In other words, at this level, much of the concern is on the thoughts of designing a database, planning the database, and producing the database's blue print. The particular software to be used for implementing the database is of little or no interest at this phase.

Normalization Process

Normalization process is the course of actions used by database developers to identify and remove databases' problems called anomalies from tables in order for data in the tables to have integrity. This process assists relational databases to be in error-free or consistent states. Normalization process uses yardsticks called normal forms (NFs) to construct new tables that are free of anomalies and that contain the same data as the old problem-stricken tables.

Normal forms (NFs) are the standard measurement tools used for normalizing tables or for reorganizing the structures of tables. Normal forms operate in a cumulative fashion or in progression in that tables in the next normal form are better than tables in the present normal form. For example, a table in second normal form (2NF) "next normal form" is better than a table in first normal form (1NF) "present normal form".

In addition to reducing unnecessary duplications of data, normalization process assists in improving databases' structures including the establishment and the enforcement of both entity (primary key) and referential (foreign key) integrities. Both integrities are used to establish relationships between tables. For easy comprehension, this textbook discusses the first three normal forms at their basic levels.

First Normal Form (1NF)

The first objective of first normal form (1NF) of normalization process is to eliminate repeating groups that can exist within the rows of tables and to make each row in the tables unique. The second objective is to identify the primary keys' columns for the tables. Typically, the primary key of a table in first normal form consists of more than one column, thus making the key a composite primary key. For each row in a table with a composite primary key to be unique, the columns that make up the primary key must allow duplications of data. However, these types of data duplications are planned or controlled to achieve the normal form.

In this section, planned or controlled means that all columns of the composite primary key for similar records (records with data values that are almost identical) must not be duplicated for those records. Otherwise, the key can no longer distinguish the records. When a table has a composite primary key, at least one of the primary key's columns for similar records in the table must contain unique data values for the primary key to accurately distinguish the records.

Repeating Groups: A repeating group is a situation in a database where several records' entries are recorded in a single row of a table. That is one row in a relation is containing the data of more than one record.

Typically, in a repeating group, some columns' entries for records sharing the single row receive no known data values (null values). This is usually the case when records, except for the first record in the group, contain the same values in those columns as the first record. The columns that are referred to as the repeating groups are the fields that contain data for all records in the table. The repeating groups for the facultyCourse table – figure 1.2 - are **Section**, **FacultyNumber**, and **FacultyName** columns. These three columns are filled with data for all records in the table. Figure 1.2 shows an example of a relation with repeating groups.

Reviewing Relational Database Model

Figure 1.2
Table Name: facultyCourse

Repeating group rows

CourseCode	CourseName	Section	Faculty Number	Faculty Name
CSC 101	Intro. To Computers	A	FAC003	Paul Mathew
		B	FAC011	John Philip
CSC 232	Principles of Programming	A	FAC003	Paul Mathew
		B	FAC006	Mary Flyes
CSC 483	Database Concepts	A	FAC001	Angela Stands

In the first two columns (**CourseCode**, **CourseName**) of the facultyCourse table, some columns' entries or columns' cells are missing data. The missing data signify that the data stored in those columns for the record immediately above the record or records with the missing data are the same as the missing data.

Removing repeating groups from a table means entering the appropriate data into all columns' cells where data are missing. Null values are not allowed. All columns' cells must be filled with data even if the data are duplicated.

Primary Keys: A primary key is either a single column or a collection of columns that uniquely identifies each row or record in a table (relation).

A primary key's job is to distinguish rows in a table by assigning each row its own identity. A table's primary key cannot contain null values and the values can only be duplicated when the table's primary key is a composite primary key. A primary key obeys one of the rules of relational database known as entity integrity. Sometimes, a table might contain two or more columns where each of the columns can individually identify each row in the table uniquely. Such columns are called candidate keys since each of the columns obeys the rules that define a primary key. The column that is chosen among these candidate keys becomes the table's primary key and those columns that are not chosen become the table's alternate keys.

Candidate Keys: A candidate key is a column that has all the properties of a primary key and qualifies to be the primary key of a table.

Alternate Keys: An alternate key is a column that has all the properties of a primary key but not chosen to be the primary key of a table.

Entity Integrity: Entity integrity is a relational database rule that says the values of a primary key of a table cannot be null and cannot be duplicated, and that duplications are only allowed when the primary key is a composite primary key.

Composite Primary Keys: A composite primary key is a primary key that consists of more than one column.

The columns of a composite primary key collectively identify each row in a table. A relation with repeating groups removed requires a composite primary key to uniquely distinguish one record from another in that relation.

Although relations with composite primary keys might still contain database anomalies, the composite keys are, usually, required to convert tables to first normal form. Figure 1.3 shows a table in first normal form (1NF). The table has no repeating groups because all its records are filled with data which makes each record in the table unique and identifiable. The primary key of the table is made up of **CourseCode**, **Section**, and

FacultyNumber columns, thus making the key a composite primary key. The **Section** column of the table is chosen as part of the primary key for the fact that a faculty member can be assigned to teach several sections of the same course.

Figure 1.3
Table Name: facultyCourse

CourseCode	CourseName	Section	FacultyNumber	FacultyName
CSC 101	Intro. To Computers	A	FAC003	Paul Mathew
CSC 101	Intro. To Computers	B	FAC011	John Philip
CSC 232	Principles of Programming	A	FAC003	Paul Mathew
CSC 232	Principles of Programming	B	FAC006	Mary Flyes
CSC 483	Database Concepts	A	FAC001	Angela Stands

Second Normal Form (2NF)

The objective of second normal form (2NF) is to remove partial dependencies from tables. Partial dependency exists in a table when a non-key column depends on a portion of the table's primary key. Partial dependency usually occurs when a table has a composite primary key. One of relational database entity integrity rules states that a non-key column must depend totally on the primary key of a table even if the key is a composite primary key. A non-key column cannot depend on a portion (part) of a table's primary key.

The facultyCourse table (figure 1.3) which is in 1NF is used to illustrate partial dependency. Entering the faculty number FAC001 which is a value in the table's **FacultyNumber** column will reveal that Angela Stands is the name of the faculty member. Following the rule of entity integrity, **FacultyNumber** column alone cannot determine any non-key column in the table. Any non-key column in the table must be determined by the table's composite primary key. In this case, the determination must be done by **CourseCode**, **Section**, and **FacultyNumber** columns collectively.

Key Columns (attributes): A key column is a field or an attribute that serves as the primary key of a table or a part of the columns that serve as the primary key of a table.

For example, in the facultyCourse table (figure 1.3), the **CourseCode**, **Section**, and **FacultyNumber** are key columns because collectively they serve as the composite primary key of the table.

Non-key columns (attributes): A non-key column is a field or an attribute that is not part of a table's primary key.

Again using the facultyCourse table (figure 1.3), **CourseName** and **FacultyName** are non-key columns because they are not part of the columns that serve as the primary key of the table.

Third Normal Form (3NF)

The objective of third normal form is to remove transitive dependencies from tables. Transitive dependency exists in a database table when a non-key column that depends on a table's primary key depends also on another non-key column in the same table. An advanced form or an extension of third normal form is the Boyce-Codd normal form (BCNF). The objective of BCNF is to remove transitive dependencies from a table where the table's primary key depends on non-key columns. Third normal form is the level where associations between tables are established.

Reviewing Relational Database Model

Foreign Keys: A foreign key is a single column or a collection of columns of a table where the values stored in those column(s) must match some values in the primary key column(s) of the associated table.

In the simplest definition, a foreign key of one table is actually the primary key of the other table when the tables are in a relationship. A foreign key is used by relational database management systems to enforce what is known as referential integrity.

Referential Integrity: Referential integrity is a database rule that says when a table's foreign key contains values, those values must match some values in the primary key of the other table when the tables are in a relationship or the foreign key values can be null.

Figure 1.4 shows a table in second normal form (2NF). The table's primary key is **StudentNumber** column. Although the **StudentNumber** column is the table's primary key, but knowing a value in the **DepartmentNumber** column also determines a value in the **DepartmentName** column. In other words, the **DepartmentNumber** column can be used to determine a department's name even though the column is not part of the primary key. For example, entering the data value "AV19" in the **DepartmentNumber** column during a query operation will reveal that the name of the department associated with the data value is "Aviation". Therefore, **DepartmentName** column depends on both the primary key column (**StudentNumber**) and the **DepartmentNumber** column. This type of problem is called transitive dependency in a relational database arena.

Figure 1.4
Table Name: studentDepartment

Student Number	Student Name	Major	Department Number	Department Name
STU090910	John Stevens	Airways Management	AV19	Aviation
STU107823	Florin Kelly	Computer Science	MC24	Mathematics and Computer Science
STU118955	Angelica Lite	Elementary Education	ED05	Education
STU123461	Johnson Slate	Economics	BA03	Business Administration

There are situations when columns – individually or collectively - of a table are not able to distinguish one row (record) from another in the table. In other words, the table's columns – individually or collectively - do not possess the properties of being candidate keys to be chosen as a primary key. In such situation, a column is created for the table to act as the table's primary key. Such a column is called a surrogate key.

Surrogate Keys: A surrogate key is a replacement (substitute) column for a primary key when a table is created with columns that lack the properties of being candidate keys.

Entity-Relationship Model

Entity-relationship model (ERM) is used in database design to give a somewhat complete representation of data to be stored in the tables of relational databases. ERM underlying functions are to indicate tables' relationships and tables' cardinalities. The model is implemented using Entity-relationship diagrams (ERDs). These diagrams are graphic symbols and they are used to represent tables (rectangle), relationships (line, diamond), and attributes (oval). In addition to the symbols, the digit (1), the letters (M, N), the dark circle symbol (•), and the crow's foot symbol (⤙) are used to represent relationships. To indicate tables' cardinalities, the digits (0 through 9), the letter N, and the crow's foot symbol (⤙) are used. The three most popular data-modeling tools used in E-R diagrams (ERDs) are Peter Chen, Crow's Foot, and Air Force IDEF1X.

Chapter One

There are three types of relationships that can exist among tables. The relationships are one-to-one denoted as 1:1, one-to-many denoted as 1:M or 1:N, and many-to-many denoted as M:N. When two tables establish a relationship, one of the tables is referred to as the parent relation (table) and the other table is referred to as the child relation (table).

Relationships: A relationship is an association between two tables and is usually established using primary keys and foreign keys of the tables in the relationship.

Parents Tables: A parent table in a relationship is the relation with a primary key in which the primary key values are being referenced by the foreign key values of the child table.

Childs Tables: A child table in a relationship is the relation that contains a foreign key in which the foreign key values reference some values in the primary key of the parent table.

Figure 1.5 shows some of the symbols used in E-R diagrams.

Figure 1.5

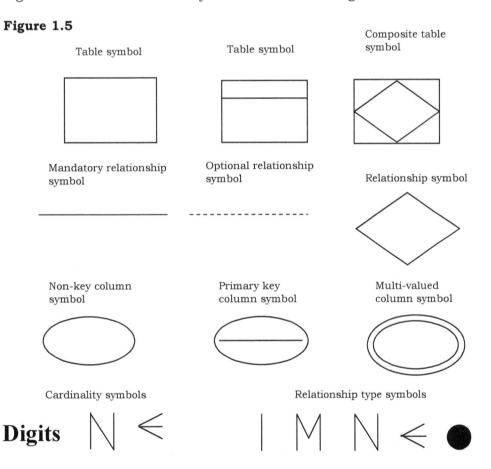

Table symbol	Table symbol	Composite table symbol
Mandatory relationship symbol	Optional relationship symbol	Relationship symbol
Non-key column symbol	Primary key column symbol	Multi-valued column symbol
Cardinality symbols		Relationship type symbols

Digits N ≤ | M N ≤ ●

> ***Note:*** The vertical bar (|) of the relationship type symbols in figure 1.5 represents digit one (1).

One-to-One Relationship (1:1)

One-to-One relationship indicates that one record (occurrence or instance) of a table, say table A, can establish a relationship (association) with only one record in the other table, say table B, and the said record in table B can only relate to that particular record of table A.

For instance, say two tables exist in an academic environment. One table contains data about presidents of colleges and universities. The other table stores data about the colleges and universities. The only type of relationship that can be established between these two tables is the one-to-one relationship. In the real world, one president is employed to manage one college or one university, and that college or university is run by that president. In other words, two or more presidents are not assigned to manage one academic institution.

To implement one-to-one relationship, make the primary key columns(s) of the first table to be the foreign key column(s) of the second table. Also, in return, make the primary key columns(s) of the second table to be the foreign key column(s) of the first table. In one-to-one relationship, each table acts as both the parent table and the child table.

Figure 1.6 shows examples of one-to-one relationship in E-R diagrams using the three data-modeling tools.

Figure 1.6

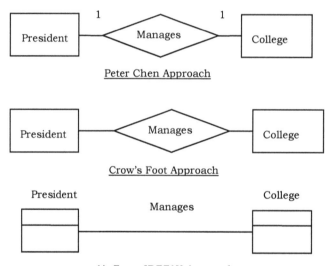

Peter Chen Approach

Crow's Foot Approach

Air Force IDEF1X Approach

One-to-Many Relationship (1:M)
One-to-Many relationship demonstrates that one record (occurrence or instance) of a table, say table A, can establish relationships (associations) with no, one, or many (several) records of a second table, say table B, where each of the said records of table B relates to that one record of table A.

Let's assume two tables exist in an academic environment. One table contains data of academic departments in a college or a university. The other table contains data of faculty members and their assigned academic departments. The type of relationship that is proper and typically suited for the two tables is one-to-many.

In a normal academic setting, a department can have several faculty members assigned to it, and each of the said faculty members relates to that one academic department. For example, if five faculty members are assigned to Computer Science department, that five members are faculty in that Computer Science department.

To implement one-to-many relationship, make the primary key column(s) of the table that has the one occurrence (record) to be the foreign key column(s) in the table that has the many occurrences (records). In this type of relationship, the table with the primary key that is being referenced is the parent table (table with the measure 1), while the child table is the one with foreign key (table with the measure M).

Figure 1.7 shows examples of one-to-many relationship in E-R diagrams using the three data-modeling tools.

Figure 1.7

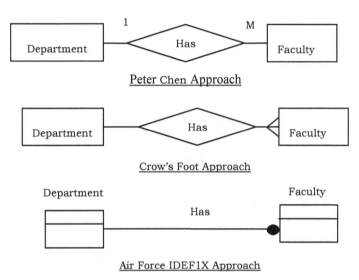

Peter Chen Approach

Crow's Foot Approach

Air Force IDEF1X Approach

Many-to-Many Relationship (M:N)
Many-to-many relationship exists between tables where no, one, or many records of one table, say table A, establish relationships with no, one, or many records of the other table, say table B and vice versa. In other words, one instance of the first table can have relationships with no, one, or several instances of the second table, and in return, an instance of the second table can have relationships with no, one, or several instances of the first table.

Let's say two tables exist in an academic setting. One of the tables contains data about courses offered by a college or a university. The other table stores data about students taking courses at the college or the university. Since students can register for more than one course if they choose to, and a course can have more than one student enrolled in it, the type of relationship in such situation is many-to-many.

Many-to-many relationship is possible in concept but it cannot be implemented in the form in which it is spoken. To implement many-to-many relationship physically, the relationship must be broken down to two or more one-to-many relationships. During the breakdown, one or more new tables are created. These new tables are called composite tables and sometimes referred to as bridge entities or link tables. These tables play the roles of intermediary tables between the two original tables that have the many-to-many relationship. In many-to-many relationship, the original tables act as both the parents' tables and childs' tables but through the bridge entity.

Bridge Entities: A bridge entity is a composite table used to implement many-to-many relationship physically. The primary key of the composite table consists of the primary keys of the original tables involved in the relationship.

Reviewing Relational Database Model

Figure 1.8 shows examples of many-to-many relationship in E-R diagrams using the three data-modeling tools.

Figure 1.8

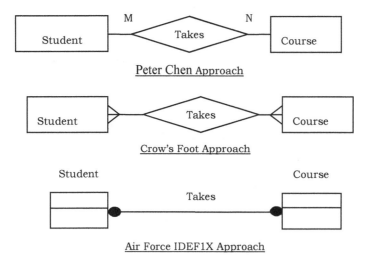

Cardinality

Cardinality is the number of records (occurrences or instances) in one table that have relationships with one record (occurrence or instance) in another table. Two values are used to represent cardinality for each table in E-R diagrams. One value denotes maximum cardinality and the other value indicates minimum cardinality for the table.

Using Crow's foot data-modeling tool, a table's cardinality is shown on the E-R diagrams' relationships lines. Values used to indicate tables' cardinalities in crow's foot data-modeling tool are digit 0, digit 1, and the crow's foot symbol, and they are placed on the side of the other table rather than on the side of the table being represented. The Crow's foot approach indicates that the value closest to the table symbol (rectangle) represents maximum cardinality and the value farther away from the table symbol denotes minimum cardinality.

With Peter Chen data-modeling tool, the values are enclosed in parentheses, separated by a comma, placed on the same side as the table they represent, and read from left to right. Within the parentheses, the value on the left indicates minimum cardinality while the value on the right denotes maximum cardinality. Values used to indicate tables' cardinalities in Peter Chen data-modeling tool are digits (0 through 9), and letter N.

Figure 1.9 shows two examples of how cardinalities are presented in E-R diagrams. One example uses the parentheses approach (Peter Chen) and the other example uses the relationship line approach (Crow's foot).

Figure 1.9

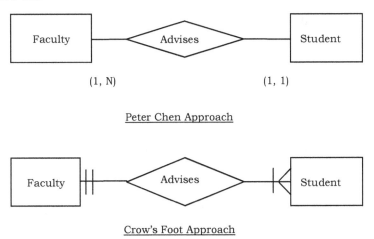

Peter Chen Approach

Crow's Foot Approach

The interpretation of the cardinality for both approaches is that a faculty member is assigned to advise at least one student (minimum) and a maximum of more than one student. In this case, no value is set as the upper limit to indicate maximum. Any number of students, as long as the number is more than one, satisfies the upper limit. On the other hand, a student is advised by one faculty member (minimum) and that faculty member only is the student's advisor (maximum).

> **Note:** In E-R diagram, when showing the cardinality of a table using Crow's Foot approach, a vertical bar (|) is used to represent digit one (1) and a circle (O) is used to represent digit zero (0) on the E-R diagram's relationship lines.

Planning Sheet

The planning sheet is the third tool used at the information-level (conceptual) design phase of database design. Although rarely used in comparison to the frequencies with which normalization process and entity-relationship model are used to illustrate the conceptual design phase, the planning sheet describes each column's requirement, including the column's data integrity constraints, that defines the structure for a table. The planning sheet is used to plan the data for a table and the data integrity constraints each column in the table must obey.

The planning sheet is also used to include the subtypes of data integrity that must be retained by each column in a table. The sheet establishes the requirement for each column and provides an effective method for defining integrity constraints that will guide the physical design phase of database design. In addition, the planning sheet may list the names of the tables that have or will have relationships (if any) with the table the sheet is describing. In enough shell, the sheet ensures the authenticity of data in a table and each table in a database should be planned using its own planning sheet.

There are two main sections in a planning sheet. The top section is used to specify the name of the database where a table belongs, the table's name, the operational function(s) of the table, the table's relationships with other tables (if any), and the types of relationships (if any) that must exist between the table and other tables. The bottom section of the sheet is used to define the specification for each column in the table which includes the column's description, the column's actual name, the column's width size where applicable, and the constraints the column's data must abide by. The sheet is used to define a table's structure, the table's content type, and the integrity constraints for that table. Figure 1.10 shows a sample of a planning sheet.

Reviewing Relational Database Model

Figure 1.10

Database Table Planning Sheet

Database Name: _____

Table Name: _____

Purpose of the Table: _____

Relationships: Associating Table Name _____ Type of Relationship _____

Associating Table Name _____ Type of Relationship _____

Attribute Specification

Description	Name	Data Type	Size	Decimal Position	Domaint	Format	Primary Key	Foreign Key	Unique	Not Null	Default	Index

Physical Design Phase

The physical design phase of database design is the process of physically creating relational databases and their objects, and establishing appropriate tables' relationships and cardinalities on storage media using particular relational database management systems such as Microsoft Access, Oracle, or SQL Server.

The transformation or conversion of the conceptual design phase to meet the data storage and access characteristics of the specific database management system and the hardware is the main objective of the physical design phase. Here, the design phase is dependent on the particular relational database software, and the physical creations of the database's individual tables are based on the specification laid out on the planning sheets for those tables. The tables' relationships and their cardinalities are physically enforced by the relational database management system using the tables' primary keys and foreign keys.

This textbook teaches relational database programming using a query language called Structured Query Language (SQL) that is integrated into relational database management systems. The relational database software of choice used to teach and discuss SQL in this textbook is Microsoft Access. In the remainder of the textbook's chapters, you will be introduced to SQL concepts, syntax, and statements. The textbook also explains basic Visual Basic for Applications (VBA) concepts, syntax, and statements, and how Microsoft Access supports SQL code writing to great depth.

Microsoft Access

In recent years, Microsoft (MS) Access has become the most popular relational database management system used in the personal computer (PC) environment. The software works superbly as front-end software and can be used as back-end software for small groups of PC users.

Beginning with MS Access 97 and to date, the software package has incorporated many SQL commands and features and has been supporting the language environment in its own way just as the language is supported by other versions of SQL. MS Access, a graphical user interface (GUI) relational database management system, supports SQL programming to a competent level that makes the learner to be professionally ready in the arena of SQL programming. Today, learning SQL using MS Access is intriguing, knowledge gathering, and developing the necessary skills just as learning the language in other SQL versions.

> **Note:** From this point on, when the text expression "Microsoft Access", "MS Access", "Microsoft Access SQL", or "MS Access SQL" is not used in a generic form in this textbook, the expression refers to MS Access 2003 software package or the package's SQL formats.

Structured Query Language (SQL)

SQL sometimes pronounced (SEEQUOL) is an industry standard query language. The query language was originally developed by IBM in the 1970s and soon after its usage became eminent in relational database design, thus making it the language of choice today for relational database programming.

SQL is a component of any relational database management system and as such, it is not considered as a complete language. Rather SQL is regarded as a sublanguage that is a built-in facet of relational database software. The language is used to create, manipulate, and maintain relational databases. SQL is a data definition, data manipulation, and data control language and it is considered a forth-generation language. A user can directly issue instructions to the language on what to do without instructing it on how to do it. In that sense SQL is regarded as a non-procedural language.

Typically, SQL is command driven and uses command-line interface. Its commands and features are grouped or divided into three subsections. One subsection called Data Definition Language (DDL) contains commands for creating and modifying (altering) objects such as tables and views. Another subsection called Data Manipulation Language (DML) contains the SQL commands used for entering, retrieving, updating, and deleting tables' data. The third subsection called Data Control Language (DCL) contains commands used to establish security controls and privileges for users.

Command-Line Interfaces: A command-line interface is an operating system's environment where commands are typed rather than being selected from command menus or command buttons.

There are various SQL standards, but the most recognizable standard in the world of SQL programming is the **American National Standards Institute** (ANSI) SQL standard (ANSI-SQL).

Activating MS Access SQL Window

The intent of this textbook is to teach SQL programming using MS Access. The first and foremost step is to explain how the SQL window is activated in MS Access.

The first step to accessing the SQL window is to start MS Access application. See figure 1.11. It is assumed that you have turned on your computer and the current window is the desktop. For demonstration purposes, Microsoft Windows XP operating system and Microsoft Access 2003 are used. Any other Microsoft Windows-based operating system beginning with MS Windows 95 to present and any version of Microsoft Access package beginning with MS Access 97 to present are suffice to start learning database programming using MS Access SQL.

Reviewing Relational Database Model

Note: See Appendix D for Windows 2000 Start menu screen display.

Figure 1.11

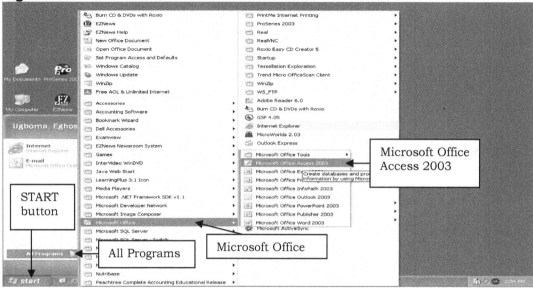

To start MS Access from your computer, click the **Start** button on the bottom left corner of the taskbar. Then point to **All Programs**. Point to **Microsoft Office**, and then click the **Microsoft Office Access 2003** command button to start the MS Access application. Clicking the **Microsoft Office Access 2003** will open the following MS Access window. See figure 1.12.

Figure 1.12

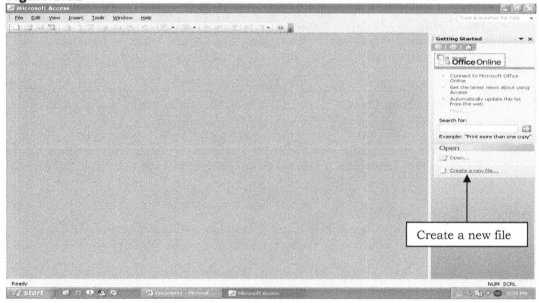

This window is used to create new databases in MS Access or to open databases that have been previously created (existing databases). But for the purpose of learning SQL programming, a new database will be created. To create a new database, click the hyperlink that says **Create a new file** on the window's right pane (Getting Started task pane). This command opens yet another window. See the figure 1.13.

Figure 1.13

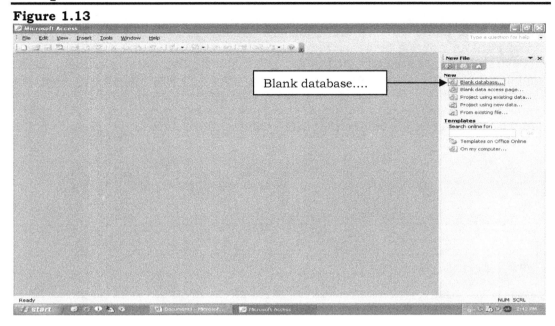

This window is used to start creating new databases' structures or to create new databases with data and other databases' creation options. For the purposes of this textbook, a database structure will be created. Click the hyperlink that says **_Blank Database..._** on the window's right pane (New File task pane) to start creating the database structure. Clicking this command button opens yet another MS Access window. See figure 1.14.

Figure 1.14

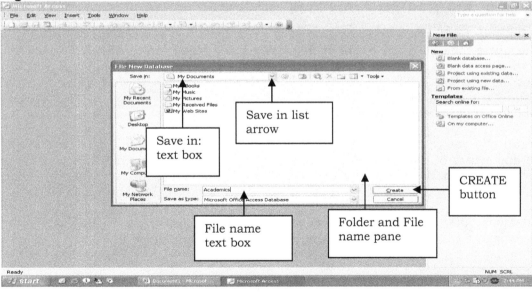

The small window with the title **File New Database** that is embedded into the larger MS Access window is where databases' structures are actually created. You can change the storage location of the database you are about to create by clicking the list arrow of the **Save in:** text box to choose a new or a different location. Alternatively, you can type the new location name in the **Save in:** text box. For demonstration purposes, the textbook uses **My Documents** default storage location.

Reviewing Relational Database Model

Next, you might want to assign a new and descriptive name to your database. To do so, you click the **File name** text box and enter the name of your choice. You can equally select and click an existing database name from Folder and File name pane, but doing so will destroy data that are contained in the database with that name. For the purpose of demonstration, the name **Academics** is entered. So the database used for demonstration here is called **Academics**. After choosing a storage location and/or a new name for the database, you then click the **Create** button to create the structure for the database. The action of the **Create** button command displays another window. See figure 1.15.

Figure 1.15

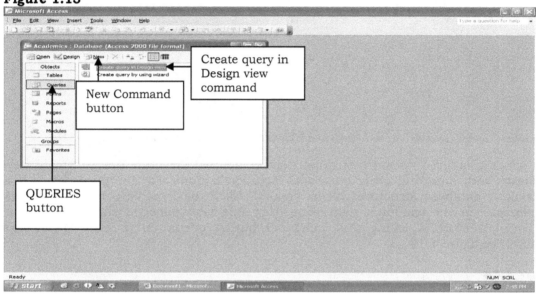

The embedded window shows the title of the database just created (**Academics**) and this is where the database objects such as tables and views are created. To access the SQL window, you must select the **Queries** button. Here you have two options. You can access the SQL window by double-clicking the **Create query in Design view** command on the right pane of the embedded window or just click the **New** command button on the menu bar of the embedded window.

Alternatively, you can used the key combination of the alternate key (Alt) and the underlined letter of the command name on the menu bar of the embedded window to activate the command. In the case of using the **New** command button of the menu bar, you can perform the command by doing the following - hold the Alt key + press letter N.

For demonstration purposes, the **New** command on the menu bar is used. Click the **New** command button and the next window is displayed. See figure 1.16.

18

Figure 1.16

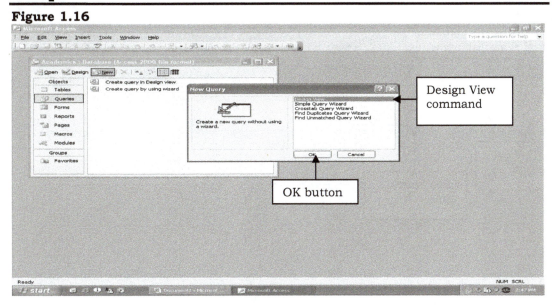

Here, yet another embedded window titled **New Query** is displayed. On this window, either double-click the ***Design View*** command on the right pane or select the command and click the **OK** button. This action displays the next MS access window. See figure 1.17.

Figure 1.17

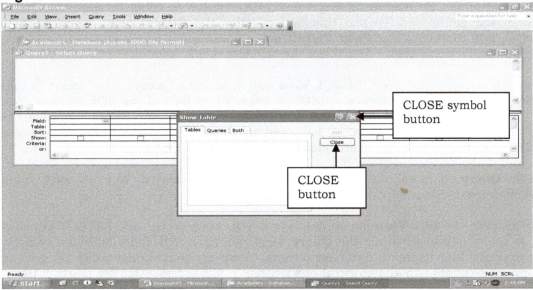

> **Note:** Double-clicking the ***Create query in Design view*** command in figure 1.15 will display this window as well, without going through figure 1.16.

Click the ***Close*** button of the embedded window titled **Show Table** to close it. Alternatively, you can use the ***Close*** symbol button on the title bar of the embedded window to close the window. The next step shows how to display MS Access SQL window. See figure 1.18.

Reviewing Relational Database Model

Figure 1.18

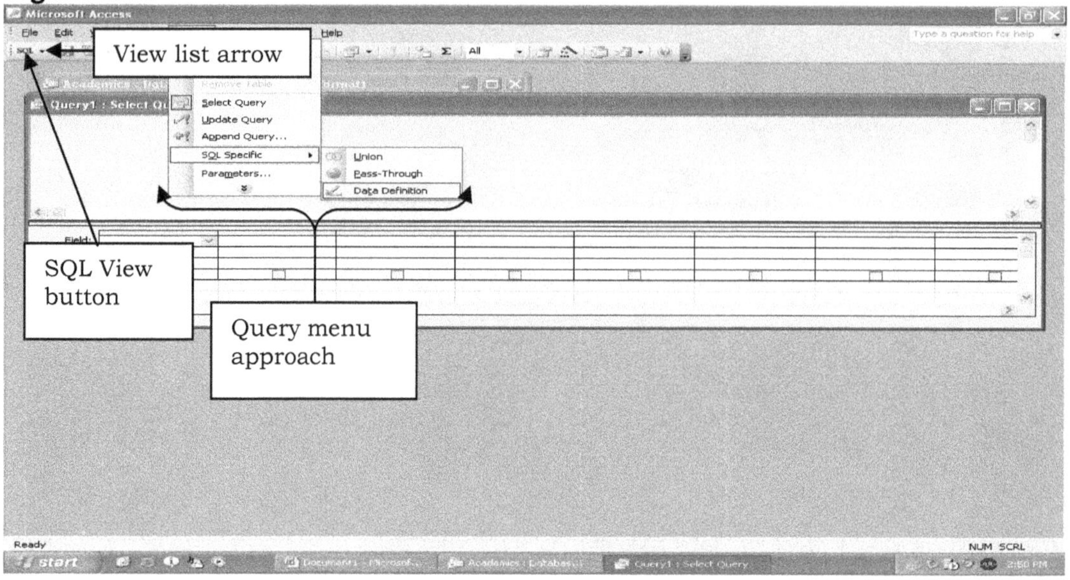

Two options are provided in MS Access to activate the SQL window. One option is to click the **SQL View** button on the standard toolbar of the MS Access window. If the **SQL View** button is not shown, click the *View* list arrow to the select the SQL View command.

The second option for displaying MS Access SQL window is going through the **Query** menu of the menu bar. To use this option, click the **Query** menu, point to *SQL Specific*, and then click the ***Data Definition*** command. For demonstration purposes, the textbook uses this option to activate the MS Access SQL window.

The only observation between the **SQL View** option and the **Query** menu option is that the **SQL View** approach displays a SELECT keyword as part of the SQL window. You have to delete the keyword to use the window to write SQL non-SELECT statements such as the CREATE TABLE statement used to create tables' structures. To write a SELECT statement, the window provides the first keyword - SELECT.

With the **Query** menu approach, a clean SQL window is displayed. You can start typing a SQL statement that is supported by MS Access.

To be specific, the **SQL View** option displays a SQL window with the SELECT keyword in it to query databases while the **Query** menu shows a SQL data definition window used to create and maintain database objects. However, both windows can be used to accomplish relational database operations written in MS Access SQL. See figure 1.19.

Figure 1.19

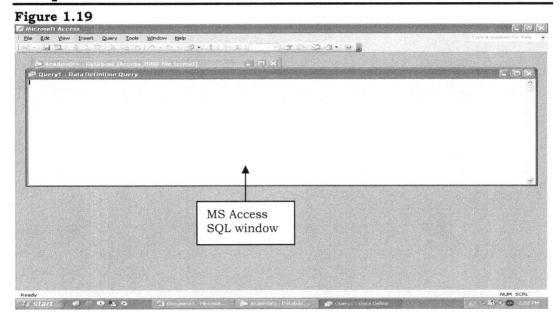

Figure 1.19 displays MS Access SQL window using the **Query** menu option. This is where you type MS Access SQL code. Figure 1.20 shows an example of MS Access SQL window that contains a CREATE TABLE statement that creates a student table.

Figure 1.20

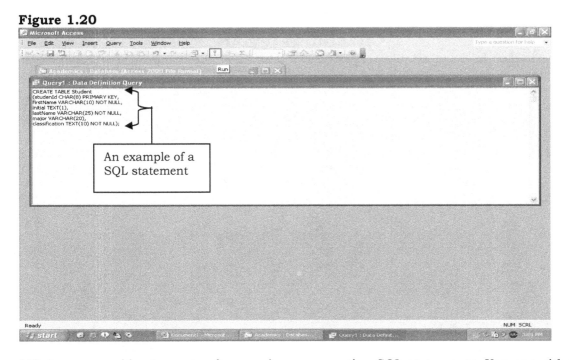

MS Access provides two ways for running or executing SQL statements. You can either use the **Run** button (! - exclamation symbol) of the standard toolbar or use the **Query** menu. It should be noted that MS Access SQL window can only run one SQL statement at a time. You cannot run two or more statements at one time. This is because the SQL window is a single-statement based window. To use the standard toolbar to run a SQL statement, just click the **Run** button after entering the statement. On the other hand, if you want to execute the SQL code using the menu, click the **Query** menu, and then click the **Run** command. See figure 1.21.

Reviewing Relational Database Model

Figure 1.21

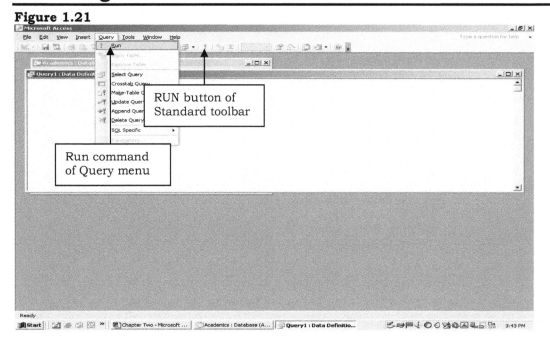

Note: To return to MS Access SQL window after a SQL statement is run, click the **View** list arrow of the standard toolbar and select the SQL View command. Alternatively, you can click the **View** menu and select the SQL View command.

Chapter Summary

This chapter explains relational database model and its concepts. The chapter also explains the characteristics of the model and the different components such as tables, views, and indexes that constitute a relational database. The three main tools – normalization process, entity-relationship model, and planning sheet - that are used at the conceptual design level are discussed. Structured Query Language, a sublanguage of relational database management system, is introduced and the language is discussed in detail in the remaining chapters of the textbook. The chapter also addresses MS Access SQL that is used to meet the requirement of the physical design level of a database. The step-by-step approach of activating MS Access SQL window is also explained.

Key Terms

Bridge Entity
Cardinality
Character
Child Table
Column
Composite Primary Key
Conceptual Design Phase
Data Control Language (DCL)
Data Definition Language (DDL)
Data independence
Data Manipulation Language (DML)
Entity-relationship Diagram
Entity-relationship Model
Foreign Key

Integrity Constraint
Many-to-many Relationship
Microsoft Access
Normal Form
Normalization Process
One-to-many Relationship
One-to-one Relationship
Parent Table
Physical Design Phase
Planning Sheet
Primary Key
Record
Relation
Relational Database Design

Chapter One

Relational Database Model   SQL
Repeating Group   Table

Chapter Review Questions

Multiple Choice Questions

1. Relational database management systems are
   - a. structures.
   - b. information systems.
   - c. software.
   - d. all of the above.

2. Which of the following is not a relational database object?
   - a. A view.
   - b. A table.
   - c. An index.
   - d. Microsoft Access.

3. A model that uses tables to store users' data is called
   - a. Entity integrity model.
   - b. Relational database model.
   - c. Normalization model.
   - d. Structured model.

4. Cardinality is indicated by using
   - a. Normalization process.
   - b. Reversed engineering.
   - c. Entity-relationship diagram.
   - d. Primary key.

5. The columns of a table are also called
   - a. records.
   - b. tuples.
   - c. fields.
   - d. rows.

6. A relation is called
   - a. data.
   - b. a table.
   - c. a row.
   - d. none of the above.

7. A tool used to identify a table's primary key is called
   - a. Entity integrity.
   - b. Structured database.
   - c. Normalization process.
   - d. Cardinality.

8. In what normal form are tables' relationships established?
   - a. 2NF
   - b. 3NF
   - c. 1NF
   - d. no normal form

9. A value in a table's foreign key column
   - a. cannot be null.
   - b. cannot be duplicated.
   - c. can be null.
   - d. can only be a numeric value.

10. The function of 2NF is to remove
   a. partial dependency.
   b. transitive dependency.
   c. repeating group.
   d. all of the above.

True or False Questions

11. Peter Chen data-modeling tool uses diamond-shaped symbol to represent relationship.
   a. True
   b. False

12. The function of a relation's planning sheet includes the definition of the relation's structure.
   a. True
   b. False

13. The physical design phase is dependent on databases' software.
   a. True
   b. False

14. SQL is used to create tables, not views.
   a. True
   b. False

15. Microsoft Access can be used as back-end software for small groups of PC users.
   a. True
   b. False

16. Data control language of SQL is used to modify tables' structures.
   a. True
   b. False

17. One of the drawbacks of relational database is having a single pool of data.
   a. True
   b. False

Fill in the blank Questions

18. A model that uses tables to store users' data is called _____.

19. A record is a collection of related _____.

20. A tool that is used to indicate cardinality in called _____.

21. We used a tool called _____ to remove repeating groups from a relation.

22. SQL stand for _____.

23. A _____ is used to uniquely identify each record in a table.

Essay Type Questions

24. Explain three benefits of relational database model?

25. In your own words, describe many-to-many relationship and cite one example to support your description?

26. Why is normalization process used in designing relational databases?

27. Explain the differences between conceptual design phase and physical design phase?

28. List some basic differences between Peter Chen tool symbols and that of the Air force tool symbols?

Chapter Two

Retrieving Data from Single Tables

Chapter Objectives

After completing this chapter, you should be able to

- Understand SELECT statements
- Perform simple retrievals on a single table
- Use ALL keyword and asterisk symbol to display data
- Eliminate records duplications when displaying data
- Use columns aliases to display data
- Perform basic mathematics as part of displayed data
- Concatenate text data
- Display null values

SELECT Statements

The SELECT statement is the most frequently used statement in SQL environment. The statement is used mostly to retrieve and display data from tables. The SELECT statement is also called a query because it is used to pose questions to a database. Querying tables to retrieve data mean writing the appropriate SELECT statements. The outcome of a query is usually what is displayed after the question has been processed. The SELECT statement is part of the data manipulation language (DML) subset of SQL. In this chapter, you will use the tables in a database called **AcademicX** to practice and understand the SELECT statement.

> **Note:** The **AcademicX** database is the practice database for this textbook. It is used in the remaining chapters – except chapters nine and ten – of this book to demonstrate the concepts learned.

Queries: A query is a question written in a format that a database recognizes and can respond to.

The complete syntax for a SELECT statement in MS Access SQL has seven clauses, namely, the SELECT clause, the FROM clause, the WHERE clause, the GROUP BY clause, the HAVING clause, the ORDER BY clause, and the WITH OWNERACCESS OPTION clause. Only the SELECT clause and the FROM clause are mandatory. In other words, the two clauses are required in a SELECT statement. The other five clauses are optional and are used based on the types of activities the user wants to perform.

Clauses: A clause is a valid portion of a SQL statement that is used to perform an action and usually begins with a keyword.

Keywords: A keyword is a word or an expression that has a special meaning in a programming language or in an application package. A keyword is a reserved word and it cannot represent anything else except for what it is defined to represent.

> **Note:** In SQL, when adjacent words are used as keywords, you must separate one word from the other by a space. This is the standard approach used in SQL environment. This space-insertion method is also used to separate individual elements in a SQL statement. In MS Access SQL, keywords are non-case sensitive. They can be written in uppercases, in lowercases, or in mixed cases. For SQL statements' syntax that are stated in this textbook, note with care the arrangement of the syntax and follow the arrangement in the order

Retrieving Data from Single Tables

presented when coding SQL statements. Words that are listed in uppercases in the syntax are keywords and are required except stated otherwise.

The required basic syntax for the SELECT statement is

SELECT [predicate] {[ALL] * | *existingColumnName, ...* | *columnExpression, ...*}
FROM *existingTableName, ...*;

The syntax for the SELECT statement with the basic optional clauses is

SELECT [predicate] {[ALL] * | *existingColumnName, ...* | *columnExpression, ...*}
FROM *existingTableName, ...*
[WHERE *rowCondition*]
[GROUP BY *existingColumnName, ...*]
[HAVING *groupCondition*]
[ORDER BY *existingColumnName, ...*]
[WITH OWNERACCESS OPTION];

where

- predicate is a condition keyword, such as DISTINCT, used to restrict records
- Symbol * is to include all columns
- *existingColumnName* is the column in the table listed in the FROM clause
- *columnExpression* is the expression formed by the combination of column(s) and data value(s). The column(s) and the data used in a column expression must be of the same data type
- *existingTableName* is the table that contains the column to be displayed
- *rowCondition* is the restriction that is applied to each record in the table
- *groupCondition* is a restriction on groups of records contained in the table
- Symbols [ ] mean items are optional
- Symbol | symbolizes **Or** Boolean operator. You can also list both *existingColumnName* and *columnExpression* or both asterisk symbol (*) and *columnExpression* in the SELECT clause
- Symbols ... mean more columns and/or columns' expressions and/or tables can be listed

Syntax: Syntax, in a computer programming environment, signifies the proper way of writing statements in a programming language or in an application package.

Predicates: A predicate is an optional keyword used as a condition in the SELECT clause of a SELECT statement to restrict the number of records to be displayed.

A predicate is either a DISTINCT keyword, a DISTINCTROW keyword, or a TOP keyword. The DISTINCT keyword and the DISTINCTROW keyword are discussed within the second subheading in the subsequent section of this chapter. The TOP keyword, which forms the foundation for the TOP clause, is discussed in detail in chapter four of this textbook. Other types of operations that can be performed with the SELECT statement, such as columns' aliases, columns' qualifiers, tables' aliases, and the IN clause are discussed in detail in this chapter and in the subsequent chapters of this textbook.

Note: The pair of curly braces used to enclose the groups of columns' items – [ALL]*, *existingColumnName*, and *columnExpression* – listed in the SELECT clause of the SELECT statement syntax is an indication that the groups are independent of the optional predicate keyword that precedes the groups in the syntax. The pair of curly braces is not required in the

Chapter Two

SELECT clause when writing a SELECT statement. Any of the groups or any correct combinations of the groups can be part of a SELECT statement that does not use an optional predicate keyword. In this textbook, whenever the syntax for a SELECT statement that includes an optional predicate keyword that precedes the groups of columns' items in the SELECT clause is written, a pair of curly braces is used to enclose the groups.

Note: If a numeric value or a date value is connected with the ampersand concatenation operator (&) to their data types' columns to form columns' expressions, the results are different from when the plus symbol (+) is used to form the columns' expressions. The ampersand operator, when used with a numeric value or a date value, appends the value to the column to form the column expression.

The SELECT clause is used to display (i) data from all columns or from selected columns, (ii) results of columns' expressions, and (iii) results of combinations of columns' data and columns' expressions. The column(s) listed in the clause must exist in the table(s) listed in the FROM clause.

The FROM clause is used to list the table(s) that contain the columns listed in the SELECT clause. The WHERE clause is used to establish the required restriction(s) for individual records contained in the table(s). The GROUP BY clause is used to group records that share common or similar characteristics in the table(s) and the column(s) used in the clause must exist in the table(s). The HAVING clause is used to establish the required restriction(s) for records grouped by the GROUP BY clause. The grouped records must exist in the table(s).

The ORDER BY clause is used to reorganize or sort data in ascending or descending order, and the column(s) used in the clause must exist in the table(s). The WITH OWNERACCESS OPTION clause is used to grant a user, in a multiuser environment, the permissions to perform certain operations on tables even if the user is not the owner of the tables. However, the operations the user can perform on those tables must be the same operations the owner of the tables can perform.

Note: For the interest of establishing users' and workgroups' accounts in a secured database and for working with a single-user environment, this textbook does not discuss the WITH OWNERACCESS OPTION clause in detail. Users' and workgroups' accounts are discussed in detail in chapter fourteen of this textbook.

When writing a SELECT statement, the clauses must be written in the order shown in the SELECT statement's syntax. The ORDER BY clause is usually, without the WITH OWNERACCESS OPTION clause, the last to be written when it is used in a SELECT statement.

Note: In Oracle, you can write the HAVING clause before the GROUP BY clause if both of them are used in a SELECT statement. However, since the HAVING clause is a condition clause that is used to restrict groups of records generated by the GROUP BY clause, the GROUP BY clause is usually written first. Oracle also supports the use of the optional ALL keyword in the SELECT clause of a SELECT statement just as MS Access SQL does. In MS Access SQL, a numeric data value is never enclosed in a pair of symbols when used in the appropriate clauses of a SELECT statement. The value is simply written as it is in the clauses where it is permitted. A text data value, when used in the appropriate clauses of a SELECT statement, must be enclosed in either double quotation marks or single quotation marks. When a date value is written in the clauses where the value is permitted in a SELECT statement, the date value usually is enclosed in a pair of number signs (#). However, there are certain MS Access SQL statements that also allow date values to be enclosed in quotation marks. For the purpose of distinguishing the text data syntax from the date data syntax, this textbook uses number signs to define the syntax for date data.

Retrieving Data from Single Tables

To practice with the SELECT statement, you must start MS Access to open the **AcademicX** database that contains the tables if MS access application is not running. If MS Access is already running on your computer, you only need to open the database to use the tables.

You navigate the application as described in chapter one on how to activate MS Access SQL window until figure 2.1 is displayed. This window is exactly the same window that is used to create databases and the one you are going to use in chapter nine to create the **Academics** database. To open an existing database, besides using the **File** menu or the **Open** button of the standard toolbar, two additional hyperlink commands can be used in MS Access 2003 to open a database. The **AcademicX** database created as a practice database is to be opened. See Figure 2.1.

> **Note:** The two databases created for this textbook have similar names. The database that is used for hands-on activities in most of the chapters is called **AcademicX** with an uppercase letter "X" ending the name, while the one you will create later in chapter nine is called **Academics** with a lowercase letter "s" ending the name. Any SQL statement written in MS Access SQL environment that is supported in Oracle can be copied to a text editor, such as Note Pad, and saved as a file with **.sql** extension. The statement can be run using Oracle database as long as the table(s) and the column(s) listed in the statement exist in the database. However, you can create the table(s) and the column(s) in Oracle database and run the statement. A text file that contains a SQL statement and saved with **.sql** extension can be run in Oracle SQL platform.

Figure 2.1

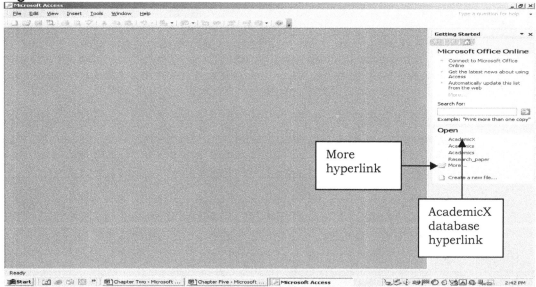

In addition to creating new databases, the **Open** section of the right pane (Getting Started task pane) of figure 2.1 is also used to open existing databases. The names of the recently opened databases are displayed as hyperlinks to access the databases if so desired. You can use the method to open a database if its name appears as a hyperlink in that section. The **More** hyperlink of the **Open** section of the figure 2.1 is used to navigate to the locations of databases that did not have their names displayed as hyperlinks.

Depending on how you installed your MS Access 2003 application, a security alert message may be displayed when you try to open an existing database. See figure 2.2.

Chapter Two

Figure 2.2

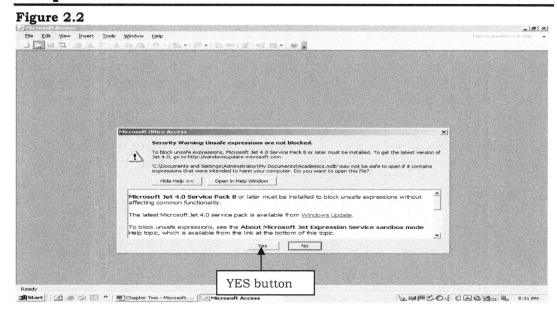

YES button

Click the **Yes** command button to continue to the next figure. See figure 2.3.

Figure 2.3

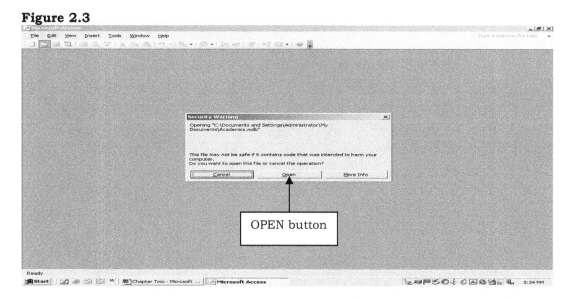

OPEN button

Click the **Open** command button to open the database.

> **Note:** Besides using different hyperlinks to create and open databases, every other step discussed in chapter one on how to activate and use the SQL window of MS Access is the same. You may refer to the **Activating Microsoft Access SQL Window** section of chapter one before continuing with this chapter.
>
> Always remember that you must start MS Access and launch the **AcademicX** practice database whenever the database is required in the textbook for practice purposes.
>
> In MS Access SQL, tables' names, columns' names, and tables' data are non case sensitive. You can list them in all uppercases, all lowercases, or mixed cases in SELECT statements. The outcomes are the same.

Retrieving Data from Single Tables

Simple Retrievals

A simple retrieval is a process where all records stored in a table are displayed. This type of data retrieval requires only the SELECT clause and the FROM clause in the SELECT statement. In a simple retrieval, data from one column, two columns, few columns, or all columns can be shown as the result of the operation. However, all records in the table queried are displayed. A simple retrieval has no restrictions or conditions placed on the records of the queried table.

To display first names (one column) of all faculty members using the facultyX table, type and run the following SELECT statement on the MS Access SQL window.

SELECT firstName
FROM facultyX;

See partial result below.

firstName
Ada
Doris
:
:
Rischi
Zenat

Figure 2.4 shows the usually way of typing a SQL statement in MS Access SQL window. That is writing one clause in one line or one clause is written in one line.

Figure 2.4

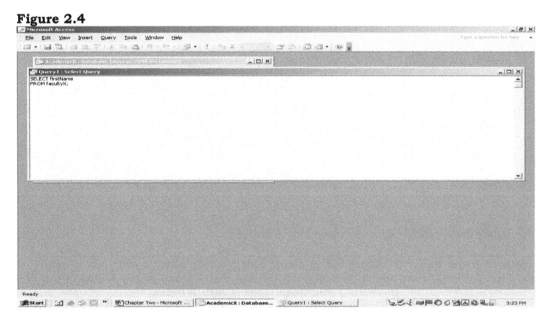

Figure 2.5 shows the displayed result in MS Access environment.

Chapter Two

Figure 2.5

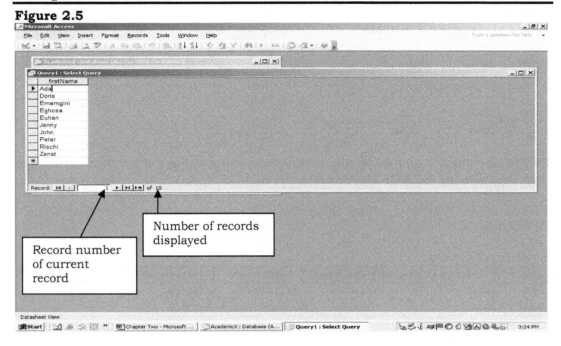

In MS Access, the result of a query shows the total number of records displayed and the record number of the current record the database pointer is actively pointing to. Usually when the result of a query is displayed in MS Access, the first record in the list is always the current record. From this point on, SELECT statements will be typed and their results will be displayed without showing MS Access SQL window.

To display first names and last names (two columns) of all faculty members using the facultyX table, type and run the following SELECT statement.

SELECT firstName, lastName
FROM facultyX;

See partial result below.

firstName	lastName
Ada	Lasking
Doris	Mea
:	:
:	:
Rischi	Ugboma
Zenat	Miller

You might have noticed that when more than one column is listed in the SELECT clause, the columns are separated by commas. This is the standard rule in SQL. Any time more than one element is listed in a clause (where allowed), the elements must be separated by commas.

To display identification numbers, first names, and last names (fewer columns) of all faculty members using the facultyX table, type and run the following SELECT statement.

SELECT facultyId, firstName, lastName
FROM facultyX;

31

Retrieving Data from Single Tables

See partial result below.

facultyId	firstName	lastName
AL501828	Ada	Lasking
DM674543	Doris	Mea
:	:	:
:	:	:
RU123098	Rischi	Ugboma
ZM567123	Zenat	Miller

To display all columns' data of faculty members' records using the facultyX table, type and run the following SELECT statement.

SELECT facultyId, firstName, initial, lastName, offPhone, departmentCode, chairId
FROM facultyX;

See partial result below.

facultyId	firstName	initial	lastName	offPhone	departmentCode	chairId
AL501828	Ada	P	Lasking	0321239876	CSCM09	EE987654
DM674543	Doris	V	Mea	0324569132	EDUD05	
:	:	:	:	:	:	:
:	:	:	:	:	:	:
RU123098	Rischi	B	Ugboma	0327555491	NASC08	
ZM567123	Zenat	J	Miller	0323751906	EDUD05	DM674543

Use of ALL Keyword and Asterisk Symbol (*)

The combination of the ALL keyword and the asterisk symbol (*) or the asterisk symbol (*) alone is used in the SELECT clause of a SELECT statement as a shortcut for including all columns' data in a table. Using one of both methods reduces the number of keystrokes usually required to type columns' names, commas, and spaces. Both methods are the fastest ways of displaying data from all columns contained in a table. However, using the asterisk symbol alone reduces the number of keystrokes.

To display data from all columns of faculty members' records using the facultyX table, type and run the following SELECT statement.

SELECT *
FROM facultyX;

See partial result below.

facultyId	firstName	initial	lastName	offPhone	departmentCode	chairId
AL501828	Ada	P	Lasking	0321239876	CSCM09	EE987654
DM674543	Doris	V	Mea	0324569132	EDUD05	
:	:	:	:	:	:	:
:	:	:	:	:	:	:
RU123098	Rischi	B	Ugboma	0327555491	NASC08	
ZM567123	Zenat	J	Miller	0323751906	EDUD05	DM674543

The result of this query is exactly the same as the result of the last query where all columns of the facultyX table are listed in the SELECT clause.

Alternatively, you can precede the asterisk symbol with the optional ALL keyword in the SELECT clause of the SELECT statement to achieve the same result.

> **Note:** The order in which columns are listed in the SELECT clause does not have to follow the structural (column) arrangement of the table. You can list a table's columns in the SELECT clause in whatever order you prefer as long as the final outcome meets your need. The columns' arrangement of the SELECT clause does not affect or change the structure of the table in which data are being displayed. The result of the action of the SELECT clause is temporary. There are no permanent changes to the table's data or to the original columns' arrangement of the table.

Other Types of Operations Performed in the SELECT Clause

Besides the listing of tables' columns, there are other different types of operations that can be achieved using the SELECT clause. In this section, five basic operations that are accomplished through the SELECT clause are discussed. These operations include (i) suppressing (eliminating) duplications of records, (ii) assigning aliases (A.K.A.) to columns, (iii) performing mathematics, (iv) concatenating (combining) text columns or concatenating text columns and text literals, and (v) displaying null values. Other types of operations that are supported by the SELECT clause that are not discussed here will be shown in the appropriate chapters in the textbook.

Eliminating Duplications of Records

MS Access SQL provides two keywords to suppress the duplications of displayed records. The keywords are DISTINCT and DISTINCTROW. To avoid the duplications of records in the result of a query, you must precede the specific column(s) in the SELECT clause with any of the keywords.

Data Duplications: Data duplication is a situation in SQL environment where the same piece of data is displayed more than once in the result of a query.

Data Suppressions: Data suppression is a process of eliminating duplicated data, where possible, in a query before displaying the result.

The SELECT clause basic syntax for eliminating records' duplications is

SELECT DISTINCT | DISINCTROW *existingColumnName*, ...
where

- *existingColumnName* is the column in the table listed in the FROM clause
- Symbol | symbolizes *Or* Boolean operator
- Symbols ... mean more columns can be listed

To display faculty members who are assigned to teach courses without duplicating their identification numbers using the courseX table, type and run the following SELECT statement.

SELECT DISTINCT facultyId
FROM courseX;

See partial result below.

facultyId
AL501828
DM674543
:
:
RU123098
ZM567123

Retrieving Data from Single Tables

> **Note:** The DISTINCT keyword suppresses the duplication of columns' data and only affects the columns listed in the SELECT clause of a SELECT statement. DISTINCTROW suppresses the duplications of records in the tables that are being queried.

To display course codes, course sections, and their assigned faculty members without duplications of records using the courseX table, type and run the following SELECT statement.

SELECT DISTINCTROW courseCode, section, facultyId
FROM courseX;

See partial result below.

courseCode	section	facultyId
BUS101	2010	JS994450
BUS101	2020	JS994450
:	:	:
:	:	:
SOC101	2010	JH682508
SOC450	2010	ES509264

In the result, each combination of the three columns appeared only once. In other words, there are no duplications of records.

> **Note:** In addition to the DISTINCT keyword, Oracle also uses UNIQUE keyword to eliminate duplications of specific records.
>
> Example:
> SELECT UNIQUE facultyId
> FROM courseX;

Assigning Aliases to Columns

Sometimes when tables are created, names given to columns may not properly reflect the data of those columns. In such situations when querying tables with ambiguous columns' names, you might want to display the results of the queries with meaningful columns' names. SQL allows the use of aliases in place of original columns' names to properly reflect the contents of those columns. When the results of the queries are displayed, the columns' aliases become the columns' headings of the displayed results.

Columns Aliases: A column alias is a temporary secondary name given to a column and used as a column heading in the result of a query.

In MS Access SQL, to assign an alias to a column, you use the AS keyword. The SELECT clause basic syntax for giving an alias to a column is

SELECT *existingColumnName* AS *alias*, ...

where

- *existingColumnName* is the column in the table listed in the FROM clause
- *alias* is the temporary and appropriate name that will be substituted for the column in a query result
- Symbol ... means more columns can be listed

Chapter Two

In MS Access SQL, to assign an alias that is not one word (include spaces) to a column, you must enclose the name in square brackets.

To display faculty members' last names with the column alias "Faculty Last Name" and their phone numbers with the column alias "Faculty_Phone", type and run the following SELECT statement.

SELECT lastName AS [Faculty Last Name], offPhone AS Faculty_Phone
FROM facultyX;

See partial result below.

Faculty Last Name	Faculty_Phone
Lasking	0321239876
Mea	0324569132
:	:
:	:
Ugboma	0327555491
Miller	0323751906

> **Note:** In Oracle, the AS keyword is optional. That is it can be omitted when substituting aliases for columns. Also in Oracle, when the columns' aliases contain spaces or you want the aliases to be displayed in particular letter cases, you must enclose them in double quotation marks. By default, Oracle converts columns' aliases made of letters to uppercase letters when the aliases are not enclosed in double quotation marks.
>
> Example:
> SELECT lastName AS "Faculty Last Name", offPhone AS "Faculty Phone"
> FROM facultyX;

Performing Mathematics

SQL permits performing computation or mathematics in the SELECT clause of a SELECT statement. Doing computation is possible only with columns defined with numeric data type or date data type. You can perform mathematics using only existing columns, only arithmetic expressions, only date expressions, or combining appropriate existing columns with the appropriate expressions. The data types of the columns must match the data types of the expressions when combining columns and expressions. The column that contains the result of such computation is called a calculated field. A calculated field is generated from performing mathematics using the SELECT clause of a SELECT statement. The field never existed in the table that is being queried.

Arithmetic Expressions: An arithmetic (numeric) expression in SQL is a mathematical form where numeric columns, date columns, numeric values, date values, and/or numeric functions, date functions are connected by numeric operators. An example of a numeric expression is 4*3+7-ROUND(7.967,1).

Calculated Fields: A calculated field, also called a computed field, is a column that contains the result of a mathematical computation.

The SELECT clause basic syntax for performing mathematics is

SELECT   *existingColumnName* | *mathematicalExpression*   *arithmeticOperator* *existingColumnName* | *mathematicalExpression...*

where

Retrieving Data from Single Tables

- *existingColumnName* is the column in the table listed in the FROM clause
- *mathematicalExpression* is numeric values or date values, their functions, or combination of the values types and their functions, and numeric operators
- *arithmeticOperator* is the numeric symbol used to connect mathematical values and/or functions
- Symbol | symbolizes *Or* Boolean operator. You can also list both *existingColumnName* and *mathematicalExpression* in the SELECT clause
- Symbols ... mean more columns and/or arithmetic expressions and/or arithmetic operators can be listed

> **Note:** Adding two date values or subtracting two date values yields a numeric value. On the contrary, adding a numeric value to a date value or subtracting a numeric value from a date value yields a date value. When subtracting two date values, the earlier date should be subtracted from the current date to generate the result in the positive form. If the current date is subtracted from the earlier date, the same numeric value is displayed but in the negative form.

To perform mathematics, arithmetic operators – also called numeric or mathematical operators - are needed to construct mathematical expressions.

There are seven (7) basic arithmetic operators in MS Access SQL. The operators are listed in figure 2.6.

Figure 2.6

Arithmetic Operator	Name	Functional Description
^ (caret)	Exponentiation	For raising a numeric value to a certain power (exponentiation)
*	Multiplication	For calculating the product of numeric values
/	Real division	For dividing numeric values and giving the result in floating point form
\	Integer division	For dividing numeric values and giving the result in integer form
mod	Modulus	For calculating the remainder of dividing numeric values
+	Addition	For calculating the sum (total) of numeric values
-	Subtraction	For calculating the difference of numeric values

Usually, when mathematical expressions are constructed with arithmetic operators of the same priority, the calculation is performed left to right. However, when different types of arithmetic operators are used in mathematical expressions, SQL uses algebraic rules called the order of precedence rules or the order of priority rules to perform the calculation. The order of precedence rules mean that the arithmetic operator with highest priority or highest superiority is performed first, followed by the operator that has the next highest priority in the order of precedence ladder, and in the order until the operator with the lowest priority is encountered. The arithmetic operator with the lowest priority is performed last.

In mathematics, a pair of parentheses is used to control the order in which the mathematics is calculated. When you want arithmetic operators with lower priorities to be performed before the operators with higher priorities, you must enclose the numeric expression with lower priority operators in parentheses. The arrangement indicates the order in which you want the calculation to be performed. A numeric expression enclosed in a pair of parentheses is done first in mathematics. If parentheses are nested within other parentheses, the mathematical expression within the innermost parentheses is performed first. In other words, mathematical expressions with nested parentheses are performed starting from the inside parentheses toward the outside parentheses.

Figure 2.7 shows arithmetic operators in their order of priority or superiority from top toward the bottom.

Figure 2.7

Order of Precedence	Operator
1	^ (exponentiation)
2	* / \ mod
3	+ -

To display faculty members' last names, their current annual salaries, their annual salaries increase of three percent, and their new salaries after the increase, type and run the following SELECT statement.

SELECT lastName AS [Last Name], annualSalary AS [Current Salary], annualSalary * 0.03 AS [Annual Increase], annualSalary + annualSalary * 0.03 AS [New Salary]
FROM facultyX;

See partial result below.

Last Name	Current Salary	Annual Increase	New Salary
Lasking	54354.80	1630.6440234375	55985.4448046875
Mea	62980.25	1889.4075	64869.6575
:	:	:	:
:	:	:	:
Ugboma	70760.15	2122.804453125	72882.952890625
Miller	46998.95	1409.9684765625	48408.9176953125

The first and second columns (lastName, annualSalary) reading from left of the query result are data in the facultyX table, while the third and fourth columns (annualSalary * 0.03, annualSalary + annualSalary * 0.03) are mathematical expressions. The results of these expressions are not stored in the facultyX table but are gotten by using data that are contained in the table. The results of these mathematical expressions are displayed in columns that are referred to as calculated fields or computed fields. All elements in the SELECT clause of the SELECT statement are assigned aliases to properly reflect their contents.

> **Note:** When mathematical expressions are written as part of a SELECT clause, SQL will generate generic columns' names as columns' headings to display the result of the query if the expressions are not given aliases. The generic names are assigned because the mathematical expressions are not actual columns and they do not exist physically in the table that is being queried.

Concatenating Text Data

MS Access SQL allows the concatenation (combination) of columns that contain text data or the concatenation of columns that contain text data and text literals (character, string). There are times when you want to combine several text columns' contents into a single column's data or to combine text columns' contents with text literals to form the data of a single column. In such situation, you have to concatenate the columns or concatenate the columns and the text literals.

Retrieving Data from Single Tables

Concatenation: Concatenation is the process of combining two or more text columns or one or more text columns with text literals to produce the data for a single column.

MS Access SQL provides two symbols to accomplish the concatenation operation. The symbols are the ampersand (&) and the plus sign (+), and they are used to connect the elements to be concatenated. The concatenating symbol being used must be typed between one element and the other element in the combination operation. MS Access SQL allows the use of both symbols in the same concatenation operation as long as each of the symbols connects its own two text data values. Using one of the concatenation symbols or both in the same concatenation operation with more than two text items to combine produce the same result.

To combine text literals including spaces to columns, you must enclose the text data in either double quotation marks or single quotation marks. The type of quotation marks you choose does not affect the outcome of the query. The results are the same. MS Access SQL also allows the use of both double quotation marks and single quotation marks in the same concatenation operation, but for different text data values.

> *Note:* When concatenating columns with text literals, SQL uses generic names as columns' headings to display the result of the query if the concatenations are not given columns' aliases. The generic names are assigned due to the fact that the concatenations are not actual columns and they do not exist physically in the table that is being queried.

To display the combined first name and last name of each faculty member using the facultyX table, type and run the following SELECT statement.

SELECT firstName & " " + lastName As [Full Name]
FROM facultyX;

See partial result below.

Full Name
Ada Lasking
Doris Mea
:
:
Rischi Ugboma
Zenat Miller

For demonstration purposes, the two concatenation symbols (&, +) are used to combine data from the first name column and the last name column. The double quotation marks are used to include two spaces to separate the last name from the first name. Without the spaces, the contents of the two columns will be joined together without distinction.

> *Note:* Oracle uses two methods to perform concatenation operations. One method uses two pipes (vertical lines) || and the other method uses the CONCAT function. Oracle allows only the use of single quotation marks to enclose text literals in concatenation operations.
>
> Example:
> SELECT firstName || ' ' || lastName AS "Full Name"
> FROM facultyX;
>   Or
> SELECT CONCAT(firstName, CONCAT(' ',lastName)) AS "Full Name"
> FROM facultyX;

Chapter Two

Displaying Null Values

When columns contain no known values, it is said that those columns contain null values. A null value is an unknown data value that can not be used to achieve a measurable calculation or result. A null value is said to be unavailable, unknown, or not applicable and it is completely different from the numeric value zero (0) and the text value space ( ).

Null Values: A null value is an unknown value in a column when the column receives no known value during data entry operation for the table where the column exists.

When tables' columns contain null values, the results of those columns, when displayed, are null. For example, displaying the chairId column of the facultyX table will show some entries to be null. This is because data were not previously entered into those columns' entries.

To display first names, last names, and department chairpersons' identification numbers using facultyX table, type and run the following SELECT statement.

SELECT firstName, lastName, chairId
FROM facultyX;

See partial result below.

firstName	lastName	chairId
Ada	Lasking	EE987654
Doris	Mea	
:	:	:
:	:	:
Rischi	Ugboma	
Zenat	Miller	DM674543

You might have noticed the null values of the chairId column. In addition, when columns that are used in mathematics contain null values, the results of the calculations are also null values.

For demonstration purposes, a table called facultyZ contains the annualSalary column where some of the faculty members' salaries are yet to be entered.

To display first names, last names, and to calculate annual salaries' increase of three (3) percent for faculty members using facultyZ table, type and run the following SELCT statement.

SELECT firstName AS [First Name], lastName AS [Last Name], annualSalary * 0.03 AS [Annual Increase]
FROM facultyZ;

See partial result below.

First Name	Last Name	Annual Increase
Ada	Lasking	
Doris	Mea	1889.4075
:	:	:
:	:	:
Rischi	Ugboma	2122.804453125
Zenat	Miller	

Retrieving Data from Single Tables

Again, you might have noticed that some of the records' annual increase calculations (the column aliased Annual Increase) are null. Those null values occurred because the annual salaries for those faculty members were not entered before the column called annualSalary is used in the computation.

> **Note:** In MS Access SQL when data values (actual values) that are being queried are not contained in a table, you can obtain the results of such values using only the SELECT clause of a SELECT statement. All other clauses can be omitted.
>
> Example:
> SELECT "Eghosa" + " " + "Maklasi" AS [FULL NAME], 62000 * 0.045 AS [FOUR AND HALF PERCENT];
>
> Notice that the SELECT statement consists only of one clause – the SELECT clause.

Chapter Summary

This chapter discusses retrieving data from single tables using basic SELECT statements. The chapter also discusses how to (i) use the optional ALL keyword and the asterisk symbol (*) to display data, (ii) eliminate duplications of records, (iii) use columns' aliases in data retrievals' operations, (iv) perform basic mathematics, (v) combine text columns and text literals, and (vi) display null values.

SELECT Statement Syntax and Statements Summary

The table below presents the SELECT statement clauses' syntax, special symbols, and keywords that are discussed in this chapter and the statements' examples for retrieving data from single tables.

Statement Type	Basic Statement Syntax	Statement Example
SELECT statement is used to retrieve and display data from a table or from joined tables	SELECT [predicate] {[ALL] * | *existingColumnName*, ... | *columnExpression*, ...} FROM *existingTableName*, ...;	SELECT facultyId FROM facultyX;
Clause Type	**Clause Syntax**	**Clause Example**
SELECT clause is used to list columns, columns' expressions, or combinations of columns and columns' expressions	SELECT [predicate] {[ALL] * | *existingColumnName*, ... | *columnExpression*, ...}	SELECT facultyId, annualSalary
FROM clause is used to list the table or the tables to be queried	FROM *existingTableName*, ...	FROM faculty
Special Symbol and Keyword	**Description**	**Statement Example**
, (comma)	Used to separate columns listed in the SELECT clause or tables listed in the FROM clause	SELECT studentId, dateFirstEnrolled FROM studentX;
& (ampersand) + (plus)	Used in the SELECT clause to concatenate or combine columns data	SELECT firstName & lastName FROM facultyX;
"" (double quotation mark) '' (single quotation mark)	Used in the SELECT clause to include spaces between concatenated or combined columns	SELECT firstName + " " + lastName FROM facultyX;

^ (caret) * (multiplication) / (real division) \ (integer division) Mod (modulus) + (addition) - (subtraction)	Used in the SELECT clause to perform mathematics or numeric calculations	SELECT facultyId, annualSalary * 0.06 AS [Annual Income Increase] FROM facultyX;
[ALL] *	Used in the SELECT clause to display all columns' data in a table	SELECT * FROM studentX; OR SELECT ALL * FROM studentX;
AS	Used in the SELECT clause to assign aliases to columns	SELECT lastName AS [Faculty Last Name], offPhone AS [Office Phone Number] FROM facultyX;
DISTINCT	Used in the SELECT clause to suppress the duplications of displayed columns' data	SELECT DISTINCT facultyId FROM courseX;
DISTINCTROW	Used in the SELECT clause to suppress the duplications of displayed records	SELECT DISTINCTROW courseCode, facultyId FROM courseX;

Key Terms

ALL
Calculated fields
Column aliases
Concatenation
Concatenation operators
DISTINCT
DISTINCTROW
FROM clause
GROUP BY clause

HAVING clause
Mathematical operators
NULL value
ORDER BY clause
SELECT clause
SELECT statement
Simple retrieval
WHERE clause

Chapter Review Questions

Multiple Choice Questions

1. The statement that is used to retrieve and display tables' data begins with the Keyword
    a. SELECT.
    b. UPDATE.
    c. DISPLAY.
    d. COMMIT.

2. A question that is posed to a database in a format that the database recognizes and can respond to is called a
    a. view.
    b. table.
    c. index.
    d. query.

3. One of the clauses that is required in a SELECT statement is the _____ clause.
    a. HAVING
    b. GROUP BY
    c. WHERE
    d. FROM

4. A keyword is a
    a. chain of characters.
    b. mathematical expression.

    c. reserved word.
    d. all of the above.

5. The FROM clause of a SELECT statement is used to list
    a. tables.
    b. views.
    c. columns.
    d. indexes.

6. The WHERE clause of a SELECT statement is used to establish restrictions
   For
    a. group of records.
    b. individual records.
    c. certain number of records.
    d. all of the above.

7. Study the following SELECT statement and point out the errors if any.
    SELECT firstName; lastName
    FROM student;

    a. SELECT clause has an error.
    b. FROM clause has an error.
    c. There are no errors in the statement.
    d. The table must not be called student.

8. The shortcut method for displaying the data of all columns in a table is to use _____
   in a SELECT clause.
    a. the asterisk symbol (*) alone
    b. the combination of the ALL keyword and the asterisk symbol (*)
    c. all of the above.
    d. none of the above

9. Study the following SELECT statement and indicate the errors if any. Assume that the
   columns listed in the SELECT clause are of numeric data type and they exist in the faculty
   table.
    SELECT annualSalary * 0.50 / 12, 6*5-3
    FROM faculty;

    a. There is an error in the SELECT clause.
    b. There is an error in the FROM clause.
    c. There are no errors in the statement.
    d. The SELECT statement needs more clauses.

10. A calculated field is a column that
    a. actually exists in a table.
    b. can be created with numeric columns of a table.
    c. contains the combination of numeric data and text data.
    d. all of the above.

True or False Questions
11. A query is not the same as a SELECT statement.
    a. True
    b. False

12. A SQL statement is usually composed of one or more valid portions that
   begin with keywords.
    a. True
    b. False

13. A simple retrieval requires no restrictions.
   a. True
   b. False

14. When used, the ALL keyword must be combined with the asterisk symbol (*) in the SELECT clause of MS Access SQL SELECT statement.
   a. True
   b. False

15. To avoid the duplications of columns' data for columns listed in the SELECT clause, you use the keyword DISTINCTROW
   a. True
   b. False

16. The arithmetic operator "**/**" is used for integer division.
   a.   True
   b.   False

17. A null value must always be of text data type.
   a.   Tue
   b.   False

Fill in the blank Questions

18. A _____ statement is an instruction that displays data contained in a table.

19. SELECT _____ lists the columns which data are to be displayed.

20. The portion of a SQL SELECT statement that shows the table name is called

_____.

21. A name that is temporarily assigned to a column in a SELECT clause is called a(n) _____.

22. To eliminate the duplications of displayed records, you use the _____ keyword.

23. The _____ is used to separate columns in a SELECT clause.

Essay Type Questions

24. Explain concatenation and give an example using a SQL statement?

25. What is a null value and how does it affect the result of a query?

26. What is the function of the MOD operator?

27. In a SELECT statement, what is the name of the second clause and its main function?

28. Define a simple retrieval and give an example using a SQL statement?

Hands-on Activities

Study the structures and the data of **AcademicX** database tables in appendix A (pages 355 through 360) and perform the following hands-on exercises.

1. Display the identification number and the country of origin of each student.

2. Display the data of all records in the courseX table.

3. Write a SQL statement to list course code and course name without duplicating records.

4. Write a SQL statement to show students' identification numbers, their last names, and dates they first enrolled for courses. Assign column alias **ID #** to the student identification number column, column alias **Student Lname** to the last name column, and column alias **First Enrollment** to the date of first enrolled column.

5. Write a SQL statement to display faculty members' identification numbers, their current monthly salaries, and their future monthly salaries once their annual salaries are increased by four and a half percent. Assign column alias **CMSAL** to the current monthly salary column and column alias **FMSAL** to the future monthly salary column.

6. Display each faculty member identification number and the remainder of the faculty member's annual salary after dividing his or her annual salary by 12. Assign column alias **Remainder Amount** to the column containing the result of the calculation.

7. Display a course code and the course name, without duplication, for each course by concatenating the course code with the course name. Precede the concatenated data with the text expression "Course Code and Name Description:" Use column alias **Course Full Name** for the column that displays the concatenated data.

8. Write a SQL statement to display students' countries of origin, the cities they reside in their countries of origin, dates they first enrolled for courses, their identification numbers, and their last names in the order specified in this question.

9. Display each faculty member monthly salary and one-third (1/3) of his or her six months (mid year) salary. Assign column alias **MonthlySalary** to the column that contains the monthly salary calculation and column alias **OneThird MidYear Salary** to the column that contains the mid year calculation.

10. Display the complete records of all books in the bookX table. Include the ALL keyword in the appropriate clause and in the right position to generate the needed result.

Chapter Three

More on Retrieving Data from Single Tables

Chapter Objectives

After completing this chapter, you should be able to

- Perform conditional retrievals using WHERE clause
- Use standard comparison operators in conditional retrievals
- Write conditions in negative forms
- Use other comparison operators in conditional retrievals
- Use logical operators in conditional retrievals
- Use parentheses in compound conditions
- Sort displayed data with tables columns
- Sort displayed data with columns positions

Conditional Retrievals

There are times when you want to query a table to return fewer records rather than all records in the table. To return fewer records means displaying only the rows that meet the condition or conditions you specified in a SELECT statement. Such a process is called a conditional retrieval. A conditional retrieval filters out the records that do not meet the conditions or criteria that are specified in a SELECT statement. In other words, restrictions are placed in the statement to limit the records to be displayed.

Conditions: A condition, in SQL environment, is a requirement that records of a table must satisfy in order to be displayed as part of the result of a query.

Conditional Retrievals: A conditional retrieval is a process where only the records that meet certain established requirements or criteria in a SELECT statement are included in the result of a query.

To achieve this type of data retrieval in SQL, you use the WHERE clause for individual records and the HAVING clause for grouped records. The HAVING clause is discussed in detail in chapter seven of this textbook.

To display individual records that satisfy the condition(s) specified in a SELECT statement, you use the WHERE clause. The basic syntax for the WHERE clause is

WHERE *rowCondition*

where

- *rowCondition* is the restriction that is applied to each record in the table

There are two types of conditional retrievals. One type uses simple conditions to display records that meet the restrictions specified in the SELECT statement, and the other type uses compound or complex conditions to list records that meet the restrictions specified in the SELECT statement.

> **Note:** In MS Access SQL, Columns' aliases cannot be used as columns' names or columns' expressions in the WHERE clause.

More on Retrieving Data from Single Tables

Conditional Retrievals Using Simple Conditions

A simple condition is a restriction in a condition clause, such as the WHERE clause, and consists of only three parts.

Simple Conditions: A simple condition is a restriction that consists of a column name or a column expression, a comparison operator, and another column name, a value, or a function in that order.

The basic syntax for a simple condition using the WHERE clause is

WHERE   *existingColumnName* | *columnExpression   comparisonOperator*
existingColumnName | value | functionName

where

- *existingColumnName* is the column in the table listed in the FROM clause
- *columnExpression* is the expression formed by the combination of column(s) and data value(s). The column(s) and the data used in a column expression must be of the same data type
- *comparisonOperator* is the comparison operator used to establish the restriction
- *value* is the literal constant or the data expression that yields a single value used in the comparison
- *functionName* is the function used in the comparison
- Symbol | symbolizes *Or* Boolean operator

In a simple condition, you can compare the data of one column to (i) the data of another column, (ii) a value, or (ii) a function. You can also compare the result of an expression to (iv) data in a column, (v) a value, or (vi) a function.

Standard Comparison Operators

To create a simple condition, you must use one of the six standard comparison operators. These operators are also called relational operators and they are the standard operators for creating simple conditions.

Comparison Operators: A comparison operator also called a relational operator is a connecting symbol used to compare the degree of relationship between two data items.

The six comparison operators are listed in figure 3.1 and their interpretations are written in both mathematical and non mathematical forms.

Figure 3.1

Comparison Operator	Mathematical Interpretation	Non-Mathematical Interpretation
=	Equal to	Exact or Match
>	Greater than	After
<	Less than	Before
>=	Greater than or Equal to	After or On
<=	Less than or Equal to	Before or On
<>	Not equal to	Not exact or No match or Different

Note: Oracle uses two additional sets of symbols to denote the Not Equal To operator. The two sets of symbols are != and ^=.

Chapter Three

Standard comparison operators are shown in their order of priority or superiority from top toward bottom. See figure 3.2.

Figure 3.2

Order of Precedence	Operator
1	> < >= <=
2	= <>

The following examples show how the WHERE clause is used to display records that meet the specified conditions.

To display identification numbers, last names, and first names of students who are sophomore using the studentX table, type and run the following SELECT statement.

SELECT studentId AS [STUDENT ID], lastName AS [LAST NAME], firstName AS [FIRST NAME]
FROM studentX
WHERE classification = "Sophomore";

See result below.

STUDENT ID	LAST NAME	FIRST NAME
FK576381	Kolly	Florence
AB778204	Bomor	Abel
AU408153	Uzueg	Andy
FA213595	Anthony	Fredrica

Records showing students who are sophomore are displayed instead of all the students' records that are contained in the studentX table. This type of restriction and display are possible because the WHERE clause is included in the SELECT statement.

To display last names, identification numbers, and dates students first enrolled for courses for those students who enrolled after August 20, 2005 using the studentX table, type and run the following SELECT statement.

SELECT lastName AS [Student Last Name], studentId AS [Student Identification Number], dateFirstEnrolled AS [First Enrolled]
FROM studentX
WHERE dateFirstEnrolled > #08/20/2005#;

See result below.

Student Last Name	Student Identification Number	First Enrolled
Actionbarrel	EA486741	8/25/2005
Johnson	EJ890321	1/20/2006
Jeffer	CJ684975	1/18/2006

Three records are displayed because they satisfied the condition.

Using Numeric Data in WHERE Clause

To specify a numeric value in the condition of a WHERE clause, you write the value without enclosing it in either a pair of quotation marks or a pair of number signs. Example:

```
SELECT *
FROM facultyX
WHERE annualSalary > 59000;
```

Using Date Data in WHERE Clause

MS Access has several date formats, but the default date format in which dates are stored is mm/dd/yyyy. mm stand for the two digits of the month, dd stand for the two digits of the day, and yyyy stand for the four digits of the year.

In MS Access SQL, to specify date data in the condition of a WHERE clause, you enclose the date data within a pair of number signs (#). This is the standard method used in this textbook. However, certain MS Access SQL statements also allow date data to be enclosed in quotation marks. Example:

```
SELECT *
FROM studentX
WHERE dateFirstEnrolled = #08/15/2004#;
```

Using Text Data in WHERE Clause

To specify character or string data in the condition of a WHERE clause, you enclose the data in either double quotation marks or single quotation marks. In most modern programming languages, single quotation marks are used to enclose character (one symbol) data, while double quotation marks are used to enclose string (usually more than one symbol) data. However, MS Access allows both sets of quotation marks to be used for any type of text (character, string) data. Example:

```
SELECT studentId AS [Identification Number]
FROM studentX
WHERE classification = 'Auditing';
                Or
SELECT studentId AS [Identification Number]
FROM studentX
WHERE initial >= "M";
```

> **Note:** Oracle uses single quotation marks to enclose both date and text (character and string) data when they are listed in the appropriate clauses where such data are permitted in SQL statements.

Other Comparison Operators

This section discusses other comparison or relational operators that can be used in the WHERE clause to establish criteria for records. The operators are sometimes referred to as special comparison operators and they are BETWEEN...AND, IN, IS NULL, and LIKE operators. These special comparison operators can be used in addition to the six standard comparison operators that are discussed in this chapter.

BETWEEN...AND Comparison Operator

The BETWEEN...AND operator is used to display columns' values that fall within a certain range of values. In MS Access SQL, a range of values includes the two values that specified the lower limit and the upper limit of the range. For example, a range of 3 to 10 includes 3 and 10 and all the values in between. The basic syntax for the operator is

BETWEEN *lowerLimitValue* AND *upperLimitValue*

where

- *lowerLimitvalue* is the beginning value for the specified range
- *upperLimitValue* is the ending value for the specified range

The lower limit of the range is written after the BETWEEN keyword and the upper limit is written after the AND keyword. This operator behaves exactly the same way as the AND logical operator. Logical operators are discussed in detail in the subsequent section of this chapter.

To display last names and annual salaries of faculty members whose annual salaries fall between 49,980.95 and 62,980.25 using the facultyX table, type and run the following SELECT statement.

SELECT lastName AS [Last Name], annualSalary AS [Annual Salary]
FROM facultyX
WHERE annualSalary BETWEEN 49980.95 AND 62980.25;

See result below

Last Name	Annual Salary
Dayet	56904.00
Miller	49980.95
Lasking	54354.80
Mea	62980.25

Reviewing the result of the SELECT statement shows that the lower limit (49,980.95) and the upper limit (62,980.25) of the specified range are included in the result.

IN Comparison Operator
The IN operator is used to return a list of values, if they exist in a table's columns, and the values must be enclosed in a pair of parentheses. The basic syntax for the IN operator is

IN (*dataValue, dataValue, ...*)

where

- *dataValue* is the value in the list
- Symbols ... mean more data values can be listed

If the list within the pair of parentheses contains only one value, the operator behaves like the Equal To comparison operator (=). If the list within the pair of parentheses contains more than one value, the operator behaves like the OR logical operator.

As Equal To Comparison Operator
To display the first name, the last name, and the user logon identification for the student whose identification number is "AB778204" using the studentX table and the IN comparison operator, type and run the following SELECT statement.

SELECT firstName AS [First Name], lastName AS [Last Name], userId AS [User Logon Identification]
FROM studentX
WHERE studentId IN ("AB778204");

More on Retrieving Data from Single Tables

See result below.

First Name	Last Name	User Logon Identification
Abel	Bomor	ab8204

Alternatively, you could have achieved the same result with the Equal To comparison operator (=) such as in

SELECT firstName AS [First Name], lastName AS [Last Name], userId AS [User Logon Identification]
FROM studentX
WHERE studentId = "AB778204";

As OR Logical Operator

To display identification numbers, course codes, sections, and letter grades for those students who have earned the letter grade "A" or "C" using the gradeX table and the IN comparison operator, type and run the following SELECT statement.

SELECT studentId, courseCode, section, letterGrade
FROM gradeX
WHERE letterGrade IN ('A', 'C');

See partial result below.

studentId	courseCode	section	letterGrade
AM609128	BUS101	2020	C
AB778204	BUS110	2010	A
:	:	:	:
:	:	:	:
CJ684975	CSC220	2010	C
FA213595	SOC450	2010	A

Alternatively, you could have gotten the same result by using the OR logical operator such as in

SELECT studentId, courseCode, section, letterGrade
FROM gradeX
WHERE letterGrade = 'A' OR letterGrade = 'C';

IS NULL Comparison Operator

The IS NULL operator is used to return columns' entries with null values. Other comparison operators cannot be used to test for null. Null means that actual value is not entered for a column entry, therefore, the value for the entry is unknown, unavailable, or missing. The basic syntax for IS NULL operator is

existingColumnName IS NULL

where

- *existingColumnName* is the column in the table listed in the FROM clause

To display identification numbers, first names, and last names of students who have no middle names' initials using the studentX table, type and run the following SELECT statement.

SELECT studentId AS STUDENT_IDENTIFICATION, firstName AS FIRST_NAME, lastName AS LAST_NAME
FROM studentX
WHERE initial IS NULL;

See result below.

STUDENT_IDENTIFICATION	FIRST_NAME	LAST_NAME
EA486741	Erasto	Actionbarrel
EM001254	Eghosa	Maklasi
CS664452	Christopher	Salat
CJ684975	Cecilia	Jeffer
PP886705	Phil	Portiskum
CC396710	Celestine	Chap

LIKE Comparison Operator

The LIKE operator is used to search and display columns' contents that are based on partial data supplied to the WHERE clause. The partial data acts as a string pattern the SQL uses to achieve the desired result. The operator is usually used with text (character, string) data, and must work with special symbols called wildcard characters if a partial (an incomplete) data value is supplied to the function.

The LIKE operator wildcard characters in MS Access SQL are asterisk symbol (*) and question mark symbol (?). The asterisk symbol (*) represents all character positions of data while the question mark symbol (?) represents any single character position of data. The basic syntax for the LIKE operator is

LIKE "*stringPattern*"

where

- *stringPattern* is the wildcard character(s), an optional pair of square brackets [], and the partial data supplied to the LIKE operator of a WHERE clause. The *stringPattern* must be enclosed in quotation marks.

> **Note:** The optional pair of square brackets [] is, usually, used to list the individual characters and/or the ranges of characters to be used in the search. Using the pair of square brackets, an example of a list of characters is [A, C, F] while an example of a renge of characters is [D – M].

To display first names and last names of students whose last names begin with the letter "A" using the studentX table, type and run the following SELECT statement.

SELECT DISTINCT firstName AS FIRST_NAME, lastName AS LAST_NAME
FROM studentX
WHERE lastName LIKE "A*";

See result below.

FIRST_NAME	LAST_NAME
Erasto	Actionbarrel
Fredrica	Anthony
Suzy	Afik

To display first names and last names of students whose last names begin with any of the following letters - "B", "J", "M", "Z", the second letter of their last names must be the

More on Retrieving Data from Single Tables

letter "e", and any sequence of letters can end their last names using the studentX table, type and run the following SELECT statement.

SELECT DISTINCT firstName AS FIRST_NAME, lastName AS LAST_NAME
FROM studentX
WHERE lastName Like "[B, J, M, Z]e*";

See result below.

FIRST_NAME	LAST_NAME
Benjamin	Benado
Cecilia	Jeffer
Doris	Mea
Kamaria	Zeberia

Reviewing the result of the SELECT statement reveals that the last names begin with the letter "B", "J", "M", or "Z" and the second letter in the last names is the letter "e".

Special comparison operators are shown in their order of priority or superiority from top toward bottom. See figure 3.3.

Figure 3.3

Order of Precedence	Operator
1	IN, IS NULL, LIKE
2	BETWEEN...AND

> **Note:** Oracle uses percent sign or symbol (%) and underscore symbol (_) as wildcard characters. The percent symbol (%) represents all character positions of data while the underscore symbol represents any single character position of data.
>
> Example:
> SELECT firstName AS FIRST_NAME, lastName AS LAST_NAME
> FROM studentX
> WHERE lastName LIKE '_e%';

Writing Conditions in Negative Forms

Usually in SQL, conditions are written in positive forms in conditions' clauses. A condition such as *annualSalary >= 49980* is considered to be in the positive form. MS Access SQL also allows writing conditions in negative forms. Conditions written in negative forms display the results of queries that are contrary to the queries' results when the conditions are written in positive forms. To write conditions in negative forms, you use the NOT logical operator.

Negating Standard Comparison Operators

To negate or write a condition using any of the six standard comparison operators (=, >, <, >=, <=. <>) in the negative form, you precede the condition in its positive form with the NOT logical operator.

The following example is a condition written in the positive form using the Greater Than or Equal To operator.

annualSalary >= 49980

To write the condition in the negative form, type

NOT annualSalary >= 49980

Notice that the NOT logical operator immediately precedes the entire condition. The logical operator is written immediately after the WHERE keyword or the HAVING keyword when used in the WHERE clause or the HAVING clause respectively. The HAVING clause is discussed in detail in chapter seven of this textbook.

To display the identification number, the last name, and the date first enrolled for the student whose identification number is "AB778204" using the studentX table and the condition in the negative form, type and run the following SELECT statement.

SELECT studentId AS STUDENT_ID, lastName AS LAST_NAME, dateFirstEnrolled as [FIRST ENROLLMENT DATE]
FROM studentX
WHERE NOT studentId <> "AB778204";

See result below.

STUDENT_ID	LAST_NAME	FIRST ENROLLMENT DATE
AB778204	Bomor	6/5/2005

Negating Other Comparison Operators
Except for the condition created with the IS NULL comparison operator, to write a condition in the negative form using any of the special comparison operators such as IN, BETWEEN...AND, and LIKE, you precede the operator with the NOT logical operator.

The following example is a condition written in the positive form using the IN comparison operator.

letterGrade IN ("A", "C")

To write the condition in the negative form, type

letterGrade NOT IN ("A", "C")

Notice that the NOT logical operator immediately precedes the IN comparison operator in the condition.

To display last names and annual salaries of faculty members whose annual salaries are outside the range of 49,980.95 and 62,980.25 using the facultyX table and the condition in the negative form, type and run the following SELECT statement.

SELECT lastName AS [Last Name], annualSalary AS [Annual Salary]
FROM facultyX
WHERE annualSalary NOT BETWEEN 49980.95 AND 62980.25;

See result below.

Last Name	Annual Salary
Maklasi	74563.55
Ugboma	70760.15
Stevenson	69852.00
Semina	45876.25
Hendix	48000.00
Erochi	68261.00

More on Retrieving Data from Single Tables

Negating IS NULL Comparison Operator

To write a condition in the negative form with the IS NULL comparison operator, you place the NOT logical operator between the IS keyword and the NULL keyword of the operator.

The following example is a condition written in the positive form using the IS NULL operator.

chairId IS NULL

To write the condition in the negative form, type

chairId IS NOT NULL

Notice that the NOT logical operator is written between the IS and the NULL keywords.

To display identification numbers, first names, middle names' initials, and last names of students who have middle names' initials using the studentX table and the condition in the negative form, type and run the following SELECT statement.

SELECT studentId AS STUDENT_IDENTIFICATION, firstName AS FIRST_NAME, initial
AS MIDDLE_NAME_INITIAL, lastName AS LAST_NAME
FROM studentX
WHERE initial IS NOT NULL;

See partial result below.

STUDENT_IDENTIFICATION	FIRST_NAME	MIDDLE_NAME_INITIAL	LAST_NAME
KZ934582	Kamaria	D	Zeberia
BB118945	Benjamin	C	Benado
:	:	:	:
:	:	:	:
DM674543	Doris	V	Mea
SA357864	Suzy	M	Afik

Conditional Retrievals Using Compound Conditions

When you want records that are to be retrieved from tables to pass more than one simple condition test or to pass one simple condition test among other simple conditions, you use a compound condition. A compound condition is a restriction whereby the condition in the condition clause, such as the WHERE clause, usually contain more than one simple condition and/or more than one logical (Boolean) operator.

Compound Conditions: A compound condition is a restriction that is usually created with more than one simple conditions connected with logical operators or one simple condition connected with the NOT logical operator.

The basic syntax for a compound condition using the WHERE clause is

WHERE   *existingColumnName | columnExpression   comparisonOperator
existingColumnName | value | functionName logicalOperator existingColumnName |
columnExpression comparisonOperator existingColumnName | value | functionName
logicalOperator...*

where

- *existingColumnName* is the column in the table listed in the FROM clause
- *columnExpression* is the expression formed by the combination of column(s) and data value(s). The column(s) and the data used in a column expression must be of the same data type
- *comparisonOperator* is the comparison operator used to establish the restriction
- *value* is the literal constant used in the comparison
- *functionName* is the function used in the comparison
- *logicalOperator* is the Boolean operator type connecting the simple conditions
- Symbol | symbolizes **Or** Boolean operator
- Symbols ... mean more simple conditions can be listed

In a compound condition, you can (i) compare the result of the evaluation of one simple condition to another, and (ii) reverse the outcome of a condition. Three standard logical operators sometimes called Boolean operators are used to create compound conditions. The operators are AND, OR, and NOT. In the simplest form, AND and OR operators are used to connect or combine two adjacent simple conditions, while the NOT operator is used to precede a single simple condition.

AND Logical Operator

The AND logical operator is used to create a compound condition where the qualifying records must satisfy all the simple conditions that constitute the compound condition. The simple conditions connected by the AND logical operator must be evaluated to be true for the qualifying records to be displayed. The AND condition is a restricted condition in that all simple conditions' tests in the compound condition must be passed by the qualifying records.

The basic syntax for the AND condition using the WHERE clause is

WHERE   *existingColumnName* | *columnExpression*   *comparisonOperator* *existingColumnName* | *value* | *functionName*   AND   *existingColumnName* | *columnExpression comparisonOperator existingColumnName* | *value* | *functionName* AND ...

where
- *existingColumnName* is the column in the table listed in the FROM clause
- *columnExpression* is the expression formed by the combination of column(s) and data value(s). The column(s) and the data used in a column expression must be of the same data type
- *comparisonOperator* is the comparison operator used to establish the restriction
- *value* is the literal constant used in the comparison
- *functionName* is the function used in the comparison
- Symbol | symbolizes **Or** Boolean operator
- AND is the logical operator connecting the simple conditions
- Symbols... mean more simple conditions can be listed

To display identification numbers, last names, and first names of students who are sophomore and first enrolled for courses before January 20, 2005 using the studentX table, type and run the following SELECT statement.

More on Retrieving Data from Single Tables

SELECT studentId AS [STUDENT ID], lastName AS [LAST NAME], firstName AS [FIRST NAME]
FROM studentX
WHERE classification = "Sophomore" AND dateFirstEnrolled < #01/20/2005#;

See result below.

STUDENT ID	LAST NAME	FIRST NAME
AU408153	Uzueg	Andy
FA213595	Anthony	Fredrica

In the result of the SELECT statement, two records from the studentX table are displayed because they are the only records that met both simple conditions of the compound condition. Notice that the AND logical operator is written between the two simple conditions in the WHERE clause.

OR Logical Operator

The OR logical operator connects two or more simple conditions and is used to display records that meet one simple condition or the other simple condition in a compound condition. In an OR condition, records that meet all the simple conditions in the compound condition are also displayed as part of the result of a query. The basic syntax for the OR condition using the WHERE clause is

WHERE *existingColumnName* | *columnExpression* *comparisonOperator* *existingColumnName* | *value* | *functionName* OR *existingColumnName* | *columnExpression* *comparisonOperator* *existingColumnName* | *value* | *functionName* OR ...

where

- *existingColumnName* is the column in the table listed in the FROM clause
- *columnExpression* is the expression formed by the combination of column(s) and data value(s). The column(s) and the data used in a column expression must be of the same data type
- *comparisonOperator* is the comparison operator used to establish the restriction
- *value* is the literal constant used in the comparison
- *functionName* is the function used in the comparison
- Symbol | symbolizes *Or* Boolean operator
- OR is the logical operator connecting the simple conditions
- Symbols... mean more simple conditions can be listed

To display last names and annual salaries of faculty members whose last names begin with the letter "M" or whose annual salaries are greater than 70,000 using the facultyX table, type and run the following SELECT statement.

SELECT lastName AS [Last Name], annualSalary AS [Annual Salary]
FROM facultyX
WHERE lastName Like "M*" OR annualSalary >= 70000;

See result below.

Last Name	Annual Salary
Maklasi	74563.55
Ugboma	70760.15

56

Last Name	Annual Salary
Miller	49980.95
Mea	62980.25

Reviewing the result of the SELECT statement reveals that the records of the faculty members displayed are those whose last names begin with the letter "M" and those whose annual salaries are more than 70,000.

NOT Logical Operator

The NOT logical operator is used to reverse the outcome of a compound condition. The operator reverses the truthfulness of the evaluation of a simple condition. The operator makes a condition that is written in the positive form to be in the negative form and vice versa. It is the only logical operator that requires one simple condition to create the required compound condition. The NOT condition is considered a compound condition because of the fact that the condition uses two operators - the NOT logical operator and a comparison operator.

The basic syntax for the NOT condition using the WHERE clause is

WHERE   NOT   *existingColumnName* | *columnExpression*   *comparisonOperator* *existingColumnName* | *value* | *functionName*

where

- *existingColumnName* is the column in the table listed in the FROM clause
- *columnExpression* is the expression formed by the combination of column(s) and data value(s). The column(s) and the data used in a column expression must be of the same data type
- *comparisonOperator* is the comparison operator used to establish the restriction
- *value* is the literal constant used in the comparison
- *functionName* is the function used in the comparison
- Symbol | symbolizes **Or** Boolean operator
- NOT is the logical operator preceding the simple condition

To display last names and annual salaries of faculty members whose annual salaries are less than 50,000 using the facultyX table and the NOT logical operator, type and run the following SELECT statement.

SELECT lastName AS [Last Name], annualSalary AS [Annual Salary]
FROM facultyX
WHERE NOT annualSalary >= 50000;

See result below.

Last Name	Annual Salary
Semina	45876.25
Miller	49980.95
Hendix	48000.00

> **Note:** In a HAVING clause, logical operators are written in the same positions as they are written in the WHERE clause. Review chapter seven to examine how the HAVING clause syntax is written.

More on Retrieving Data from Single Tables

> **Note:** One of the methods of recognizing a compound condition is when the condition uses two or more logical and comparison operators. The basic form for the logical conditions listed in this section follows the standard comparison operators' rule. To review how logical operators are written using special comparison operators such as IN, BETWEEN...AND, LIKE, and IS NULL, refer to the sections titled **Other Comparison Operators** and **Writing Conditions in the Negative Form** of this chapter.

Using Parentheses in Compound Conditions

When compound conditions are created with different logical operators, the conditions are evaluated based on algebraic order of precedence also called the order of priority. As in mathematics, pairs of parentheses are used to control the order in which the logical conditions are performed when different types of logical operators are used. When you want logical conditions with lower priorities to be performed before those with higher priorities, you enclose the logical conditions with lower priorities in parentheses. A logical condition that is enclosed in a pair of parentheses is evaluated first. If parentheses are nested within other parentheses, the condition within the innermost parentheses is performed first.

Logical operators are shown in their order of priority or superiority from top toward bottom. See figure 3.4.

Figure 3.4

Order of Precedence	Operator
1	NOT
2	AND
3	OR

To display last names and annual salaries of faculty members whose last names begin with the letter "M" and are department chairpersons or whose annual salaries are greater than 65,000 using the facultyX table, type and run the following SELECT statement.

SELECT lastName AS [Last Name], annualSalary AS [Annual Salary]
FROM facultyX
WHERE lastName Like "M*" AND chairId IS NULL OR annualSalary > 65000;

See result below.

Last Name	Annual Salary
Maklasi	74563.55
Ugboma	70760.15
Stevenson	69852.00
Mea	62980.25
Erochi	68261.00

In the SELECT statement, the AND condition produces two records (Maklasi and Mea) and the OR condition produces the other three records. Based on the order of precedence, the AND condition was evaluated first.

Now let's run the same query again, but this time you want the OR condition, which is of lower priory to the AND condition, to evaluate first. To accomplish the action, you must enclose the OR condition in a pair of parentheses. Type and run the following SELECT statement.

Chapter Three

SELECT lastName AS [Last Name], annualSalary AS [Annual Salary]
FROM facultyX
WHERE lastName Like "M*" AND (chairId IS NULL OR annualSalary > 65000);

See result below.

Last Name	Annual Salary
Maklasi	74563.55
Mea	62980.25

In the SELECT statement, the OR condition is evaluated first because the condition is enclosed in parentheses. The records retrieved by the OR condition must be evaluated again by the AND operator to make sure that the faculty members whose last names begin with the letter "M" are displayed.

Figure 3.5 shows arithmetic operators, concatenation operators, comparison operators, and logical operators in their order of priority.

Figure 3.5

Name of Operator	Order of Precedence	Symbol of Operator
Arithmetic Operators	1	^ (exponentiation)
	2	* / \ mod
	3	+ -
Concatenation Operators	4	& +
Standard Comparison Operators	5	> < >= <=
	6	= <>
Other Comparison Operators	7	IN, IS NULL, LIKE
	8	BETWEEN...AND
Logical Operators	9	NOT
	10	AND
	11	OR

Sorting Queries Results

Usually, data stored in tables are displayed in the order in which they are entered. For example, if Zeneth Paul's record was entered into a table before Andy Anderson's record, when the table is queried to include both records, Zeneth Paul's record is listed before Andy Anderson's record. To display resulting records in a particular order, you must sort or rearrange the result so that the desired order of arrangement is obtained.

Sorting: Sorting is the process of reorganizing or rearranging displayed data records in a particular order.

To sort records, you use the ORDER BY clause. The ORDER BY clause rearranges or reorganizes displayed data in either ascending order (ASC) or descending order (DESC). The order can be in a numerical, alphabetical, or date form. Ascending order means incrementing from low to high (0 to 9, A to Z, earlier to present) and descending order means decrementing from high to low (9 to 0, Z to A, present to earlier).

By default, when no sort order is specified in the ORDER BY clause, the result of the query is listed in ascending order based on the values of the primary key of the table that is being queried. The ascending order ASC keyword is only used to reverse the action of the descending order (DESC) if the descending sort action has been previously applied to a table. In MS Access SQL, you can reorganize the result of a query with one column or with one column position. You can also reorganize the result with more than one column or with more than one column position.

More on Retrieving Data from Single Tables

The basic syntax for the ORDER BY clause is

ORDER BY *existingColumnName, ... | columnPosition, ...* [ASC | DESC]

where

- *existingColumnName* is the column in the table listed in the FROM clause
- *columnPosition* is the numeric position of the column in the SELECT clause beginning with the leftmost column as position 1 and subsequent columns as position 2, position 3 and so on in that order
- Symbols [ ] mean items are optional
- Symbol | symbolizes *Or* Boolean operator
- Symbols ... mean more columns and/or columns' positions can be listed

> **Note:** If you are using actual columns to sort, the columns do not have to be listed in the SELECT clause as long as they exist in the table that is being sorted. However, if you are using columns' positions to sort, you must list the appropriate columns in the SELECT clause of the SELECT statement.

Sorting with Columns

The usual method of reorganizing displayed data of a SELECT statement is to list the sort columns in the ORDER BY clause. This is the most frequently used approach for rearranging displayed records in the order desired.

To display first names, middle names' initials, and last names of students who enrolled for courses on or before August 25, 2004 using the studentX table and sort with the middle name initial, type and run the following SELECT statement.

SELECT firstName AS FIRST_NAME, initial AS NAME_INITIAL, lastName AS LAST_NAME
FROM studentX
WHERE dateFirstEnrolled <= #08/25/2004#
ORDER BY initial;

See result below.

FIRST_NAME	NAME_INITIAL	LAST_NAME
Phil		Portiskum
Christopher		Salat
Andy	C	Uzueg
Benjamin	C	Benado
Suzy	M	Afik

The resulting records are sorted in ascending order using the middle name initial column.

Sorting with Columns Positions

Columns' positions can be used to specify the order in which data records are displayed in the result of a query. Columns' positions are the physical locations of columns, numbered from left to right beginning with the numeric digit 1, in the SELECT clause of a SELECT statement. Only integer values (whole numbers) must be used in denoting the physical locations of columns listed in a SELECT clause when columns' positions are to be used to rearrange displayed records.

To display identification numbers, last names and annual salaries for faculty members whose annual salaries are in the range of 50,000 to 68,000 using the facultyX table, and sort with the annual salary using a column position and in descending order, type and run the following SELECT statement.

SELECT facultyId AS [Identification Number], lastName AS [Last Name], annualSalary AS [Annual Salary]
FROM facultyX
WHERE annualSalary BETWEEN 50000 AND 68000
ORDER BY 3 DESC;

See result below.

Identification Number	Last Name	Annual Salary
DM674543	Mea	62980.25
PD002312	Dayet	56904.00
AL501828	Lasking	54354.80

The annual salary column is the third column - counting from left the columns listed in the SELECT clause, whence the digit three (3) is used in the ORDER BY clause. You can specify more than one column and/or more than one column position in the ORDER BY clause.

In MS Access SQL, when displaying sorted data in ascending order, the data are listed in the following sequence.

- NULL values
- Numeric values
- Date values
- Text (character and string) values

When displaying sorted data in descending order, the data are listed in he following sequence.

- Text (character and string) values
- Date values
- Numeric values
- NULL values

Note: In addition to columns and columns' positions, Oracle allows also the use of columns' aliases in the ORDER BY clause.

Example:
SELECT facultyId AS Identification_Number, lastName AS Last_Name,
annualSalary AS Annual_Salary
FROM facultyX
WHERE annualSalary BETWEEN 50000 AND 68000
ORDER BY Annual_Salary DESC;

By default and in ascending order, Oracle lists data in the following sequence: numeric values, date values, character values, and NULL values. In descending order, data are listed in the following sequence: NULL values, character values, date values, and numeric values.

Sort Keys

The columns and/or columns' positions used in an ORDER BY clause are called sort keys. Usually, there are three common types of sort keys. The keys are primary sort key, secondary sort key and tertiary sort key. However, a fourth type called multiple columns' sort key also exists.

Sort Keys: A sort key is a column or a column position listed in the ORDER BY clause and used to reorganize the result of a query.

Primary Sort Keys

When one column or one column position is used to reorganize displayed data, the column or the column position is referred to as the primary sort key. The primary sort key controls the final reorganization (final desired arrangement) of the result of a query.

Secondary Sort Keys

When two columns or two columns' positions are used to reorganize the displayed data, the leftmost one is called the primary sort key and the rightmost one is called the secondary sort key. The main goal of the secondary sort key is to further reorganize records, usually the records' positions of the result of a query, within the sort of the primary sort key. The secondary sort key is used to resolve positions' conflicts when there are records that have identical data in the primary sort.

Tertiary Sort Keys

There are times when three columns or three columns' positions are used to reorganize the result of a query. In such situation, the leftmost one is called the primary sort key, the one following the primary sort key (the middle one) is called the secondary sort key, and the rightmost one is referred to as the tertiary sort key. The main goal of the tertiary sort key is to further reorganize records, usually the records' positions of the result of a query, within the sort of the secondary sort key. The tertiary sort key is used to resolve positions' conflicts when there are records that have identical data in the secondary sort.

Examples of primary, secondary, and tertiary sort keys are shown in the following SELECT statement.

SELECT facultyId AS [Identification Number], lastName AS [Last Name], annualSalary AS [Annual Salary]
FROM facultyX
WHERE annualSalary BETWEEN 50000 AND 68000
ORDER BY 3, lastName, facultyId;

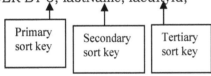

Primary sort key   Secondary sort key   Tertiary sort key

In the SELECT statement, the resulting records are first sorted in ascending order using the annual salary column - third position in the SELECT clause. The records are further sorted with last name column in ascending order if there are records with the same salary value. Finally, the records are further sorted in ascending order with the faculty identification number if there are matching last names.

Multiple Columns Sort Keys

When more than three columns or more than three columns' positions are used to reorganize data from a table, such columns or columns' positions are commonly referred to as multiple columns' sort key.

Chapter Summary

This chapter discusses conditional retrieval using the WHERE clause to retrieve qualifying records as queries' results. The chapter also explains simple and compound conditions and how they are written in the WHERE clause of a SELECT statement. Furthermore, the chapter discusses in detail how to (i) use comparison or relational operators in conditional retrievals, (ii) write conditions in negative forms, (iii) use special comparison operators in conditional retrievals, (iv) use logical or Boolean operators in conditional retrievals, and (v) use parentheses in compound conditions. In addition, this chapter explains sorting or displaying data in an organized form using both columns and columns' positions, and mentions the different types of sort keys.

SELECT Statement Syntax and Statements Summary

The table below presents the SELECT statements' syntax, conditions, operators, special symbols, and keywords discussed in this chapter and the SQL statements' examples for retrieving data from tables.

Clause Type	Basic Clause Syntax	Clause Example
WHERE clause is used to retrieve records that meet the specified conditions	WHERE rowCondition	WHERE classification = "Sophomore"
ORDER BY clause is used to reorganize or rearrange displayed data either in ascending or descending order	ORDER BY existingColumnName, ... | columnPosition, ... [ASC | DESC]	ORDER BY facultyId

Condition Type	Clause Syntax	Clause Example
A simple condition is a restriction that consists of three parts	WHERE existingColumnName | columnExpression comparisonOperator existingColumnName | value | functionName	WHERE annualSalary >= 68000
A compound condition is a restriction that consists of one simple condition or more than one simple conditions	WHERE existingColumnName | columnExpression comparisonOperator existingColumnName | value | functionName logicalOperator existingColumnName | columnExpression comparisonOperator existingColumnName | value | functionName logicalOperator ...	WHERE lastName = "Mea" AND annualSalary <= 50000

Operator Type	Description	Statement Example
Simple condition comparison operators are =, >, <, >=, <=, <>, IN, IS NULL, LIKE, BETWEEN...AND	Used in conditions' clauses, such as the WHERE clause, to construct simple conditions	SELECT studentId, lastName dateFirstEnrolled FROM studentX WHERE studentId = "FK576381" ;
Compound condition logical operators are AND, OR, NOT	Used in conditions' clauses, such as the WHERE clause, to construct compound conditions	SELECT studentId, lastName dateFirstEnrolled FROM studentX WHERE state = "Texas" OR state = "Florida";

Special Symbols and Keyword	Description	Statement Example
, (comma)	Used in the ORDER BY clause to separate columns and/or columns' positions	SELECT facultyId AS [Identification Number], lastName AS [Last Name], annualSalary AS [Annual Salary] FROM facultyX WHERE annualSalary BETWEEN 50000 AND 68000 ORDER BY 3, lastName, facultyId;

ASC	Used in the ORDER BY clause to display records in ascending order	SELECT facultyId, annualSalary * 0.06 AS [Annual Income Increase] FROM facultyX ORDER BY facultyId ASC;
DESC	Used in the ORDER BY clause to display records in descending order	SELECT facultyId, annualSalary * 0.06 AS [Annual Income Increase] FROM facultyX ORDER BY facultyId DESC;

Key Terms

AND
ASC
BETWEEN...AND
Columns' names
Columns' positions
Comparison operators
Compound conditions
Conditional retrieval
DESC

IN
IS NULL
LIKE
Logical operators
NOT
OR
ORDER BY clause
Simple conditions
WHERE Clause

Chapter Review Questions

Multiple Choice Questions

1. In a SQL environment, a process where only records that meet certain established conditions are listed is called a
   - a. conditional list.
   - b. conditional retrieval.
   - c. conditional display.
   - d. conditional manipulation.

2. There are _____ standard comparison operators used in SQL programming.
   - a. two
   - b. four
   - c. six
   - d. eight

3. To specify a numeric data value in the condition of a WHERE clause, you write the value
   - a. enclosed in double quotation marks.
   - b. enclosed in single quotation marks.
   - c. enclosed in a pair of number symbol.
   - d. without enclosing it in any pair of symbols.

4. Which of the following operators is not used in the WHERE clause?
   - a. NOT NULL.
   - b. IS NULL.
   - c. IN.
   - d. LIKE.

5. The _____ operators are used to connect two or more simple conditions.
   - a. comparison
   - b. relational
   - c. unary
   - d. logical (Boolean)

6. Which of the following is not a logical (Boolean) operator?
     a. NOT.
     b. AND.
     c. >=.
     d. none of the above.

7. Assume that the student table exists and the listed columns are contained in the table. Study the following SELECT statement and tell the output.
     SELECT firstName, lastName
     FROM student
     WHERE lastName LIKE "?e*";

     a. Displays records that have last names that begin with the letter "e".
     b. Displays records where the letter "e" is the second letter of last names.
     c. Displays records with full names having the letter "e" as the first letter.
     d. none of the above.

8. To rearrange displayed records, you use the _____ clause.
     a. ORDER BY
     b. SORT BY
     c. SELECT
     d. GROUP BY

9. Which of the following is not a valid sort key name in MS Access SQL?
     a. Primary sort key.
     b. Secondary sort key.
     c. Tertiary sort key.
     d. binary sort key.

10. Which of the following comparison operators will execute last?
     a. =.
     b. >.
     c. <=.
     d. <.

True or False Questions

11. In a simple condition, you can compare the data of one column to a function.
     a. True
     b. False

12. Comparison operators are connecting symbols that can be used with the WHERE clause.
     a. True
     b. False

13. In MS Access SQL, the date data value is enclosed in a pair of parentheses.
     a. True
     b. False

14. A condition in a WHERE clause can be written in both positive and negative forms.
     a. True
     b. False

15. MS Access SQL only sort displayed data in ascending order.
     a. True
     b. False

16. In MS Access SQL, columns' positions can be used to rearrange displayed data.
   a. True
   b. False

17. In MS Access SQL, the two wildcard characters used with the LIKE operator are asterisk and ampersand symbols.
   a. Tue
   b. False

Fill in the blank Questions

18. A _____ is a situation where records meeting the specified criteria are displayed.

19. The clause used to list displayed records in a particular order is called _____.

20. AND and OR operators belong to an operator's group called _____.

21. The BETWEEN...AND operator is an example of a _____.

22. The NOT operator is used to construct a _____.

23. To test for null values, you use the _____ operator.

Essay Type Questions

24. List three comparison operators and explain their meanings in non mathematical terms?

25. What is the effect of parentheses when used in a compound condition?

26. Describe the function of the ORDER BY clause and write a valid SELECT statement that contains the clause?

27. Explain the operational function of both primary and secondary sort keys?

28. How is a simple condition written without the NOT operator differs from another simple condition written with the NOT operator?

Hands-on Activities

Study the structures and the data of **AcademicX** database tables in appendix A (pages 355 through 360) and perform the following hands-on exercises.

1. Display the identification number and the last name of each faculty member whose annual salary is less than or equal to $50,500.

2. Display identification numbers, first names, and last names of students whose country of origin is the British Virgin Islands.

3. Write a SQL statement to list the complete records of faculty members whose first names begin with the letter "J" and earn monthly salaries of $4000 or less.

4. Write a SQL statement to show students' identification numbers, their last names, and dates they first enrolled for students who enrolled after January 31, 2004 and are from the state of Texas. Assign column alias **ID #** to the student identification number column, column alias **Student Lname** to the last name column, and column alias **First Enrollment** to the date of first enrolled column.

5. Write a SQL statement to display the complete records of faculty members whose middle names' initials is the letter "M" or the letter "V" and they are department chairpersons.

6. Display the identification numbers of faculty members whose monthly salaries fall within the range of $5,000 and $5,800.

7. Display the course code, course section, and course name of each course that has a course code that begins with the letter "C" and the identification number of the faculty member assigned to teach the course.

8. Write a SQL statement to display all records in the positionX table. Show the displayed result in descending order using the academic position column.

9. Display academic positions of faculty members whose minimum annual salaries fall within the range of $51,000 and $61,500. The result should be listed in ascending order.

10. Display the isbn, name, cost price, selling price, profit, and the classification of each book that has a net profit of less than $7.00. Rearrange the result first by book classification and then by profit using columns' positions and in ascending order. Assign column alias *Net Profit* to the column that displays the profit.

Chapter Four

Retrieving Data from Multiple Tables

Chapter Objectives

After completing this chapter, you should be able to

- Understand theta join
- Retrieve data based on equality join
- Use tables aliases to display data
- Retrieve data based on self join
- Retrieve data based on Cartesian join
- Retrieve data based on non-equality join
- Retrieve data based on outer joins
- Explain relational algebra
- Use SET operators
- Perform TOP-N analysis

Data Generated from Two or More Tables

A situation may arise when queries' results are gotten from more than one table. MS Access SQL provides ways of obtaining such results. In this chapter, you are introduced to different methods of retrieving data from multiple tables. The join operations discussed here are the means of displaying data generated from multiple tables.

Theta Join

Theta join is a join that is created when standard comparison operators (>, <, =, >=, <=, <>) and/or special comparison operators (IN, IS NULL, BETWEEN...AND) are used in the join conditions of the tables that are being joined. Theta join is further divided into two classes, namely, equality join and non-equality join.

Equality Join

Equality join also called equijoin, simple join, or inner join is a join operation that generates a result that is based on a common column that exists between the tables that are used in the join operation. The common column is usually the primary key and the corresponding foreign key of the tables. The table that contains the primary key used in the operation is called the parent table and the table that contains the corresponding foreign key used in the operation is called the child table. These columns must have identical structure and are specified in the join condition. Records that are displayed in an equality join operation must have identical values or matching values in the primary key and the corresponding foreign key of the tables that are being joined.

To create this type of join, the Equal To operator (=) is used to establish the condition that searches the specified columns for the matching records. The operator compares the values of the foreign key to that of the corresponding primary key to find a match. If a match exists, the corresponding records that have the same common column value are joined and displayed, as a single record. If no match is found, the result of the query is null. In MS Access SQL, equality join is established using (i) the WHERE clause, or (ii) the INNER JOIN...ON clause.

The two methods display data from tables where the tables have columns with identical structures even if the columns are not serving as the tables' primary keys and foreign

Retrieving Data from Multiple Tables

keys. However, using non-primary keys' columns and non-foreign keys' columns in the join conditions of equality join operations can generate incorrect results.

For example, the first names' columns and the last names' columns of both facultyX and studentX tables in the **AcademicX** database have identical structures and identical columns' names. Using these columns in the join condition of the WHERE clause or the INNER JOIN...ON clause of a query generates a result, even though the columns do not serve as the primary keys and the foreign keys of the tables that are being queried. However, the result may be inaccurate.

Retrieving Data Based on Equality Join Using WHERE clause

The WHERE clause is the traditional method of creating equality join. The basic syntax for the WHERE clause to create equality join is

WHERE *existingTableForeignKey* = *existingTablePrimaryKey*

where

- *existingTableForeignKey* is the foreign key column that exists in the child table listed in the FROM clause
- *existingTablePrimaryKey* is the primary key column that exists in the parent table listed in the FROM clause

> **Note:** Primary key and foreign key columns can be from the same table (as in self join) or from different tables. Tables that are involved in a join operation must be listed in the FROM clause and the tables must be separated by commas when using the traditional WHERE clause approach.

To display identification numbers, last names, and first names of faculty members, and department codes and department names in which faculty members are assigned using both facultyX and departmentX tables, type and run the following SELECT statement.

SELECT facultyId AS [FACULTY ID], lastName AS [FACULTY LAST NAME], firstName AS [FACULTY FIRST NAME], departmentX.departmentCode AS [DEPARTMENT ID], departmentName AS [DEPARTMENT NAME]
FROM facultyX, departmentX
WHERE facultyX.departmentCode = departmentX.departmentCode;

See partial result below.

FACULTY ID	FACULTY LAST NAME	FACULTY FIRST NAME	DEPARTMENT ID	DEPARTMENT NAME
EM001254	Maklasi	Eghosa	BUSA02	Business Administration
JS994450	Semina	John	BUSA02	Business Administration
:	:	:	:	:
:	:	:	:	:
ES509264	Stevenson	Euhan	SOCC06	Social Science
JH682508	Hendix	Jenny	SOCC06	Social Science

From the SELECT statement, you might have noticed that the fourth column, aliased [DEPARTMENT ID] listed in the SELECT clause consists of a table name and the required column name. The same method is used in the WHERE clause of the statement.

When tables that are used in a join operation have columns of the same names and structure, you must qualify the columns if they are to be used in a SELECT statement. Not qualifying the columns generates an error message when the SELECT statement that contains the columns is run. MS Access SQL treats columns with the same names listed in a SELECT statement and not qualified as ambiguous since SQL does not know exactly which of the tables' columns you are referring to in the SELECT statement. To qualify a column, you begin by typing the name of the table that contains the column, followed by a period (.), and finally the column. The combination of the three parts is called a column qualifier.

Columns Qualifiers: A column qualifier is a column name that is formed by preceding a column with a table name and a period.

Qualifying columns' names in a SELECT statement has additional merit. Usually, the result of a query without columns' qualifiers is gotten in a process by which the computer system searches through the tables in a database sequentially to retrieve the required data from the columns listed in the SELECT clause.

For example, if the column that is being sought is in a table located at position ten of the database tables' arrangement, the computer system has to search the needed column beginning from the table at position one through the table at position nine to finally reach the desired table. This process wastes the computer system's time and engages the processor in additional work. This type of query processing is sequential. But when columns' names are qualified, the system accesses the specified columns directly without searching several tables. This is due to the fact that tables' names are the first elements of columns' qualifiers and they exclusively inform the computer system the tables to search. This saves the system's time and the processor works less. The data displayed using columns' qualifiers are located directly in the database without searching tables sequentially.

For example, to qualify the department code column of the departmentX table, you type *departmentX.departmentCode*.

Retrieving Data Based on Equality Join Using INNER JOIN...ON Clause

In addition to using the WHERE clause to create equality join, MS Access SQL also uses the INNER JOIN...ON clause to create equality join. The basic syntax for the INNER JOIN...ON clause is

FROM *existingTableName* INNER JOIN *existingTableName*
ON *existingTableForeignKey* = *existingTablePrimaryKey*

where

- *existingTableName* are the tables listed in the FROM clause
- *existingTableForeignKey* is the foreign key column that exists in the child table listed in the FROM clause
- *existingTablePrimaryKey* is the primary key column that exists in the parent table listed in the FROM clause

The INNER JOIN keywords are used in the FROM clause to separated one table (say child table) from another (say parent table). The condition that identifies the columns to be used is created with the ON portion of the INNER JOIN...ON clause.

Retrieving Data from Multiple Tables

> **Note:** In MS Access SQL, to use the INNER JOIN...ON clause in join operations, columns that are used in the SELECT statements must be qualified and the clause does not support special comparison operators (IN, IS NULL, LIKE, BETWEEN...AND)

To display identification numbers, first names, and last names of faculty members who are also students using both facultyX and studentX tables, type and run the following SELECT statement.

SELECT facultyX.facultyId AS FACULTY_ID, studentX.firstName AS FACULTY_FIRST_NAME, studentX.lastName AS FACULTY_LAST_NAME
FROM facultyX INNER JOIN studentX
ON facultyX.facultyId = studentX.studentId;

See result below.

FACULTY_ID	FACULTY_FIRST_NAME	FACULTY_LAST_NAME
DM674543	Doris	Mea
EM001254	Eghosa	Maklasi

> **Note:** Although, there is no direct relationship between the facultyX table and the studentX table, the tables' primary keys are unique in their own rights without conflicts. Writing such queries' statements, in MS Access SQL environment, are allowed and running the statements produce the desired results. This textbook uses such approach and the proper tables to simplify queries' statements, where appropriate, to arrive at the needed solutions.

Alternatively, the above result can be achieved using facultyX, studentX, and courseX tables. The courseX table has relationships with both facultyX and studentX tables. The following SELECT statement consists of the three tables, and when run, yields the same result as the last SELECT statement.

SELECT DISTINCT facultyX.facultyId AS FACULTY_ID, facultyX.firstName AS FACULTY_FIRST_NAME, facultyX.lastName AS FACULTY_LAST_NAME
FROM facultyX INNER JOIN (courseX INNER JOIN studentX
ON courseX.facultyId=studentX.studentId)
ON courseX.facultyId=facultyX.facultyId;

Assigning Aliases to Tables

Like columns' aliases, tables can be given alternative names or aliases. These aliases are temporary and do not change the original names of tables. Assigning aliases to tables reduce the number of keystrokes required to enter tables' names. This is advantageous especially when qualifying columns' names in both the SELECT clause and the WHERE clause. The FROM clause is used to assign aliases to tables and each alias must follow the name of the table it is assigned to in the clause. In MS Access SQL, an optional AS keyword can be used when assigning aliases to tables.

Tables Aliases: A table alias is a temporary secondary name given to a table and can be used to reference the table in a SELECT statement.

The basic syntax for assigning table alias is

FROM *existingTableName* [AS] *tableAlias*, ...

where

Chapter Four

- *existingTableName* is the table to be given the alias
- *tableAlias* is the alternative and temporary name that is assigned to the table
- Symbols [ ] mean item is optional
- Symbols ... mean more tables can be listed

Note: The AS keyword is optional when creating an alias name for a table.

The following SELECT statement shows how tables' aliases are created and used. The facultyX table is assigned the alias F and the studentX table is assigned the alias S. Also notice how the aliases are used to refer to columns in their respective tables both in the SELECT clause and in the WHERE clause.

SELECT F.facultyId AS FACULTY_ID, S.firstName AS FACULTY_FIRST_NAME, S.lastName AS FACULTY_LAST_NAME
FROM facultyX F INNER JOIN studentX S
ON F.facultyId = S.studentId;

Although, you can assign aliases of several characters long (up to 64 characters) to tables, it is usually preferable to give aliases that are shorter than tables' actual names. In the SELECT statement, instead of writing tables' full names in the columns' qualifiers, the names are shortened to one letter each. This reduces the number of keystrokes and saves typing time.

Note: In addition to using the traditional WHERE clause to perform equality join, Oracle uses three other methods to display data in equality join operations. The methods use NATURAL JOIN keywords, JOIN...USING clause, and JOIN...ON clause. NATURAL JOIN keywords and the JOIN...USING clause join tables that have the same columns' names and structures.

Example:
SELECT facultyId AS FACULTY_ID, annualSalary AS FACULTY_SALARY
FROM facultyX NATURAL JOIN studentX;

If the common columns from the tables to be joined have the same name and are listed in the SELECT clause, the columns must not be qualified when using the NATURAL JOIN keywords or the JOIN...USING clause.

Creating Self Join Using Equal To Comparison Operator
Self join is created by joining a table to itself to display the table's joined records. This type of join is also called recursive join or unary join. To create self join, the sole table used in the join operation must appear more than once in the FROM clause, must be given aliases, and the columns used in the join operation must be qualified. This type of join can be created using (i) the WHERE clause, or (ii) the INNER JOIN...ON clause.

Creating Self Join Using WHERE Clause
The basic syntax for the WHERE clause, using the FROM clause, to create self join is

FROM *existingTableName* [AS] *tableAlias*, *existingTableName* [AS] *tableAlias*
WHERE *existingTableForeignKey* = *existingTablePrimaryKey*

where

- *existngTableName* is the sole table
- *tableAlias* is the alternative and temporary name that is assigned to the table

- *existingTableForeignKey* is the foreign key column that exists in the child table listed in the FROM clause
- *existingTablePrimaryKey* is the primary key column that exists in the parent table listed in the FROM clause
- Symbols [ ] mean items are optional

> **Note:** The aliases that are assigned to the sole table must not be the same otherwise an error message is generated.

To display identification numbers and full names of faculty members who are not department chairpersons along with their chairpersons' identification numbers and the chairpersons' full names using the facultyX table, type and run the following SELECT statement.

SELECT FX.facultyId AS ID, FX.firstName & " " & FX.lastName AS FACULTY_NAME,
FX.chairId AS CHAIR_ID, FY.firstName & " " & FY.lastName AS CHAIRPERSON_NAME
FROM facultyX AS FX, facultyX AS FY
WHERE FX.chairId = FY.facultyId;

See result below.

ID	FACULTY_NAME	CHAIR_ID	CHAIRPERSON_NAME
ZM567123	Zenat Miller	DM674543	Doris Mea
AL501828	Ada Lasking	EE987654	Ememgini Erochi
JS994450	John Semina	EM001254	Eghosa Maklasi
JH682508	Jenny Hendix	ES509264	Euhan Stevenson
PD002312	Peter Dayet	RU123098	Rischi Ugboma

You might have noticed from the SELECT statement that the facultyX table appeared twice in the FROM clause with different aliases. You also might have noticed how the tables' aliases are used in columns' qualifiers in both the SELECT clause and the WHERE clause. Without the tables' aliases, self join is impossible. The aliases fool the computer system to think that the tables are different.

Creating Self Join Using INNER JOIN...ON Clause

The basic syntax for the INNER JOIN...ON clause to create self join is

FROM *existingTableName* [AS] *tableAlias* INNER JOIN *existingTableName* [AS] *tableAlias*
ON *existingTableForeignKey* = *existingTablePrimaryKey*

where

- *existngTableName* is the sole table
- *tableAlias* is the alternative and temporary name that is assigned to the table
- *existingTableForeignKey* is the foreign key column that exists in the child table listed in the FROM clause
- *existingTablePrimaryKey* is the primary key column that exists in the parent table listed in the FROM clause
- Symbols [ ] mean items are optional

To perform the last self join operation using the INNER JOIN...ON clause, type and run the following SELECT statement.

```
SELECT FX.facultyId AS ID, FX.firstName & " " & FX.lastName AS FACULTY_NAME,
FX.chairId AS CHAIR_ID, FY.firstName & " " & FY.lastName AS CHAIRPERSON_NAME
FROM facultyX AS FX INNER JOIN facultyX AS FY
ON FX.chairId = FY.facultyId;
```

> **Note:** The main advantage of using the INNER JOIN...ON clause is that it frees up the WHERE clause from being used as a join condition clause. Rather, it allows you to use the WHERE clause to create a search condition to further restrict records in a join operation. In other words, the WHERE clause is used in addition to the INNER JOIN...ON clause to filter out unqualified records.

Cartesian Join

Cartesian join is used to produce the result of a query known as a Cartesian product. This type of join is commonly used for statistics or to produce a large number of records for data testing or for data analysis purposes. The join combines each record from the first table specified in the operation to every record in the second table specified in the operation. The total number of records generated by the join is equivalent to multiplying the number of records in the first table by the number of records in the second table. The total number of columns in the query is the sum of the number of columns selected from both tables.

Cartesian Products: A Cartesian product is a query result where each record from one table concatenates with every record in the other table.

The simplest way to create Cartesian join is by omitting the WHERE clause in the SELECT statement that is used to join the tables. MS Access SQL also provides an alternative method for generating a Cartesian product.

Creating Cartesian Join by Omitting WHERE Clause

To generate and display a query result based on Cartesian join using faculty identification number column from facultyX table, and department code column and department chairperson identification number column from departmentX table, type and run the following SELECT statement.

```
SELECT F.facultyId AS FACULTY, D.departmentCode AS DEPARTMENT, D.chairId AS CHAIR
FROM facultyX F, departmentX D;
```

See partial result below.

FACULTY	DEPARTMENT	CHAIR
EM001254	SOCC06	ES509264
EM001254	BUSA02	EM001254
:	:	:
:	:	:
EE987654	NASC08	RU123098
EE987654	CSCM09	EE987654

Notice that each row of the facultyX table (in this case the facultyId column) concatenated with every row in the departmentX table (in this case both the departmentCode and chaired columns).

Creating Cartesian Join Using Alternative Methods

The alternative approach of generating a Cartesian product is to use a subquery with the EXISTS operator. To generate and display a query result based on Cartesian join

Retrieving Data from Multiple Tables

using the alternative approach and using the same columns as in the last SELECT statement, type and run the following SELECT statement.

SELECT F.facultyId AS FACULTY, D.departmentCode AS DEPARTMENT, D.chairId AS CHAIR
FROM facultyX F, departmentX D
WHERE EXISTS (SELECT *
              FROM facultyX F, departmentX D
              WHERE F.departmentCode NOT IN (D.departmentCode));

The result of the join is obtained using a nested query construct and a multiple-row operator – the EXISTS operator. The result of the SELECT statement is exactly the same as without the WHERE clause. Subqueries and the EXISTS operator are discussed in detail in chapter eight of this textbook.

A situation may arise when you want to concatenate each record that meets a specified condition from one table with every record in another table. To achieve such results in MS Access SQL, you use a subquery that is embedded in the FROM clause of a SELECT statement. Such a subquery creates a temporary table called an inline view.

To concatenate and display each identification number for those faculty members who are students using the facultyX table with every record that consists of course code, course section, and letter grade using the gradeX table, type and run the following SELECT statement.

SELECT V.facultyId, courseCode, section, letterGrade
FROM (SELECT F.facultyId
      FROM facultyX F, gradeX G
      WHERE G.studentId = F.facultyId) V, gradeX;

See partial result below.

facultyId	courseCode	Section	letterGrade
DM674543	BUS101	2010	AU
DM674543	BUS101	2010	B
:	:	:	:
:	:	:	:
EM001254	NAS250	2010	I
EM001254	SOC450	2010	A

In the query result, the record of each faculty member who is also a student from the temporary table (inline view) called "V" concatenated with every record of the gradeX table.

> **Note:** In addition to omitting the WHERE clause, Oracle also uses the CROSS JOIN keywords in the FROM clause to create Cartesian join.
>
> Example:
> SELECT F.facultyId AS FACULTY, D.departmentCode AS DEPARTMENT, D.chairId AS CHAIR
> FROM facultyX F CROSS JOIN departmentX D;

Chapter Four

Using AND Logical Operator in Join Operations

Sometimes it is necessary to further restrict records that are displayed for equality join operations. To obtain such results, you include search conditions constructed with the AND logical operator to the join conditions.

WHERE Clause Approach

To display identification numbers and full names of faculty members who are not department chairpersons with annual salaries of less than or equal to 49980.95, along with their chairpersons' identification numbers and the chairpersons' full names using the facultyX table, type and run the following SELECT statement.

SELECT FX.facultyId AS ID, FX.firstName & " " & FX.lastName AS FACULTY_NAME, FX.chairId AS CHAIR_ID, FY.firstName & " " & FY.lastName AS CHAIRPERSON_NAME
FROM facultyX AS FX, facultyX AS FY
WHERE FX.chairId = FY.facultyId
AND FX.annualSalary <= 49980.95;

See result below.

ID	FACULTY_NAME	CHAIR_ID	CHAIRPERSON_NAME
JS994450	John Semina	EM001254	Eghosa Maklasi
ZM567123	Zenat Miller	DM674543	Doris Mea
JH682508	Jenny Hendix	ES509264	Euhan Stevenson

In the SELECT statement, the WHERE clause is used to create both the join condition and the search condition but with the help of the AND logical operator.

INNER JOIN...ON Clause Approach

Alternatively, you can achieve the same result by typing and running the following SELECT statement.

SELECT FX.facultyId AS ID, FX.firstName & " " & FX.lastName AS FACULTY_NAME, FX.chairId AS CHAIR_ID, FY.firstName & " " & FY.lastName AS CHAIRPERSON_NAME
FROM facultyX AS FX INNER JOIN facultyX AS FY
ON FX.chairId = FY.facultyId
WHERE FX.annualSalary <= 49980.95;

In the above SELECT statement, the INNER JOIN...ON clause is used to create the join condition and the WHERE clause is used to create the search condition.

Non-Equality Join

Non-equality join (non-equijoin) is a join where the join condition is created using other standard comparison operators (>, <, >=, <=, <>) including the IN, IS NULL, and BETWEEN...AND special comparison operators. There are situations when the desired queries' results do not have to be records having exact values in the common columns of the tables that are being joined. Non-equality join is used to search for values within ranges in columns' entries (cells) and to display records with no matching values in their common columns. This type of join can be created using (i) the WHERE clause and (ii) the INNER JOIN...ON clause.

The syntax for the two methods is similar to the syntax for the equality join shown earlier in this chapter except that the Equal To operator (=) cannot be used.

Retrieving Data from Multiple Tables

Retrieving Data Based on Non-Equality Join Using WHERE Clause

Using the WHERE clause, you can create non-equality join with standard comparison operators, except for the Equal To operator (=).

To display academic positions of faculty members based on their annual salaries along with the concatenation of their first and last names using both positionX and facultyX tables, type and run the following SELECT statement.

SELECT academicPosition AS POSITION, firstName + " " + lastName AS FULL_NAME
FROM positionX, facultyX
WHERE annualSalary BETWEEN minAnnualSalary AND maxAnnualSalary;

See partial result below.

POSITION	FULL_NAME
Full Professor	Eghosa Maklasi
Full Professor	Rischi Ugboma
⋮	⋮
⋮	⋮
Assistant Professor	Peter Dayet
Instructor	Zenat Miller

Retrieving Data Based on Non-Equality Join Using INNER JOIN...ON Clause

In MS Access SQL, the INNER JOIN...ON clause is also used to create non-equality join using standard comparison operators, except for the Equal To operator (=).

To display the result of the last query using INNER JOIN...ON clause approach, type and run the following SELECT statement.

SELECT P.academicPosition AS POSITION, F.firstName + " " + F.lastName AS FULL_NAME
FROM positionX P INNER JOIN facultyX F
ON F.annualSalary >= P.minAnnualSalary AND F.annualSalary <= P.maxAnnualSalary;

Creating Self Join Using Other Comparison Operators

Self join can also be created using special comparison operators. This type of join can also be created using (i) the WHERE clause, or (ii) the INNER JOIN...ON clause. The basic syntax is similar to the ones shown earlier on the section that discusses creating self join with the Equal To comparison operator. The only difference is that the Equal To comparison operator is replaced with special comparison operators in the join condition of the tables that are being joined.

Creating Self Join Using WHERE Clause

To concatenate and display chairpersons' full names along with the concatenation of full names of faculty members they chair in textual expressions using the facultyX table, type and run the following SELECT statement.

SELECT FX.firstName & " " & FX.lastName & " is the chairperson for " & " " & FY.firstName & " " & FY.lastName AS SUPERVISOR
FROM facultyX AS FX, facultyX AS FY
WHERE FY.chairId IS NOT NULL
AND FX.facultyId IN (FY.chairId);

See result below.

SUPERVISOR
Eghosa Maklasi is the chairperson for John Semina
Rischi Ugboma is the chairperson for Peter Dayet
Euhan Stevenson is the chairperson for Jenny Hendix
Doris Mea is the chairperson for Zenat Miller
Ememgini Erochi is the chairperson for Ada Lasking

Here the WHERE clause used to establish the join condition uses the IS NOT NULL comparison operator, the IN comparison operator, and the AND logical operator in order to achieve the needed result.

Creating Self Join Using INNER JOIN...ON Clause

To perform the same self join as in the last SELECT statement using the INNER JOIN...ON clause, type and run the following SELECT statement.

```
SELECT FX.firstName & "  " & FX.lastName & " is the chairperson for " & "  " &
FY.firstName & "  " & FY.lastName AS SUPERVISOR
FROM facultyX AS FX INNER JOIN facultyX AS FY
ON FY.chairId = FX.facultyId
AND FX.facultyId <> FY.facultyId;
```

Outer Join

Equality join, non-equality join, and self join display data contained in joined tables where the records from the joined tables satisfy the join conditions. But, there are times when records that fail to meet the join conditions are included in queries' results. To obtain such results, you must join the tables using outer join statements. There are three types of outer joins, namely, left outer join, right outer join, and full outer join.

Creating Left Outer Join

Left outer join is a join where all records from the left table are displayed even if some or all the records have no corresponding matching records with the right table in the operation. The unmatched records generated by the left table are matched with null records from the right table to complete the operation. MS Access SQL uses the LEFT JOIN...ON clause to create left outer join.

Retrieving Data Using LEFT JOIN...ON Clause

The basic syntax for the LEFT JOIN...ON clause is

FROM *existingLeftTableName* LEFT JOIN *existingRightTableName*
ON *existingTableForeignKey* = *existingTablePrimaryKey*

where

- *existingLeftTableName* is the table listed on the left of the FROM clause
- *existingRighttTableName* is the table listed on the right of the FROM clause
- *existingTableForeignKey* is the foreign key column that exists in the child table listed in the FROM clause
- *existingTablePrimaryKey* is the primary key column that exists in the parent table listed in the FROM clause

Retrieving Data from Multiple Tables

The LEFT JOIN keywords are used in the FROM clause to separate the right table from the left table. The condition that identifies the columns to be used is written in the ON portion of the clause.

To display first and last names of faculty members along with their department chairpersons' identification numbers as well as those who do not have department chairpersons using both facultyX and departmentX tables, type and run the following SELECT statement.

```
SELECT F.firstName & " " & F.lastName AS [FULL NAME], D.chairId AS CHAIR_ID
FROM facultyX AS F LEFT JOIN departmentX AS D
ON F.chairId = D.chairId
ORDER BY 1;
```

See partial result below.

FULL NAME	CHAIR_ID
Ada Lasking	EE987654
Doris Mea	
⋮	⋮
⋮	⋮
Rischi Ugboma	
Zenat Miller	DM674543

In the SELECT statement, the ORDER BY clause is used to sort the result of the query. The clause is not required if no sort is needed. The records with null values in the CHAIR_ID column have no department chairpersons.

Creating Left Outer Join Using Alternative Methods

One alternative way of creating left outer join is using the UNION operator to combine the results of two queries. The following UNION statement yields the same result as the LEFT JOIN...ON clause approach that is discussed in the last demonstration.

```
SELECT firstName + " " + lastName AS FULL_NAME, NULL AS CHAIRPERSON_ID
FROM facultyX
WHERE chairId IS NULL
UNION
SELECT firstName & " " & lastName, D.chairId
FROM facultyX F, departmentX D
WHERE F.chairId = D.chairId;
```

You might have noticed that the SELECT statement (top statement) for the left table is written first in the UNION statement. This is a good programming practice. The first and last names of the faculty members are gotten from the facultyX table (left table), while the chairpersons' identification numbers are retrieved from the departmentX table (right table). The two WHERE clauses serve as join conditions. The UNION operator and other Set operators are discussed in detail in the following section of this chapter.

Creating Right Outer Join

Right outer join is a join where all records from the right table of the join operation are displayed even if some or all the records have no corresponding matching records with the left table in the operation. The unmatched records generated by the right table are matched with null records from the left table to complete the operation. MS Access SQL uses the RIGHT JOIN...ON clause to create right outer join.

Chapter Four

Retrieving Data Using RIGHT JOIN...ON Clause

The basic syntax for the RIGHT JOIN...ON clause is similar to that of the LEFT JOIN...ON clause. Replace the LEFT JOIN keywords of left outer join syntax with the RIGHT JOIN keywords to get the syntax for right outer join.

The RIGHT JOIN keywords are used in the FROM clause to separate the right table from the left table. The condition that identifies the columns to be used is written in the ON portion of the clause.

To display first and last names of faculty members who are also students as well as those who are not enrolled as students using both studentX and facultyX tables, type and run the following SELECT statement.

SELECT S.firstName & " " & S.lastName AS [STUDENT NAME], F.firstName + " " +
F.lastName AS [FACULTY NAME]
FROM studentX AS S RIGHT JOIN facultyX AS F
ON S.studentId = F.facultyId;

See partial result below.

STUDENT NAME	FACULTY NAME
	Ada Lasking
Doris Mea	Doris Mea
:	:
:	:
	Ememgini Erochi
Eghosa Maklasi	Eghosa Maklasi

Creating Right Outer Join Using Alternative Methods

An alternative way of creating right outer join is using the UNION operator to combine the results of two queries. The following UNION statement yields the same result as the RIGHT JOIN...ON clause approach that is discussed in the last demonstration.

SELECT S.firstName + " " + S.lastName AS [STUDENT NAME], F.firstName + " " +
F.lastName AS [FACULTY NAME]
FROM studentX S, facultyX F
WHERE studentId = facultyId
UNION
SELECT NULL AS [STUDENT NAME], F.firstName + " " + F.lastName AS [FACULTY NAME]
FROM facultyX F
WHERE facultyId NOT IN (SELECT studentId
                        FROM studentX, facultyX
                        WHERE studentId = facultyId)
ORDER BY 2;

In the SELECT statement, both the UNION operator and a subquery are used to obtain the needed result.

Creating Full Outer Join

The result of full outer join are records from both the left table and the right table that are involved in the join operation where there are matching values in the common column(s) of the tables, as well as, records from both tables where there are no matching values or null values in the common column(s). MS Access SQL uses alternative methods to create full outer join. One of the alternative methods uses the

Retrieving Data from Multiple Tables

UNION operator. The UNION operator vertically concatenates both the results of left outer join and right outer join to generate the result of full outer join.

Retrieving Data Using Full Outer Join

To display first and last names of all students whether they are faculty members or not, and first and last names of all faculty members whether they are students or not using both studentX and facultyX tables, type and run the following SELECT statement.

```
SELECT S.firstName & " " & S.lastName AS [STUDENT NAME], F.firstName & " " & F.lastName AS [FACULTY NAME]
FROM studentX S LEFT JOIN facultyX F
ON S.studentId = F.facultyId
UNION
SELECT S.firstName & " " & S.lastName, F.firstName & " " & F.lastName
FROM studentX S RIGHT JOIN facultyX F
ON S.studentId = F.facultyId;
```

See partial result below.

STUDENT NAME	FACULTY NAME
	Jenny Hendix
	John Semina
:	:
:	:
Celestine Chap	
Doris Mea	Doris Mea

Note: Oracle uses two methods to create outer join. One method is traditional and it uses the plus symbol (+) in the WHERE clause to accomplish both left outer join and right outer join. The plus symbol is used to indicate the table lacking the matching records and to include null records to complete the operation. The plus symbol must be specified to the right of the column used in the WHERE clause for the table that is lacking the matching records and the symbol must be enclosed in a pair of parentheses. Example:

```
SELECT F.firstName || ' ' || F.lastName AS "FULL NAME", D.chairId AS CHAIR_ID
FROM facultyX F, departmentX D
WHERE F.chairId = D.chairId (+);
```

The second method uses the keywords LEFT OUTER JOIN for left outer join, RIGHT OUTER JOIN for right outer join, and FULL OUTER JOIN for full outer join. Like MS Access SQL, the keywords are placed between the tables that are being joined in the FROM clause. Example:

```
SELECT F.firstName || ' ' || F.lastName AS "FULL NAME", D.chairId AS CHAIR_ID
FROM facultyX F LEFT OUTER JOIN departmentX D
ON F.chairId = D.chairId;
```

Retrieving Data by Joining More Than Two Tables

There are times when the results displayed by queries are gotten by joining more than two tables. Such operations can be achieved by using the WHERE clause or the nested INNER JOIN...ON clause.

WHERE Clause Approach

To use the WHERE clause to join three or more tables, the tables are listed in the FROM clause and separated by commas. All the join conditions that link the tables together are written in the WHERE clause.

To display first and last names of faculty members who are also students and the department names to which they are assigned using departmentX , facultyX, and studentX tables, type and run the following SELECT statement.

```
SELECT F.firstName & "  " & F.lastName AS [FACULTY NAME], departmentName AS
[DEPARTMENT NAME]
FROM departmentX D, facultyX F, studentX S
WHERE F.departmentCode = D.departmentCode
AND studentId = facultyId
ORDER BY 1;
```

See result below.

FACULTY NAME	DEPARTMENT NAME
Doris Mea	Education
Eghosa Maklasi	Business Administration

The tables in the SELECT statement can be listed in any order in the FROM clause as long as the conditions in the WHERE clause are written correctly.

INNER JOIN...ON Clause Approach

To display the result of a query that uses three or more tables, two options of nested INNER JOIN...ON clause are available in MS Access SQL. One option (option 1) allows the writing of the nested INNER JOIN...ON clauses by placing an open parenthesis symbol [(] after each INNER JOIN keywords and placing a close parenthesis symbol [)] after each ON portion of the nested INNER JOIN...ON clauses. With option 1, the ON portion of the inner INNER JOIN...ON clause is written before the ON portion of the outer INNER JOIN...ON clause. With the second option (option 2), all the open parentheses' symbols of the nested INNER JOIN...ON clauses are written immediately after the FROM keyword in the FROM clause. The close parenthesis symbol is written after each ON portion of the nested INNER JOIN...ON clauses. With option 2, the ON portion of the outer INNER JOIN...ON clause is written before the ON portion of the inner INNER JOIN...ON clause. The number of INNER JOIN...ON clauses needed in such a query, using any of the two options, is always one less than the number of tables that are being joined. For example, if five tables are used in the join operation, the number of INNER JOIN...ON clauses listed in the SELECT statement is four (5-1).

The following two examples, using option 1 and option 2 respectively, display the same result as the last SELECT statement.

Option 1
```
SELECT F.firstName & "  " & F.lastName AS [FACULTY NAME], departmentName AS
[DEPARTMENT NAME]
FROM departmentX D INNER JOIN (facultyX F INNER JOIN studentX S
                              ON S.studentId = F.facultyId)
ON F.departmentCode = D.departmentCode
ORDER BY 1;
```

Option 2
```
SELECT F.firstName & "  " & F.lastName AS [FACULTY NAME], departmentName AS
[DEPARTMENT NAME]
FROM (departmentX D INNER JOIN facultyX F ON F.departmentCode =
D.departmentCode) INNER JOIN studentX S ON S.studentId = F.facultyId
ORDER BY 1;
```

Retrieving Data from Multiple Tables

Notice that both facultyX and studentX tables, using option 1, are enclosed in a pair of parentheses after the first INNER JOIN keywords. With option 2, the complete INNER JOIN...ON clause for both departmentX and facultyX tables is enclosed in a pair of parentheses.

The following two examples, using four tables, demonstrate how option 1 and option 2 of the nested INNER JOIN...ON clause approach are applied.

To display last names and first names of faculty members who are also students and have taken some courses and have earned letter grades using facultyX, studentX, courseX, and gradeX tables, type and run the following SELECT statement.

Option 1
SELECT DISTINCT F.lastName AS [Last Name], F.firstName AS [First Name]
FROM facultyX F INNER JOIN (studentX S INNER JOIN (courseX C INNER JOIN gradeX
G ON G.studentId = C.studentId) ON C.facultyId = S.studentId)
ON S.studentId = F.facultyId;

See result below.

Last Name	First Name
Maklasi	Eghosa
Mea	Doris

The result of the last SELECT statement can also be achieved using option 2 below.

Option 2
SELECT DISTINCT F.lastName AS [Last Name], F.firstName AS [First Name]
FROM ((facultyX F INNER JOIN studentX S ON S.studentId = F.facultyId)
INNER JOIN courseX C ON C.facultyId = S.studentId)
INNER JOIN gradeX G ON G.studentId = C.studentId;

> **Note:** In MS Access SQL, INNER JOIN...ON, LEFT JOIN...ON, and RIGHT JOIN...ON clauses can be placed inside another INNR JOIN...ON clause. However, Oracle does not nest JOIN...ON clause when performing the joining of three or more tables. Instead, Oracle connects the tables using the JOIN keyword, and each join must be followed immediately by its own ON portion of the clause.
>
> Example:
> SELECT F.firstName || ' ' || F.lastName AS "FACULTY NAME", departmentName AS "DEPARTMENT NAME"
> FROM departmentX D JOIN facultyX F
> ON F.departmentCode = D.departmentCode
> JOIN studentX S
> ON F.facultyId = S.studentId
> ORDER BY 1;

Relational Algebra

Relational algebra establishes a theoretical way of creating nonphysical tables by manipulating the data in physical tables. The resulting tables exist hypothetically, but not physically. To convert such tables to their physical forms in MS Access, you must apply the save operation on them to make them retrievable from storage media. Once saved, the data of these one-time hypothetical tables can be manipulated just as any other physical table in relational database environment. There are nine standard relational algebra operators used to create hypothetical tables. The operators are

SELECT (SELECTION), PROJECT (PROJECTION), JOIN, UNION, UNION ALL, INTERSECT, DIFFERENCE, PRODUCT, and DIVIDE. The results of SELECT, PROJECT, and JOIN operators are common occurrences in queries. The remaining six operators are referred to as SET operators.

SELECT Operator

The SELECT operator is used to display a horizontal subset of a table. This operator returns some or fewer records from a table. In MS Access SQL, the inclusion of the WHERE clause and/or any other condition clause in a SELECT statement is the result of a SELECT operator. If a table that has ten records returns fewer records after being queried, that result is an example of the SELECT operation. The result of the SELECT operator can include all columns of the table that is being queried. The following example uses the WHERE clause to demonstrate the SELECT operator.

To display first and last names, and the annual salaries for faculty members who are department chairpersons using the facultyX table, type and run the following SELECT statement.

SELECT firstName AS [FIRST NAME], lastName AS [LAST NAME], annualSalary AS [ANNUAL INCOME]
FROM facultyX
WHERE chairId IS NULL;

See result below.

FIRST NAME	LAST NAME	ANNUAL INCOME
Eghosa	Maklasi	74563.55
Rischi	Ugboma	70760.15
Euhan	Stevenson	69852.00
Doris	Mea	62980.25
Ememgini	Erochi	68261.00

The result of the query shows the records that meet the specified search condition. All records stored in the facultyX table are not displayed.

PROJECT Operator

The PROJECT operator is used to display a vertical subset of a table. This operator returns some or fewer columns from a table rather than all the columns contained in the table. In MS Access SQL, excluding the WHERE clause from a SELECT statement is performing the PROJECT operator. If a table that has six columns returns fewer columns after being queried, that result is an example of the PROJECT operation. The result of PROJECT operator can include all records of the table that is being queried. The following example demonstrates the PROJECT operator.

To display identification numbers and last names for all students using the studentX table, type and run the following SELECT statement.

SELECT studentId AS [ID#], lastName AS [LAST NAME]
FROM studentX;

See partial result below.

ID#	LAST NAME
AB778204	Bomor
AM609128	Manny

Retrieving Data from Multiple Tables

ID#	LAST NAME
:	:
:	:
EJ890321	Johnson
FA213595	Anthony

The result of the query shows two columns even though the studentX table contains seven columns.

JOIN Operator

The JOIN operator and its different subtypes are discussed in the first part of this chapter. You may revisit the sections entitled "Theta Join" and "Outer Join" to familiarize yourself once again with the different types of JOIN operations.

SET Operators

SET operators are operators used to join the results of queries. These operators are used to perform special types of join operations by combining the results of queries. SET operators are part of the nine standard relational algebra operators and they are UNION, UNION ALL, INTERSECT, DIFFERENCE, PRODUCT, and DIVIDE.

UNION Operator

The UNION operator is used to display all records retrieved from SELECT statements that are written for the operation without duplicating the records. The operator is used to create the UNION statement. The tables that are involved in the UNION operation must be union-compatible. That is the columns listed in the SELECT statements, particularly in the SELECT clauses, of the operation must have identical columns' definitions. In UNION operation, the positions of the tables in the SELECT statements do not matter.

UNION Statements: A UNION statement is a SQL instruction used to display, without duplicating records, the records contained in the tables listed in the SELECT statements of the UNION operation.

The basic syntax for the UNION operator statement is

selectStatement UNION *selectStatement* UNION...;
where

- *selectStatement* is a SELECT statement
- Symbols ... mean more SELECT statements and UNION operators can be listed

> *Note:* The SELECT statements used in SET operators' activities can contain all the valid clauses associated with a SELECT statement. The basic syntax for all SET operators is similar. The differences in their syntax are the names of the operators.

To display the combined result of a SELECT statement that retrieves students' identification numbers and students' last names with another SELECT statement that retrieves faculty identification numbers and faculty members' last names using both studentX and facultyX tables, type and run the following UNION statement.

SELECT studentId AS [ID#], lastName AS [LAST NAME]
FROM studentX

UNION
SELECT facultyId, lastName
FROM facultyX;

See partial result below.

ID#	LAST NAME
CC396710	Chap
CJ684975	Jeffer
:	:
:	:
ES509264	Stevenson
ZM567123	Miller

UNION ALL Operator

Like the UNION operator, the UNION ALL operator displays all records retrieved from SELECT statements that are written for the operation, except that the UNION ALL operator also displays duplicate records if such records exist. The tables that are involved in this operation must be union-compatible and also the positions of the tables in the SELECT statements do not matter.

UNION ALL Statements: A UNION ALL statement is a SQL instruction used to display, with duplicated records if they exist, the records contained in the tables listed in the SELECT statements of the UNION ALL operation.

The following UNION ALL statement performs the same operation as the UNION statement discussed earlier.

SELECT studentId AS [ID#], lastName AS [LAST NAME]
FROM studentX
UNION ALL
SELECT facultyId, lastName
FROM facultyX;

INTERSECT Operator

The INTERSECT operator produces a table that contains records common to tables used in the SELECT statements of the operation. The results of the operator are matching records from the tables used in the operation. The operator is used to create the INTERSECT statement. The tables used in the operation must be union-compatible and the positions of the tables in the SELECT statements do not matter. MS Access SQL does not support the INTERSECT keyword used to accomplish the operation. Rather it uses alternative methods to achieve the same results.

INTERSECT Statements: An INTERSECT statement is a SQL instruction used to display the records that are common to the tables listed in the SELECT statements of the INTERSECT operation.

The basic syntax for the INTERSECT operator statement using one of the alternative methods is

SELECT [predicate] {[ALL] * | *existingColumnName, … | columnExpression, …*}
FROM *tableA*
WHERE *primaryKeyOfTableA* = ANY (SELECT *primaryKeyOfTableA*
                    FROM *tableA, tableB*

Retrieving Data from Multiple Tables

$$WHERE\ primaryKeyOfTableA = primaryKeyOfTableB)$$

where

- Predicate is a condition keyword, such as DISTINCT, used to restrict records
- Symbol * is to include all columns
- *existingColumnName* is the column in the table listed in the first FROM clause (reading from top to bottom)
- *columnExpression* is the expression formed by the combination of column(s) and data value(s). The column(s) and the data used in a column expression must be of the same data type
- *tableA* and *tableB* are the tables being queried
- *primaryKeyOfTableA* is the primary key of *tableA*
- *primaryKeyOfTableB* is the primary key of *tableB*
- Symbols [ ] mean item is optional
- Symbol | symbolizes **Or** Boolean operator. You can also list both *existingColumnName* and *columnExpression* or both asterisk symbol (*) and *columnExpression* in the first SELECT clause (reading from top to bottom)
- Symbols ... mean more columns and/or columns' expressions can be listed

Note: The column(s), column expression, columns' expressions, or their combinations listed in the first SELECT clause of the INTERSECT operator statement must be union-compatible. The *primaryKeyOfTableA* in the condition of the second WHERE clause (reading from top to bottom) can also be regarded as a foreign key since it references the *primaryKeyOfTableB*.

To display identification numbers, first names, and last names of individuals whose records appear in both facultyX and studentX tables, type and run the following INTERSECT statement.

```
SELECT facultyId AS ID, firstName AS FIRST_NAME, lastName AS LAST_NAME
FROM facultyX
WHERE facultyId = ANY (SELECT facultyId
                       FROM facultyX, studentX
                       WHERE facultyId = studentId);
```

See result below.

ID	FIRST_NAME	LAST_NAME
EM001254	Eghosa	Maklasi
DM674543	Doris	Mea

The alternative method discussed here uses a nested query construct and a multiple-row operator - the =ANY operator. Records that are based on matching identification numbers from both facultyX and studentX tables are listed. Substituting the multiple-row IN operator for the =ANY operator in the INTERSECT statement generates the same result. Multiple-row operators are discussed in detail in chapter eight of this textbook.

Note: Oracle uses the INTERSECT keyword to perform the INTERSECT operation.

```
Example:
SELECT facultyId AS ID, lastName AS LAST_NAME
FROM facultyX
INTERSECT
SELECT studentId, lastName
FROM studentX;
```

DIFFERENCE Operator

The DIFFERENCE operator produces a table that contains only records found in the first SELECT statement (first table) of the operation, but those records are not found in the second SELECT statement (second table). The operator removes all records that are common to the results of the SELECT statements (tables) and displays only the unmatched records that are contained in the result of the first SELECT statement. The operator subtracts the result of the right SELECT statement (right table) from the result of the left SELECT statement (left table).

The DIFFERENCE operator is used to create the DIFERENCE statement. Tables that are used in this operation must be union-compatible and the positions of the tables in the SELECT statements matter. This operator is a subtraction operator and swapping the positions of the SELECT statements in the operation produce different results.

DIFFERENCE Statements: A DIFFERENCE statement is a SQL instruction used to display records contained in the table listed in one SELECT statement of the DIFFERENCE operation but those records are not found in the table listed in the other SELECT statement of the DIFFERENCE operation.

MS Access SQL does not support the MINUS keyword used for the operation, and as such, it allows the use of alternative methods to obtain the result of the DIFFERENCE operator.

The basic syntax for the DIFFERENCE operator statement using one of the alternative methods is

SELECT [predicate] {[ALL] * | *existingColumnName, … | columnExpression, …*}
FROM *tableA*
WHERE *primaryKeyOfTableA* <> ALL (SELECT *primaryKeyOfTableA*
       FROM *tableA, tableB*
       WHERE *primaryKeyOfTableA* = *primaryKeyOfTableB*)

where

- Predicate is a condition keyword, such as DISTINCT, used to restrict records
- Symbol * is to include all columns
- *existingColumnName* is the column in the table listed in the first FROM clause (reading from top to bottom)
- *columnExpression* is the expression formed by the combination of column(s) and data value(s). The column(s) and the data used in a column expression must be of the same data type
- *tableA* and *tableB* are the tables being queried
- *primaryKeyOfTableA* is the primary key of *tableA*
- *primaryKeyOfTableB* is the primary key of *tableB*
- Symbols [ ] mean item is optional
- Symbol | symbolizes **Or** Boolean operator. You can also list both *existingColumnName* and *columnExpression* or both asterisk symbol (*) and *columnExpression* in the first SELECT clause (reading from top to bottom)
- Symbols … mean more columns and/or columns' expressions can be listed

Note: The column(s), column expression, columns' expressions, or their combinations listed in the first SELECT clause of the DIFFERENCE operator statement must be union-compatible. The *primaryKeyOfTableA* in the condition of the second WHERE clause (reading from top to bottom) can also be regarded as a foreign key since it references the *primaryKeyOfTableB*.

Retrieving Data from Multiple Tables

To display identification numbers, first names, and last names of records that are in the facultyX table but not among the records in the studentX table, type and run the following DIFFERENCE statement.

SELECT facultyId AS ID, firstName AS FIRST_NAME, lastName AS LAST_NAME
FROM facultyX
WHERE facultyId <> ALL (SELECT facultyId
                     FROM facultyX, studentX
                     WHERE facultyId = studentId);

See partial result below.

ID	FIRST_NAME	LAST_NAME
ES509264	Euhan	Stevenson
PD002312	Peter	Dayet
:	:	:
:	:	:
JH682508	Jenny	Hendix
EE987654	Ememgini	Erochi

One alternative method of achieving the DIFFERENCE operation is using a nested query and a multiple-row operator – the <>ALL operator. In the DIFFERENCE statement, records that are in the facultyX table but do not exist in the studentX table are displayed. Matching or common records in both tables are eliminated or are not part of the displayed result.

> **Note:** Oracle uses the MINUS keyword to perform the DIFFERENCE operation.
>
> Example:
> SELECT facultyId AS ID, lastName AS LAST_NAME
> FROM facultyX
> MINUS
> SELECT studentId, lastName
> FROM studentX;

PRODUCT Operator

The PRODUCT operator produces Cartesian products. The operator is used to create the PRODUCT statement. Cartesian join and Cartesian product are discussed in the beginning part of this chapter. You may revisit the section on join operations to familiarize yourself with the Cartesian join operator.

PRODUCT Statements: A PRODUCT statement is a SQL instruction used to display the concatenation of records contained in the tables listed in the SELECT statement of the PRODUCT operation.

DIVIDE Operator

The DIVIDE operator is the most difficult of all SET operators to implement using SQL programming language. Usually, textbooks discuss the operator in concept and hardly show how to obtain the result of the operator in a SQL environment. However, this textbook goes to great depth to demonstrate how to achieve the DIVIDE operation in MS Access SQL environment. The operator is used to create the DIVIDE statement.

The DIVIDE operation involves dividing one column of a table into two columns of another table (two columns divide by one column). The column of the one-column table must be a common column with one of the columns of the two-column table that is being divided. The tables' common columns are the matching columns. Typically, the dividing one-column table will contain two or more records that are identical to some values in the matching column of the two-column table. The result of this operation is/are the data from the non-matching column of the two-column table that is/are common to all records in the dividing one-column table.

DIVIDE Statements: A DIVIDE statement is a SQL instruction used to display data from the table that is being divided listed in the SELECT statement of the DIVIDE operation, and those data are common to all records in the dividing table listed in the SELECT statement of the DIVIDE operation.

MS Access SQL uses alternative methods to achieve the operation. One way of achieving the DIVIDE operation in MS Access SQL is to create a temporary table by embedding a subquery in the FROM clause of a SELECT statement. The subquery (inner query) must include the GROUP BY clause. The outer query must include both the GROUP BY clause and the HAVING clause. The GROUP BY clause and the HAVING clause are discussed in detail in chapter seven of this textbook.

The basic syntax for the DIVIDE operator statement using the temporary table (inline view) approach is

SELECT [predicate] *nonMatchingColumnName*
FROM *tableA*, (SELECT *nonMatchingColumnName*, COUNT(*nonMatchingColumnName*)
        AS *columnAlias*
        FROM *tableB, tableC*
        WHERE *primaryKeyOfTableB* = *primaryKeyOfTableC*
        GROUP BY *nonMatchingColumnName*) AS *inlineViewName*
GROUP BY *inlineViewName.nonMatchingColumnName*
HAVING MAX(*inlineViewName.columnAlias*) > 1 AND MAX(*inlineViewName.columnAlias*)
= COUNT(*primaryKeyOfTableA*);

where

- Predicate is a condition keyword, such as DISTINCT, used to restrict records
- *nonMatchingColumnName* is the column that is not common to the two tables used in the division operation and it is also the column that displays the data being sought in the operation
- *tableA, tableB,* and *tableC* are the tables being queried
- *primaryKeyOfTableA* is the primary key of *tableA*
- *primaryKeyOfTableB* is the primary key of *tableB*
- *primaryKeyOfTableC* is the primary key of *tableC*
- *inlineViewName* is the alias name given to the temporary table
- *columnAlias* is the column alias assigned to the column with the multiple-row function in the temporary table (inline view)

> **Note:** *tableA* and *tableC* are the same table but must be given different tables' aliases. The *primaryKeyOfTableB* in the condition of the WHERE clause of the temporary table can also be regarded as a foreign key since it references the *primaryKeyOfTableC*.

To display the common letter grades, where possible, for selected students using both studentZ and gradeX tables, type and run the following DIVIDE statement.

Retrieving Data from Multiple Tables

```
SELECT DISTINCT letterGrade AS [COMMON LETTER GRADE FOR QUERIED
STUDENTS]
FROM studentZ Z, (SELECT letterGrade, COUNT(letterGrade) AS Total
                FROM gradeX G, studentZ Y
                WHERE G.studentId = Y.studentId
                GROUP BY letterGrade) AS Div_Op
GROUP BY Div_Op.letterGrade
HAVING MAX(Div_Op.Total) > 1 AND MAX(Div_Op.Total) = COUNT(Z.studentId);
```

See result below.

COMMON LETTER GRADE FOR THE QUERIED STUDENTS
B
C

In the DIVIDE statement, the dividing one column is the student identification number column from the studentZ table and the two columns that are being divided are the student identification number column and the letter grade column of the gradeX table. The non-matching column, in this case, is the letter grade column of the gradeX table. The temporary table is assigned the alias name Div_Op and is created in the FROM clause of the SELECT statement. The Div_Op table contains two columns (letterGrade and COUNT(letterGrade) alias Total) which are used to assist in achieving the needed result. The resulting table of the operation contains the common letter grades for the students that are queried. Records from the dividing column relate to the same data (B, C) in the non-matching column of the two-column table. Data B and C are common or matching values that are shared among the records queried in the studentZ table.

> **Note:** All SET operators use the columns or the columns' aliases listed in the SELECT clause of the first SELECT statement as columns' headings to display their results. In the case of columns' aliases, it is not necessary, especially with UNION and UNION ALL operators, to repeat the aliases again in the subsequent SELECT statements of the operations, except a particular SQL requires such repetitions.

Using Non-Existing Columns in SET Operators

There are times when combining several pairs of columns from tables are impossible, especially in a set operation, when the tables do not have matching number of union-compatible columns. MS Access SQL allows the use of numeric data, text data including spaces, or the NULL keyword to substitute for such unmatched number of union-compatible columns. However, these data must be chosen with care to properly reflect meaningful representation of their usage.

To display, through UNION operation, the result of a SELECT statement that displays faculty identification numbers and their last names for those faculty members who are also students to the result of a SELECT statement that displays the total number of faculty members who are students using both studentX and facultyX tables, type and run the following UNION statement.

```
SELECT facultyId AS FACULTY_ID, F.lastName AS LAST_NAME, " " AS [TOTAL
NUMBER OF RECORDS DISPLAYED]
FROM studentX S, facultyX F
WHERE studentId = facultyId UNION
SELECT NULL, NULL, COUNT(facultyId)
FROM studentX, facultyX
WHERE studentId = facultyId
ORDER BY 1 DESC;
```

See result below.

FACULTY_ID	LAST_NAME	TOTAL NUMBER OF RECORDS DISPLAYED
EM001254	Maklasi	
DM674543	Mea	
		2

Notice that the last column in the SELECT clause of the first SELECT statement in the UNION operation is not an actual column in the tables used in the statement. A space enclosed in double quotation marks is used instead to substitute for a column. Similarly, The SELECT clause of the second SELECT statement in the UNION operation uses the NULL keyword twice to represent null values. The keyword is used to substitute for the first two columns in the statement.

Performing TOP-N Analysis

Displaying a specific number of records from a table or joined tables is referred to as TOP-N analysis. The function of TOP-N analysis is different from the function of the WHERE clause in a SELECT statement. With the WHERE clause, records that meet the specified conditions in the clause are displayed. On the contrary, TOP-N analysis displays a specific number of records that are based on a numeric integer value or on a percentage.

In MS Access SQL, the TOP clause is used to achieve the analysis. This clause is listed as part of the SELECT clause of a SELECT statement. The TOP clause accomplishes the display of (i) the exact number of records from table(s) or (ii) a certain percent of records from table(s). To display the needed records in a particular order, the ORDER BY clause is required. To display a specific number of records, you substitute an integer value for the *n* in the syntax. To display a certain percent of records, you substitute an integer value for *n* in the syntax and include the PERCENT keyword after the integer value.

The basic syntax for the TOP clause using the SELECT clause of a SELECT statement is

SELECT [predicate] TOP *n* [PERCENT] {[ALL] *, existingColumnName, ... | columnExpression, ...}

where

- predicate is a condition keyword, such as DISTINCT, used to restrict records
- *n* is an integer representing the exact number of records to be displayed
- Symbol * is to include all columns
- *existingColumnName* is the column in the table listed in the FROM clause
- *columnExpression* is the expression formed by the combination of column(s) and data value(s). The column(s) and the data used in a column expression must be of the same data type
- Symbols [ ] mean items are optional
- Symbol | symbolizes **Or** Boolean operator. You can also list both *existingColumnName* and *columnExpression* in the SELECT clause of the statement
- Symbols ... mean more columns and/or columns' expressions can be listed

You must include the DESC keyword for descending order in the ORDER BY clause to display the upper records that are contained in tables. Also to display the bottom records contained in tables, you either omit the DESC keyword in the ORDER BY clause or include the ASC keyword for ascending order in the ORDER BY clause.

Retrieving Data from Multiple Tables

To display identification numbers, fist names, last names, academic positions, and annual salaries of the three highest paid faculty members using both facultyX and positionX tables, type and run the following SELECT statement.

SELECT DISTINCT TOP 3 facultyId AS ID, firstName AS FNAME, lastName AS LNAME,
academicPosition AS POSITION, annualSalary AS [ANNUAL INCOME]
FROM facultyX, positionX
WHERE annualSalary >= minAnnualSalary AND annualSalary <= maxAnnualSalary
ORDER BY annualSalary DESC;

See result below.

ID	FNAME	LNAME	POSITION	ANNUAL INCOME
EM001254	Eghosa	Maklasi	Full Professor	74563.55
RU123098	Rischi	Ugboma	Full Professor	70760.15
ES509264	Euhan	Stevenson	Full Professor	69852.00

To display, using the same columns and tables as in the last SELECT statement, fifteen percent (15%) of the records beginning with the lowest annual salary, type and run the following SELECT statement.

SELECT DISTINCT TOP 15 PERCENT facultyId AS ID, firstName AS FNAME, lastName
AS LNAME, academicPosition AS [POSITION], annualSalary AS [ANNUAL INCOME]
FROM facultyX, positionX
WHERE annualSalary>=minAnnualSalary AND annualSalary<=maxAnnualSalary
ORDER BY annualSalary ASC;

See result below.

ID	FNAME	LNAME	POSITION	ANNUAL INCOME
JS994450	John	Semina	Instructor	45876.25
JH682508	Jenny	Hendix	Instructor	48000.00

Chapter Summary

This chapter explains Theta join, equality join, self join, Cartesian join, and non-equality join. The chapter also explains the different outer joins, relational algebra, SET operators that include UNION, UNION ALL, INTERSECT, DIFFERNCE, PRODUCT, and DIVIDE and how their operations are achieved in MS Access SQL. The chapter concludes with explaining TOP-N analysis and how it is used to display a specified number of records (top or bottom records) from tables.

JOIN Syntax and Statements Summary

The table below presents the joins' syntax, set operators, and keywords discussed in this chapter and the SQL statements' examples for retrieving data from tables.

Clause Type	Clause Syntax	Clause Example
INNER JOIN...ON clause is used to join records from tables	FROM *existingTableName* INNER JOIN *existingTableName* ON *existingTableForeignKey* = *existingTablePrimaryKey*	FROM facultyX INNER JOIN studentX ON facultyX.facultyId = studentX.studentId
LEFT JOIN...ON clause is used to display all records of the left table of a join operation	FROM *existingTableName* LEFT JOIN *existingTableName* ON *existingTableForeignKey* = *existingTablePrimaryKey*	FROM facultyX AS F LEFT JOIN departmentX AS D ON F.chairId = D.chairId

RIGHT JOIN...ON clause is used to display all records of the right table of a join operation	FROM *existingTableName* RIGHT JOIN *existingTableName* ON *existingTableForeignKey* = *existingTablePrimaryKey*	FROM studentX AS S RIGHT JOIN facultyX AS F ON S.studentId = F.facultyId
Join	**Description**	**Statement Example**
Equality Join	Used to generate a result that is based on matching values in the common column that exists between the tables involved in the join operation	SELECT facultyId AS [FACULTY ID], lastName AS [FACULTY LAST NAME], firstName AS [FACULTY FIRST NAME], departmentX.departmentCode AS [DEPARTMENT ID], departmentName AS [DEPARTMENT NAME] FROM facultyX, departmentX WHERE facultyX.departmentCode = departmentX.departmentCode;
Self Join	Used to join a table to itself to generate a result	SELECT FX.firstName & " " & FX.lastName & " is the chairperson for " & " " & FY.firstName & " " & FY.lastName AS SUPERVISOR FROM facultyX AS FX, facultyX AS FY WHERE FY.chairId IS NOT NULL AND FX.facultyId IN (FY.chairId);
Cartesian Join	Used to generate a result that is the concatenation of each record of the first table to every records of the second table in the join operation	SELECT F.facultyId AS FACULTY, D.departmentCode AS DEPARTMENT, D.chairId AS CHAIR FROM facultyX F, departmentX D; Or SELECT F.facultyId AS FACULTY, D.departmentCode AS DEPARTMENT, D.chairId AS CHAIR FROM facultyX F, departmentX D WHERE EXISTS (SELECT * FROM facultyX F, departmentX D WHERE F.departmentCode NOT IN (D.departmentCode));
Non-equality Join	Used to generate a result that is based on non-matching values of the common column that exists between the tables involved in the join operation	SELECT academicPosition AS POSITION, firstName + " " + lastName AS FULL_NAME FROM positionX, facultyX WHERE annualSalary BETWEEN minAnnualSalary AND maxAnnualSalary;
Left Outer Join	Used to generate a result that contains all records of the left table as well as matching records of the right table in the join operation	SELECT F.firstName & " " & F.lastName AS [FULL NAME], D.chairId AS CHAIR_ID FROM facultyX AS F LEFT JOIN departmentX AS D ON F.chairId = D.chairId ORDER BY 1;
Right Outer Join	Used to generate a result that contains all records of the right table as well as matching records of the left table in the join operation	SELECT S.firstName & " " & S.lastName AS [STUDENT NAME], F.firstName + " " + F.lastName AS [FACULTY NAME] FROM studentX AS S RIGHT JOIN facultyX AS F ON S.studentId = F.facultyId;
Full Outer Join	Used to generate a result that contains all matching records as well as non-matching records from the tables involved in the join operation	SELECT S.firstName & " " & S.lastName AS [STUDENT NAME], F.firstName & " " & F.lastName AS [FACULTY NAME] FROM studentX S LEFT JOIN facultyX F ON S.studentId = F.facultyId UNION SELECT S.firstName & " " & S.lastName, F.firstName & " " & F.lastName FROM studentX S RIGHT JOIN facultyX F ON S.studentId = F.facultyId;
Relational Algebra Operator	**Description**	**Statement Example**
SELECT	Used to display some or fewer records from a table	SELECT firstName AS [FIRST NAME], lastName AS [LAST NAME], annualSalary AS [ANNUAL INCOME] FROM facultyX WHERE chairId IS NULL;

Retrieving Data from Multiple Tables

PROJECT	Used to display some or fewer columns from a table	SELECT studentId AS [ID#], lastName AS [LAST NAME] FROM studentX;
UNION	Used to display all records from tables involved in the operation without records' duplications	SELECT studentId AS [ID#], lastName AS [LAST NAME] FROM studentX UNION SELECT facultyId, lastName FROM facultyX;
UNION ALL	Used to display all records from tables involved in the operation with records' duplications	SELECT studentId AS [ID#], lastName AS [LAST NAME] FROM studentX UNION ALL SELECT facultyId, lastName FROM facultyX;
INTERSECT	Used to display records that are common to the tables involved in the operation	SELECT facultyId AS ID, firstName AS FIRST_NAME, lastName AS LAST_NAME FROM facultyX WHERE facultyId = ANY (SELECT facultyId FROM facultyX, studentX WHERE facultyId = studentId);
DIFFERENCE	Used to display non-common records that are contained in the first table but not in the second table of the operation	SELECT facultyId AS ID, firstName AS FIRST_NAME, lastName AS LAST_NAME FROM facultyX WHERE facultyId <> ALL (SELECT facultyId FROM facultyX, studentX WHERE facultyId = studentId);
DIVIDE	Used to display common columns' values after dividing one-column table into two-column table involved in the operation	SELECT DISTINCT letterGrade AS [COMMON LETTER GRADE FOR QUERIED STUDENTS] FROM studentZ Z, (SELECT letterGrade, COUNT(letterGrade) AS Total FROM gradeX G, studentZ Y WHERE G.studentId = Y.studentId GROUP BY letterGrade) AS Div_Op GROUP BY Div_Op.letterGrade HAVING MAX(Div_Op.Total) > 1 AND MAX(Div_Op.Total) = COUNT(Z.studentId);

Keyword	Description	Statement Example
AS	Optionally used in the FROM clause to assign aliases to tables	SELECT F.lastName, F.offPhone FROM facultyX AS F;
TOP	Used in the SELECT clause to display exact number of records or certain percentage of records from a table	SELECT DISTINCT TOP 3 facultyId AS ID, firstName AS FNAME, lastName AS LNAME, academicPosition AS POSITION, annualSalary AS [ANNUAL INCOME] FROM facultyX, positionX WHERE annualSalary >= minAnnualSalary AND annualSalary <= maxAnnualSalary ORDER BY annualSalary DESC;
PERCENT	Used with the TOP keyword in the SELECT clause to indicate that the records to be displayed are in percentage measure	SELECT DISTINCT TOP 15 PERCENT facultyId AS ID, firstName AS FNAME, lastName AS LNAME, academicPosition AS [POSITION], annualSalary AS [ANNUAL INCOME] FROM facultyX, positionX WHERE annualSalary>=minAnnualSalary And annualSalary<=maxAnnualSalary ORDER BY annualSalary ASC;

Key Terms

Cartesian join
DIFFERENCE operator
DIVIDE operator
Equality join

Full outer join
INNER JOIN...ON clause
INTERSECT operator
LEFT JOIN...ON clause

Left outer join
Non-equality join
PROJECT operator
RIGHT JOIN...ON clause
Right outer join

SELECT operator
Theta join
TOP-N analysis
UNION operator

Chapter Review Questions

Multiple Choice Questions

1. The _____ operator is used to create equality join in the WHERE clause.
   - a. >=
   - b. <=
   - c. <>
   - d. =

2. Which of the following is not a component of a column qualifier?
   - a. table name.
   - b. semicolon.
   - c. period.
   - d. column name.

3. Which of the following operators is supported by INNER JOIN...ON clause?
   - a. AND.
   - b. IN.
   - c. BETWEEN...AND.
   - d. LIKE.

4. To assign an alias to a table, you use the _____ clause.
   - a. SELECT
   - b. WHERE
   - c. FROM
   - d. GROUP BY

5. Self join is also known as
   - a. recursive join.
   - b. unary join.
   - c. all of the above.
   - d. none of the above.

6. Which of the following joins does not display records from the joining tables where records from those tables satisfy the join conditions?
   - a. equality join.
   - b. non-equality join.
   - c. self join.
   - d. outer join.

7. The _____ operator is used to display a horizontal subset of a table.
   - a. SELECT
   - b. PROJECT
   - c. INTERSECT
   - d. DIVIDE

8. Which of the following is not a SET operator?
   - a. INTERSECT.
   - b. DIVIDE.
   - c. PROJECT.
   - d. UNION.

9. The TOP clause used to implement the TOP-N analysis is embedded in the _____ clause.
    a. HAVING
    b. ORDER BY
    c. FROM
    d. SELECT

10. To display a specific number of records that is based on actual number or percentage, you use the _____ clause.
    a. WHERE
    b. SELECT
    c. HAVING
    d. GROUP BY

True or False Questions

11. Theta join is divided into equality join and non-equality join.
    a. True
    b. False

12. In MS Access SQL, the INNER JOIN...ON clause does not support non-equality join.
    a .True
    b .False

13. Assigning aliases to tables usually reduce the number of keystrokes typed.
    a. True
    b. False

14. A Cartesian product is the result of a query where each record of one table concatenates with one record of another table.
    a. True
    b. False

15. Right outer join displays null records from the left table to complete the join operation.
    a. True
    b. False

16. In MS Access SQL, SET operators are used to separate the results of queries.
    a. True
    b. False

17. The AS keyword is optional when creating an alias for a table.
    a. Tue
    b. False

Fill in the blank Questions

18. Theta join is a join created when _____ are used.

19. Equality join is also called _____.

20. A join whereby a table is joined to itself is called _____.

21. A join that concatenates each record of the first table to every record of the second table is called _____.

22. _____ is a join that uses other comparison operators except for the equal to (=) comparison operator.

23. The RIGHT JOIN...ON clause is used to create _____ join.

Chapter Four

Essay Type Questions

24. Describe how the INTERSECT operator differs from the DIVIDE operator?

25. Explain concatenation of the PRODUCT operator and give an example using a SQL statement?

26. Explain the differences between UNION and UNION ALL operators and write a SQL statement for each?

27. What is the function of Left outer join and write a valid SQL statement to demonstrate how the join is achieved?

28. What is a table alias and how does it differ from a column alias? List all possible differences.

Hands-on Activities

Study the structures and the data of *AcademicX* database tables in appendix A (pages 355 through 360) and perform the following hands-on exercises.

1. Using the INNER JOIN...ON clause approach, display identification numbers of faculty members and the department codes in which the faculty members are assigned.

2. Using the self join approach, display identification numbers and last names of faculty members who are department chairpersons and whose individual annual salary is $69,000 or less. Eliminate records' duplications.

3. Write a SQL statement to concatenate each department code to every academic position. Rearrange the result in ascending order by department code.

4. Write a SQL statement to concatenate each identification number of faculty members who are also students with every record that consists of the course code and the course name taught by the faculty member whose identification number is "PD002312". Eliminate records' duplications.

5. Using the WHERE clause approach, write a SQL statement to display faculty members' academic positions and the concatenation of their first and last names for those faculty members whose annual salaries are less than $50,000. Assign column alias **Full Name** to the concatenated column.

6. Using the INNER JOIN...ON clause approach, write a SQL statement to display a result, in a concatenated expression format, first and last names of faculty members who are also students and their countries of origin. The result should be displayed using the following expression example, "Henry Matthew is from the British Virgin Islands". Assign column alias **Country of Origin** to the concatenated column expression.

7. Using the WHERE clause approach, display students' first and last names, names of courses, and letter grades for the courses the students have earned the letter grade "A".

8. Using the INNER JOIN...ON clause approach, write the SQL statement to solve the same problem as question 7.

9. Using the UNION operator, display first and last names of students who have earned the letter grade "AU" and first and last names of faculty members who taught those courses. The result should be sorted by last name in ascending order.

10. Display the first thirty (30) percent of students' records for those students who have earned the letter Grade "C". The result should include the students' identification numbers, their last names, and names of the courses for which the students have earned the letter grade "C". Using the course name column, sort the result in ascending order.

Chapter Five

Single-Row Functions

Chapter Objectives
After completing this chapter, you should be able to
- Understand the underlying principles of functions
- Understand single-row functions
- Use text case-conversion single-row functions
- Use character manipulation single-row functions
- Use numeric single-row functions

Functions

A function is a block or collection of programming instructions which task is pre-known. A function can, depending on its syntax, accept no value, one value, or more values as its actual arguments and it must return a single value as its result. Two types of functions are used in programming arena. One type is called built-in functions and the other type is called programmer- or user-defined functions. Both types can further be classified as single-row and multiple-row functions. The codes of built-in functions are incorporated into the programming language before the language is distributed for use and that is the type that is being discussed in this textbook. Programmer-defined functions are written by programmers during programs' development and their codes are part of the programs. Programmer-defined functions are outside the scope of this textbook, and as such, they are not addressed.

MS Access SQL supports dozens of functions, but this chapter discusses the ones that are most commonly used in MS Access SQL environment

The general syntax for a function is the function name followed by a pair of parentheses with optional actual argument(s) separated by commas placed within the parentheses.

The general syntax for a function is

functionName([*actualArgument*], ...)

where

- *functionName* is the function that is being used
- *actualArgument* is the optional data item that is passed to the function to use to perform the assigned task
- Symbols [ ] mean item is optional
- Symbols ... mean more actual arguments can be listed

A function might require no (zero) actual arguments to perform its assigned task. In such situation, no data items are passed to the function as its actual arguments when the function is called. In case a function requires an actual argument, the argument can be a single column, an expression, combination of columns, combination of expressions, combination of columns and expressions enclosed in a pair of parentheses. You can also specify more than one actual argument in the pair of parentheses if that is a function's requirement. When a function requires more than one actual argument, the arguments must be separated by commas.

Single-Row Functions

Actual Arguments: An actual argument is a data item supplied to a function to use to perform its assigned task. The data item must be enclosed in a pair of parentheses following the function name.

The following is an example of MS Access function using a single actual argument:

UCASE(lastName)

The pair of parentheses is mandatory as it is the standard means of supplying a data item, which is the actual argument, to a function.

> ***Note:*** Data altered by functions listed in the SELECT clause and conditions' clauses of a SELECT statement are changed temporarily. Functions do not permanently change the original form of data stored in tables. Whenever functions are allowed to be used in conditions' clauses, you can specify the functions on either side or both sides of the comparison operators that are used in the conditions.
>
> In MS Access SQL when data values that are being queried are not contained in a table, you can obtain the results of such values with functions that use the values as their actual arguments by including the functions in the SELECT clause of a SELECT statement that consists of only the SELECT clause. All other clauses can be omitted.
>
> Example:
> SELECT UCASE("Stevenson");
>
> Notice that the SELECT statement consists only of one clause – the SELECT clause.

Single-Row Functions

Single-row functions are functions that return one record for each row processed in a single table or joined tables. Single-row functions are categorized into text (string, character) functions, numeric functions, date and time functions, and non-categorized functions.

Text Functions

String or character functions are used to manipulate text data. These functions accept text data as their input and can return text and numeric data as their output. Text functions are further divided into case conversion and character manipulation functions. When text functions return text data as their values, the results are aligned to the left by default. When the functions return numeric data as their values, the results are aligned to the right by default.

Case Conversion Functions

Case conversion functions are used to convert or change characters, usually letters of the alphabet, from one case to another. Other printable symbols, such as digits (numbers) and special symbols such as the question mark (?) are not affected as these symbols have no case variations. The basic syntax for a case conversion function in a SELECT clause or in a WHERE clause is

textFunctionName(*actualArgument*)

where

- *textFunctionName* is the text function that is being used
- *actualArgument* is the text data item that is being converted

Uppercase Conversion

In MS Access SQL, the UCASE function is used to convert letters of the alphabet to uppercase letters. The function changes all letters in the text data to uppercase. The basic syntax for this function is

UCASE(*existingColumnName* | *"textExpression"*)

where

- *existingColumnName* is the column in the table listed in the FROM clause
- *textExpression* is the text value enclosed in quotation marks
- Symbol | symbolizes **Or** Boolean operator. You can also concatenate columns and/or text expressions as the function's actual argument

To display last names and first names of department chairpersons in uppercase letters along with a text expression that displays the text "CHAIR PERSON" also in uppercases using the facultyX table, type and run the following SELECT statement.

SELECT UCase(lastName) AS [Last Name], UCase(firstName) AS [First Name], UCase("chair person") AS [Academic Status]
FROM facultyX
WHERE chairId IS NULL;

See result below.

Last Name	First Name	Academic Status
MAKLASI	EGHOSA	CHAIR PERSON
UGBOMA	RISCHI	CHAIR PERSON
STEVENSON	EUHAN	CHAIR PERSON
MEA	DORIS	CHAIR PERSON
EROCHI	EMEMGINI	CHAIR PERSON

You might have noticed that the names in the result of the query are displayed in uppercases even though the names are stored in the facultyX table in mixed cases. That is the job of the UCASE function.

Lowercase Conversion

In MS Access SQL, the LCASE function is used to convert letters of the alphabet to lowercase letters. The function changes all letters in the text data to lowercase. The basic syntax for the LCASE function is similar to that of the UCASE function. Substitute the function name LCASE for UCASE in the uppercase conversion syntax to obtain that of lowercase conversion.

To display identification numbers, last names, and dates first enrolled for courses for students whose first names is "Benjamin" and last names is "Benado" using the studentX table and searching in lowercases, type and run the following SELECT statement.

SELECT studentId AS [STUDENT ID], lastName AS [LAST NAME], dateFirstEnrolled AS [ENROLLMENT DATE]
FROM studentX
WHERE LCASE(firstName) = "benjamin" AND LCASE(lastName) = "benado";

Single-Row Functions

See result below.

STUDENT ID	LAST NAME	ENROLLMENT DATE
BB118945	Benado	8/15/2004

In the result of the query, the last name is displayed exactly as it is in the studentX table - mixed cases. This is because the function is used in the WHERE clause to search for the required record and not in the SELECT clause. Here, the LCASE function converts all data entries in both first name and last name columns of the table to lowercases before comparing each column entries to the data listed on the right sides of the comparison operators in the WHERE clause.

> **Note:** When functions are used in conditions' clauses, the functions' data must match the values that are being compared both in types and in forms.

Mixed Case Conversion

MS Access SQL allows the nesting of one text function inside another text function to achieve the mixed case conversion. To convert text data to mixed cases whereby the first letter of each piece of data begins with uppercase or capital letter, you can nest other appropriate text functions within the UCASE function.

To display last names in uppercases, lowercases, and mixed cases for students whose first names is "Benjamin" and last names is "Benado" using the studentX table and searching in lowercases, type and run the following SELECT statement.

```
SELECT UCASE(lastName) AS [UPPERCASE], LCASE(lastname) AS [LOWERCASE],
UCASE(MID(lastName,1,1)) & MID(lastName,2,LEN(lastName)) AS [MIXED CASE]
FROM studentX
WHERE LCASE(firstName) = "benjamin" AND LCASE(lastName) = "benado";
```

See result below.

UPPERCASE	LOWERCASE	MIXED CASE
BENADO	benado	Benado

In the result of the query, two other text functions (MID and LEN), in addition to the UCASE function, are used to display the last name in mixed cases. Although, students' last names are entered in the table in mixed cases, the nested functions did perform the required task. MID, LEN, and other character manipulation functions are discussed in the following section of this chapter.

> **Note:** To use the nesting function approach to achieve the mixed case conversion, the text data that is being converted must be in the appropriate case so that the effect of the conversion will be noticed.

STRCONV Function

The STRCONV function is the other function used to convert letters of the alphabet to uppercases, lowercases, and mixed cases. The basic syntax for the STRCONV function is

STRCONV(*existingColumnName* | *"textExpression"*, *conversionTypeDigit*)

where

- *existingColumnName* is the column in the table listed in the FROM clause
- *textExpression* is the text value enclosed in quotation marks

- Symbol | symbolizes *Or* Boolean operator. You can also concatenate columns and/or text expressions as the function's actual argument
- *conversionTypeDigit* is an integer that specifies the type of case conversion to be returned.

If the *conversionTypeDigit* is 1, the text data is converted to uppercase. If it is 2, the text data is converted to lowercases and if the *conversionTypeDigit* is 3, the text data is converted to mixed cases.

To display department chairpersons' first names in lowercases, their last names in uppercases and stated text expressions in mixed cases indicating the department each person heads using both departmentX and facultyX tables, type and run the following SELECT statement.

SELECT DISTINCT STRCONV(firstName, 2) AS [FIRST NAME IN LOWERCASES], STRCONV(lastName, 1) AS [LAST NAME IN UPPERCASES], STRCONV("is the chair person for ", 3) + departmentName + STRCONV(" department", 3) AS [ACADEMIC STATUS IN MIXED CASES]
FROM facultyX F INNER JOIN departmentX D
ON F.departmentCode = D.departmentCode
WHERE F.chairId IS NULL;

See result below.

FIRST NAME IN LOWERCASES	LAST NAME IN UPPERCASES	ACADEMIC STATUS IN MIXED CASES
doris	MEA	Is The Chair Person For Education Department
eghosa	MAKLASI	Is The Chair Person For Business Administration Department
ememgini	EROCHI	Is The Chair Person For computer science Department
euhan	STEVENSON	Is The Chair Person For Social Science Department
rischi	UGBOMA	Is The Chair Person For Natural Science Department

Notice that every word of each entry in the third column of the result begins with an uppercase letter or a capital letter. That is an example of a mixed case conversion text data. With the STRCONV function, you can perform any or all of the case conversions discussed in this chapter.

> **Note:** Oracle uses UPPER, LOWER, and INITCAP functions to convert text data to uppercases, lowercases, and mixed cases respectively.
>
> Example:
> SELECT LOWER(lastName), UPPER(firstName), INITCAP('FACULTY MEMBER')
> FROM facultyX
> WHERE chaired IS NULL;

Character Manipulation Functions

Character manipulation functions are used to alter the forms of text data besides converting text data to upper, lower, and mixed cases. This category of text functions is used to return portion - subset of a string or substring – of text data, determine the number of characters in text data, return the beginning position of the first occurrence of text data within another text data, remove leading and trailing spaces from text data, pad text data from left and right with spaces, replace instances of text data or the text data with another text data, reverse the spelling of text data, indicate the position of the first occurrence of a text symbol that is being sought, and reverses the positions of characters in text data and so on.

Single-Row Functions

Generating Substrings

In MS Access SQL, there are three functions used to return a portion (substring) of a text data or string. The functions are LEFT, RIGHT, and MID.

LEFT Function - This function returns as its output a substring that contain a specific number of characters beginning from the left side of the text data item that is enclosed as the actual argument of the function. The LEFT function requires two actual arguments. The basic syntax for this function is

LEFT(*existingColumnName* | *"textExpression"*, *numberOfCharacter*)

where

- *existingColumnName* is the column in the table listed in the FROM clause
- *textExpression* is the text value enclosed in quotation marks
- Symbol | symbolizes **Or** Boolean operator. You can also combine both *existingColumnName* and *textExpression* in the function's actual argument
- *numberOfCharacter* is a numeric value of integer type that specifies the number of characters to be returned.

To display the first three symbols of identification numbers and the first four symbols of last names of faculty members who are not department chairpersons using the facultyX table, type and run the following SELECT statement.

SELECT LEFT(facultyId, 3) AS [FIRST THREE SYMBOLS], LEFT(lastName, 4) AS [FIRST FOUR SYMBOLS]
FROM facultyX
WHERE chairId IS NOT NULL;

See result below.

FIRST THREE SYMBOLS	FIRST FOUR SYMBOLS
JS9	Semi
PD0	Daye
ZM5	Mill
AL5	Lask
JH6	Hend

RIGHT Function - This function returns a substring that contains a specific number of characters beginning from the right side of the text data item that is enclosed as the actual argument of the function. This function requires two actual arguments.

The basic syntax for this function is similar to that of the LEFT function. Substitute the function name RIGHT for the function name LEFT in the LEFT function syntax to obtain the syntax for the RIGHT function.

To display the last three symbols of identification numbers and the last four symbols of last names of faculty members who are department chairpersons using the facultyX table, type and run the following SELECT statement.

SELECT RIGHT(facultyId, 3) AS [LAST THREE SYMBOLS], RIGHT(lastName, 4) AS [LAST FOUR SYMBOLS]
FROM facultyX
WHERE chairId IS NULL;

Chapter Five

See result below.

LAST THREE SYMBOLS	LAST FOUR SYMBOLS
254	Lasi
098	Boma
264	Nson
543	Mea
654	Ochi

MID Function - This function returns a substring that contains a specific number of characters beginning from a specified character position of the text data item that is enclosed as the actual argument of the function up to a specified length. This function requires three actual arguments. The basic syntax for the MID function is

MID(*existingColumnName* | *"textExpression"*, *beginningCharacterPosition, numberOfCharacter*)

where

- *existingColumnName* is the column in the table listed in the FROM clause
- *textExpression* is the text value enclosed in quotation marks
- Symbol | symbolizes **Or** Boolean operator. You can also concatenate columns and/or text expressions as the function's actual argument
- *beginningCharacterPosition* is a numeric value of integer type that specify the starting character position to begin searching for the required text
- *numberOfCharacter* is a numeric value of integer type that specifies the number of characters to be returned.

Note: The character at the starting character position of the function's actual argument is included in the result.

To display the three symbols of identification numbers beginning with the second character and the letter grade for students with the letter grade of "F" using the gradeX table, type and run the following SELECT statement.

SELECT MID(studentId, 2, 3) AS [PARTIAL STUDENT ID], letterGrade AS [STUDENT LETTER GRADE]
FROM gradeX
WHERE letterGrade IN ("F")
ORDER BY studentId;

See result below.

PARTIAL STUDENT ID	STUDENT LETTER GRADE
B11	F
C39	F
J68	F
J89	F

The query displays the symbols at character positions 2, 3, and 4 of the studentId column.

Note: For LEFT and RIGHT functions, if the actual argument *numberOfCharacter* is equal to or greater than the number of characters contained in the text data that is being searched, the entire text data is returned. For MID function, if the actual argument *numberOfCharacter*

Single-Row Functions

is equal to or greater than the number of characters remaining in the text data that is being searched, the entire text starting from the beginning character position is returned.

The beginning character position for the MID function cannot be zero (0) and the lengths of LEFT, RIGHT, and MID functions cannot be negative numeric values. If no substring is found, a null value is returned. Oracle uses the SUBSTR function to extract portions of text data.

Example:
SELECT SUBSTR(facultyId, 1, 3) AS "FIRST THREE SYMBOLS", SUBSTR(lastName, 2, 5) AS "FIRST MIDDLE FOUR SYMBOLS"
FROM facultyX
WHERE chairId IS NULL;

LEN Function

The LEN function is used to return the number of characters contained in a text data value. This function returns a value of numeric integer data type and the value can be used in mathematics. The basic syntax for this function is

LEN(*existingColumnName* | "*textExpression*")

where

- *existingColumnName* is the column in the table listed in the FROM clause
- *textExpression* is the text value enclosed in quotation marks
- Symbol | symbolizes **Or** Boolean operator. You can also concatenate columns and/or text expressions as the function's actual argument

To display first names and last names of students and the total number of characters for each student's first name and last name for those students who have earned the letter grade "A" using both studentX and gradeX tables, type and run the following SELECT statement.

SELECT DISTINCT firstName AS FIRST_NAME, lastName AS LAST_NAME, LEN(firstName + lastName) AS [NUMBER OF CHARACTERS IN BOTH NAMES]
FROM gradeX G INNER JOIN studentX S
ON G.studentId = S.studentId
WHERE letterGrade IN ('A')
ORDER BY lastName, firstName;

See result below.

FIRST_NAME	LAST_NAME	NUMBER OF CHARACTERS IN BOTH NAMES
Erasto	Actionbarrel	18
Suzy	Afik	8
Fredrica	Anthony	15
Abel	Bomor	9
Christopher	Salat	16

INSTR Function

This function is used to return the beginning numeric position of the first occurrence of a character within a text data item that is enclosed as the actual argument of the function. The value returned by this function is of numeric integer data type and the value can be used in mathematics. The basic syntax for the INSTR function is

INSTR([*beginningCharacterPosition*], *textDataBeingSearched*,
"*textDataBeingCompared*" [, *compareDigit*])

where

- *beginningCharacterPosition* is the optional starting character position and must be a numeric value of integer type
- *textDataBeingSearched* is a column, text expression, or concatenation of column(s) and/or text expression(s).
- *textDataBeingCompared* is the text value that is being compared to the *textDataBeingSearched* and must be enclosed in quotation marks
- *compareDigit* is the optional type of comparison to perform and must be a numeric value of integer type
- Symbols [ ] mean items are optional

If *textDataBeingSearched* is a text expression, the expression must be enclosed in quotation marks.

The INSTR function performs forward searching. That is from left to right. There are three types of comparisons that can be accomplished using the function. The comparisons are binary, textual, and database and are represented by 0, 1, and 2 respectively. 0 is used for binary comparison, 1 for textual comparison, and 2 for database comparison. If omitted, the optional compare (-1) is used. You can only specify one type of comparison within the INSTR function. If the left most actual argument of the function is omitted, the comparison search will go through all character positions in the text data that is being searched. In MS Access SQL, to use the compare portion (the third actual argument counting from left) of the function, you must also use the left most argument of the function.

To display last names of students who have earned the letter grade "B" and return the character positions of the first occurrence of the letter "a" in their last names starting with the second character positions of their last names using both studentX and gradeX tables, type and run the following SELECT statement.

SELECT DISTINCT lastName AS LAST_NAME, INSTR(2, lastName,'a', 1) AS [CHARACTER POSITION]
FROM gradeX G, studentX S
WHERE G.studentId = S.studentId
AND letterGrade = 'B';

See partial result below.

LAST_NAME	CHARACTER POSITION
Actionbarrel	8
Kolly	0
:	:
:	:
Salat	2
Zeberia	7

The entries with zeros (0) in the second column (CHARACTER POSITION) indicate that the letter being searched is not found.

Single-Row Functions

INSTRREV Function

The INSTRREV function is similar to the INSTR function except that the INSTRREV function searches for the first occurrence of the specified character backward (right to left). The value returned by this function is of numeric integer data type and the value can be used in mathematics. The basic syntax for the INSTRREV function is

INSTRREV(*textDataBeingSearched*, "*textDataBeingCompared*"
[, *beginningCharacterPosition*, *compareDigit*])

where

- *textDataBeingSearched* is a column, a text expression, or concatenation of column(s) and/or text expression(s).
- *textDataBeingCompared* is the text value that is being compared to the *textDataBeingSearched* and must be enclosed in quotation marks
- *beginningCharacterPosition* is the optional starting character position and must be a numeric value of integer type
- *compareDigit* is the optional type of comparison to perform and must be a numeric value of integer type
- Symbols [ ] mean items are optional

If *textDataBeingSearched* is a text expression, the expression must be enclosed in quotation marks.

To display the combined first names and last names of students with the last name "Mea" and return the character positions of the first occurrence of the letter "o" in the combined names in reversed order using the studentX table, type and run the following SELECT statement.

SELECT DISTINCT firstName + " " + lastName AS NAME, INSTRREV(firstName + " " + lastName,'o') AS [CHARATER POSITION]
FROM studentX
WHERE LCASE(lastName) = LCASE('MEA');

See result below.

NAME	CHARATER POSITION
Doris Mea	2

STRCOMP Function

The STRCOMP function compares the ASCII values of the characters contained in the first (left) text data to the ASCII values of the characters contained in the second (right) text data. The function compares the two text data character position by character position. If the first text data is less than the second text data, the integer value -1 is returned. If they are equal, the integer value 0 is returned and if the first text data is larger than the second text data, the integer value 1 is returned. If any of the two text data is null, the null value is returned.

The basic syntax for this function is

STRCOMP(*textDataBeingCompared*, *textDataBeingComparedTo*
[, *compareDigit*])

where

- *textDataBeingCompared* is a column, a text expression, or concatenation of column(s) and/or text expression(s).
- *textDataBeingComparedTo* is a column, a text expression, or concatenation of column(s) and/or text expression(s)
- *compareDigit* is the optional type of comparison to perform and must be a numeric value of integer type
- Symbols [ ] mean item is optional

If *textDataBeingCompared* and *textDataBeingComparedTo* are text expressions, the expressions must be enclosed in quotation marks.

To display first names and last names of students who have earned the letter grade "F" and return the numeric status of comparing their first names to their last names using both studentX and gradeX tables, type and run the following SELECT statement.

SELECT DISTINCT firstName AS [FIRST NAME], lastName AS [LAST NAME], STRCOMP(firstName, lastName, 2) AS [NUMERIC STATUS]
FROM gradeX G, studentX S
WHERE G.studentId = S.studentId
AND letterGrade = 'F';

See result below.

FIRST NAME	LAST NAME	NUMERIC STATUS
Benjamin	Benado	1
Cecilia	Jeffer	-1
Celestine	Chap	-1
Efosa	Johnson	-1

STRING Function

The STRING function is used to return a specified number of a particular printable character symbol including a space. The function can be used to increase the original character position of text data and to format output. The function can also be used with other appropriate function to pad text data to the left, right, or both. The basic syntax for the STRING function is

STRING(*totalNumber*, "*characterSymbol*")

where

- *totalNumber* is a numeric value of integer type that specifies the total number of the character symbol to be returned
- *characterSymbol* is the character to be displayed and must be enclosed in quotation marks

To display first names and last names of faculty members and show department chairpersons by including five asterisk symbols (*) to the right of their last names using the facultyX table, type and run the following UNION statement.

SELECT firstName AS [FACULTY FIRST NAME], lastName AS [FACULTY LAST NAME]
FROM facultyX
WHERE chairId IS NOT NULL
UNION

Single-Row Functions

```
SELECT  firstName, lastName + STRING(5, '*')
FROM facultyX
WHERE chairId IS  NULL
ORDER BY 2;
```

See partial result below.

FACULTY FIRST NAME	FACULTY LAST NAME
Peter	Dayet
Ememgini	Erochi*****
:	:
:	:
Jenny	Hendix
Euhan	Stevenson*****

SPACE Function

The SPACE function is used to temporarily increase the number of character positions originally reserved for columns. This function is usually used to format output such as padding text data to the left, right, or both. The basic syntax for this function is

SPACE(*totalNumber*)

where

- *totalNumber* is a numeric value of integer type that specifies the total number of spaces to be returned or to be added to the text data

To display first names of faculty members who are not department chairpersons with leading fifteen spaces to each of the names using the facultyX table, type and run the following SELECT statement.

```
SELECT SPACE(15) + firstName AS [FIRST NAME]
FROM facultyX
WHERE chairId IS NOT NULL;
```

See result below.

FIRST NAME
John
Peter
Zenat
Ada
Jenny

STRREVERSE Function

This function is used to spell text data backward. The STRREVERSE function reverses the character positions of the original text. The last character becomes the first and the second to the last character becomes the second character and in that order until the first character becomes the last. The character positions of the characters between the first and the last characters of the function's actual argument are also affected.

The basic syntax for the STRREVERSE function is

STRREVERSE(*existingColumnName* | "*textExpression*")

110

where

- *existingColumnName* is the column in the table listed in the FROM clause
- *textExpression* is the text value enclosed in quotation marks
- Symbol | symbolizes **Or** Boolean operator. You can also concatenate columns and/or text expressions as the function's actual argument

To display first names of students who have earned the letter grade "F" and spell their names backward using both studentX and gradeX tables, type and run the following SELECT statement.

```
SELECT firstName AS [STUDENT FIRST NAME], STRREVERSE(firstName ) AS [NAME
SPELLED BACKWARD]
FROM gradeX G, studentX S
WHERE G.studentId = S.studentId
AND letterGrade = "F";
```

See result below.

STUDENT FIRST NAME	NAME SPELLED BACKWARD
Benjamin	nimajneB
Efosa	asofE
Cecilia	ailiceC
Celestine	enitseleC

LTRIM, RTRIM, and TRIM Functions

These functions are primarily used to remove leading spaces, trailing spaces, or both from text data. The LTRIM function removes leading spaces, the RTRIM function removes trailing spaces, and the TRIM function removes both leading and trailing spaces. The basic syntax for these functions is

LTRIM | RTRIM | TRIM(*existingColumnName* | *"textExpression"*)

where

- *existingColumnName* is the column in the table listed in the FROM clause
- *textExpression* is the text value enclosed in quotation marks
- Symbol | symbolizes **Or** Boolean operator. You can also concatenate columns and/or text expressions as the function's actual argument

To remove trailing spaces and display last names and first names of students who audited courses with the letter grade "AU" using both studentX and gradeX tables, type and run the following SELECT statement.

```
SELECT DISTINCT RTRIM(lastName) AS LNAME, RTRIM(firstName) AS FNAME
FROM gradeX G INNER JOIN studentX S
ON G.studentId = S.studentId
WHERE G.letterGrade = "AU";
```

See result below.

LNAME	FNAME
Maklasi	Eghosa
Mea	Doris

Single-Row Functions

> **Note:** The LTRIM and RTRIM functions behave differently in Oracle. In Oracle, they are used to remove portions of text data from the left side and the right side of the text data respectively.
>
> Example:
> SELECT firstName, lastName, LTRIM(offPhone, '032')
> FROM facultyX;

REPLACE Function

The REPLACE function is used to search and replace an instance of text data or the entire text data. The REPLACE function is a substitution function and it is used to substitute one piece of data for another. The basic syntax for this function is

REPLACE(*textDataBeingSearched*, "*textDataBeingReplaced*", "*substituteTextData*" [, *beginningCharacterPosition*, *numberOfSubstitution*, *compareDigit*])

where

- *textDataBeingSearched* is a column, a text expression, or concatenation of column(s) and/or text expression(s).
- *textDataBeingReplaced* is the portion to be replaced and must be enclosed in quotation marks
- *substitueTextData* is the text data to replace *textDataBeingReplaced* and must be enclosed in quotation marks
- *beginningCharacterPosition* is the optional starting character position and must be a numeric value of integer type
- *numberOfSubstitution* is the optional number of times the replacement is performed if the portion is found in several locations within the text data that is being searched
- *compareDigit* is the optional type of comparison to perform and must be a numeric value of integer type
- Symbols [ ] mean items are optional

If *textDataBeingSearched* is a text expression, the expression must be enclosed in quotation marks.

To display first names and last names of faculty members whose last names is "Ugboma" after the first three letters of their last names have been replaced with "Bl" using the facultyX table, type and run the following SELECT statement.

SELECT firstName AS FIRST_NAME, REPLACE(LastName,"Ugb", "Bl") AS [CHANGE OF LAST NAME]
FROM facultyX
WHERE LCASE(lastName) = "ugboma" AND LCASE(firstName) = "rischi";

See result below.

FIRST_NAME	CHANGE OF LAST NAME
Rischi	Bloma

The REPLACE function substitutes the text value "Bl" for the text value "Ugb" in the last name of the record whose first name is Rischi. It is assumed that only one record of such information exists in the table.

Removing Portions of Text Data

In MS Access SQL, there is no function for removing portions of text data. But there are times when you would want to remove portions of text data. In such situations, you must adopt mathematical methods using any of the three functions - LEFT, RIGHT, MID - or their combinations where appropriate with either the INSTR function, the INSTRREV function, or the REPLACE function to help in obtaining the desired results. The necessary computations to remove the not needed portions of text data are all your logic and creations.

To display last names and post office box numbers for students whose addresses include post office box numbers but without the expression "P. O." using the studentX table, type and run the following SELECT statement.

SELECT   lastName   AS   LAST_NAME,   MID(address,INSTRREV(address,".")+1, LEN(address)-INSTRREV(address,".")) AS [POST OFFICE ADDRESS]
FROM studentX
WHERE address Like ("P. O.*");

See result below.

LAST_NAME	POST OFFICE ADDRESS
Zeberia	Box 2008
Maklasi	Box 6753
Manny	Box 675
Jeffer	Box 1020
Chap	Box 874

You might have noticed that the removal of the specified portion in the query is accomplished by using nested functions. INSTRREV and LEN functions are nested within the MID function. INSTRREV and LEN functions are used to compute the starting character position in the text data value that is being queried and the number of characters to retrieve.

Nesting single-row functions is discussed in detail in chapter six of this textbook. You can obtain the same result by using the REPLACE function as in the following SELECT statement.

SELECT lastName AS LAST_NAME, REPLACE(address, "P. O.", "") AS [POST OFFICE ADDRESS]
FROM studentX
WHERE address Like ("P. O.*");

To display the result of the query again, this time without post office numbers but with the expression "P. O. Box", type and run the following SELECT statement.

SELECT lastName AS LAST_NAME, LEFT(address,INSTRREV(address," ") - 1) AS [POST OFFICE ADDRESS]
FROM studentX
WHERE address Like ("P. O.*");

See result below.

LAST_NAME	POST OFFICE ADDRESS
Zeberia	P. O. Box
Maklasi	P. O. Box

Single-Row Functions

LAST_NAME	POST OFFICE ADDRESS
Manny	P. O. Box
Jeffer	P. O. Box
Chap	P. O. Box

You can also obtain the same result by using the REPLACE function as in the following SELECT statement.

SELECT   lastName   AS   LAST_NAME,   REPLACE(address, MID(address,INSTRREV(address, "x") + 1, LEN(address)), "") AS [POST OFFICE ADDRESS]
FROM studentX
WHERE address Like ("P. O.*");

> **Note:** There are other functions' combinations that can be used to accomplish the same results as the ones presented above. To obtain the desired results, records' entries must be specified in a consistent manner especially in columns where entries are similar. You must also understand how data are entered in tables. However, always consider the LEFT function, the RIGHT function, the MID function, the INSTR function, the INSTRREV function, the REPLACE function, and the functions' correct combinations to remove the unwanted portions of text data from the results of queries.

Padding Text Data

MS Access SQL has no defined standard function for padding characters in text data. However, you can perform the padding function by concatenating the STRING function, the SPACE function, the LTRIM function, the RTRIM function or any correct combinations of these functions with other functions that are used to display queries' results. Aligning text data to the right is the same as padding the text data on the left, and aligning text data to the left is the same as padding the text data on the right.

To display, by aligning their last names to the right with ten leading spaces, students who have earned the letter grade "AU" using both studentX and gradeX tables, type and run the following SELECT statement.

SELECT DISTINCT SPACE(10) + RTRIM(lastName) AS LNAME
FROM gradeX G INNER JOIN studentX S
ON G.studentId = S.studentId
WHERE G.letterGrade = "AU";

See result below.

LNAME
Maklasi
Mea

In the query, the SPACE function inserts leading ten spaces to the last name by using concatenation process. The RTRIM function removes the trailing spaces from the last name. The same result can be obtained if the STRING function is substituted for the SPACE function. In the query, you can also obtain the same result by replacing SPACE(10) with STRING(10,' ').

> **Note:** Oracle uses LPAD and RPAD functions to pad characters to the left and right of text data respectively.

> Example:
> SELECT RPAD(firstName, 10, ' '), LPAD(lastName, 10, ' ')
> FROM facultyX;

ASC Function

The ASC function returns the ASCII character code (numeric integer value) that is assigned to a printable character. The returned value can be used in mathematics. The basic syntax for this function is

ASC(*existingColumnName* | *"textExpression"*)

where

- *existingColumnName* is the column in the table listed in the FROM clause
- *textExpression* is the text value enclosed in quotation marks
- Symbol | symbolizes **Or** Boolean operator

> **Note:** If the column data or the text expression that is being used as the function's actual argument contains more than one character, the ASCII character code for the first character in the data is returned.

To display students' last names and return the ASCII character codes of the first letters of their last names for students who have earned the letter grade "I" using both studentX and gradeX tables, type and run the following SELECT statement.

SELECT lastName AS LAST_NAME, ASC(lastName) AS [FIRST LETTER ASCII VALUE]
FROM gradeX G, studentX S
WHERE G.studentId = S.studentId
AND letterGrade = "I";

See result below.

LAST_NAME	FIRST LETTER ASCII VALUE
Manny	77
Anthony	65

CHR Function

The CHR function returns the character symbol of the ASCII character code (numeric integer value) that is specified as the function's actual argument. The normal range of values for this function is 0 through 255. The CHR function is the opposing function to the ASC and vice versa. The two functions are used to reverse the tasks each of them has performed. The basic syntax for this function is

CHR(*integerValue*)

where

- *integerValue* is the ASCII character code of the character that is being sought

To display students' last names, return the ASCII character codes of the first letters of their last names, and reverse the ASCII character codes to the first letters of their last names, for students who have earned the letter grade "I" using both studentX and gradeX tables, type and run the following SELECT statement.

Single-Row Functions

SELECT lastName AS LAST_NAME, ASC(lastName) AS [CODE FOR FIRST LETTER OF LAST NAME], CHR(ASC(lastName)) AS [FIRST LETTER OF LAST NAME]
FROM gradeX AS G, studentX AS S
WHERE G.studentId=S.studentId And letterGrade="I";

See result below.

LAST_NAME	CODE FOR FIRST LETTER OF LAST NAME	FIRST LETTER OF LAST NAME
Manny	77	M
Anthony	65	A

STR Function

The STR function converts numeric (integer and floating-point) values to text data. The function returns numeric values in text data form. Even though the results of the function are regarded as text, MS Access allows the function's output to be used in mathematics. That is after the conversion the values are aligned to the left as text but can still be used in mathematical computations.

The basic syntax for this function is

STR(*numericValue*)

where

- *numericValue* is the integer or floating-point value to be transformed to text data

To display last names of faculty members who have enrolled for courses and return their annual salaries as text data using both facultyX and studentX tables, type and run the following SELECT statement.

SELECT facultyId AS [FACULTY ID], STR(annualSalary) AS [ANNUAL INCOME CONVERTED TO TEXT]
FROM studentX S INNER JOIN facultyX F
ON S.studentId = F.facultyId;

See result below.

FACULTY ID	ANNUAL INCOME CONVERTED TO TEXT
DM674543	62980.25
EM001254	74563.55

Numeric Functions

Numeric functions are mathematical or arithmetic functions that are used to perform mathematical computations and to alter the appearance of numeric values. The functions can be used in numeric expressions to obtain the desired output from queries. MS Access supports a number of arithmetic functions. Each of the numeric functions that are discussed here, except for the ROUND function, require a single actual argument. The values returned by numeric functions are aligned to the right by default.

ROUND Function

The ROUND function returns a numeric value that is rounded to a specific number of decimal positions. This function supports two actual arguments.

The basic syntax for the ROUND function is

116

ROUND(*existingColumnName* | *numericExpression* [, *numberOfDecimalPlaces*])

where

- *existingColumnName* is the column of numeric data type in the table listed in the FROM clause
- *numericExpression* is the numeric value or numeric expression that is being used
- *numberOfDecimalPlaces* is the optional number of decimal positions being sought
- Symbols [ ] mean item is optional
- Symbol | symbolizes **Or** Boolean operator. You can also combine numeric columns and/or numeric expressions as the functions' actual arguments

The actual argument *numberOfDecimalPlaces* cannot be a negative integer value. If the actual argument is zero (0) or omitted, the ROUND function returns a numeric integer value. This function rounds the decimal position that is requested to the nearest whole number. The ROUND function checks the position on the immediate right of the decimal position that is being sought. If the value at that position is 5 or above, the function rounds the desired decimal position to the nearest whole number and displays the numeric value up to the desired decimal positions. If the value of the position on the immediate right of the desired decimal position is less than 5, no rounding is performed, but the numeric value is displayed up to the specified decimal positions.

To display identification numbers, annual salaries, and annual salaries to one decimal position for faculty members who are assigned to Education department, using both facultyX and departmentX tables, type and run the following SELECT statement.

SELECT facultyId AS ID, annualSalary AS ANNUAL_INCOME, ROUND(annualSalary, 1)
AS ANNUAL_INCOME_ROUNDED
FROM facultyX F, departmentX D
WHERE F.departmentCode = D.departmentCode
AND departmentName = 'Education';

See result below.

ID	ANNUAL_INCOME	ANNUAL_INCOME_ROUNDED
ZM567123	49980.95	49981
DM674543	62980.8	62980.8

Note: Oracle also allows the actual argument *numberOfDecimalPlaces* to be a negative integer value. The ROUND function refers to the left side (integer part) of the decimal point if the integer value of the actual argument is negative. -1 means the first digit of the integer part, -2 means the second digit of the integer part and so on until the digit to the immediate left of the decimal position is reached.

Example:
SELECT facultyId, ROUND(annualSalary, -1)
FROM facultyX;

INT and FIX Functions

INT and FIX functions are used to return the integer parts of numeric values, usually of floating-point types. However, if the numeric value that is used as the functions' actual argument is negative, INT and FIX functions behave differently. If the actual argument is negative, the INT function returns a value that is less than or equal to the integer part of the actual argument. With the actual argument negative, the FIX function returns a value that is greater or equal to the integer part of the actual argument.

The basic syntax for the two functions is

INT | FIX (*existingColumnName* | *numericExpression*)

where

- *existingColumnName* is the column of numeric data type in the table listed in the FROM clause
- *numericExpression* is the numeric value or numeric expression that is being used
- Symbol | symbolizes **Or** Boolean operator. You can also combine numeric columns and/or numeric expressions as the functions' actual arguments

To display identification numbers, annual salaries, and integer parts of their annual salaries for faculty members who are assigned to Computer Science department, using both facultyX and departmentX tables, type and run the following SELECT statement.

SELECT facultyId AS ID, annualSalary AS ANNUAL_INCOME, INT(annualSalary) AS INTEGER_PART_OF_ANNUAL_INCOME
FROM facultyX F, departmentX D
WHERE F.departmentCode = D.departmentCode
AND departmentName = 'Computer Science';

See result below.

ID	ANNUAL_INCOME	INTEGER_PART_OF_ANNUAL_INCOME
AL501828	54354.15	54354
EE987654	68261.39	68261

The same result can be obtained with the ROUND function if the actual argument that represents the number of decimal positions is zero (0) or omitted.

ABS Function

The ABS function is used to return the absolute value of a numeric value. An absolute value is a numeric value in its positive form. A zero (0) value is regarded as a neutral value which means that it can be preceded by either the plus sign (+), minus sign (-), or it can be written without a sign preceding it to yield the same absolute value. The basic syntax for this function is similar to that of the INT function and the FIX function. Substituting the function name ABS for INT or FIX gives the syntax for ABS function.

To display identification numbers, annual salaries in negative forms, and reverse annual salaries to positive forms for faculty members who are assigned to Business Administration department, using both facultyX and departmentX tables, type and run the following SELECT statement.

SELECT facultyId AS ID, (-annualSalary) AS ANNUAL_INCOME_IN_NEGATIVE, ABS(-annualSalary) AS ANNUAL_INCOME_IN_POSITIVE
FROM facultyX F, departmentX D
WHERE F.departmentCode = D.departmentCode
AND departmentName = 'Business Administration';

See result below.

ID	ANNUAL_INCOME_IN_NEGATIVE	ANNUAL_INCOME_IN_POSITIVE
EM001254	-74563.55	74563.55
JS994450	-45876.25	45876.25

FORMATNUMBER Function

The FORMATNUMBER function is used to alter or change the appearance of values of numeric data type. The function displays the required results with comma symbols as separators for each numeric value that is quantified in thousands.

The basic syntax for this function is

FORMATNUMBER(*existingColumnName* | *numericExpression* [, *numberOfDecimalPlaces*])

where

- *existingColumnName* is the column of numeric data type in the table listed in the FROM clause
- *numericExpression* is the numeric value or numeric expression that is being used
- *numberOfDecimalPlaces* is the optional numeric integer that specifies the number of digit required after decimal point.
- Symbols [ ] mean item is optional
- Symbol | symbolizes **Or** Boolean operator. You can also combine numeric columns and/or numeric expressions as the functions' actual arguments

If the value for *numberOfDecimalPlaces* actual argument is omitted, the result is displayed using the system setting (usually two digits to the right of the decimal point or two decimal positions). If the value of the actual argument is zero (0), this means that no decimal positions of the result should be displayed.

To display identification numbers, first names, and annual salaries formatted to two decimal positions of faculty members whose last names is "Mea" using the facultyX table, type and run the following SELECT statement.

SELECT facultyId AS ID, firstName AS [NAME], FORMATNUMBER(annualSalary, 2) AS [FORMATTED SALARY]
FROM facultyX
WHERE lastName="Mea";

See result below.

ID	NAME	FORMATTED SALARY
DM674543	Doris	62,980.25

Chapter Summary

This chapter teaches single-row functions. The functions discussed are classified into two groups, namely, text functions and numeric functions. For the text functions, the distinctions between text case-conversion functions and character manipulation functions are explained and how they are used to attain the needed results. The chapter introduces some numeric functions and shows how the functions are written in MS Access SQL statements to obtain the necessary output.

Single-Row Functions Syntax and SQL Statements Summary

The table below presents single-row functions' syntax discussed in this chapter and the SQL statements' examples for retrieving data from tables.

Description	Function General Syntax	Function Example
A function is a block of programming instructions that performs a specific task	*functionName([actualArgument], ...)*	UCASE(lastName)
Case Conversion Functions		
Function Name and Description	**Function Syntax**	**Statement Example**
LCASE and UCASE functions are used to convert letters of the alphabet to lowercases' and uppercases' letters respectively	LCASE | UCASE(*existingColumnName* | *textExpression*)	SELECT LCASE(firstName), UCASE(lastName) FROM studentX;
STRCONV function is used to convert letters of the alphabet to lower, upper, and mixed cases' letters	STRCONV(*existingColumnName* | *textExpression, conversionTypeDigit*)	SELECT STRCONV(firstName, 3), STRCONV(lastName, 3) FROM facultyX WHERE charId IS NULL;
Character Manipulation Functions		
Function Name and Description	**Function Syntax**	**Statement Example**
LEFT and RIGHT functions are used to return a specific number of characters beginning from the left side or the right side of the text being searched respectively	LEFT | RIGHT(*existingColumnName* | *textExpression, numberOfCharacter*)	SELECT LEFT(firstName, 3) AS [First Three Characters], RIGHT(lastName, 2) AS [Last Two Characters] FROM facultyX WHERE charId IS NULL;
MID function is used to return a specific number of characters beginning from a specific character position of the text being searched	MID(*existingColumnName* | *textExpression, beginningCharacterPosition, numberOfCharacter*)	SELECT MID(studentId, 2, 3) AS [Partial Student Id] FROM gradeX WHERE letterGrade = "F" ORDER BY studentId;
LEN function is used to calculate the number of characters contained in a text value	LEN(*existingColumnName* | *textExpression*)	SELECT DISTINCT LEN(firstName + lastName) AS [Total Number of Characters] FROM studentX;
INSTR function is used to return the beginning numeric position of the first occurrence of a specific character in a text value	INSTRREV([*beginningCharacterPosition*], *textDataBeingSearched, textDataBeingCompared* [, *compareDigit*])	SELECT DISTINCT lastName, INSTR(2, lastName, 'a', 1) AS Character_Position FROM gradeX G, studentX S WHERE G.studentId = S.studentId AND letterGrade = "B";
INSTRREV function, searching backward, is used to return the beginning numeric position of the first occurrence of a specific character in a text value	INSTR(*textDataBeingSearched, textDataBeingCompared* [, *beginningCharacterPsition, compareDigit*])	SELECT DISTINCT firstName, INSTRREV(firstName, 'o') AS Character_Position FROM studentX WHERE studentId = "DM674543";

STRCOMP function is used to compare, position by position, the ASCII values of characters contained in two text values	STRCOMP(*textDataBeingCompared*, *textDataBeingComparedTo* [, *compareDigit*])	SELECT DISTINCT firstName, lastName, STRCOMP(firstName, lastName, 2) AS Numeric_Status FROM gradeX G, studentX S WHERE G.studentId = S.studentId AND letterGrade = "F";
STRING function is used to return a specified number of a particular printable symbol including a space	STRING(*totalNumber*, *characterSymbol*)	SELECT lastName + STRING(5, '*') FROM facultyX WHERE chairId IS NOT NULL;
SPACE function is used to increase the number of character positions for a column	SPACE(*totalNumber*)	SELECT SPACE(10) +firstName AS [First Name] FROM facultyX WHERE chairId IS NULL;
STRREVERSE function is used to spell a text value backward	STRREVERSE(*existingColumnName* | *textExpression*)	SELECT firstName, STRREVERSE(firstName) AS [Name Spelled Backward] FROM gradeX G, studentX S WHERE G.studentId = S.studentId AND letterGrade = "F";
LTRIM, RTRIM, TRIM functions are used to remove leading spaces, trailing spaces, or both from a text value respectively	LTRIM | RTRIM | TRIM(*existingColumnName* | *textExpression*)	SELECT DISTINCT RTRIM(lastName) AS LNAME FROM gradeX G INNER JOIN studentX S ON G.studentId = S.studentId WHERE G.letterGrade = "AU";
REPLACE function is used to search and replace an instance of a text value or the entire text value	REPLACE(*textDataBeingSearched*, *textDataBeingReplaced*, *substituteTextData* [, *beginningCharacterPosition*, *numberOfSubstitution*, *compareDigit*])	SELECT firstName, REPLACE(lastName, "Ugb", "Bl") AS [New Last Name] FROM facultyX WHERE facultyId IN ("RU123098");
ASC function is used to return the ASCII numeric character code of a printable character	ASC(*existingColumnName* | *textExpression*)	SELECT DISTINCT lastName, ASC(lastName) AS [First Letter ASCII Value] FROM gradeX G, studentX S WHERE G.studentId = S.studentId AND G.letterGrade = "I";
CHR function is used to return the character symbol of an ASCII numeric character code	CHR(*integerValue*)	SELECT DISTINCT ASC(lastName), CHR(ASC(lastName)) FROM gradeX G, studentX S WHERE G.studentId = S.studentId AND G.letterGrade = "I";
STR function is used to convert numeric values to text data	STR(*numericValue*)	SELECT facultyId, STR(annualSalary) AS [Salary Converted To Text] FROM studentX S INNER JOIN facultyX F ON S.studentId = F.facultyId;
Numeric Functions		
Function Name and Description	**Function Syntax**	**Statement Example**
ROUND function is used to return a numeric value rounded to a specific number of decimal positions	ROUND(*existingColumnName* | *numericExpression* [, *numberOfDecimalPlaces*])	SELECT facultyId, annualSalary, ROUND(annualSalary, 1) AS ANNUAL_INCOME_ROUNDED FROM facultyX F, departmentX D WHERE F.departmentCode = D.departmentCode AND departmentName = 'Education';
INT and FIX functions are used to return the integer part of a numeric value – usually of a floating point value	INT | FIX (*existingColumnName* | *numericExpression*)	SELECT facultyId, annualSalary, INT(annualSalary, 1) AS ANNUAL_INTEGER_PART FROM facultyX F, departmentX D WHERE F.departmentCode = D.departmentCode AND departmentName = 'Computer Science';

ABS function is used to return a numeric value to its positive (absolute) form	ABS(*existingColumnName* | *numericExpression*)	SELECT facultyId, (-annualSalary) AS NEGATIVE_FORM, ABS(-annualSalary) AS BACK_TO_POSITIVE FROM facultyX F, departmentX D WHERE F.departmentCode = D.departmentCode AND departmentName = 'Business Administration';
FORMATNUMBER function is used to alter the appearance of a numeric value	FORMATNUMBER(*existingColumnName* | *numericExpression* [, *numberOfDecimalPlaces*])	SELECT facultyId, firstName, FORMATNUMBER(annualSalary, 2) AS [FORMATTED SALARY] FROM facultyX WHERE facultyId="DM674543";

Key Terms

ABS
CHR
FORMATNUMBER
Functions
Generating substrings
INT
LCASE
LEN
Numeric functions

Padding text data
ROUND
Single-Row functions
STRCONV
STRING
Text functions
TRIM
UCASE

Chapter Review Questions

Multiple Choice Questions

1. A function returns _____ value(s).
   - a. four
   - b. three
   - c. two
   - d. one

2. A data item that is supplied to a function to use to perform its task is called
   - a. formal parameter.
   - b. actual argument.
   - c. a seed.
   - d. a case.

3. Data used by functions that are listed in the conditions' clauses of a SELECT statement are changed
   - a. temporarily.
   - b. permanently.
   - c. all of the above.
   - d. none of the above.

4. Which of the following functions converts string data to mixed case?
   - a. MIXCASE function.
   - b. UCASE function.
   - c. STRCONV function.
   - d. LCASE function.

5. Which of the following is not a character manipulation function?
   - a. LEFT function.
   - b. MID function.
   - c. RIGHT function.
   - d. CHARACTER function.

6. In MS Access SQL, to calculate the number of characters in a text value you use _____ function.
   a. COUNT
   b. LEN
   c. ADD
   d. SELECT

7. The _____ function is used to remove trailing spaces from a text value.
   a. TRIM
   b. LTRIM
   c. RTRIM
   d. LRTRIM

8. The FIX function requires _____ actual argument(s).
   a. one
   b. two
   c. three
   d. four

9. Values returned by numeric functions are aligned to the _____ by default.
   a. center
   b. left
   c. right
   d. none of the above

10. Which of the following functions returns the character symbol of an ASCII character code?
    a. INT function.
    b. STR function.
    c. ASC function.
    d. CHR function.

True or False Questions

11. A function's task is pre-known.
    a. True
    b. False

12. Single-row functions return one record for a block of rows processed in a single table.
    a. True
    b. False

13. MS Access SQL does not support case conversion functions.
    a. True
    b. False

14. The STRING function returns a specific number of a printable character symbol.
    a. True
    b. False

15. An absolute value is a numeric value in the negative form.
    a. True
    b. False

16. The FORMATNUMBER function changes the appearance of numeric data values.
    a. True
    b. False

17. In MS Access SQL, the substitution function is the REPLACE function.
    a. Tue
    b. False

Fill in the blank Questions

18. A single function that can convert letters of the alphabet to uppercases, lowercases, and mixed cases is called _____.

19. _____ returns a text value that contains a specific number of characters beginning from a specified character position.

20. To return the number of _____ contained in a text value, you use the LEN function.

21. The _____ function is used to remove leading spaces from a text value.

22. The ABS function is used to return the _____ of a numeric value.

23. As discussed in this chapter, to alter the appearance of a numeric value, you use the _____ function.

Essay Type Questions

24. Define a single-row function and write the general syntax of a single-row function as discussed in this chapter?

25. Explain text padding and list the functions that MS Access SQL uses to right align text data?

26. Explain the differences between SPACE and STRING functions and write a valid SQL statement that uses the two functions?

27. Describe the behavior of both INT and FIX functions when they use negative numeric values to complete their tasks?

28. Explain how the ASC function differs from the CHR function?

Hands-on Activities

Study the structures and the data of **AcademicX** database tables in appendix A (pages 355 through 360) and perform the following hands-on exercises.

1. Using the STRCONV function, display in uppercase letters, first and last names of faculty members whose first and last names begin with the letter "E".

2. Display first names and last names of students where the total number of characters in both names is ten or less.

3. Write a SQL statement to list first and last names of students who have earned the letter grade "B" in any course and the letter "E" is the second letter in their last names. Sort the result by last name in ascending order.

4. Write a SQL statement to show faculty members' identification numbers and their annual salaries for those faculty members who hold instructor positions. The salaries should be preceded and trailed by five asterisk symbols and assign column alias **Annual_Salary** to the salary column. Sort the result in descending order using the faculty identification number column.

5. Write a SQL statement to display the first letters of first and last names and the ASCII values of the letters for faculty members who are department chairpersons. Use any column alias of your choice to display the result.

6. Display identification numbers and annual salaries of faculty members who are also students. Format their annual salaries to include leading dollar sign ($), commas, and two decimal positions. Assign column alias **Annual Salary** to the salary column.

7. Write a SQL statement to display identification numbers and annual salaries of faculty members who are not department chairpersons. The annual salaries should be rounded to zero decimal position and displayed as strings (text). Assign column alias of your choice to the salary column.

8. Display the absolute value, a value that is less or equal to the integer part, and a value that is greater or equal to the integer part of the monthly salary of the faculty member whose identification number is "AL501828". The monthly salary must be entered as a negative value. Round the absolute value to two decimal positions.

9. Write a SQL statement to display identification numbers (spelled backward) and last names (spelled backward) of faculty members who are also students.

10. Write a SQL statement to perform the same operation as in question 9 for faculty members who are department chairpersons.

Chapter Six

More on Single-Row Functions

Chapter Objectives

After completing this chapter, you should be able to

- Use date single-row functions
- Use time single-row functions
- Convert data from one type to another
- Use non-categorized single-row functions
- Nest single-row functions
- Display data not contained in tables

Date and Time Functions

Date and time functions are used to (i) determine current and future dates and time periods, (ii) determine how much time has elapsed between dates or between time periods, and (iii) change the appearance of date data and time data. Date and time data are stored as serial numbers and as such, they can be used to perform date and time mathematics. Their results can be used as numeric expressions or as parts of numeric expressions in calculations.

Most date functions are based on types of time periods called intervals. The intervals determine how the results of date functions are gotten. Date intervals are measured in years, quarters, months, weeks, days, hours, minutes, and so on. In this section, date and time functions are divided into two classes, namely, nonargument-based functions and argument-based functions.

Dates Intervals: A date interval is the type of time period on which a date function bases its calculations.

Nonargument-based Functions

Date and time functions, as well as other functions, that are referred to as nonargument-based functions require no actual arguments to perform their assigned tasks. No data items are supplied to the functions and the pair of parentheses does not contain data. The general syntax for this class of functions is

functionName()

where

- *functionName* is the function that is being used

> **Note:** In MS Access SQL when data values that are being queried are not contained in a table, you can obtain the results of such values with functions that use the values as their actual arguments by including the functions in the SELECT clause of a SELECT statement that consists of only the SELECT clause. All other clauses can be omitted.
>
> Example:
> SELECT DATE(), NOW();
>
> Notice that the SELECT statement consists only of one clause – the SELECT clause.

More on Single-Row Functions

DATE and NOW Functions

DATE and NOW functions return the current date of the computer system. In addition, the NOW function also returns the current time of the computer system. The basic syntax for the DATE function is DATE() and the basic syntax for the NOW function is NOW().

To display a computer system's current date using the studentX table, type and run the following SELECT statement.

SELECT DATE() AS [A COMPUTER SYSTEM CURRENT DATE]
FROM studentX
WHERE studentId = "CS664452";

See result below.

A COMPUTER SYSTEM CURRENT DATE
8/3/2005

Notice that the SELECT statement uses the test for one record in the table to display the result. This is how such operation is achieved in MS Access SQL when a table is used. The result of the query may differ depending on the current date of the computer system that is being used.

TIME and TIMER Functions

The TIME function returns the current time of the computer system. The TIMER function returns the total number of seconds that has elapsed since midnight based on the current time of a computer system. The TIMER function returns also fractional portion of the calculated seconds. The basic syntax for the TIME function is TIME() and the basic syntax for the TIMER function is TIMER().

To display a computer system's current time and how many seconds have elapsed since midnight based on the computer system's time using the studentX table, type and run the following SELECT statement.

SELECT TIME() AS [COMPUTER SYSTEM CURRENT TIME], TIMER() AS [HOW MANY SECONDS HAVE PASSED SINCE MIDNIGHT]
FROM studentX
WHERE studentId LIKE ("CS664452");

See result below.

COMPUTER SYSTEM CURRENT TIME	HOW MANY SECONDS HAVE PASSED SINCE MIDNIGHT
10:09:01 PM	79741.7265625

Again, the SELECT statement uses the test for one record in the table to display the result. The result of the query may differ depending on the current date of the computer system that is being used.

> **Note:** A computer system's current date is not necessarily the actual current date. If the computer's date is set incorrectly, the function displays the wrong date as the current date. The same applies to a computer system's time. In MS Access SQL, other methods of displaying time data, besides using the NOW function and the TIME function, are to include time intervals, time format modes, or time format symbols as part of date data formats in the SELECT clause of a SELECT statement. See figures 6.1, 6.4, and 6.6 for time intervals, time format modes, and time format symbols respectively.

Argument-based Functions

Argument-based functions are functions that require data items to perform their assigned tasks. These functions require a minimum of one data item or one actual argument. The general syntax for an argument-based function is

functionName(actualArgument, ...)

where

- *functionName* is the function that is being used
- *actualArgument* is the data item that is being passed to the function to use to perform the assigned task
- Symbols ... mean more actual argument can be listed

The actual argument can be a single column, an expression, combination of columns, combination of expressions, combination of columns and expressions enclosed in parentheses. You can also specify more than one actual argument in parentheses if that is a function's requirement. When a function requires more than one actual argument, the arguments must be separated by commas.

DATEADD Function

This function is used to determine a certain date based on a specified time period. The certain date can be gotten either by addition or by subtraction. This function can be used to add time period to a date or to subtract time period from a date. The basic syntax for the DATEADD function is

DATEADD("*typeOfTimePeriod*", *numberOfTimePeriod*, *existingColumnName* | #*dateExpression*#)

where

- *typeOfTimePeriod* is the type of interval being sought and must be enclosed in quotation marks
- *numberOfTimePeriod* is the number of intervals to be added or subtracted
- *existingColumnName* is the column of date data type in the table listed in the FROM clause
- *dateExpression* is the date being used and must be enclosed in a pair of number signs (#)
- Symbol | symbolizes **Or** Boolean operator

Note: The addition operation is performed when the actual argument *numberOfTimePeriod* is positive, and the subtraction operation is performed when it is negative. In MS Access SQL, date values listed in a SELECT statement can also be enclosed using either the double quotation marks or the single quotation marks.

Figure 6.1 lists the valid symbols used as intervals in MS Access.

Figure 6.1

Interval	Interpretation
yyyy	Year
q	Quarter
m	Month
y	Day of year
d	Day

More on Single-Row Functions

Interval	Interpretation
w	Weekday
ww	Week of year
h	Hour
n	Minute
s	Second

To display identification numbers, first enrollment dates, and dates corresponding to the scheduled placement tests that come up in four months for students whose identification numbers begin with the letter "F" using the studentX table, type and run the following SELECT statement.

SELECT studentId AS STUDENT_ID, dateFirstEnrolled AS DATE_FIRST_ENROLLED, DATEADD('m',4,dateFirstEnrolled) AS PLACEMENT_TEST_DATE
FROM studentX
WHERE studentId LIKE ("F*");

See result below.

STUDENT_ID	DATE_FIRST_ENROLLED	PLACEMENT_TEST_DATE
FA213595	1/10/2005	5/10/2005
FK576381	1/20/2005	5/20/2005

To display first names, last names, first enrollment dates, and rejection dates that have elapsed for three months before first enrollment dates for students whose identification numbers begin with the letter "P" using the studentX table, type and run the following SELECT statement.

SELECT firstName AS FIRST_NAME, lastName AS LAST_NAME, dateFirstEnrolled AS DATE_FIRST_ENROLLED, DATEADD('m',-3,dateFirstEnrolled) AS REJECTD_DATE
FROM studentX
WHERE studentId LIKE ("P*");

See result below.

FIRST_NAME	LAST_NAME	DATE_FIRST_ENROLLED	REJECTD_DATE
Phil	Portiskum	8/15/2004	5/15/2004

The day of year interval symbol "y" is in fact the day of the month being queried. For example, if the numeric integer 4 is used as the *numberOfTimePeriod* actual argument using the "y" interval symbol, four days is added to the queried date before displaying the calculated date. The "y" symbol behaves like the "d" symbol.

The following is a SELECT statement that displays the date #8/9/2005# using the date #8/5/2005# after four day is added to the date #8/5/2005#.

SELECT (#08/05/2005#) AS CURRENT_DATE, DATEADD('y',4,#08/05/2005#) AS NEW_DATE
FROM studentX
WHERE studentId IN ("EM001254");

See result below.

CURRENT_DATE	NEW_DATE
8/5/2005	8/9/2005

> **Note:** By default, MS Access displays date in mm/dd/yyyy format. You can enter or display date data in any MS Access valid date formats such as the dd-mon-yy format. Oracle uses the ADD_MONTH function to add months to dates.
>
> Example:
> SELECT studentId AS STUDENT_ID, dateFirstEnrolled AS DATE_FIRST_ENROLLED, ADD_MONTHS(dateFirstEnrolled, 4) AS PLACEMENT_TEST_DATE
> FROM studentX
> WHERE studentId LIKE ("F%");

DATEDIFF Function

The DATEDIFF function is used to return how much time has elapsed between dates. This function returns a numeric integer value as its output. The basic syntax for the DATEDIFF function is

DATEDIFF("*typeOfTimePeriod*", *existingColumnName1* | #*dateExpression1*#, *existingColumnName2* | #*dateExpression2*# [, *firstDayOfTheWeek*, *firstWeekOfTheYear*])

where

- *typeOfTimePeriod* is the type of interval being sought and must be enclosed in quotation marks
- *existingColumnName1* is the column of date data type in the table that is being subtracted from
- *dateExpression1* is the date being used and being subtracted from and must be enclosed in a pair of number signs (#)
- *existingColumnName2* is the column of date data type in the table that is being subtracted
- *dateExpression2* is the date being used and being subtracted and must be enclosed in a pair of number signs (#)
- *firstDayOfTheWeek* is the optional type of calculation needed based on the numeric integer values that represent the days of the week
- *firstWeekOfTheYear* is the optional type of calculation needed based on the numeric integer that represent the first week of the year being sought
- Symbols [ ] mean items are optional
- Symbol | symbolizes **Or** Boolean operator

The *typeOfTimePeriod* actual argument uses the same intervals as those listed for the DATEADD function in figure 6.1. Figure 6.2 lists the numbers used as the *firstDayOfTheWeek* actual argument and the days of the week they represent.

Figure 6.2

Number	Interpretation
0	System day setting
1	Sunday
2	Monday
3	Tuesday
4	Wednesday
5	Thursday
6	Friday
7	Saturday

MS Access defaults the day to Sunday if the value for the *firstDayOfTheWeek* actual argument is not specified in the DATEDIFF function.

More on Single-Row Functions

Figure 6.3 lists the digits used as the *firstWeekOfTheYear* actual argument and the weeks of the year they represent.

Figure 6.3

Number	Significance
0	Uses the system setting
1	Starts with the week in which January 1 occurs
2	Starts with the first week that has at least four days in the new year
3	Starts with the first full week of the year

MS Access defaults to the week in which January 1 occurs if the value for the *firstWeekOfTheYear* actual argument is not specified in the DATEDIFF function.

> **Note:** If *existingColumnName1* or *dateExpression1* and *existingColumnName2* or *dateExpression2* are equal, Zero (0) is returned as the result of the date calculation. If *existingColumnName1* or *dateExpression1* actual argument is an earlier date than *existingColumnName2* or *dateExpression2* actual argument, the result of the calculation is positive, otherwise the result is negative.

To display students' identification numbers, their last names, and how many weeks have elapsed between the first time they enrolled for courses and the computer system's current date, for students whose identification numbers begin with the three symbols "CS6" using the studentX table, type the and run following SELECT statement.

SELECT studentId AS [STUDENT ID], lastName AS [LAST NAME], dateFirstEnrolled AS [ENROLLMENT DATE], DATEDIFF('ww', dateFirstEnrolled, DATE(), 3) AS [HOW MANY WEEKS ELAPSED]
FROM studentX
WHERE studentId LIKE ("CS6*");

See result below.

STUDENT ID	LAST NAME	ENROLLMENT DATE	HOW MANY WEEKS ELAPSED
CS664452	Salat	1/10/2004	82

The result of the query may differ depending on the current date of the computer system that is being used.

> **Note:** Oracle uses the MONTHS_BETWEEN function to determine how much time has elapsed between dates.
>
> Example:
> SELECT studentId AS "STUDENT ID", MONTHS_BETWEEN('01-Jan-06', dateFirstEnrolled)
> FROM studentX
> WHERE studentId LIKE ('CS6%');

YEAR, MONTH, and DAY Functions

YEAR, MONTH and DAY functions return numeric integer values that represent the year of the date data being queried, month of the year (1 through 12), and the day of the month (1 through 31) respectively. For the months of the year, 1 represents January, 2 represents February and so on until December which is presented by 12.

The basic syntax for YEAR, MONTH, and DAY functions is

YEAR | MONTH | DAY(*existingColunmName* | #*dateExpression*#)

where

- *existingColumnName* is the column of date data type in the table listed in the FROM clause
- *dateExpression* is the date being used and must be enclosed in a pair of number signs (#)
- Symbol | symbolizes *Or* Boolean operator

To display identification numbers, dates of first enrollment, numeric integer values that represent year, month, and day of the month of first enrollment for students whose last names is "Bomor" using the studentX table, type and run the following SELECT statement.

SELECT studentId, dateFirstEnrolled AS [DATE], YEAR(dateFirstEnrolled) AS [YEAR], MONTH(dateFirstEnrolled) AS [NUMBER OF MONTH], DAY(dateFirstEnrolled) AS [NUMBER OF DAY]
FROM studentX
WHERE UCASE(lastName) = "BOMOR";

See result below.

studentId	DATE	YEAR	NUMBER OF MONTH	NUMBER OF DAY
AB778204	6/5/2005	2005	6	5

WEEKDAY Function

The WEEKDAY function returns the numeric representations of days of the week (1 through 7). For days of the week, 1 represents Sunday, 2 represents Monday and so on until Saturday which is represented by 7. The basic syntax for the WEEKDAY function is

WEEKDAY(*existingColunmName* | #*dateExpression*# [, *firstDayOfTheWeek*])

where

- *existingColumnName* is the column of date data type in the table listed in the FROM clause
- *dateExpression* is the date being used and must be enclosed in a pair of number signs (#)
- *firstDayOfTheWeek* is the optional type of calculation needed based on the numeric integer values that represent the days of the week
- Symbols [ ] mean item is optional
- Symbol | symbolizes *Or* Boolean operator

Refer to figure 6.2 for the numbers representing the values for *firstDayOfTheWeek* actual argument.

To display identification numbers, dates of first enrollment, numeric integer values that represent the day of the week of first enrollment for students whose last names is "Bomor" using the studentX table, type and run the following SELECT statement.

SELECT studentId, dateFirstEnrolled AS [DATE], WEEKDAY(dateFirstEnrolled, 1) AS [DAY OF THE WEEK]
FROM studentX
WHERE UCASE(lastName) = "BOMOR";

More on Single-Row Functions

See result below.

studentId	DATE	DAY OF THE WEEK
AB778204	6/5/2005	1

MONTHNAME Function

The MONTHNAME function converts the numeric representations of months of the year (1 through 12) to their proper names respectively. The basic syntax for the MONTHNAME function is

MONTHNAME(*numericIntegerForMonth* [, *booleanValue*])

where

- *numericIntegerForMonth* is the integer value representing the month that is being queried
- *booleanValue* is the optional Boolean value (TRUE or FALSE)
- Symbols [ ] mean item is optional

If the optional *booleanValue* actual argument is specified in the function, the TRUE values means to abbreviate the name of the data being sought and the FALSE value means to display the full name of the data. If the *booleanValue* actual argument is omitted, the month's full name is displayed.

To display the full name of the month in the date #08/07/2005#, using the studentX table, type and run the following SELECT statement.

SELECT DISTINCT (#08/07/2005#) AS [DATE], MONTHNAME(08,FALSE) AS [MONTH NAME]
FROM studentX
WHERE UCASE(lastName) = "BOMOR";

See result below.

DATE	MONTH NAME
8/7/2005	August

WEEKDAYNAME Function

The WEEKDAYNAME function converts the numeric representations of days of the week (1 through 7) to their proper names respectively. The basic syntax for the WEEKDAYNAME function is

WEEKDAYNAME(*numericIntegerForWeek* [, *booleanValue*, *firstDayOfTheWeek*])

where

- *numericIntegerForWeek* is the integer value representing the day of the week being queried
- *booleanValue* is the optional Boolean value (TRUE or FALSE)
- *firstDayOfTheWeek* is the optional type of calculation needed based on the numeric integer values that represent the days of the week
- Symbols [ ] mean items are optional

If the optional *booleanValue* actual argument is specified in the function, the TRUE value means to abbreviate the name of the data being sought and the FALSE value means to display the full name of the data. If the *booleanValue* actual argument is omitted, the full name of the day is displayed. Refer to figure 6.2 for the numbers representing the values for the *firstDayOfTheWeek* actual argument.

To display the full name of the day of the week in the date #08/07/2005#, using the studentX table, type and run the following SELECT statement.

SELECT DISTINCT (#08/07/2005#) AS [DATE], WEEKDAYNAME(WEEKDAY(#08/07/2005#), FALSE,1) AS [WEEKDAY NAME IN FULL] FROM studentX
WHERE UCASE(lastName) = "BOMOR";

See result below.

DATE	WEEKDAY NAME IN FULL
8/7/2005	Sunday

The SELECT statement uses a nested function approach to get the correct day of the week. In the statement, the WEEKDAY (inner) function is used to return the numeric representation of the day and the WEEKDAYNAME (outer) function is used to display the name of the day that the numeric value represents.

Alternatively, you could have obtained the same result by using only the SELECT clause of the SELECT statement.

Determining Next or Previous Occurrence of Day of the Week

MS Access SQL does not provide a function that determines the next or previous occurrence of a particular day of the week in a date that is being queried. However, by performing basic arithmetic of adding a numeric integer of range 1 to 7 to a date or subtracting an integer of the range from a date, one can obtain the desired result. Adding a value of the range to a date determines the future occurrence of a particular day in the date while using a value of the range to subtract the day from a date determines the previous occurrence of a particular day in the date.

The day in the date being used is always the day zero. For example if the day in the date is Friday, therefore Friday is counted as zero, the next day which is Saturday is 1, Sunday is 2, and in that order. The actual value to be added or subtracted from a date to determine the next occurrence or the previous occurrence of a particular day is calculated by counting beginning with the first non-zero day until the digit that represents the day that is being determined is counted or reached. To obtain the date for the following Monday using Friday as the day in the date being queried, you must add 3 to the Friday date. Similarly, to display the Wednesday date prior to the Friday date, you must subtract 2 from the Friday date.

The following SELECT statement is used to obtain the next occurrence of the day in the date #10/20/2006# by performing the necessary addition to the date value. Type and run the SELECT statement.

SELECT DISTINCT (#10/20/2006#) AS [DATE], (#10/20/2006#) + 7 AS [NEXT OCCURENCE OF THE DAY IN THE DATE]
FROM studentX
WHERE STRCONV(lastName,2) = "mea";

More on Single-Row Functions

See result below.

DATE	NEXT OCCURRENCE OF THE DAY IN THE DATE
10/20/2006	10/27/2006

The following SELECT statement is used to obtain the next occurrence of a particular day of the week by adding four days to the date #10/20/2006#. The result of the query includes the full names of the days of the week as well as the dates. Type and run the SELECT statement.

SELECT WEEKDAYNAME(WEEKDAY(#10/20/2006#), FALSE, 1) & ", " & (#10/20/2006#) AS [DATE], WEEKDAYNAME(WEEKDAY(#10/20/2006# + 4), FALSE, 1) & ", " & #10/20/2006# + 4 AS [NEXT OCCURRENCE OF A DAY AFTER ADDING FOUR DAYS];

See result below.

DATE	NEXT OCCURRENCE OF A DAY AFTER ADDING FOUR DAYS
Friday, 10/20/2006	Tuesday, 10/24/2006

The following SELECT statement is used to obtain the previous occurrence of a particular day of the week by subtracting two days from the date #10/20/2006#. The result of the query includes the full names of the days of the week as well as the dates. Type and run the SELECT statement.

SELECT WEEKDAYNAME(WEEKDAY(#10/20/2006#), FALSE, 1) & ", " & (#10/20/2006#) AS [DATE], WEEKDAYNAME(WEEKDAY(#10/20/2006# - 2), FALSE, 1) & ", " & #10/20/2006# - 2 AS [PREVIOUS OCCURRENCE OF A DAY AFTER SUBTRACTING TWO DAYS];

See result below.

DATE	PREVIOUS OCCURRENCE OF A DAY AFTER SUBTRACTING TWO DAYS
Friday, 10/20/2006	Wednesday, 10/18/2006

Notice that the last two SELECT statements consist of only the SELECT clause. In MS Access SQL, data that are not gotten from a table can be queried using most functions and the results of such functions can be displayed by using only the SELECT clause of a SELECT statement.

> **Note:** Oracle uses the NEXT_DAY function with the name of the day to be determined as one of the function's values to reveal the next occurrence of the particular day in a date.
>
> Example
> SELECT NEXT_DAY(dateFirstEnrolled, 'FRIDAY') AS "NEXT OCCURRENCE"
> FROM studentX
> WHERE studentId = 'FA213595';

FORMATDATETIME Function

The FORMATDATETIME function is used to change the appearance of date data and time data from their default format configurations. The function is used to format date data and time data. The basic syntax for this function is

FORMATDATETIME(*existingColunmName* | *#dateExpression#* [, *formatMode*])

where

- *existingColumnName* is the column of date data type in the table listed in the FROM clause
- *dateExpression* is the date being used and must be enclosed in a pair of number signs (#)
- *formatMode* is the optional numeric integers that represent the date or time format desired
- Symbols [ ] mean item is optional
- Symbol | symbolizes *Or* Boolean operator

Figure 6.4 lists the numbers used as the *formatMode* actual argument and the type of date and time they represent.

Figure 6.4

formatMode	Number	Significance
System setting	0	Displays a date and/or time. If there is a date part, display it as a short date. If there is a time part, display it as a long time. Both parts are displayed if they are included in the system's setting.
Long date	1	Displays a date using the long date format specified in your computer's regional settings.
Short date	2	Displays a date using the short date format specified in your computer's regional settings.
Long time	3	Displays a time using the time format specified in your computer's regional settings.
Short time	4	Displays a time using the 24-hour format (hh:mm).

If the value for the *formatMode* actual argument is omitted or is zero (0), the system's date and time settings are used.

To display identification numbers, first names, last names and, dates of first enrollment and dates for the next occurrences of the days in the dates of first enrollment for students whose first names begin with the letter "F" using the studentX table, type and run the following SELECT statement.

```
SELECT studentId AS [ID], firstName + "   " + lastName AS [FULL NAME],
FORMATDATETIME(dateFirstEnrolled,1)          AS          [DATE          ENROLLED],
FORMATDATETIME((dateFirstEnrolled+7),1)  AS  [NEXT  OCCURRENCE  OF  DAY
ENROLLED]
FROM studentX
WHERE STRCONV(firstName,2) LIKE ("f*");
```

See result below.

ID	FULL NAME	DATE ENROLLED	NEXT OCCURRENCE OF DAY ENROLLED
FK576381	Florence Kolly	Thursday, January 20, 2005	Thursday, January 27, 2005
FA213595	Fredrica Anthony	Monday, January 10, 2005	Monday, January 17, 2005

Data Types Conversion Functions

Data types' conversion functions are used to convert data from one type to another. Although, MS Access performs most data conversion tasks implicitly, there are times you might want to manipulate data values for one data type to obtain a single value for another data type. In such situation, you must explicitly tell MS Access SQL to do the conversion. The basic syntax for all data types' conversion functions discussed in this chapter is similar.

More on Single-Row Functions

The basic syntax for data types' conversion functions is

dataTypeConversionName(existingColumnName | dataExpression)

where

- *dataTypeConversionName* is the conversion function that is being used
- *existingColumnName* is the column of data type in the table to be converted
- *dataExpression* is the data being converted
- Symbol | symbolizes **Or** Boolean operator

Figure 6.5 lists the data type conversion functions and their assigned tasks.

Figure 6.5

Function Name	Return Type	Significance
CBool	Boolean	Converts valid data to Boolean data type
CByte	Byte	Converts valid data to byte data type
CCur	Currency	Converts valid data to currency data type
CDate	Date	Converts valid data to date data type
CDbl	Double	Converts valid data to double-precision data type
CDec	Decimal	Converts valid data to floating-point data type
CInt	Integer	Converts valid data to integer data type. Fractions are rounded
CLng	Long	Converts valid data to long integer data type. Results are rounded
CSng	Single	Converts valid data to single-precision data type
CStr	String	Converts valid data to text (string) data type
CVar	Variant	Converts valid numeric data to double-precision data type and valid non-numeric data to string data type

Note: A valid data value means that the value being converted falls within the range and type recognized by the converting function. If the value passed to the converting function is outside the range of the data type, an error occurs.

To convert the sum of two floating-point values (1.098 and 38.895) and display the result as an integer value using the studentX table, type and run the following SELECT statement.

SELECT CINT(1.098 + 38.895) AS [CONVERTING REAL VALUES TO INTEGER VALUE]
FROM studentX
WHERE studentId="DM674543";

See result below.

CONVERTING REAL VALUES TO INTEGER VALUE
40

Again, to obtain a single value as the result of such operation, one record in a table is tested. This is one of the standard means for generating results for data that are not contained in tables in MS Access SQL environment.

Alternatively, you could have obtained the same result by using only the SELECT clause of the SELECT statement.

Non-Categorized Single-Row Functions

These are single-row functions that do not fall within any of the groups discussed in this chapter. These functions, although unclassified, are used to resolve many issues in MS Access SQL environment. This section discusses the non-categorized single-row functions that are frequently used in database programming.

ISNULL Function

The ISNULL function is used to determine whether columns' entries contain null values or not. The function returns the Boolean value TRUE which is represented by numeric digit -1 if the column entry contains a null value. The function returns the Boolean value FALSE which is represented by numeric digit 0 if the column entry contain non-null value.

The basic syntax for the ISNULL function is

ISNULL(*existingColumnName* | *dataExpression*)

where

- *existingColumnName* is the column of numeric, text, or date data type in the table listed in the FROM clause
- *dataExpression* is the numeric data, text data, or date data being used
- Symbol | symbolizes **Or** Boolean operator

If the *dataExpression* actual argument is a text data value, the value must be enclosed in quotation marks. If the actual argument is a date data value, the value must be enclosed in a pair of number signs.

To display identification numbers, first names, middle names' initials, last names, and determine whether the entries for middle names' initials are null or not, for faculty members whose last names is "Maklasi" using the facultyX table, type and run the following SELECT statement.

SELECT facultyId, firstName, initial, lastName, ISNULL(initial) AS [initial status]
FROM facultyX
WHERE lastName IN ("Maklasi");

See result below.

facultyId	firstName	initial	lastName	initial status
EM001254	Eghosa		Maklasi	-1

You might have noticed that the displayed record has no middle name initial. This is indicated by the numeric digit -1 (TRUE) which means the entry is null.

NZ Function

The NZ function is used to force columns' entries that contain null values to contain non-null values. The function is used to substitute known values for null values and its formation is a decision statement that is equivalent to the IF...THEN decision statement. The function is helpful when performing mathematical computations that might generate invalid results due to null values.

More on Single-Row Functions

The basic syntax for the NZ function is

NZ(*existingColumnName* | *dataExpression* [, *substituteData*])

where

- *existingColumnName* is the column of valid data type in the table listed in the FROM clause
- *dataExpression* is the numeric data, text data, or date data being used
- *substituteData* is the optional value being used as the replacement data
- Symbols [ ] mean item is optional
- Symbol | symbolizes **Or** Boolean operator

If the *dataExpression* actual argument is a text data value, the value must be enclosed in quotation marks. If the actual argument is a date data value, the value must be enclosed in a pair of number signs, and if a value is not supplied for the *substituteData* actual argument, a zero-length text (string) is returned.

To display identification numbers, first names, middle names' initials, last names, and replace the entries for middle names' initials with the letter "P" where they are null for faculty members whose last names is "Maklasi" using the facultyX table, type and run the following SELECT statement.

SELECT facultyId, firstName, NZ(initial, 'P') AS [middle initial], lastName
FROM facultyX
WHERE UCASE(lastName) ='MAKLASI';

See result below.

facultyId	firstName	middle initial	lastName
EM001254	Eghosa	P	Maklasi

In the result of the query, the function is used to assign the letter "P" to the null entries of the column called initial.

> **Note:** Oracle uses the NVL function to substitute a known value for a null value.
>
> Example:
> SELECT facultyId, firstName, NVL(initial, 'P') AS "middle initial", lastName
> FROM facultyX
> WHERE UPPER(lastName) ='MAKLASI';

IIF Function

The IIF function allows two options to be specified based on whether columns' entries contain null values or not. This function is considered as an advanced form of the NZ function and its formation is a decision statement that is equivalent to the IF...THEN...ELSE decision statement. The function allows the substitution of a column entry whether or not the entry contains a null value.

The basic syntax for the IIF function is

IIF(*conditionExpression, dataDisplayedIfTrue, dataDisplayedIfFalse*)

where

- *conditionExpression* is the logical test to be evaluated in order to determine which of the two options to display
- *dataDisplayedIfTrue* is the value to be displayed if the *conditionExpression* actual argument evaluates to be true
- *dataDisplayedIfFalse* is the value to be displayed if the *conditionExpression* actual argument evaluates to be false

If *dataDisplayedIfTrue* and *dataDisplayedIfFalse* actual arguments are text data values, the values must be enclosed in quotation marks. If the actual arguments are date data values, the values must be enclosed in pairs of number signs.

If the column entry being tested is not null, the value for the *dataDisplayedIfTrue* actual argument is displayed. However, if the column entry contains null value, the value for the *dataDisplayedIfFalse* actual argument is displayed.

To display first and last names of the last four faculty members in descending order based on their first names and indicate those who have no middle names' initials with the text expression "No Initial" using the facultyX table, type and run the following SELECT statement.

SELECT TOP 4 firstName, lastName, IIF(initial,initial,'No Initial') AS [middle initial]
FROM facultyX
ORDER BY firstName DESC;

See result below.

firstName	lastName	middle initial
Zenat	Miller	J
Rischi	Ugboma	B
Peter	Dayet	No Initial
John	Semina	No Initial

The last two records in the result have no middle names' initials. The IIF function in the SELECT statement substituted the text expression "No Initial" for the faculty members with no middle names' initials.

> **Note:** Oracle uses NVL2 function to obtain similar results.
>
> Example:
> SELECT facultyId, firstName, lastName, NVL2(initial,initial,'No Initial')
> FROM facultyX
> WHERE firstName LIKE ('E%')
> ORDER BY firstName DESC;

CHOOSE Function

The CHOOSE function allows more than two options to be specified for a test. This function can be considered as an extension or an advanced form of the IIF function and it is used to write a decision statement. The statement is equivalent to the IF...THEN...ELSEIF decision statement. The CHOOSE function can contain any number of options or actions. The basic syntax for this function is

CHOOSE(*existingColumnName* | *numericExpression*, *dataDisplayedIf1*, *dataDisplayedIf2*, ...)

where

More on Single-Row Functions

- *existingColumnName* is the column of numeric data type in the table listed in the FROM clause
- *numericExpression* is the numeric value or numeric expression being used
- *dataDisplayedIf1* is the value to be displayed if the *existingColumnName* or *numericExpression* actual argument evaluates to 1
- *dataDisplayedIf2* is the value to be displayed if the *existingColumnName* or *numericExpression* actual argument evaluates to 2
- Symbol | symbolizes *Or* Boolean operator
- Symbols ... mean more options can be listed

The *existingColumnName* actual argument or the *numericExpression* actual argument must evaluate to a numeric integer value. The value must be integer 1 or of higher integer and the integer value must correspond to an option numeric position listed in the function. If the *existingColumnName* or the *numericExpression* actual argument is 1, the data for the first option on the list is displayed, if 2, the data for the second option on the list is displayed and in that order until the last option of the list is reached and displayed.

If the value of the *existingColumnName* or the *numericExpression* actual argument is a floating-point value, the value is rounded to the nearest whole number on the integer part. The options are chosen based on the values of the *existingColumnName* or the *nuericExpression* actual argument. If the values of the arguments are zero (0) or the values are greater than the number of options listed, a null value is returned. If the *dataDisplayedIf1* and *dataDisplayedIf2* actual arguments are text data values, the values must be enclosed in quotation marks. If the actual arguments are date data values, the values must be enclosed in pairs of number signs.

To display academic positions based on numericNumbering column using the positionX table, type and run the following SELECT statement.

SELECT CHOOSE (numericNumbering, "Assistant Professor", "Associate Professor", "Full Professor", "Instructor") AS [ACADEMIC POSITIONS]
FROM positionX;

See result below.

ACADEMIC POSITIONS
Assistant Professor
Associate Professor
Full Professor
Instructor

> **Note:** Oracle can use any of the following two functions - DECODE, CASE - to obtain the same results as the CHOOSE function.
>
> Example:
> SELECT DECODE(numericNumbering, 1, 'Assistant Professor', 2, 'Associate Professor', 3, 'Full Professor', 'Instructor') AS 'ACADMIC POSITIONS'
> FROM positionX;

FORMATCURRENCY and FORMATPERCENT Functions

FORMATCURRENCY and FORMATPERCENT functions are used to alter or change the appearance of values of numeric data type to currency and percent respectively. The FORMATCURRENCY function displays the needed results with dollar symbols ($) and comma symbols while the FORMATPERCENT function displays the needed results with percent symbol (%) and comma symbols. The comma symbols are used as separators for numeric values that are quantified in thousands. The basic syntax for these two functions is

FORMATCURRENCY | FORMATPERCENT(*existingColumnName* | *numericExpression* [, *numberOfDecimalPlaces*])

where

- *existingColumnName* is the column of numeric data type in the table listed in the FROM clause
- *numericExpression* is the numeric value or numeric expression being used
- *numberOfDecimalPlaces* is the optional numeric integer that specifies the number of digit required after decimal point.
- Symbols [ ] mean item is optional
- Symbol | symbolizes **Or** Boolean operator. You can also combine numeric columns and/or numeric expressions as the functions' actual arguments

If the value for the *numberOfDecimalPlaces* actual argument is omitted, the value is displayed using the system setting. The system setting is usually two digits to the right of the decimal point or two decimal positions. If the value of the actual argument is zero (0), no decimal portion of the value is displayed.

To display identification numbers, first names, and annual salaries formatted to currency with two decimal positions, twenty percent of annual salaries formatted to currency with one decimal position, and the percentage of the twenty percent of annual salaries with no decimal positions for faculty members whose last names is "Mea" using the facultyX table, type and run the following SELECT statement.

SELECT facultyId AS ID, firstName AS NAME, FORMATCURRENCY(annualSalary, 2) AS [SALARY IN CURRENCY FORMAT], FORMATCURRENCY(annualSalary * 0.20, 1) AS [PART SALARY], FORMATPERCENT(annualSalary * 0.20 / annualSalary, 0) AS [PERCENT OF PART SALARY ON ANNUAL SALARY]
FROM facultyX
WHERE lastName="Mea";

See result below.

ID	NAME	SALARY IN CURRENCY FORMAT	PART SALARY	PERCENT OF PART SALARY ON ANNUAL SALARY
DM674543	Doris	$62,980.25	$12,596.1	20%

FORMAT Function
The FORMAT function is used to change or alter the appearance of the results of queried data. This function can be applied to numeric, text, and date data types. The basic syntax for the FORMAT function is

FORMAT(*existingColumnName* | *dataExpression* [, "*formatStyle*"])

where

- *existingColumnName* is the column of the data in the table listed in the FROM clause
- *dataExpression* is the data being used

More on Single-Row Functions

- *formatStye* is the optional formatting symbols used to change the appearance(s) of displayed data and must be enclosed in quotation marks
- Symbols [ ] mean item is optional
- Symbol | symbolizes *Or* Boolean operator

If the *dataExpression* actual argument is a text data value, the value must be enclosed in quotation marks. If the actual argument is a date data value, the value must be enclosed in a pair of number signs.

Figure 6.6 lists the symbols that are commonly used in the FORMAT function.

Figure 6.6

Format Symbol	Significance
Text	
@	Displays a text character at the position indicated or a space if there is no character to display
&	Displays a text character at the position indicated or nothing if there is no character to display
<	Converts text data to lowercase
>	Converts text data to uppercase
Numeric	
$	Includes a floating dollar symbol
#	Displays a numeric digit at the position indicated or nothing if there is no digit to display
0	Displays a numeric digit at the position indicated or a zero (0) if there is no digit to display
, (comma)	Displays a comma at the position indicated
. (period)	Specifies the number of decimal positions to include
Date	
d	Displays the numeric digit representing the day of the month without leading zero (0)
dd	Displays the numeric digit representing the day of the month with leading zero (0)
ddd	Displays the first three letter abbreviation representing the day of the week
dddd	Displays the full name representing the day of the week
w	Displays the numeric digit representing the day of the week
ww	Displays the numeric digit representing the week of the year
m	Displays the numeric digit representing the month of the year without leading zero (0)
mm	Displays the numeric digit representing the month of the year with leading zero (0)
mmm	Displays the first three letter abbreviation representing the month of the year
mmmm	Displays the full name representing the month of the year
yy	Displays the last two digit representing the year
yyyy	Displays the four digits representing the year
Time	
h	Displays the numeric digit representing the hours of the day without leading zero (0)
hh	Displays the numeric digit representing the hours of the day with leading zero (0)
m	Displays the numeric digit representing the minutes of the hour without leading zero (0)
mm	Displays the numeric digit representing the minutes of the hour with leading zero (0)
s	Displays the numeric digit representing the seconds of the minute without leading zero (0)

Format Symbol	Significance
ss	Displays the numeric digit representing the seconds of the minute with leading zero (0)
: (colon)	Separates hours from minutes and minutes from seconds when two or more of the different time symbols are used

Note: Using the time symbols in a FORMAT function displays the time in 24-hour format by default, therefore A.M. or P.M. is not required.

To display identification numbers, first names in uppercases, annual salaries formatted to currency, system date formatted, system time formatted, and the percentage of twenty percent of annual salaries with no decimal positions for faculty members whose last names is "Mea" using the facultyX table, type and run the following SELECT statement.

SELECT facultyId AS ID, FORMAT(firstName,">") AS NAME, FORMAT(annualSalary,'$###,###.00') AS [ANNUAL INCOME], FORMAT(DATE(), "dddd, dd mmmm, yyyy") AS [SYSTEM DATE], FORMAT(NOW(),"hh:mm:ss") AS [SYSTEM TIME], FORMAT(annualSalary*0.2/annualSalary,'##%') AS [PERCENTAGE]
FROM facultyX
WHERE lastName="Mea";

See result below.

ID	NAME	ANNUAL INCOME	SYSTEM DATE	SYSTEM TIME	PERCENTAGE
DM674543	DORIS	$62,980.25	Thursday, 11 August, 2005	22:09:41	20%

The results of the date and time may differ depending on the computer system that is being used.

Note: All MS Access formatting functions display their data as text data, and as a result, the displayed data are aligned to the left. Oracle uses TO_CHAR function to achieve the same output.

Example:
SELECT facultyId AS ID, firstName AS FIRST_NAME, TO_CHAR(annualSalary,'$999,999.00') AS ANNUAL_INCOME, TO_CHAR(SYSDATE, 'DD Month, YYYY') AS SYSTEM_DATE
FROM facultyX
WHERE lastName="Mea";

Nesting Single-Row Functions

Single-row functions can be placed inside one another. In other words, single-row functions can be the actual arguments of other single-row functions. However, care must be taking when nesting functions as some functions are not compatible especially when they generate results of different data types. Single-row functions can be embedded within each other to any level of depth. Nested functions are evaluated from the innermost level to the outermost level.

The basic syntax for nested function using two level nesting is

functionName(functionName([actualArgument], ...))

where

More on Single-Row Functions

- *functionName* is the function that is being used
- *actualArgument* is the optional data item being passed to the function to use to perform the assigned task
- Symbols [ ] mean item is optional
- Symbols... mean more actual argument can be listed

To display identification numbers, first names in uppercases, and monthly salaries, based on adding the length of last names to the square of the numeric ASCII representations of first letters of last names for students whose first names begin with the letter "E" using the studentX table, type and run the following SELECT statement.

SELECT studentId AS ID, FORMAT(firstName,">") AS NAME, FORMATCURRENCY(ASC(MID(lastName, 1, 1)) ^ 2 + LEN(LastName), 2) AS [WORKING STUDENT]
FROM studentX
WHERE firstName LIKE "E*";

See result below.

ID	NAME	WORKING STUDENT
EA486741	ERASTO	$4,237.00
EM001254	EGHOSA	$5,936.00
EJ890321	EFOSA	$5,483.00

In the query, MID function is the actual argument for the ASC function. ASC, MID, and LEN functions are the actual argument for the FORMATCURRENCY function.

Displaying Results of Data Not Contained in Tables

There are times when you want to write SELECT statements to display results that are not gotten from data contained in tables or to display such results using functions. MS Access SQL allows you to display such data either by writing the SELECT statement to contain only a SELECT clause or by using a table that exists in a database. When using a table to perform such types of database activities, you must use a condition clause, usually the WHERE clause, to restrict the displayed result to one record. If functions' actual arguments are not data that are gotten from tables, you can display the results of such functions by using only the SELECT clause of a SELECT statement.

To display the number of days that have elapsed between October 28, 2004 and February 8, 2005 using the studentX table, type and run the following SELECT statement.

SELECT FORMATDATETIME(#10/28/2004#, 1) AS [FIRST DATE], FORMATDATETIME(#08-Feb-05#, 1) AS [SECOND DATE], DATEDIFF('d', #28-Oct-04#, #02/08/2005#) AS [NUMBER OF DAYS ELAPSED]
FROM studentX
WHERE studentId = 'EM001254';

See result below.

FIRST DATE	SECOND DATE	NUMBER OF DAYS ELAPSED
Thursday, October 28, 2004	Tuesday, February 08, 2005	103

You might have noticed that the date data are not contained in the studentX table and the WHERE condition clause is used to restrict the result to one record. You must make sure that the data value that is being compared to in the condition clause is not duplicated in the column that is being compared.

In the SELECT statement, the studentId column is the column that is being compared and the data value "EM001254" is the value that the studentId column is being compared to. Different date formats (mm/dd/yyyy and dd-mon-yy) are used to demonstrate that valid date formats can be used in the same SELECT statement.

Alternatively, writing only the SELECT clause of the SELECT statement yields the same result.

> **Note:** Oracle uses a system table called DUAL to achieve the same result.
>
> Example:
> SELECT TO_CHAR(SYSDATE, 'Month DD, YYYY') AS "DATE"
> FROM DUAL;

Chapter Summary

This chapter explains date and time single-row functions. The chapter, in addition, shows how to (i) convert data from one type to another, (ii) change the appearance of displayed data using formatting functions, (iii) substitute for null values, (iv) nest functions, and (v) display the results of data that are not gotten from existing tables.

Single-Row Functions Syntax and SQL Statements Summary

The table below presents the single-row functions' syntax discussed in this chapter and the SQL statements' examples for retrieving data from tables.

Description	Function General Syntax	Function Example
A function is a block of programming instructions that performs a specific task	*functionName*([*actualArgument*], ...)	DATE() Or NZ(initial, 'P')
A nonargument-based function is a function that requires no actual arguments	*functionName*()	TIME()
An argument-based function is a function that requires actual arguments	*functionName*(*actualArgument*,...)	ISNULL(initial)

Function Name and Description	Function Syntax	Statement Example
DATE function is used to return the current date of a computer system	DATE()	SELECT DATE() AS [Current Date] FROM studentX WHERE studentId LIKE ("CS664452");
NOW function is used to return both the current date and the current time of a computer system	NOW()	SELECT NOW() AS DATE_TIME FROM studentX WHERE studentId LIKE ("CS664452");
DATEADD function is used to determine a certain date based on a specified time period	DATEADD("*typeOfTimePeriod*", *numberOfTimePeriod*, *existingColumnName* | *dateExpression*)	SELECT studentId AS ID, dateFirstEnrolled AS ENROLLED, DATEADD('m',4,dateFirstEnrolled) AS TEST_DATE FROM studentX WHERE studentId LIKE ("F*");

More on Single-Row Functions

DATEDIFF function is used to return how much time has elapsed between dates	DATEDIFF("*typeOfTimePeriod*", *existingColumnName1* | *dateExpression1*, *existingColumnName2* | *dateExpression2* [, *firstDayOfTheWeek*, *firstWeekOfTheYear*])	SELECT studentId AS ID, DATEDIFF('ww', dateFirstEnrolled, DATE(), 3) AS [MWEEKS] FROM studentX WHERE studentId LIKE ("CS6*");
YEAR function is used to return the numeric integer value that represents the year in the date being queried	YEAR(*existingColunmName* | *dateExpression*)	SELECT studentId, dateFirstEnrolled, YEAR(dateFirstEnrolled) AS [YEAR] FROM studentX WHERE UCASE(lastName) = "BOMOR";
MONTH function is used to return the numeric integer value that represents the month in the year being queried	MONTH(*existingColunmName* | *dateExpression*)	SELECT studentId, dateFirstEnrolled, MONTH(dateFirstEnrolled) AS [MONTH] FROM studentX WHERE UCASE(lastName) = "BOMOR";
DAY function is used to return the numeric integer value that represents the day in the month being queried	WEEKDAY(*existingColunmName* | *dateExpression*)	SELECT studentId, dateFirstEnrolled, DAY(dateFirstEnrolled) AS [DAYS] FROM studentX WHERE UCASE(lastName) = "BOMOR";
WEEKDAY function is used to return the numeric representations of days of the week	WEEKDAY(*existingColunmName* | *dateExpression* [, *firstDayOfTheWeek*])	SELECT studentId, dateFirstEnrolled, WEEKDAY(dateFirstEnrolled, 1) AS [WEEKS] FROM studentX WHERE UCASE(lastName) = "BOMOR";
MONTHNAME function is used to convert the numeric representations of months of the year to their actual names	MONTHNAME(*numericIntegerForMonth* [, *booleanValue*])	SELECT DISTINCT (#08/07/2005#) AS [DATE], MONTHNAME(08,FALSE) AS [MNAME] FROM studentX WHERE UCASE(lastName) = "BOMOR";
WEEKDAYNAME function is used to convert the numeric representations of days of the week to their actual names	WEEKDAYNAME(*numericIntegerForWeek* [, *booleanValue*, *firstDayOfTheWeek*])	SELECT DISTINCT (#08/07/2005#) AS [DATE], WEEKDAYNAME(WEEKDAY(#08/07/2005#) , FALSE,1) AS [WEEKDAY NAME IN FULL] FROM studentX WHERE UCASE(lastName) = "BOMOR";
TIME function is used to return the current time of a computer system	TIME()	SELECT TIME() AS DATE_TIME FROM studentX WHERE studentId LIKE ("CS664452");
TIMER function is used to return the total number of seconds that has elapsed since midnight based on a computer system's current time	TIMER()	SELECT TIMER() AS HOW_MANY_SECONDS FROM studentX WHERE studentId LIKE ("CS664452");
FORMATDATETIME function is used to alter the appearances of date and time data	FORMATDATETIME(*existingColunmName* | *dateExpression* [, *formatMode*])	SELECT studentId, firstName + " " + lastName AS FULL_NAME, FORMATDATETIME(dateFirstEnrolled,1) AS DENROLLED, FORMATDATETIME((dateFirstEnrolled+7),1) AS [OCCURRENCE OF DAY ENROLLED] FROM studentX WHERE STRCONV(firstName,2) LIKE ("f*");
ISNULL function is used to determine whether column entries contain null values	ISNULL(*existingColumnName* | *dataExpression*)	SELECT facultyId, firstName, initial, lastName, ISNULL(initial) AS [initial status] FROM facultyX WHERE lastName IN ("Maklasi");

NZ function is used to substitute actual values for column entries that contain null values	NZ(*existingColumnName* | *dataExpression* [, *substituteData*])	SELECT facultyId, firstName, NZ(initial, 'P') AS [middle initial], lastName FROM facultyX WHERE UCASE(lastName) ='MAKLASI';
IIF function is used to substitute actual values for column entries whether the column entries contain null values or not	IIF(*conditionExpression*, *dataDisplayedIfTrue*, *dataDisplayedIfFalse*)	SELECT TOP 4 firstName, lastName, IIF(initial,initial,'No Initial') AS [middle initial] FROM facultyX ORDER BY firstName DESC;
CHOOSE function is used to specify more than two options for a decision test	CHOOSE(*existingColumnName* | *numericExpression*, *dataDisplayedIf1* [, *dataDisplayedIf2*, …])	SELECT CHOOSE (numericNumbering, "Assistant Professor", "Associate Professor", "Full Professor", "Instructor") AS [ACADEMIC POSITIONS] FROM positionX;
FORMATCURRENCY function is used to alter the appearances of numeric data to currency	FORMATCURRENCY(*existingColumnName* | *numericExpression* [, *numberOfDecimalPlaces*])	SELECT facultyId, firstName, FORMATCURRENCY(annualSalary, 2) AS [FSALARY] FROM facultyX WHERE lastName="Mea";
FORMATPERCENT function is used to alter the appearances of numeric data to include the percent symbol	FORMATPERCENT(*existingColumnName* | *numericExpression* [, *numberOfDecimalPlaces*])	SELECT facultyId, firstName, FORMATPERCENT(annualSalary * 0.20 / annualSalary, 0) AS [PERCENTOFSAL] FROM facultyX WHERE lastName="Mea";
FORMAT function is used to alter the appearance of any data type value	FORMAT(*existingColumnName* | *dataExpression* [, *formatStyle*])	SELECT FORMAT(firstName,">") AS NAME, FORMAT(annualSalary,'$###,###.00') AS AINCOME, FORMAT(annualSalary*0.2/annualSalary,'# #%') AS [PERCENTAGE] FROM facultyX WHERE facultyId="EM001254";
Data Type Conversion Functions		
Description	**Function Syntax**	**Statement Example**
Data type conversion functions are used to transform data from one type to other	*dataTypeConversionName*(*existingColumnName* | *dataExpression*)	SELECT CINT(1.098 + 38.895) AS [CONVERTING REAL VALUES TO INTEGER VALUE] FROM studentX WHERE studentId="DM674543";

Key Terms

Argument-based
CHOOSE
Data type conversion
Date functions
DATEADD
DATEDIFF
DAY
FORMAT
IIF

Intervals
ISNULL
MONTH
Nonargument-based
TIME
Time functions
WEEKDAY
YEAR

Chapter Review Questions

Multiple Choice Questions

1. Date data are stored as
   - a. algebraic equations.
   - b. serial numbers.
   - c. geometrical patterns.
   - d. strings.

2. The TIME function is a _____ function.
   - a. string
   - b. argument-based
   - c. nonargument-based
   - d. character-based

3. Assume that the studentX table exists and the table contains a column called studentId. Study the following SELECT statement and tell the output.

   SELECT DATE()
   FROM studentX
   WHERE studentId LIKE ("AB12345");

   - a. The display shows the computer system's current date.
   - b. The display shows the date the student with the ID "AB12345" enrolled.
   - c. The display shows the dates all students contained in the table enrolled.
   - d. all of the above.

4. The WEEKDAY function returns
   - a. the full names of the days of the week.
   - b. the abbreviations of the names of the weeks.
   - c. the days, the time intervals, and dates.
   - d. the numeric representations of the days of the week.

5. Which of the following is not the symbol used to enclosed date data in MS Access SQL?
   - a. parenthesis.
   - b. double quotation mark.
   - c. single quotation mark.
   - d. number sign.

6. Which of the following data type conversion functions converts numeric data to double-precision data type and nonnumeric data to string data type?
   - a. CByte function.
   - b. CVar function.
   - c. CBool function.
   - d. CDbl function.

7. The _____ function is used to substitute known values for null values.
   - a. ISNULL
   - b. CDec
   - c. NZ
   - d. IS NOT NULL

8. Which of the following functions is used to construct the IF...THEN decision statement?.
   - a. IIF function.
   - b. CHOOSE function.
   - c. FORMAT function.
   - d. NZ function.

9. Which of the following symbols is displayed as part of the result of the FORMATCURRENCY function?
   a. comma symbol.
   b. number sign.
   c. percent symbol.
   d. all of the above.

10. Which function can be used to alter the appearance of numeric, text, and date data values?
    a. FORMATDATENUMBER function.
    b. FORMATNUMBERTEXT function.
    c. FORMATDATETIME function.
    d. FORMAT function.

True or False Questions

11. Date intervals are measured in days only.
    a. True
    b. False

12. The DATEDIFF function returns a numeric value as its result.
    a. True
    b. False

13. Data type conversion functions convert one data type to another.
    a. True
    b. False

14. To convert a data value to a string data type, you use the CSng function.
    a. True
    b. False

15. The CHOOSE function allows more than two options to be specified for a test.
    a. True
    b. False

16. The IIF function allows one option based on whether columns' entries contain null values or not.
    a. True
    b. False

17. In MS Access SQL, a single-row function can be placed inside another single-row function.
    a. Tue
    b. False

Fill in the blank Questions

18. A function that uses no actual argument is called a _____.

19. The _____ returns both the current date and time of a computer system.

20. To determine how much time has elapsed between dates, you use the _____ function.

21. When the Boolean value TRUE is used in the MONTHNAME function, it is an indication that the month name should be _____.

22. To convert an integer value to a single-precision data type using the data type conversion functions' group, you use the _____ function.

23. The _____ function is used to determine whether the entry of a column contains null.

More on Single-Row Functions

Essay Type Questions

24. Describe the advantage(s) of the FORMAT function over the FORMATDATETIME function? Write a SQL statement that uses the FORMAT function?

25. When is it convenient to use the CHOOSE function and point out the differences between the function and the IIF function?

26. Explain the differences between FORMATCURRENCY and FORMATPERCENT functions and write a valid SQL statement that uses the two functions?

27. Explain the mathematics used to calculate the next occurrence of a particular day and write a SELECT statement that supports your answer?

28. What is a nested function and write a SELECT statement that shows an example of a nested function?

Hands-on Activities

Study the structures and the data of **AcademicX** database tables in appendix A (pages 355 through 360) and perform the following hands-on exercises.

1. Write a SELECT statement to display identification numbers and how many years have elapsed between the dates that students from United Kingdom first enrolled and the computer system's current date. The year should be calculated using Sunday as the first day of the week and use the first full week of the year. Assign column alias **Number Of Years Gone By** to the column that contains the number of years.

2. Based on four-year graduation period, display identification numbers, last names, and dates students from Texas suppose to graduate. Assign column alias **Graduation** to the column that contains the dates. Sort the result in ascending order using the dateFirstEnrolled column.

3. Write a SQL statement to display the current time of a computer system. Use column alias of your choice.

4. Write a SQL statement to display the computer system's current date and the next occurrence of the day in the date using the long date format. Use columns' aliases of your choice.

5. Write the solution to question 4 using the FORMAT function.

6. Display identification numbers and annual salaries of faculty members who are also students. Format their annual salaries to include leading dollar sign ($), commas, and two decimal positions using the FORMAT function. Assign column alias **Annual Salary** to the salary column.

7. Write a SQL statement that displays identification numbers of faculty members who have no middle names' initials and substitute the word "None" for their middle names' initials. Assign column alias **Middle_Name_Initial** to the middle name initial column.

8. Display identification numbers and middle names' initials of students who have earned the letter grade "B" or better in any course, and the second character of their identification numbers is "J". If the qualifying students have no middle names' initials, substitute the word "Good" for their middle names' initials. If they have middle names' initials, keep the initials. Assign columns' aliases of your choice.

9. Write a SQL statement to display identification numbers and monthly salaries of faculty members who are associate professors. Round their monthly salaries to two decimal positions.

10. Write a SELECT statement to convert the result of the following floating-point values (564.98, 832.09, and 409.67) to currency data type using the data type conversion functions' group. The result should be displayed once (not duplicated). Use column alias of your choice.

Chapter Seven

Multiple-Row Functions and Results Sets

Chapter Objectives

After completing this chapter, you should be able to

- Understand multiple-row functions
- Use SUM and AVG functions
- Use COUNT function
- Use MAX and MIN functions
- Use GROUP BY clause
- Use STDEV and VAR functions
- Use FIRST and LAST functions
- Use HAVING clause
- Nest multiple-row functions
- Summarize data for grouped Records (Results Sets)

Functions

A function is a block or collection of programming instructions which task is pre-known. A function can, depending on its syntax, accept no value, one value, or more values as its actual arguments and it must return a single value as its result. Two types of functions are used in programming arena. One type is called built-in functions and the other type is called programmer- or user-defined functions. Both types can further be classified as single-row and multiple-row functions. The codes of built-in functions are incorporated into the programming language before the language is distributed for use and that is the type that is being discussed in this textbook. Programmer-defined functions are written by programmers during programs' development and their codes are part of the programs. Programmer-defined functions are outside the scope of this textbook, and as such, they are not addressed.

MS Access SQL supports dozens of functions, but this chapter discusses the ones that are most commonly used in MS Access SQL environment. The general syntax for a function is the function name followed by a pair of parentheses with optional actual argument(s) separated by commas placed within the parentheses. The general syntax for a function is

functionName([*actualArgument*], ...)

where

- *functionName* is the function that is being used
- *actualArgument* is the optional data item that is passed to the function to use to perform the assigned task
- Symbols [ ] mean item is optional
- Symbols ... mean more actual arguments can be listed

A function might require no (zero) actual arguments to perform its assigned task. In such situation, no data items are passed to the function as its actual arguments when the function is called. In case a function requires an actual argument, the argument can be a single column, an expression, combination of columns, combination of expressions, or combination of columns and expressions enclosed in a pair of parentheses. You can also specify more than one actual argument in the pair of parentheses if that is a function's requirement. When a function requires more than one actual argument, the arguments must be separated by commas.

The following is an example of MS Access function using one actual argument.

COUNT(lastName)

The pair of parentheses is mandatory as it is used to supply the data which is the actual argument to a function.

Note: Data altered by functions listed in the SELECT clause and conditions' clauses of a SELECT statement are changed temporarily. Functions do not permanently change the original form of data stored in tables. Whenever functions are allowed to be used in conditions' clauses, you can specify the functions on either side or both sides of the comparison operators of the conditions. In MS Access SQL when data values that are being queried are not contained in a table, you can obtain the results of such values with functions that use the values as their actual arguments by including the functions in the SELECT clause of a SELECT statement that consists of only the SELECT clause. All other clauses can be omitted.

Example:
SELECT DATE(), NOW();

Notice that the SELECT statement consists only of one clause – the SELECT clause.

Multiple-Row Functions

Multiple-row functions are group functions. Multiple-row functions are also called aggregate, statistics, or summary functions and they work across groups of rows to return one record for each group processed in a table or joined tables. Multiple-row functions, except for the COUNT(*) function, ignore null values.

Although, many multiple-row functions can be applied to all types of data, but there are few that can only work with values of numeric data type. These functions cannot be applied to values of other data types, except when performing mathematics with date data. The functions that are exclusively used for numeric data type are SUM, AVG, STDEV (STDEVP), and VAR (VARP).

SUM and AVG Functions

The SUM function returns the total or the sum of a collection of numeric values. Generally, the SUM function adds numbers – positive or negative – to arrive at a single value. The AVG function returns the average or the mean value of a collection of numeric values.

The basic syntax for these functions is

SUM | AVG(*existingColumnName* | *numericExpression*)

where

- *existingColumnName* is the column of numeric data type in the table listed in the FROM clause
- *numericExpression* is the numeric value or numeric values connected by arithmetic operator(s)
- Symbol | symbolizes **Or** Boolean operator

Chapter Seven

> **Note:** When numeric values are used as the actual argument, you must connect the values with arithmetic operators. Example: 4 * 6 -1

To display total and average salaries for all faculty members using the facultyX table, type and run the following SELECT statement.

SELECT SUM(annualSalary) AS [TOTAL ANNUAL SALARY FOR ALL FACULTY], AVG(annualSalary) AS [AVERAGE OF TOTAL ANNUAL SALARIES FOR ALL FACULTY] FROM facultyX;

See result below.

TOTAL ANNUAL SALARY FOR ALL FACULTY	AVERAGE OF TOTAL ANNUAL SALARIES FOR ALL FACULTY
601533.68	60153.368

The query returns one value for the total annual salary for all faculty members and one value for the average annual salary for all faculty members.

COUNT Function
The COUNT function is used to return the number of records in a table or joined tables. The returned value is based on the type of actual argument supplied to the function. The actual argument determines how the records are to be counted. If the actual argument is a column in a table, the COUNT function returns the number of records that have non-null values in that column.

However, if the actual argument is the asterisk symbol (*), the COUNT function returns a number that includes all records in the queried table. In this function, the meaning of the asterisk symbol is to use any column in the table that is being queried and count both the non-null and the null entries of that column. With the asterisk symbol as the COUNT function's actual argument, the numeric value returned by the function corresponds to the total number of records in the queried table.

The basic syntax for this function is

COUNT(* | *existingColumnName*)

where

- Symbol * is to count all records
- *existingColumnName* is the column of any data type in the table listed in the FROM clause
- Symbol | symbolizes **Or** Boolean operator

To display the number of faculty members who have middle names' initials and the total number of faculty members using the facultyX table, type and run the following SELECT statement.

SELECT COUNT(initial) AS [COUNT FACULTY WITH MIDDLE INITIAL], COUNT(*) AS [COUNT ALL RECORDS] FROM facultyX;

See result below.

COUNT FACULTY WITH MIDDLE INITIAL	COUNT ALL RECORDS
6	10

Multiple-Row Functions and Results Sets

The result of the SELECT statement reveals that six faculty members have middle names' initials. The first COUNT function ignores the null entries of the column called initial in the facultyX table. The second COUNT function counts both the non-null and the null entries of any column of the facultyX table. From the result, the number returned for all faculty members is 10 and the value indicates that four faculty members have no middle names' initials.

MAX and MIN Functions

The MAX function returns the value of the highest measure - largest value or maximum value - among a group of values, and the MIN function returns the values of the lowest measure - smallest value or minimum value - among a group of values. The basic syntax for these functions is

MAX | MIN(*existingColumnName* | *dataExpression*)

where

- *existingColumnName* is the column of any data type in the table listed in the FROM clause
- *dataExpression* is either the combination of columns of the same data type or combination of data values to columns of the same data type
- Symbol | symbolizes *Or* Boolean operator

To display maximum and minimum letter values of middle names' initials, maximum and minimum string values of combined first and last names, and latest and earliest dates of enrollment for students using the studentX table, type and run the following SELECT statement.

SELECT MAX(initial) AS [INITIAL OF HIGHEST VALUE], MIN(initial) AS [INITIAL OF LOWEST VALUE], MAX(LCASE(firstName) & UCASE(lastName)) AS [COMBINED NAMES OF HIGHEST VALUE], MIN(LCASE(firstName) & UCASE(lastName)) AS [COMBINED NAMES OF LOWEST VALUE], MAX(dateFirstEnrolled) AS [LATEST DATE], MIN(dateFirstEnrolled) AS [EARLIEST DATE]
FROM studentX;

See result below.

INITIAL OF HIGHEST VALUE	INITIAL OF LOWEST VALUE	COMBINED NAMES OF HIGHEST VALUE	COMBINED NAMES OF LOWEST VALUE	LATEST DATE	EARLIEST DATE
V	A	suzyAFIK	abelBOMOR	1/20/2006	1/10/2004

GROUP BY Clause

When results of multiple-row functions should be displayed based on specified or defined groups, rather than having one record representing the result of all groups in a table, you use the GROUP BY clause. The GROUP BY clause is used to divide records into specific groups so that the results generated by the query can be grouped. In SQL environment, creating groups mean records that share common characteristics are put together. The basic syntax for the GROUP BY clause is

GROUP BY *existingColumnName*, ... | *columnPosition*, ...

where

- *existingColumnName* is the column in the table listed in the FROM clause
- *columnPosition* is the numeric position of the column in the SELECT clause beginning with the leftmost column as position 1 and subsequent columns as position 2, position 3 and so on in that order
- Symbol | symbolizes *Or* Boolean operator
- Symbols ... mean more columns and/or columns' positions can be listed

In MS Access SQL, when using the GROUP BY clause in a SELECT statement, the following steps should be observed.

- Columns that are used in the GROUP BY clause do not have to be listed in the SELECT clause, as long as the columns are contained in the table being queried
- Columns that are used as actual arguments for multiple-row functions that are listed in the SELECT clause can be listed in the GROUP BY clause
- Individual columns that are not used as actual arguments for multiple-row functions but are listed independently in the SELECT clause that contains multiple-row functions must be listed in the GROUP BY clause
- Exclude records that are not needed in the grouping using the WHERE condition clause before grouping the required records
- Data of individual records cannot be displayed when the SELECT clause contains at least one multiple-row function
- Columns' aliases cannot be used in the GROUP BY clause
- Results are displayed in ascending order based on the order (arrangement) of the columns listed in the GROUP BY clause
- Use the ORDER BY clause to change or rearrange the order of display of the GROUP BY clause

To display academic positions, total annual salaries of faculty members in groups based on academic positions and the number of faculty members in each group using both facultyX and positionX tables, type and run the following SELECT statement.

SELECT academicPosition AS [POSITION], SUM(annualSalary) As [TOTAL ANNUAL SALARY BY POSITION], COUNT(academicPosition) AS [HOW MANY IN EACH GROUP]
FROM facultyX, positionX
WHERE annualSalary BETWEEN minAnnualSalary AND maxAnnualSalary
GROUP BY academicPosition;

See result below.

POSITION	TOTAL ANNUAL SALARY BY POSITION	HOW MANY IN EACH GROUP
Assistant Professor	111258.15	2
Associate Professor	62980.25	1
Full Professor	283438.08	4
Instructor	143857.2	3

The last column of the result indicates that there are two Assistant Professors, one Associate Professor, four Full Professors, and three Instructors. The total annual salary for each group based on academic positions is also shown in the second column of the result.

The following SELECT statement uses the academicPosition column as the actual argument of the COUNT function as well as the column for grouping in the GROUP BY clause. Type and run the SELECT statement.

Multiple-Row Functions and Results Sets

```
SELECT COUNT(academicPosition) AS [HOW MANY IN EACH GROUP]
FROM facultyX, positionX
WHERE annualSalary BETWEEN minAnnualSalary AND maxAnnualSalary
GROUP BY academicPosition;
```

See result below.

HOW MANY IN EACH GROUP
2
1
4
3

STDEV (STDEVP) Function

The STDEV(STDEVP) function is used to compute the standard deviation for a group of numeric values. This function calculates how close a value is to the average or the mean of a group of numeric values. The basic syntax for this function is

STDEV | STDEVP(*existingColumnName* | *numericExpression*)

where

- *existingColumnName* is the column of numeric data type in the table listed in the FROM clause
- *numericExpression* is the numeric value or numeric values connected by arithmetic operators
- Symbol | symbolizes *Or* Boolean operator

To display academic positions, annual average salaries of faculty members in groups based on academic positions and the standard deviation for each group using both facultyX and positionX tables, type and run the following SELECT statement.

```
SELECT academicPosition AS [POSITION], AVG(annualSalary) AS [ANNUAL AVERAGE
SALARY BY POSITION], NZ(STDEV(annualSalary), 0) AS [STANDARD DEVIATION]
FROM facultyX, positionX
WHERE annualSalary BETWEEN minAnnualSalary AND maxAnnualSalary
GROUP BY academicPosition;
```

See result below.

POSITION	ANNUAL AVERAGE SALARY BY POSITION	STANDARD DEVIATION
Assistant Professor	55629.075	1803.01622600852
Associate Professor	62980.25	0
Full Professor	70859.52	2676.71679909051
Instructor	47952.4	2052.76395196818

Notice the standard deviation for the Associate Professor group is nothing or zero (0). There is only one faculty member in that group, and thus, the closeness to the mean is 100%.

> **Note:** Oracle uses STDDEV function to perform standard deviations for numeric data.
>
> Example:
> SELECT academicPosition AS "POSITION", AVG(annualSalary) AS "ANNUAL AVERAGE SALARY BY POSITION", STDDEV(annualSalary) AS "STANDARD DEVIATION"

```
FROM facultyX, positionX
WHERE annualSalary BETWEEN minAnnualSalary AND maxAnnualSalary
GROUP BY academicPosition;
```

VAR (VARP) Function

The VAR (VARP) function determines the variance of a group of numeric values. That is how data values are spaced out in a group or how wide the data values are scattered among themselves. This function performs its calculation using the maximum and minimum values of the specified column as its base of measurement. If data values are in close proximity, the variance is small otherwise the variance is not so small. The basic syntax for the VAR function is similar to that of the STDEV function. Substitute the VAR|VARP keywords for the STDEV|STDEVP keywords to obtain the syntax for the VAR function.

To display academic positions, minimum and maximum annual salaries of faculty members in groups based on academic positions and the variance for each group using both facultyX and positionX tables, type and run the following SELECT statement.

```
SELECT academicPosition AS [POSITION], MIN(annualSalary) AS [SMALLEST VALUE],
MAX(annualSalary) AS [LARGEST VALUE], NZ(VAR(annualSalary), 0) AS [VARIANCE]
FROM facultyX, positionX
WHERE annualSalary BETWEEN minAnnualSalary AND maxAnnualSalary
GROUP BY academicPosition;
```

See result below.

POSITION	SMALLEST VALUE	LARGEST VALUE	VARIANCE
Assistant Professor	54354.15	56904	3250867.51125
Associate Professor	62980.25	62980.25	0
Full Professor	68261.39	74563.55	7164812.82253333
Instructor	45876.25	49980.95	4213839.8425

The variance for the Associate Professor group is nothing or zero (0) since the minimum and maximum values for the group are the same. Notice that the annual salaries of Assistant Professors are closer in number than the annual salaries of Instructors. Similarly, the annual salaries of Instructors are closer in number than that of Full Professors.

> **Note:** Oracle uses VARIANCE function to determine values for variance.
>
> Example:
> SELECT academicPosition AS "POSITION", MIN(annualSalary) AS "SMALLEST VALUE",
> MAX(annualSalary) AS "LARGEST VALUE", VARIANCE(annualSalary) AS "VARIANCE"
> FROM facultyX, positionX
> WHERE annualSalary BETWEEN minAnnualSalary AND maxAnnualSalary
> GROUP BY academicPosition;

FIRST and LAST Functions

The FIRST function returns the first data value as determined by the computer system in a group of values of a specified column, and the LAST function returns the last data value also as determined by the computer system in a group of values of a specified column. In other words, the values returned by the functions are random values. The values are chosen by the computer system arbitrarily and they do not always correspond to the arrangement of data in the specified column.

Multiple-Row Functions and Results Sets

For example, if the first data value in a text column arrangement is "ADA", the FIRST function might display a different value from the column as the first data. To display or return the correct data value of a specific column, include the ORDER BY clause in the SELECT statement that uses the functions.

The basic syntax for these functions is

FIRST | LAST(*existingColumnName* | *dataExpression*)

where

- *existingColumnName* is the column of any data type in the table listed in the FROM clause
- *dataExpression* is either the combination of columns of the same data type or combination of data values to columns of the same data type
- Symbol | symbolizes **Or** Boolean operator

To display the first data value and the last data value of the first name column of faculty members according to the computer system's logical arrangement using the facutyX table, type and run the following SELECT statement.

SELECT FIRST(firstName) AS [FIRST OF FIRST NAME], LAST(FirstName) AS [LAST OF FIRST NAME]
FROM facultyX;

See result below.

FIRST OF FIRST NAME	LAST OF FIRST NAME
Eghosa	Ememgini

HAVING Clause

Like the WHERE clause, the HAVING clause is also a condition clause. Unlike the WHERE clause, the HAVING clause is used to restrict or filter out groups of records that do not meet the specified criteria or conditions. The main difference between the WHERE clause and the HAVING clause is that the WHERE clause is used to restrict individual records while the HAVING clause is used to restrict grouped records. In addition, the HAVING clause works with group functions while the WHERE clause does not support group functions.

The HAVING clause can only be used to restrict grouped records when a SELECT statement includes the GROUP BY clause. You cannot use the HAVING clause without the GROUP BY clause. However, you can use the GROUP BY clause without the HAVING clause. It is fair to say that the HAVING clause works for the GROUP BY clause to display records' groups that meet the specified conditions. The WHERE clause is used to restrict individual records before grouping them and the HAVING clause is used to restrict grouped records after grouping the records. The basic syntax for the HAVING clause is

HAVING *groupFunction*(*existingColumnName*) | *groupFunction*(*columnExpression*) *comparisonOperator existingColumnName* | *value* | *groupFunction*(*existingColumnName* | *columnExpression*)

where

- *groupFunction* is the multiple-row function being used
- *existingColumnName* is the column in the table listed in the FROM clause
- *columnExpression* is the expression formed by combining column(s) with value(s) of the same data type
- *comparisonOperator* is the comparison operator used to establish the restriction
- *value* is the literal constant used in the comparison
- Symbol | symbolizes **Or** Boolean operator

The HAVING clause uses the same comparison and logical operators as the WHERE clause. See figures 3.1, 3.2, 3.3, and 3.4 in chapter three of this textbook to review the operators.

To display academic positions, average annual salaries of faculty members in groups based on academic positions, and the highest paid faculty members whose annual salaries are equal to the average annual salary of the group they belong to using both facultyX and positionX tables, type and run the following SELECT statement.

SELECT academicPosition AS [POSITION], AVG(annualSalary) AS [AVERAGE ANNUAL SALARY], MAX(annualSalary) AS [HIGHEST PAID]
FROM facultyX, positionX
WHERE annualSalary BETWEEN minAnnualSalary AND maxAnnualSalary
GROUP BY academicPosition
HAVING MAX(annualSalary) = AVG(annualSalary);

See result below.

POSITION	AVERAGE ANNUAL SALARY	HIGHEST PAID
Associate Professor	62980.25	62980.25

> **Note:** In its simplest form, the value (being compared) on the left side of the comparison operator in the condition of the HAVING clause must be gotten using a multiple-row function. The value (being compared to) on the right side of the comparison operator in the condition of the HAVING clause can be (i) gotten using a multiple-row function, (ii) a single value, or (iii) an expression that yields a single value.

Nesting Multiple-Row Functions

Like single-row functions, multiple-row functions can be nested. Unlike single-row functions which have no limitation on the degree of depth on which the functions are nested, multiple-row functions, in MS Access SQL, cannot be nested within themselves. However, you can nest multiple-row functions within single-row functions and vice versa.

To display department codes, department names, and the total annual salary for each department formatted to currency and rounded to zero decimal position using both facultyX and departmentX tables, type and run the following SELECT statement.

SELECT F.departmentCode AS [DEPARTMENT CODE], departmentName AS [DEPARTMENT NAME], FORMATCURRENCY(ROUND(SUM(annualSalary), 0), 0) AS [TOTAL ANNUAL SALARY FOR EACH DEPARTMENT]
FROM facultyX F, departmentX D
WHERE F.departmentCode = D.departmentCode
GROUP BY F.departmentCode, departmentName;

Multiple-Row Functions and Results Sets

See result below.

DEPARTMENT CODE	DEPARTMENT NAME	TOTAL ANNUAL SALARY FOR EACH DEPARTMENT
BUSA02	Business Administration	$120,440
CSCM09	Computer Science	$122,616
EDUD05	Education	$112,961
NASC08	Natural Science	$127,665
SOCC06	Social Science	$117,852

Notice that the innermost function of the SELECT statement is the SUM group function and the other two functions are single-row functions. Since FORMATCURRENCY, by default, includes two decimal positions to a displayed value, the rightmost zero in the nested function expression is included in the expression so that the FORMATCURRENCY function displays the result with no decimal positions.

> *Note:* Oracle allows the nesting of multiple-row functions to two-level depth only.
>
> Example:
> SELECT MAX(AVG(annualSalary)) AS "MAXIMUM OF AVERAGE"
> FROM facultyX
> GROUP BY departmentCode;

Summarizing Data for Grouped Records - Results Sets

There are situations when summarized data are needed in results' sets that are based on grouping records and aggregates within tables for statistical purposes. MS Access SQL provides ways of finding totals, subtotals, grand totals, and producing cross tabulations for tables. MS Access SQL also provides ways to understand how summarized data are gotten. In addition, MS Access SQL lists the different sets of groups in a results' set. The results' set is obtained by combining the appropriate SELECT statements with the UNION or UNION ALL operator. The specified SELECT statements must use multiple-row functions and the GROUP BY clause.

> *Note:* In MS Access SQL, a UNION or UNION ALL statement consists of two or more SELECT statements.

The number of columns listed in the GROUP BY clause of the first SELECT statement of the UNION or UNION ALL statement determines how many SELECT statements are needed to achieve the results' set. The logic for accomplishing the operation is that the columns listed in the GROUP BY clause of the succeeding SELECT statement must be one less than the columns listed in the GROUP BY clause of the previous SELECT statement and in that order until the last SELECT statement of the UNION or UNION ALL statement is written.

The elimination or removal of columns must be done from right to left and the removed columns must be replaced with either a NULL keyword for a null value, a numeric value, a text value, or a date value in the SELECT clause of that particular SELECT statement. However, these values must be chosen with care to reflect meaningful interpretations of the displayed results. The last SELECT statement of the UNION or UNION ALL statement must be grouped either by the NULL keyword to represent null values, positions of numeric data values, positions of text data values, or positions of date data values in the SELECT clause of the last SELECT statement.

The ORDER BY clause can be used to reorganize the results of the operation. Sorting must be done using the columns listed in the SELECT clause of the first SELECT statement of the UNION or UNION ALL statement. If reorganizing the results' set is done by using the last SELECT statement of the UNION or UNION ALL statement, use columns' positions with MS Access 2003 to display more accurate representations of the results' set. You can use columns and columns' positions with any other existing MS Access versions.

When summarizing data for grouping and aggregates, the actual arguments of multiple-row functions listed in the SELECT clause of a SELECT statement cannot be used in the GROUP BY clause of that statement, otherwise the wrong results' set is generated. The basic syntax for UNION or UNION ALL operator is discussed in chapter four of this textbook.

Finding Totals, Subtotals, and Grand Totals

To generate totals, subtotals, and grand totals, the number of SELECT statements needed in the UNION or UNION ALL statement is equal to the number of columns listed in the GROUP BY clause of the first SELECT statement of the UNION or UNION ALL statement plus one $(k + 1)$

where

k represents the number of columns listed in the GROUP BY clause of the first SELECT statement.

The number of groupings obtained is also $k + 1$. The number of UNION or UNION ALL operators needed to combine the SELECT statements is equal to the number of columns (k) listed in the GROUP BY clause.

> *Note:* The UNION or UNION ALL operator and GROUP BY clause become more complex and time consuming as the number of columns listed in the GROUP BY clause increases. With this approach, the system searches through all the tables listed in the SELECT statements. Remember that the UNION operator eliminates records' duplication, therefore, to avoid unnecessary removal of records from a results' set, you should always include primary key columns in the operation when using the UNION operator to obtain the needed result.

Generating Totals

Finding total is calculating and displaying the sum of individual numeric column entries.

To display faculty members' identification numbers, their annual salaries, and the total annual salary for all faculty members using the facultyX table, type and run the following UNION ALL statement.

```
SELECT facultyId AS FACULTY_ID, SUM(annualSalary) AS ANNUAL_SALARY
FROM facultyX
GROUP BY facultyId
UNION ALL
SELECT "TOTAL", SUM(annualSalary)
FROM facultyX
GROUP BY 1;
```

Multiple-Row Functions and Results Sets

See partial result below.

FACULTY_ID	ANNUAL_SALARY
AL501828	54354.80078125
DM674543	62980.25
:	:
:	:
RU123098	70760.1484375
ZM567123	49980.94921875
TOTAL	601532.9453125

Grouping 1 - faculty records or regular records

Grouping 2 - summary record (sum)

In the UNION ALL statement, one column (facultyId) is listed in the GROUP BY clause of the first SELECT statement, therefore, two SELECT statements are needed for the operation and two groupings are displayed - regular faculty records from the facultyX table and the calculated total for the annual salaries of all faculty members. The SUM function is used with the column called annualSalary to find the total annual salary for the faculty members. The column expression "TOTAL" of the second SELECT statement is not a column in the facultyX table. However, it reflects what the last row of the result represents. Usually, to display a single total for records in a table, you need only one column to be listed in the GROUP BY clause of the first SELECT statement of the UNION or UNION ALL statement.

The following UNION ALL statement uses three SELECT statements to generate the same result as the last UNION ALL statement, even though only one column is listed in the GROUP BY clause of the first SELECT statement. The middle SELECT statement is used to include a null record for readability purposes only and, therefore, it does not contain actual columns. Without including the box and comment of the second SELECT statement, type and run the following UNION ALL statement

```
SELECT facultyId AS FACULTY_ID, SUM(annualSalary) AS ANNUAL_SALARY
FROM facultyX
GROUP BY facultyId
UNION ALL
    SELECT NULL, NULL
    FROM facultyX
    GROUP BY NULL
UNION ALL
SELECT "TOTAL", SUM(annualSalary)
FROM facultyX
GROUP BY 1;
```

Included for readability purposes

See partial result below.

FACULTY_ID	ANNUAL_SALARY
EE987654	68261
JH682508	48000
:	:
:	:
JS994450	45876.25
PD002312	56904
TOTAL	601532.9453125

NULL record to separate summary record (sum) from regular records

163

> **Note:** Oracle uses ROLLUP operator with the GROUP BY clause to generate Total result set.
>
> Example:
> SELECT facultyId AS FACULTY_ID, SUM(annualSalary) AS SALARY
> FROM facultyX
> GROUP BY ROLLUP (facultyId);

Generating Subtotals and Grand Totals

Subtotals are subsets of grand totals and grand totals are gotten by adding subtotals. To generate subtotals and grand totals, two or more columns must be listed in the GROUP BY clause of the first SELECT statement of the UNION ALL statement.

To display faculty members' departments, their identification numbers, their annual salaries, and their total annual salaries based on departments along with the grand total for all faculty members using both departmentX and facultyX tables, type and run the following UNION ALL statement.

```
SELECT departmentName AS DEPARTMENT, facultyId AS FACULTY_ID, NULL AS
SUMMARY, SUM(annualSalary) AS SALARY
FROM facultyX F, departmentX D
WHERE F.departmentCode = D.departmentCode
GROUP BY departmentName, facultyId
UNION ALL
SELECT departmentName, NULL, "Subtotal", SUM(annualSalary)
FROM facultyX F, departmentX D
WHERE F.departmentCode = D.departmentCode
GROUP BY departmentName
UNION ALL
SELECT NULL, NULL, "Grand Total", SUM(annualSalary)
FROM facultyX
GROUP BY NULL
ORDER BY 1 DESC, 2 DESC;
```

See partial result below.

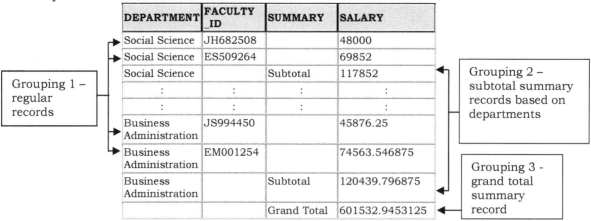

DEPARTMENT	FACULTY_ID	SUMMARY	SALARY
Social Science	JH682508		48000
Social Science	ES509264		69852
Social Science		Subtotal	117852
:	:	:	:
:	:	:	:
Business Administration	JS994450		45876.25
Business Administration	EM001254		74563.546875
Business Administration		Subtotal	120439.796875
		Grand Total	601532.9453125

Grouping 1 – regular records

Grouping 2 – subtotal summary records based on departments

Grouping 3 - grand total summary record

The results' set is displayed using the following data arrangements. Grouping 1 displays regular records from the tables. Grouping 2 shows the subtotal for each group and grouping 3 shows the grand total of all the groups.

Multiple-Row Functions and Results Sets

> **Note:** Oracle uses ROLLUP operator with the GROUP BY clause to generate Subtotal and Grand Total results' sets.
>
> Example:
> SELECT departmentCode AS DEPARTMENT, facultyId AS FACULTY_ID, SUM(annualSalary)
> AS SALARY
> FROM facultyX
> GROUP BY ROLLUP (departmentCode, facultyId);

Generating Cross-tabulation Results Sets

Cross-tabulation results' sets are sets gotten by the possible combinations of columns listed in the GROUP BY clause of the first SELECT statement. Cross-tabulation, in addition to extra records, produces subtotals and a grand total. Possible columns' combinations of the columns listed in the GROUP BY clause of the first SELECT statement are used to produce the results' sets. The formula for achieving cross-tabulation is 2^k (2 raised to power k). k is the number of columns listed in the GROUP BY clause of the first SELECT statement.

For example, if the number of columns listed in the GROUP BY clause is 2, therefore, k is also 2. The total number of SELECT statements that is involved in the operation is 2^2 (2 * 2). This means that four SELECT statements are required for the UNION or UNION ALL statement. The number of possible combinations for the results' sets is also four. Again, the number of UNION or UNION ALL operators to be used is one less than the total number of SELECT statements in the UNION or UNION ALL statement.

To display department names, the annual salary for each academic position within the department, the average annual salary for each department, the average annual salary for every position irrespective of the department, and the average salary for all departments using facultyX, departmentX, and positionX tables, type and run the following UNION ALL statement.

SELECT   departmentName   AS   DEPARTMENT, academicPosition   AS   POSITION,
AVG(annualSalary) AS AVERAGE_SALARY
FROM facultyX F, departmentX D, positionX P
WHERE F.departmentCode = D.departmentCode
AND annualSalary BETWEEN minAnnualSalary AND maxAnnualSalary
GROUP BY departmentName, academicPosition
UNION ALL
SELECT departmentName, NULL, AVG(annualSalary)
FROM facultyX F, departmentX D, positionX P
WHERE F.departmentCode = D.departmentCode
AND annualSalary BETWEEN minAnnualSalary AND maxAnnualSalary
GROUP BY departmentName
UNION ALL
SELECT NULL, academicPosition, AVG(annualSalary)
FROM facultyX, positionX
WHERE annualSalary BETWEEN minAnnualSalary AND maxAnnualSalary
GROUP BY academicPosition
UNION
SELECT NULL, NULL, AVG(annualSalary)
FROM facultyX
GROUP BY NULL
ORDER BY 1 DESC, 2 DESC;

Chapter Seven

See partial result below.

DEPARTMENT	POSITION	AVERAGE_SALARY
Natural Science	Full Professor	70760.1484375
Natural Science	Assistant Professor	56904
Natural Science		63832.07421875
:	:	:
:	:	:
computer science	Full Professor	68261
computer science	Assistant Professor	54354.80078125
Computer science		61307.900390625
	Instructor	47952.3997395833
	Full Professor	70859.173828125
	Associate Professor	62980.25
	Assistant Professor	55629.400390625
		60153.29453125

Grouping 1 – regular records

Grouping 2 – sub-average summary records

Grouping 3 – cross-tabulation records

Grouping 4 – grand average summary record

Grouping 3 is the additional rows created by the cross-tabulation operation. These additional rows are called cross-tabulation records and in the result of the query, they display the average annual salaries for Instructors, Full Professors, Associate Professors, and Assistant Professors respectively.

> **Note:** Oracle uses CUBE operator with the GROUP BY clause to generate Cross-tabulation result set.
>
> Example:
> SELECT departmentCode AS DEPARTMENT, facultyId AS FACULTY_ID, AVG(annualSalary) AS AVSALARY
> FROM facultyX
> GROUP BY CUBE (departmentCode, facultyId);

Generating Results Sets for Multiple Columns Grouping Using One Statement

MS Access SQL allows the generating of different results' sets by grouping columns and using one UNION or one UNION ALL statement. This type of query assists in analyzing data produced by grouping columns listed in the SELECT clause of the first SELECT statement to several groups.

The number of columns that is listed in the SELECT clause of the first SELECT statement determines the number of SELECT statements needed in the UNION or UNION ALL statement. The number of columns also determines the total number of results' sets for all the columns' groups. The number of UNION or UNION ALL operators needed in the operation is always one less than the number of columns listed in the SELECT clause of the first SELECT statement.

To display department names and faculty academic positions within each department as one column group and display faculty academic positions, faculty identification numbers, and their annual salaries as another column group using departmentX, facultyX, and positionX tables, type and run the following UNION ALL statement.

SELECT D.departmentName AS DEPARTMENT, P.academicPosition AS POSITION, NULL AS ID, NULL AS SALLARY
FROM departmentX D, facultyX F, positionX P
WHERE F.departmentCode = D.departmentCode
AND F.annualSalary BETWEEN P.minAnnualSalary AND P.maxAnnualSalary
GROUP BY D.departmentName, P.academicPosition

Multiple-Row Functions and Results Sets

```
UNION ALL
SELECT NULL, P.academicPosition, F.facultyId, SUM(annualSalary)
FROM facultyX F, positionX P
WHERE F.annualSalary BETWEEN P.minAnnualSalary AND P.maxAnnualSalary
GROUP BY P.academicPosition, F.facultyId
ORDER BY 1 DESC, 2 DESC;
```

See partial result below.

DEPARTMENT	POSITION	ID	SALLARY
Education	Instructor		
Education	Associate Professor		
⋮	⋮	⋮	⋮
⋮	⋮	⋮	⋮
	Assistant Professor	AL501828	54354.80078125
	Assistant Professor	PD002312	56904

Grouping 1 – department and position grouping

Grouping 2 – position and faculty ID grouping

The result is divided into two different column groupings. Notice that the columns in the SELECT clause of the first SELECT statement are departmentName and academicPosition. These columns formed the first column group. The third and the fourth columns in that SELECT clause are null columns. The second column group is formed by academicPosition and facultyId columns of the SELECT clause of the second SELECT statement. The second SELECT statement also displays the annual salary for each faculty member using the SUM group function.

> **Note:** Oracle uses GROUPING SETS operator with the GROUP BY clause to generate results' sets for multiple columns' groupings using one statement.
>
> Example:
> SELECT departmentCode AS DEPARTMENT, chairId AS CHAIRPERSON_ID, facultyId AS FACULTY_ID, SUM(annualSalary) AS SALARY
> FROM facultyX
> GROUP BY GROUPING SETS ((departmentCode, chairId), (chairId, facultyId));

Generating Results Sets for Composite Columns

MS Access SQL also allows the computations of composite columns. The number of SELECT statements that is required for the operation is equal to the number of columns listed in the SELECT clause of the first SELECT statement. The number of results' set grouping is equal to the number of SELECT statements required. As always, the number of UNION or UNION ALL operators is one less than the number of SELECT statements that is needed in the UNION or UNION ALL statement.

Composite Columns: A composite column is a collection or group of columns that are treated as a unit. The columns that make up a composite column behave as a single column and generate a single value.

To display department codes, faculty academic positions in each department, the chairperson's identification number for faculty members in each department, the annual salaries' subtotal for faculty members within a department, and the annual salaries' grand total for all department using both facultyX and positionX tables, type and run the following UNION ALL statement

```
SELECT F.departmentCode AS DEPARTMENT, P.academicPosition AS POSITION,
F.chairId AS CHAIRED_BY, SUM(F.annualSalary) AS ANNUAL_SALLARY
FROM facultyX F, positionX P
```

167

WHERE F.annualSalary BETWEEN P.minAnnualSalary AND P.maxAnnualSalary
GROUP BY F.departmentCode, P.academicPosition, F.chairId
UNION ALL
SELECT F.departmentCode, NULL, NULL, SUM(F.annualSalary)
FROM facultyX F
GROUP BY F.departmentCode
UNION ALL
SELECT NULL, NULL, NULL, SUM(F.annualSalary)
FROM facultyX F
GROUP BY NULL
ORDER BY 1 DESC, 2 DESC, 3 DESC;

See partial result below.

DEPARTMENT	POSITION	CHAIRED_BY	ANNUAL_SALLARY
NASC08	Full Professor		70760.1484375
NASC08	Assistant Professor	RU123098	56904
NASC08			127664.1484375
:	:	:	:
:	:	:	:
BUSA02	Instructor	EM001254	45876.25
BUSA02	Full Professor		74563.546875
BUSA02			120439.796875
			601532.9453125

Grouping 1 – regular records

Grouping 2 – subtotal summary records

Grouping 3 – grand total summary record

Note: Oracle uses ROLLUP operator with the GROUP BY clause to generate results' set for composite columns.

Example:
SELECT departmentCode AS DEPARTMENT, chairId AS CHAIRPERSON_ID, facultyId AS FACULTY_ID, AVG(annualSalary) AS AVSALARY
FROM facultyX
GROUP BY ROLLUP (departmentCode, (chairId, facultyId));

The academicPosition and chairId columns are the composite column in the UNION ALL statement. Notice that the two columns are replaced with null values in the SELECT clause of the second SELECT statement. That is an indication that the two columns constitute a composite column. The third column (CHAIRED_BY), besides the null entries recorded in the column for the subtotal rows and the grand total row, where identification numbers are missing indicates that those professors are department chairpersons.

Generating Results Sets By Concatenating Columns
Results' sets can be obtained by concatenating columns to form different concatenated groupings. Combining or concatenating columns to generate tables' data for analysis is one method for producing the needed results' sets

To display, in different groupings, department codes, chairpersons' identification numbers, and faculty identification numbers in each department, and the average annual salary for faculty members within a department using the facultyX, type and run the following UNION ALL statement

```
SELECT departmentCode, chairId, facultyId, AVG(annualSalary) AS [AVERAGE
ANNUAL SALARY]
FROM facultyX
GROUP BY departmentCode, chairId, facultyId
UNION ALL
SELECT departmentCode, chairId, null, AVG(annualSalary)
FROM facultyX
GROUP BY departmentCode, chairId
UNION ALL
SELECT departmentCode, null, facultyId, AVG(annualSalary)
FROM facultyX
GROUP BY departmentCode, facultyId
UNION ALL
SELECT departmentCode, NULL, NULL, AVG(annualSalary)
FROM facultyX
GROUP BY departmentCode
UNION ALL
SELECT NULL, NULL, NULL, NULL
FROM facultyX
GROUP BY NULL
ORDER BY 1 DESC, 2 DESC, 3 DESC;
```

See partial result below.

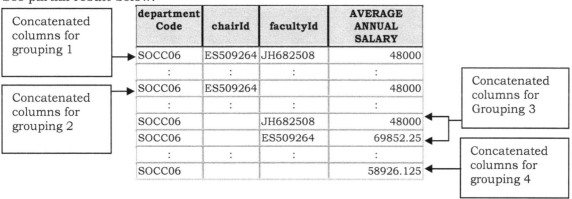

Notice the different columns' combination for each grouping in the results' set. Grouping 4 displays the average annual salary for the particular department. The last SELECT statement in the UNION ALL statement can be omitted since it does not display actual data value(s). The ORDER BY clause is used for rearranging the results' set.

Note: Oracle uses ROLLUP and CUBE operators with the GROUP BY clause to generate results' set for concatenated columns.

Example:
```
SELECT          departmentCode,    chairId,    facultyId,    AVG(annualSalary)    AS
AVERAGE_ANNUAL_SALARY
FROM facultyX
GROUP BY departmentCode, ROLLUP (chairId), CUBE(facultyId);
```

Chapter Summary

This chapter explains multiple-row functions which are also called group, aggregate, statistics, or summary functions. The chapter demonstrates how these functions are used with numeric, text, and date data types, and the degree in which the functions can

Chapter Seven

be nested. The chapter also uncovers two new clauses and their functional activities in SQL programming. The clauses are GROUP BY and HAVING clauses. Finally, the chapter shows and demonstrates how to summarize and aggregate data such as subtotals, grand totals, and cross tabulations for grouped records.

Multiple-Row Functions Syntax and SQL Statements Summary

The table below presents the multiple-row functions' syntax, and the GROUP BY clause syntax and the HAVING clause syntax discussed in this chapter and the SQL statements' examples for retrieving data from tables.

Clause Type	Clause Syntax	Clause and Statement Example
GROUP BY clause is used to group records	GROUP BY *existingColumnName* | *columnPosition*, ...	GROUP BY chairId SELECT MIN(annualSalary) AS MIN_SAL, MAX(annualSalary) AS MAX_SAL FROM facultyX, positionX WHERE annualSalary BETWEEN minAnnualSalary AND maxAnnualSalary GROUP BY academicPosition;
HAVING clause is used to restrict groups of records after the records have being grouped	HAVING *groupFunction(existingColumnName)* | *groupFunction(columnExpression)* *comparisonOperator* *existingColumnName* | *value* | *groupFunction(existingColumnName* | *columnExpression)*	HAVING MAX(annualSalary) = AVG(annualSalary) SELECT AVG(annualSalary) AS AVG_SAL, MAX(annualSalary) AS MAX_SAL FROM facultyX, positionX WHERE annualSalary BETWEEN minAnnualSalary AND maxAnnualSalary GROUP BY academicPosition HAVING MAX(annualSalary) = AVG(annualSalary);
Description	**Function General Syntax**	**Function Example**
A function is a block of programming instructions that performs a specific task	*functionName([actualArgument],...)*	DATE() Or SUM(annualSalary)
A nonargument-based function is a function that requires no actual arguments	*functionName()*	TIME()
An argument-based function is a function that requires actual arguments	*functionName(actualArgument,...)*	AVG(annualSalary)
Function Name and Description	**Function Syntax**	**Statement Example**
SUM function is used to return the total value of a collection of numeric values	SUM(*existingColumnName* | *numericExpression*)	SELECT SUM(annualSalary) AS SAL_TOTAL FROM facultyX;
AVG function is used to return the average value of a collection of numeric values	AVG(*existingColumnName* | *numericExpression*)	SELECT AVG(annualSalary) AS SAL_AVERAGE FROM facultyX;
COUNT function is used to return the number of records in a table	COUNT(*existingColumnName* | *)	SELECT COUNT(initial) AS STUD_INITIAL, COUNT(*) AS TOTAL_RECORD FROM studentX;
MAX function is used to return the highest value among a collection of values	MAX(*existingColumnName* | *dataExpression*)	SELECT MAX(initial) AS MAX_INITIAL FROM studentX;

Multiple-Row Functions and Results Sets

MIN function is used to return the lowest value among a collection of values	MIN(*existingColumnName dataExpression*)		SELECT MIN(initial) AS MIN_INITIAL FROM studentX;
STDEV(STDEVP) function is used to compute the standard deviation for a group of numeric values	STDEV|STDEVP(*existingColumnName numericExpression*)		SELECT AVG(annualSalary) AS [AAVERAGE], STDEV(annualSalary) AS [SDEVIATION] FROM facultyX, positionX WHERE annualSalary BETWEEN minAnnualSalary AND maxAnnualSalary GROUP BY academicPosition;
VAR(VARP) function is used to determine the variance for a group of numeric values	VAR|VARP(*existingColumnName numericExpression*)		SELECT MIN(annualSalary) AS MIN_SAL, MAX(annualSalary) AS MAX_SAL, VAR(annualSalary) AS G_VARIANCE FROM facultyX, positionX WHERE annualSalary BETWEEN minAnnualSalary AND maxAnnualSalary GROUP BY academicPosition;
FIRST function is used to return the first value in a group of values as determined by the computer system	FIRST(*existingColumnName dataExpression*)		SELECT FIRST(firstName) AS FIRST_NAME FROM studentX;
LAST function is used to return the last value in a group of values as determined by the computer system	LAST(*existingColumnName dataExpression*)		SELECT LAST(firstName) AS LAST_NAME FROM studentX;

Key Terms

AVG
Composite columns
COUNT
Cross-tabulation
FIRST
GROUP BY clause
HAVING clause
LAST
MAX

MIN
Multiple-row functions
Results' set
STDEV(STDEVP)
SUM
Summarizing data
UNION ALL
VAR(VARP)

Chapter Review Questions

Multiple Choice Questions

1. Which of the following multiple-row functions does not ignore null values?
   - a. STDEV( ).
   - b. MAX( ).
   - c. AVG( ).
   - d. COUNT(*).

2. The _____ function can only be applied to numeric data values.
   - a. VAR
   - b. MIN
   - c. LAST
   - d. FIRST

3. Multiple-row functions work on
   - a. an individual record.
   - b. groups of records.
   - c. all of the above.
   - d. none of the above.

4. Which of the following names is not used for multiple-row functions?
    a. aggregate function.
    b. statistics function.
    c. binary function.
    d. summary function.

5. To return the number of records in a table, you use the _____ function.
    a. SUM
    b. COUNT
    c. ADD
    d. MAX

6. In MS Access SQL, aliases cannot be used in a _____ clause.
    a. SELECT
    b. FROM
    c. GROUP BY
    d. none of the above

7. In MS Access SQL, the HAVING clause can be used in a SELECT statement only when the _____ clause is used.
    a. GROUP BY
    b. ORDER BY
    c. WHERE
    d. none of the above

8. Multiple-row functions can be nested within
    a. multiple-row functions.
    b. single-row functions.
    c. two depth-level of multiple-row functions.
    d. all of the above.

9. In MS Access SQL, a results' set is achieved by combining the appropriate SELECT statements with the _____ operator.
    a. PROJECT
    b. SELECT
    c. INTERSECT
    d. UNION

10. In MS Access SQL, if the number of columns listed in the GROUP BY clause of the first SELECT statement is two, how many SELECT statements are needed to calculate total (sum)?
    a. one.
    b. two.
    c. three.
    d. four.

True or False Questions

11. Multiple-row functions are group functions.
    a. True
    b. False

12. A COUNT function that uses an existing column as its actual argument returns the number of records that have non-null values in that column.
    a. True
    b. False

13. The MIN function returns the value of the highest measure.
    - a. True
    - b. False

14. Grouped records in MS Access SQL must share common characteristics.
    - a. True
    - b. False

15. The HAVING clause is not a condition clause.
    - a. True
    - b. False

16. A composite column is a group of columns that are treated as a unit.
    - a. True
    - b. False

17. In MS Access SQL, to determine how data are spaced out in a group, you use the STDEVP function.
    - a. Tue
    - b. False

Fill in the blank Questions

18. A data value supplied to a function to use to perform its assigned task is called a(n) _____.

19. The COUNT function that does not ignore null values is the _____.

20. Grouped records share _____.

21. The _____ function is used to determine how data are spaced in a group.

22. In MS Access SQL, to achieve a results' set, you use _____ operator.

23. Multiple-row functions are also called _____ functions.

Essay Type Questions

24. State the similarities and differences between the WHERE clause and the HAVING clause?

25. Explain cross-tabulation results' sets and what is the main purpose of the results' sets?

26. Explain the function of the GROUP BY clause and write a valid SELECT statement that supports your explanation?

27. How does the group function called FIRST behave in a SELECT statement that contains the ORDER BY clause and how does the function behave when the clause is omitted from the statement?

28. Define a numeric multiple-row function and list two functions to support your definition?

Hands-on Activities

Study the structures and the data of **AcademicX** database tables in appendix A (pages 355 through 360) and perform the following hands-on exercises.

1. Write a SELECT statement to display how many academic positions exist. Assign column alias **NumberOfAcademicPosition** to the column that displays the result.

2. Display the total number of books that have titles that begin with the letter "P". Assign column alias of your choice.

3. Write a SQL statement to display both the total cost and the total retail price of books. Format the results to currency with leading dollar symbols ($) and to two decimal positions. Assign columns' aliases of your choice.

4. Write a SQL statement to display both the maximum cost and the minimum cost of computer science textbooks. Assign column alias *MaximumValue* to the maximum value and column alias *MinimumValue* to the minimum value.

5. Display twenty percent (20%) of the total selling prices of all textbooks in each group. The result should be sorted in ascending order and displayed in currency with leading dollar symbol ($) and to zero decimal position. Assign column alias *20_Percent* to the column that displays the result..

6. Display academic positions and sums of annual salaries of faculty members in each academic position. Format the sums of the annual salaries to include leading dollar signs ($), commas, and two decimal positions using the FORMAT function. Assign column alias *Position* to the academic position column and column alias *AnnualSalaryByPosition* to the salary column.

7. Write a SQL statement to perform the same operation as in question 6, but to display the information for each group where the total annual salary for that group is less than $150,000.

8. Using the INNER JOIN...ON clause, other appropriate clauses (except for the WHERE clause), and the FORMATCURRENCY function, display total and average annual salaries of faculty members who are also students in each academic position. Format the results to one decimal position. Assign columns' aliases of your choice.

9. Using the WHERE clause and other appropriate clauses (except for the INNER JOIN...ON clause), write a SQL statement to display the identification number of each student and the total number of letter grades of the letter "A" and of the letter "B" he or she has earned so far if the student has earned two or more letter grades of the letter "B" or better. Assign column alias *GoodLetterGrades* to the total number of letter grades' column.

10. Write a SELECT statement to display each student identification number, the letter grade if the student has earned the letter grade "A" in any course, the total number (subtotal) of the letter grade "A" the student has earned so far, and the total number (grand total) of the letter grade "A" for all students who have earned that letter grade. Assign columns' aliases of your choice.

Chapter Eight

Subqueries

Chapter Objectives
After completing this chapter, you should be able to
- Understand subqueries
- Define functions of subqueries
- Use single-row subqueries
- Use multiple-row subqueries
- Use multiple-column subqueries
- Avoid NULL values in subqueries
- Use IS NULL operator in subqueries
- Distinguish between correlated and uncorrelated subqueries
- Nest subqueries

Nested Queries
A nested query also called a subquery is a SELECT statement that is nested or embedded within a clause of another SQL statement. A subquery can be placed inside (i) another SELECT statement, (ii) a SELECT...INTO statement, (iii) an INSERT...INTO statement, (iv) a DELETE statement, or (v) an UPDATE statement. Usually, a subquery is connected to the statement that contains it through the condition clauses - WHERE and HAVING, but there are times when the link between a subquery and the SELECT statement that contains it is established through the SELECT clause and/or through the FROM clause of the SELECT statement

> **Note:** When a query is placed inside another SELECT statement, the query is called a subquery and the SELECT statement that contains it is called an outer query, a main query, or a parent query. A subquery can also be referred to as inner query, inner SELECT statement, nested SELECT statement, or sub-SELECT statement.

Although subqueries can be embedded into other SQL statements, however, the focus of this chapter is to discuss subqueries that are contained or nested inside other SELECT statements. That is queries within other queries. You should remember that a query is a SELECT statement.

A subquery is a valid SELECT statement that does not include the ORDER BY clause. A subquery must be enclosed in a pair of parentheses to separate it from the SELECT statement (outer query) that contains it. A subquery must be placed on the right side of the comparison operator when it is connected to a SELECT statement (outer query) with a WHERE clause or a HAVING clause.

Functions of Subqueries
A subquery is used to determine data values that are not known to the user, but the values exist in the table being queried. A subquery uses values in columns of a table to display data values that exist in the database. Again, the values are not known to the user querying the database table. Usually, a subquery is first evaluated before the outer query is evaluated and the data values retrieved by the subquery are used as an input to the outer query. The outer query uses the input to display the needed records. However, when a subquery is connected to the outer query using the WHERE clause or

Subqueries

the HAVING clause, the result(s) returned by the subquery are used to complete the clause condition.

The basic syntax for a subquery statement using an outer query as part of the syntax is

SELECT [predicate] {[ALL] * | *existingColumnName*, ... | *columnExpression*, ...}
FROM *existingTableName*
WHERE *existingColumnName*, ... *subqueryOperator* (SELECT *existingColumnName*, ...
FROM *existingTableName*);

where

- Predicate is a condition keyword, such as DISTINCT, used to restrict records
- Symbol * is to include all columns
- *existingColumnName* is the column in the table listed in the FROM clause
- *columnExpression* is the expression formed by the combination of column(s) and data value(s). The column(s) and the data used in a column expression must be of the same data type
- *existingTableName* is the table that contains the column to be displayed
- *subqueryOperator* is the comparison operator used to connect the subquery to the outer query
- Symbols [ ] mean item is optional
- Symbol | symbolizes **Or** Boolean operator. You can also list both *existingColumnName* and *columnExpression* or both * and *columnExpression* in the SELECT clause of the statement
- Symbols ... mean more columns and/or columns' expressions can be listed

In the syntax, the SELECT statement that is enclosed in a pair of parentheses is the subquery.

There are three types of subqueries. They are single-row subquery, multiple-row subquery, and multiple-column subquery. These subqueries can further be classified into correlated and uncorrelated subqueries.

Single-Row Subqueries

A single-row subquery is used to return a single record that is used as the input to the outer or parent query when the result of the outer query is based on a single unknown value. The single value may not be known to the user, but the value exists in the table that is being queried. The result returned by the subquery must be a single-value or one-column entry record. The outer query uses the record to generate the final output which can be one or more records of one or several columns. Comparison operators also called relational operators are used to connect a single-row subquery to the outer query. In the subquery environment, these operators are called single-row operators.

Figure 8.1 lists the six single-row operators used to create single-row subqueries.

Figure 8.1

Single-Row Operator	Interpretation
=	Used to determine whether the value that is being tested in the condition clause of the outer query is equal to the value returned by a subquery
>	Used to determine whether the value that is being tested in the condition clause of the outer query is greater than the value returned by a subquery

176

Chapter Eight

Single-Row Operator	Interpretation
<	Used to determine whether the value that is being tested in the condition clause of the outer query is less than the value returned by a subquery
>=	Used to determine whether the value that is being tested in the condition clause of the outer query is greater than or equal to the value returned by a subquery
<=	Used to determine whether the value that is being tested in the condition clause of the outer query is less or equal to the value returned by a subquery
<>	Used to determine whether the value that is being tested in the condition clause of the outer query is different from (not equal to) the value returned by a subquery

The value returned by the subquery is the value on the right side of the single-row operator and it is the value that other values are compared to in the condition clause of the outer query. In other words, the value is the base on which the data of the column listed in the condition clause of the outer query is judged.

> **Note:** Oracle uses two additional sets of symbols to denote the Not Equal To operator. The two sets of symbols are != and ^=.

A single-row subquery can be placed in the WHERE clause, the HAVING clause, and the SELECT clause of a SELECT statement.

Single-Row Subquery Placed in WHERE Clause
The WHERE clause is a condition clause that is used to remove individual records that fail to meet the condition specified in the WHERE clause of the outer query from being part of the result. When a single-row subquery is placed in a WHERE clause, only the outer query records which columns' values correspond to the condition set by using the single value returned by the subquery are displayed. When a subquery is placed in the condition clause of the outer query, the column listed in the SELECT clause of the subquery must be structural compatible in definition to the column listed in the condition clause of the outer query.

The following SELECT statement is used as a subquery in the subsequent SELECT statement. First let's display, among other data, the annual salary for the faculty member whose identification number is "EE987654" using the SELECT statement. The faculty member's annual salary is use as the base for comparing other faculty members annual salaries later.

To display the annual salary of the faculty member whose identification number is "EE987654", using the facultyX table, type and run the following SELECT statement.

SELECT facultyId AS [FACULTY ID], FORMATCURRENCY(annualSalary) AS [ANNUAL INCOME]
FROM facultyX
WHERE facultyId = "EE987654";

See result below.

FACULTY ID	ANNUAL INCOME
EE987654	$68,261.39

Notice the annual salary of the queried faculty member. The salary is used as the result of the subquery in the following SELECT statement.

177

Subqueries

To display last names, first names, middle names' initials, and annual salaries of faculty members whose annual salaries are higher than the annual salary of the faculty member whose identification number is "EE987654" using the facultyX table, type and run the following SELECT statement.

```
SELECT lastName AS [LAST NAME], firstName AS [FIRST NAME], NZ(initial, "") AS
[MIDDLE INITIAL], FORMATCURRENCY(annualSalary) AS [ANNUAL INCOME]
FROM facultyX
WHERE annualSalary > (SELECT annualSalary
                FROM facultyX
                WHERE facultyId = "EE987654");
```

See result below.

LAST NAME	FIRST NAME	MIDDLE INITIAL	ANNUAL INCOME
Maklasi	Eghosa		$74,563.55
Ugboma	Rischi	B	$70,760.89
Stevenson	Euhan	S	$69,852.25

In the SELECT statement, the subquery is evaluated first to determine the annual salary of the faculty member with the identification number "EE987654". The result is then used to determine those faculty members whose annual salaries are higher than that of the faculty member with identification number "EE987654".

Notice that the subquery is placed on the right side of the single-row operator in the WHERE clause of the outer query, and as such, the single value generated by the subquery is also placed on the right side of the operator to complete the WHERE condition of the outer query. In this situation, the annual salary of faculty member with identification number "EE987654" is used to complete the condition of the WHERE clause of the outer query.

Also notice that the column called annualSalary appeared in both the WHERE clause of the outer query and in the SELECT clause of the subquery. That is the usual method of connecting the subquery to the outer query. The connection arrangement is that the structural definition of the columns in those clauses must be identical.

> **Note:** An error occurs when a single-row subquery tries to generate more than one record as the intending result. One way to avoid single-row subquery errors is to use columns where individual values or combination of values are unique (not duplicated) in the condition clause of the subquery as in the last SELECT statement.

Single-Row Subquery Placed in HAVING Clause
The HAVING clause is a condition clause that is used to remove grouped records that fail to meet the condition specified in the HAVING clause of the outer query from being part of the result. When a single-row subquery is placed in a HAVING clause, only the grouped records of the outer query which columns' values correspond to the condition set by using the single value returned by the subquery are displayed. Anytime the value returned by a single-row subquery is to be compared with a group function, that comparison must be performed by using the HAVING condition clause.

To display department codes and average annual salaries grouped by department codes for those departments which average annual salaries are greater than the annual salary of the faculty member whose identification number is "DM674543" using the facultyX table, type and run the following SELECT statement.

SELECT departmentCode AS [DEPATMENT CODE], FORMAT(AVG(annualSalary), "$###,###.00") AS [AVERAGE ANNUAL SALARY]
FROM facultyX
GROUP BY departmentCode
HAVING AVG(annualSalary) > (SELECT annualSalary
                FROM facultyX
                WHERE facultyId = "DM674543");

See result below.

DEPATMENT CODE	AVERAGE ANNUAL SALARY
NASC08	$63,832.45

The result indicates that the average annual salary for faculty members in the Natural Science department (NASC08) is higher than the annual salary of the faculty member whose identification number is "DM674543".

You might have noticed that the column in the SELECT clause of the subquery is not an actual argument of a group function. It is not enclosed in a pair of parentheses and it is not preceded by a function name. It is a column by itself. This is due to the fact that the subquery is generating a value for a single record - faculty member with the identification number of "DM674543". You could have obtained the same result if the column is used as an actual argument with a group function such as SUM, AVG, MAX, and MIN. Since the value that is being determined is a single value, any of the appropriate group functions will have the same effect.

Single-Row Subquery Placed in SELECT Clause
In addition to using the conditions' clauses, a single-row subquery can also be embedded in the SELECT clause of a SELECT statement. However, the record generated by the subquery is duplicated for every record that is displayed by the outer query. Nesting a single-row subquery in the SELECT clause of a SELECT statement is usually for statistical comparisons only.

> **Note:** When single-row subqueries are placed inside the SELECT clause of a SELECT statement, the subqueries must be separated from one another and from columns listed in the SELECT clause by commas.

To display identification numbers, annual salaries, and the average annual salary for all faculty members with the letter "M" as the second character symbol in their identification numbers using facultyX table, type and run the following SELECT statement.

SELECT facultyId AS ID, FORMATCURRENCY(annualSalary) AS ANNUAL_INCOME,
    (SELECT FORMAT(AVG(annualSalary), "$###,###.00")
    FROM facultyX) AS AVERAGE_SALARY_OF_ALL_FACULTY_MEMBER
FROM facultyX
WHERE facultyId LIKE ("?M*");

See result below.

ID	ANNUAL_INCOME	AVERAGE_SALARY_OF_ALL_FACULTY_MEMBER
EM001254	$74,563.55	$60,153.37
ZM567123	$49,980.95	$60,153.37
DM674543	$62,980.25	$60,153.37

Subqueries

The result of the subquery is duplicated for every record that is returned by the outer query. The result of a subquery that is placed in the SELECT clause of a SELECT statement is usually used for comparison purposes.

Multiple-Row Subqueries

A multiple-row subquery is a nested query that can return more than one record as the input to the outer query when the result of the outer query is based on unknown values. The values may not be known to the user, but the values exist in the table that is being queried. The result returned by the subquery can be a single value or several values. The outer query uses the returned values as input to generate the final output which can be one or more records of one or several columns. A multiple-row subquery can be placed in the WHERE clause or the HAVING clause of an outer query.

To connect a multiple-row subquery to the outer query, use the comparison operators known as multiple-row operators. Figure 8.2 lists the four multiple-row operators used to construct multiple-row subqueries.

Figure 8.2

Multiple-Row Operator	Interpretation
IN	Equal to any value in the list generated by the subquery
ANY	Compare value to each value in the list generated by the subquery
SOME	The same function as ANY operator
ALL	Compare value to every value in the list generated by the subquery

Among the multiple-row operators, the IN operator is most frequently used. For ANY, SOME, and ALL multiple-row operators to return sets of values rather than single values, you must combine each operator with any of the single-row operators. Such combinations assist in obtaining the needed results. See figure 8.3.

Figure 8.3

Multiple-Row Operator	Interpretation
>ANY	Greater than or higher than any value in the list generated by the subquery
<ANY	Less than or lower than any value in the list generated by the subquery
=ANY	Equal to any value in the list generated by the subquery. The same function as IN operator
>SOME	The same function as >ANY operator
<SOME	The same function as <ANY operator
>ALL	Greater than or higher than all values in the list generated by the subquery
<ALL	Less than or lower than all values in the list generated by the subquery

Multiple-Row Subquery Placed in WHERE Clause

Like single-row subqueries, multiple-row subqueries can be nested using the WHERE clause of outer queries. The only difference is that you must use multiple-row operators to connect multiple-row subqueries to outer queries.

The following SELECT statements show how IN, >ALL, and <ANY operators are used to create multiple-row subqueries respectively.

Chapter Eight

To display identification numbers and annual salaries of faculty members whose individual annual salary is the same (equal) as the average annual salary of any faculty group based on academic positions using both facultyX and positionX tables, type and run the following SELECT statement.

SELECT facultyId AS ID, FORMAT(annualSalary,'$###,###,###.00') AS SALARY
FROM facultyX
WHERE annualSalary IN (SELECT AVG(annualSalary)
                    FROM facultyX, positionX
                    WHERE annualSalary BETWEEN minAnnualSalary
                    AND maxAnnualSalary
                    GROUP BY academicPosition);

See result below.

ID	SALARY
DM674543	$62,980.25

To display identification numbers and annual salaries of faculty members whose individual annual salary is higher than the annual salaries of every faculty member in the Social Science ("SOCC06") department using the facultyX table, type and run the following SELECT statement.

SELECT facultyId AS ID, FORMAT(annualSalary, '$###,###,###.00') AS SALARY
FROM facultyX
WHERE annualSalary >ALL (SELECT annualSalary
                    FROM facultyX
                    WHERE departmentCode = "SOCC06");

See result below.

ID	SALARY
EM001254	$74,563.55
RU123098	$70,760.89

To display identification numbers and annual salaries of faculty members whose individual annual salary is less than the lowest annual salary of any department grouped by department code using the facultyX table, type and run the following SELECT statement.

SELECT facultyId AS ID, FORMAT(annualSalary,'$###,###,###.00') AS SALARY
FROM facultyX
WHERE annualSalary <ANY (SELECT MIN(annualSalary)
                    FROM facultyX
                    GROUP BY departmentCode);

See result below.

ID	SALARY
JS994450	$45,876.25
ZM567123	$49,980.95
AL501828	$54,354.15
JH682508	$48,000.00

Subqueries

Multiple-Row Subquery Placed in HAVING Clause

You can also embed multiple-row subqueries into outer queries by using the HAVING clause of outer queries. The following SELECT statement demonstrates how such a subquery is created using the HAVING condition clause.

To display department codes and the sum of faculty members' annual salaries of individual department grouped by department codes for those departments with total annual salaries higher than twice the average annual salary of any department using facultyX table, type and run the following SELECT statement.

```
SELECT               departmentCode            AS           DEPARTMENT_CODE,
FORMATCURRENCY(SUM(annualSalary)) AS TOTAL_SALARY_BY_DEPARTMENT
FROM facultyX
GROUP BY departmentCode
HAVING SUM(annualSalary) >ANY  (SELECT  AVG(annualSalary) * 2
                               FROM facultyX
                               GROUP BY departmentCode);
```

See result below.

DEPARTMENT_CODE	TOTAL_SALARY_BY_DEPARTMENT
BUSA02	$120,439.80
CSCM09	$122,615.54
NASC08	$127,664.89
SOCC06	$117,852.25

EXISTS Operator

The EXISTS operator is a special operator that does not retrieve data by quantifying their values, rather it checks whether specific data values in the outer query exist in the subquery. The EXISTS operator is a condition operator that returns the Boolean value TRUE if the specified data values are contained in the subquery or returns the Boolean value FALSE if the specified data values are not found in the subquery. The basic syntax for the EXISTS operator using both outer and inner queries' construct and the WHERE clause is

```
SELECT [predicate] {[ALL] * | existingColumnName, ... | columnExpression, ...}
FROM existingTableName
WHERE EXISTS (SELECT existingColumnName, ...
FROM existingTableName);
```

where

- Predicate is a condition keyword, such as DISTINCT, used to restrict records
- Symbol * is to include all columns
- existingColumnName is the column in the table listed in the FROM clause
- columnExpression is the expression formed by the combination of column(s) and data value(s). The column(s) and the data used in a column expression must be of the same data type
- existingTableName is the table that contains the column to be displayed
- Symbols [ ] mean item is optional
- Symbol | symbolizes **Or** Boolean operator. You can also list both existingColumnName and columnExpression or both * and columnExpression in the SELECT clause of the statement
- Symbols ... mean more columns and/or columns' expressions can be listed

To display identification numbers, first names, and last names of faculty members who are taking courses as students using facultyX table, studentX table, and the EXISTS operator, type and run the following SELECT statement.

```
SELECT facultyId, firstName, lastName
FROM facultyX F
WHERE EXISTS (SELECT studentId
              FROM studentX S
              WHERE F.facultyId = S.studentId);
```

See result below.

facultyId	firstName	lastName
DM674543	Doris	Mea
EM001254	Eghosa	Maklasi

In the query, the EXISTS operator checks to determine whether any faculty identification number exists as student identification number in the subquery. The operator returns the Boolean value TRUE to the outer query because two faculty members are also registered as students. The outer query's responsibility is to display the matching records.

> **Note:** When using the EXISTS operator, MS Access SQL allows, if desired, the listing of more than one column, asterisk symbol (*), any text data value such as "X", "PAUL", "8", or spaces in the SELECT clause of the subquery. To use a text data value in the SELECT clause of the subquery, the value must be enclosed in quotation marks.

The following three SELECT statements display the same result as in the last query. The statements use different arrangements that conform with the EXISTS operator in the SELECT clause of the subquery.

```
SELECT facultyId, firstName, lastName
FROM facultyX F
WHERE EXISTS (SELECT studentId, dateFirstEnrolled
              FROM studentX S
              WHERE F.facultyId = S.studentId);
```

Notice that the two columns (studentId, dateFirstEnrolled) from the studentX table of the subquery are listed in the SELECT clause of the subquery.

```
SELECT facultyId, firstName, lastName
FROM facultyX F
WHERE EXISTS (SELECT *
              FROM studentX S
              WHERE F.facultyId = S.studentId);
```

In the last query, the all columns' symbol (*) is used in the SELECT clause of the subquery.

```
SELECT facultyId, firstName, lastName
FROM facultyX F
WHERE EXISTS (SELECT 'X'
              FROM studentX S
              WHERE F.facultyId = S.studentId);
```

Subqueries

The query uses the character value "X" in the SELECT clause of the subquery.

Multiple-Column Subqueries

A multiple-column subquery is a subquery that returns the values of more than one column to the outer query. The outer query uses the columns' values as its input to determine the final output. In MS Access SQL, this type of subquery can only be embedded in the FROM clause of the outer query. However, with the use of the EXISTS operator in both WHERE and HAVING clauses of an outer query, MS Access SQL allows the listing of more than one column in the SELECT clause of a subquery to create a multiple-column subquery.

Note: In addition to nesting subqueries in the FROM clause of the outer query, Oracle also allows the nesting of multiple-column subqueries in WHERE and HAVING clauses of the outer query. Oracle uses the IN operator to establish the connection between a multiple-column subquery and the outer query when using the WHERE clause or the HAVING clause.

Example:
SELECT isbn AS "BOOK ISBN", bookTitle AS "TITLE OF BOOK", costPrice AS "COST OF BOOK", classification AS "BOOK CLASS"
FROM bookX
WHERE (classification, costPrice) IN (SELECT classification, MAX(costPrice)
                                       FROM bookX
                                       GROUP BY classification);

Multiple-Column Subquery Placed in FROM Clause

Embedding a multiple-column subquery inside the FROM clause of an outer query creates a temporary table. This temporary table is called an inline view and the table can be referenced by any clause of the outer query. If the contents of the inline view are summary data or the inline view contains grouped data, the data are referenced as individual values in the outer query. In other words, an individual grouped value is referenced and used just as a single value in the SELECT statement.

Inline Views: An inline view is a short-term table that is created when a query is embedded in the FROM clause of a SELECT statement.

To display identification numbers, last names, and monthly salaries for faculty members whose individual monthly salary is greater than the average monthly salary of their department using both facultyX table and an inline view, type and run the following SELECT statement.

SELECT F.facultyId AS ID, F.lastName AS LAST_NAME, ROUND(F.annualSalary / 12, 2) AS MONTHLY_SALARY, ROUND(G.MONTHLY_AVERAGE_BY_DEPARTMENT, 2) AS MONTHLY_AVERAGE_BY_DEPARTMENT
FROM facultyX F, (SELECT departmentCode, AVG(annualSalary / 12) AS
                         MONTHLY_AVERAGE_BY_DEPARTMENT
                  FROM facultyX
                  GROUP BY departmentCode) G
WHERE F.departmentCode = G.departmentCode
AND F.annualSalary /12 > G.MONTHLY_AVERAGE_BY_DEPARTMENT;

See result below.

ID	LAST_NAME	MONTHLY_SALARY	MONTHLY_AVERAGE_BY _DEPARTMENT
EM001254	Maklasi	6213.63	5018.32
RU123098	Ugboma	5896.74	5319.37

ID	LAST_NAME	MONTHLY_SALARY	MONTHLY_AVERAGE_BY_DEPARTMENT
ES509264	Stevenson	5821.02	4910.51
DM674543	Mea	5248.35	4706.72
EE987654	Erochi	5688.45	5108.98

In the query, the inline view is called G. The SELECT statement embedded in the FROM clause creates the inline view which is a temporary table. The inline view is the subquery. Notice also that the column alias of the inline view is used as a column in both the SELECT clause and the WHERE condition clause of the outer query. This is allowed in SQL programming. The query uses the traditional method of joining tables – that is the use of the WHERE clause.

> **Note:** Whenever an inline view is created using columns listed in the SELECT clause of the outer query, the columns must be qualified in the SELECT clause or/and condition clauses of the outer query. In addition, an inline view must be assigned a table alias so the temporary table can be referenced in the outer query.

Now, let's write the last query again but this time replacing the WHERE clause with the INNER JOIN...ON clause to display monthly and average monthly salaries in currency with two decimal positions. Type and run the following SELECT statement.

```
SELECT      F.facultyId    AS    ID,    F.lastName    AS    LAST_NAME,
FORMATCURRENCY(F.annualSalary    /    12)    AS    MONTHLY_SALARY,
FORMAT(G.MONTHLY_AVERAGE_BY_DEPARTMENT,    "$###,###.00")    AS
MONTHLY_AVERAGE_BY_DEPARTMENT
FROM facultyX F INNER JOIN (SELECT departmentCode, AVG(annualSalary /
                  12) AS
                  MONTHLY_AVERAGE_BY_DEPARTMENT
                  FROM facultyX
                  GROUP BY departmentCode) G
ON F.departmentCode = G.departmentCode
AND F.annualSalary /12 > G.MONTHLY_AVERAGE_BY_DEPARTMENT;
```

See result below.

ID	LAST_NAME	MONTHLY_SALARY	MONTHLY_AVERAGE_BY_DEPARTMENT
EM001254	Maklasi	$6,213.63	$5,018.32
RU123098	Ugboma	$5,896.74	$5,319.37
ES509264	Stevenson	$5,821.02	$4,910.51
DM674543	Mea	$5,248.35	$4,706.72
EE987654	Erochi	$5,688.45	$5,108.98

Multiple-Column Subquery Placed in WHERE Clause

MS Access SQL provides an alternative approach of nesting a multiple-column subquery in the WHERE clause of the outer query. With the use of the EXISTS operator, you can list more than one column in the SELECT clause of the subquery. The following SELECT statement demonstrates how the WHERE clause is used to create a multiple-column subquery.

To display isbns, titles, cost prices, and classifications for the least expensive books in their respective groups based on classifications using the bookX table, type the following SELECT statement.

Subqueries

```
SELECT   A.isbn   AS   [BOOK   ISBN],   A.bookTitle   AS   [TITLE   OF   BOOK],
FORMATCURRENCY(A.costPrice) AS [BOOK COST PRICE], A.classification AS [BOOK
CLASS]
FROM bookX A
WHERE EXISTS (SELECT classification, MIN(costPrice)
                FROM bookX B
                WHERE A.classification = B.classification
                GROUP BY classification
                HAVING MIN(A.costPrice) = MIN(B.costPrice))
ORDER BY classification;
```

See result below.

BOOK ISBN	TITLE OF BOOK	BOOK COST PRICE	BOOK CLASS
09978423	Introduction to Marketing	$29.95	Business Administration
06142546	Database Design	$25.95	Computer Science
03821069	Basic Physics	$38.90	Natural Science
05588332	Basic Criminology	$31.60	Social Science

You might have noticed that two columns (classification and costPrice) are listed in the SELECT clause of the subquery which is connected, through the WHERE clause, to the outer query. This multiple-column listing is made possible by the EXISTS operator.

Multiple-Column Subquery Placed in HAVING Clause

Like the WHERE clause, MS Access SQL also provides an alternative method of nesting a multiple-column subquery in the HAVING clause of the outer query. With the use of the EXISTS operator, you can list more than one column in the SELECT clause of the subquery. The following SELECT statement demonstrates how the HAVING clause is used to create a multiple-column subquery.

To display classifications and cost prices for the least expensive books in their respective groups based on classifications and cost prices using the bookX table, type and run the following SELECT statement.

```
SELECT classification AS [BOOK CLASS], FORMATCURRENCY(A.costPrice) AS [COST
OF BOOK]
FROM bookX A
GROUP BY classification, costPrice
HAVING EXISTS (SELECT classification, MIN(costPrice)
                FROM bookX B
                WHERE A.classification = B.classification
                GROUP BY classification
                HAVING MIN(A.costPrice) = MIN(B.costPrice))
ORDER BY classification;
```

See result below.

BOOK CLASS	COST OF BOOK
Business Administration	$29.95
Computer Science	$25.95
Natural Science	$38.90
Social Science	$31.60

Again, two columns (classification and costPrice) are listed in the SELECT clause of the subquery. The link between the subquery and the HAVING condition clause of the outer query is made possible by the EXISTS operator.

Subqueries in Compound Conditions

Subquries are allowed to be used in each of the simple conditions that constitute a compound condition. Remember that a compound condition is created by connecting two or more simple conditions with AND or OR logical operators. A compound condition is also created by placing the NOT logical operator in front of a simple condition. The following SELECT statement demonstrates the use of subqueries in the AND logical condition.

To display titles and selling prices of books in the computer science classification which selling prices are higher than the average selling prices of books in all classifications using the bookX table, type and run the following SELECT statement.

```
SELECT bookTitle AS [TITLE OF BOOK], FORMAT(sellingPrice, "$###.00") AS [RETAIL PRICE]
FROM bookX
WHERE classification IN (SELECT classification
                FROM bookX
                WHERE classification = "Computer Science")
AND sellingPrice >ALL (SELECT AVG(sellingPrice)
                FROM bookX
                GROUP BY classification);
```

See result below.

TITLE OF BOOK	RETAIL PRICE
SQL Programming	$50.25
Programming with Java	$56.90

Notice that there are two subqueries in the WHERE clause of the SELECT statement. The first subquery returns books in the computer science category and the second subquery returns the selling prices that are higher than the average selling prices of books in all categories. Since the AND logical operator is used, the qualifying records must meet or pass the two simple conditions.

NULL Values in Subqueries

When a null value is returned by a subquery, the outer query displays no record. This type of problem is usually corrected by substituting the null value with any other non-null value. The following SELECT statement displays no record due to the fact that the record that is being queried in the subquery returns a null value. In the example, the student whose identification number is "CJ684975" has no middle name initial, and as such, the column entry for that student middle name initial contains a null value.

```
SELECT firstName, lastName, initial
FROM studentX
WHERE  initial = (SELECT initial
                FROM studentX
                WHERE studentId = "CJ684975");
```

Now let's write the SELECT statement again, but this time the null value generated by the subquery is substituted by an actual (non-null) value. Type and run the following SELECT statement.

```
SELECT firstName, lastName, initial
FROM studentX
WHERE initial = (SELECT NZ(initial,"C")
                FROM studentX
                WHERE studentId = "CJ684975");
```

See result below.

firstName	lastName	initial
Benjamin	Benado	C
Andy	Uzueg	C

The outer query of the above SELECT statement returns two records. This result is due to the fact that the null value that is contained in the student middle name initial is replaced with the data value "C".

> **Note:** MS Access SQL supports the use of either an actual value in the table being queried by the subquery or a valid value that is not contained in the table as a substitute for a null value. The choice of the substitute value, within the table or outside the table, depends on the types of results the user is requesting. When generating results with a query that contains a subquery, null values substitutions can be specified only in the subquery.

IS NULL Comparison Operator in Subqueries

Although, null values create problems in subqueries, there are times when searching for null values in the condition clauses of a subquery are needed for the outer query to display the needed result. This type of search approach is accomplished by using the IS NULL comparison operator.

To display first and last names, course codes, sections, and letter grades for the first four students who have no middle names' initials using both studentX and gradeX tables, type and run the following SELECT statement.

```
SELECT TOP 4 firstName, lastName, courseCode, section, letterGrade
FROM studentX S INNER JOIN gradeX G
ON G.studentId = S.studentId
WHERE G.studentId IN (SELECT studentId
                FROM studentX
                WHERE initial IS NULL);
```

See result below.

firstName	lastName	courseCode	section	letterGrade
Erasto	Actionbarrel	BUS101	2010	B
Christopher	Salat	BUS110	2010	C
Eghosa	Maklasi	CSC220	2010	AU
Phil	Portiskum	CSC355	2010	WP

In the SELECT statement, the null values of the middle name initial column of the studentX table in the subquery are used to return the identification numbers of the students who had no middle names' initials to the outer query. The outer query uses that data to display the needed records.

Correlated Subqueries versus Uncorrelated Subqueries

Subqueries can further be classified as correlated and uncorrelated subqueries. Usually, when a SELECT statement that contains a subquery is run, the subquery is evaluated first. The result of the subquery is passed to the outer query as the outer query's input. The outer query, in turn, uses the input to generate the final result. In an environment where a subquery is evaluated first, such a subquery is called uncorrelated subquery. An uncorrelated subquery is an inner query that is executed first and the result passed to the outer or query.

> **Note:** If a subquery has a condition clause and the columns listed in the condition clause of the subquery are contained in the table or tables listed in the FROM clause of the subquery, then the subquery is an uncorrelated subquery. Also, if a subquery contains no condition clause, that subquery is also an uncorrelated subquery.

By comparison, a correlated subquery uses a different approach to display the needed records. With a correlated subquery, each record in the table of the outer query is processed to check whether the record exists in the table of the inner query. With correlated subquery, the outer query is executed first and execution is done for each record stored in table of the outer query. The execution of a record in the outer query checks the inner query to determine whether the record exists.

For example, if there are five records in the table of the outer query, the query executes five times, one for each record. The execution of each record in the table of the outer query is compared to the records in the table of the inner query to determine whether that record exists in the table of the inner query. If the record exists, the outer query displays the record as specified in the SELECT clause of the outer query. If not, the next record in the table of the outer query is executed for the next comparison. The execution of the outer query continues in that fashion until all the records in the table of the outer query are processed.

> **Note:** Anytime, at least one column, in the table of the outer query is referenced or listed in the condition clause of the subquery, that subquery is a correlated subquery.

One way of creating a correlated subquery is using the EXISTS operator in the outer query condition clause to establish an association with the subquery. The following SELECT statement contains a correlated subquery. Type and run the SELECT statement.

```
SELECT firstName, lastName
FROM studentX S
WHERE EXISTS (SELECT studentId
              FROM gradeX G
              WHERE S.studentId = G.studentId
              AND letterGrade = "F");
```

See result below.

firstName	lastName
Benjamin	Benado
Efosa	Johnson
Cecilia	Jeffer
Celestine	Chap

In the SELECT statement, you might have noticed that the identification number column (S.studentId) that is contained in the studentX table of the outer query is listed in the WHERE clause of the subquery. That makes the subquery a correlated subquery.

Subqueries

Four records are displayed as the result of the correlated subquery. Each record of the studentX table of the outer query is executed and the student identification number for that record is checked to determine whether the record exists in the gradeX table of the subquery. In addition, if the student identification number exists in the table of the subquery, the student must have earned at least one letter grade of "F" for his or her record to be displayed.

Nesting Subqueries

In MS Access SQL environment, you can nest subqueries within other subqueries. Subqueries can be embedded inside outer subqueries using FROM, WHERE, or HAVING clauses of the outer subqueries. In nested subqueries, typically the innermost ones are evaluated first. The evaluations of nested subqueries are performed beginning with the innermost ones and the evaluations proceed toward the outer subqueries.

Nested Subqueries: A nested subquery is an inner query that is entirely written inside another inner query.

The basic syntax, using the first three clauses, for a nested subquery statement to the second-level depth is

SELECT [predicate] {[ALL] * | *existingColumnName*, ... | *columnExpression*, ...}
FROM *existingTableName*
WHERE *existingColumnName*, ... *subqueryOperator* (SELECT *existingColumnName*, ...
      FROM *existingTableName*
      WHERE *existingColumnName*, ... *subqueryOperator* (SELECT
            existingColumnName, ...
            FROM *existingTableName*));

where

- Predicate is a condition keyword, such as DISTINCT, used to restrict records
- Symbol * is to include all columns
- *existingColumnName* is the column in the table listed in the FROM clause
- *columnExpression* is the expression formed by the combination of column(s) and data value(s). The column(s) and the data used in a column expression must be of the same data type.
- *existingTableName* is the table that contains the column to be displayed
- *subqueryOperator* is the comparison operator that is used to connect the inner subquery to the outer subquery and to connect the outer subquery to the outer query
- Symbols [ ] mean item is optional
- Symbol | symbolizes ***Or*** Boolean operator. You can also list both *existingColumnName* and *columnExpression* or both * and *columnExpression* in the SELECT clause of the statement
- Symbols ... mean more columns and/or columns' expressions can be listed

The following SELECT statement demonstrates how a subquery can be nested inside another subquery.

To display identification numbers, first names, middle names' initials, and last names of faculty members who are also students and teach less than two courses using facultyX, studentX, and courseX tables, type and run the following SELECT statement.

```
SELECT facultyId AS FACULTY_ID, firstName AS FIRST_NAME, IIF(initial, initial, "") AS
MIDDLE_INITIAL, lastname AS LAST_NAME
FROM facultyX
WHERE facultyId =ANY (SELECT studentId
                FROM studentX
                WHERE studentId =ANY (SELECT facultyId
                              FROM courseX
                              GROUP BY facultyId
                              HAVING COUNT(facultyId) < 2));
```

See result below.

FACULTY_ID	FIRST_NAME	MIDDLE_INITIAL	LAST_NAME
DM674543	Doris	V	Mea

In the SELECT statement, the innermost subquery returns the identification numbers of faculty members who are assigned to teach less than two courses using the courseX table to the outer subquery. The outer subquery checks to determine whether the student identification numbers in the studentX table matches any of the faculty identification numbers that are returned by the nested subquery. If identification numbers match are found, the outer subquery returns the student identification numbers to the outer query. The outer query then checks to determine whether faculty identification numbers from the facultyX table match any of the student identification numbers that are returned by the outer subquery. If identification numbers match are found, the outer query displays the final result.

The result of the last SELECT statement can also be obtained through other SELECT statements' constructs. The following SELECT statement achieves the same result as the last SELECT statement by nesting a subquery in the FROM clause of the outer subquery. This approach uses an inline view.

```
SELECT facultyId AS FACULTY_ID, firstName AS FIRST_NAME, IIF(initial, initial, "") AS
MIDDLE_INITIAL, lastname AS LAST_NAME
FROM facultyX
WHERE facultyId =ANY (SELECT studentId
                FROM studentX S, (SELECT facultyId
                              FROM courseX
                              GROUP BY facultyId
                              HAVING COUNT(facultyId) < 2) G
                WHERE S.studentId = G.facultyId);
```

Chapter Summary

This chapter teaches subqueries, their functions, and how to construct them in SQL SELECT statements. The chapter discusses different types of subqueries from single-row subqueries, to multiple-row subqueries, to multiple-column subqueries. Subqueries operators and the EXISTS operator are explained and how the operators differ from the EXISTS operator. The chapter also explains the differences between correlated and uncorrelated subqueries. The chapter concludes by explaining how subqueries are embedded inside other subqueries.

Subqueries Syntax and Statements Summary

The table below presents subqueries' syntax and subqueries' operators discussed in this chapter and the SQL statements' examples for retrieving data from tables.

Statement Description	Basic Statement Syntax	Statement Example
A subquery is used to retrieve values that are not known to the user, but the values exist in the table being queried	SELECT [predicate] {[ALL] * | *existingColumnName*, ... | *columnExpression*, ...} FROM *existingTableName* WHERE *existingColumnName*, ... *subqueryOperator* (SELECT *existingColumnName*, ... FROM *existingTableName*);	SELECT facultyId, firstName, lastName FROM facultyX F WHERE EXISTS (SELECT studentId FROM studentX S WHERE F.facultyId = S.studentId);

Operators		
Single-Row Operator		

Operator Type	Description	
=	Used to determine whether the value that is being tested in the condition clause of the outer query is equal to the value returned by a subquery	
>	Used to determine whether the value that is being tested in the condition clause of the outer query is greater than the value returned by a subquery	
<	Used to determine whether the value that is being tested in the condition clause of the outer query is less than the value returned by a subquery	
>=	Used to determine whether the value that is being tested in the condition clause of the outer query is greater than or equal to the value returned by a subquery	
<=	Used to determine whether the value that is being tested in the condition clause of the outer query is less or equal to the value returned by a subquery	
<>	Used to determine whether the value that is being tested in the condition clause of the outer query is different from (not equal to) the value returned by a subquery	

Multiple-Row Operator		

Operator Type	Description	
IN	Used to determine whether the value that is being tested in the condition clause of the outer query is equal to any of the values returned by the subquery	
>ALL	Used to determine whether the value that is being tested in the condition clause of the outer query is greater than all the values returned by the subquery	
<ALL	Used to determine whether the value that is being tested in the condition clause of the outer query is less than all the values returned by the subquery	
>ANY	Used to determine whether the value that is being tested in the condition clause of the outer query is greater than any of the values returned by the subquery	
<ANY	Used to determine whether the value that is being tested in the condition clause of the outer query is less than any of the values returned by the subquery	
>SOME	Same as the >ANY operator	
<SOME	Same as the <ANY operator	
EXISTS	Used to determine whether the record contained in the outer query exists also in the subquery	

Subquery Classification		

Subquery Class	Description	Statement Example
Correlated Subquery	A subquery where each row (record) in the table of the outer query is processed first to check whether the record exists in the table of the inner query. A subquery where the condition clause of the inner query contains, at least, one column from the table listed in the outer query	SELECT firstName, lastName FROM studentX S WHERE EXISTS (SELECT studentId FROM gradeX G WHERE S.studentId = G.studentId AND letterGrade = "F");
Uncorrelated Subquery	A subquery where the inner query is executed first and the result passed to the outer query as input. A subquery where the inner query contain no condition clause or the condition clause uses only the columns of the table listed in the inner query	SELECT TOP 4 firstName, lastName, courseCode, section, letterGrade FROM studentX S INNER JOIN gradeX G ON G.studentId = S.studentId WHERE G.studentId IN (SELECT studentId FROM studentX WHERE initial IS NULL);

Key Terms

Subqueries	HAVING clause
Single-row operators	IS NULL operator
Multiple-row operators	NULL
Correlated	Compound condition
Uncorrelated	SELECT clause
Single-row subquery	FROM clause
Multiple-row subquery	GROUP BY clause
EXISTS operator	Multiple-column subquery
WHERE clause	Inline view

Chapter Review Questions

Multiple Choice Questions

1. Which of the following is not true? A subquery can be connected to a SELECT statement through
   - a. condition clauses.
   - b. FROM clause.
   - c. ORDER BY clause.
   - d. SELECT clause.

2. A subquery must be enclosed in a pair of
   - a. curly braces.
   - b. square brackets.
   - c. single quotation marks.
   - d. parentheses.

3. Assume that the facultyX table exists and the table contains a column called facultyId. Study the following SELECT statement and tell the output.

   ```
   SELECT facultyId
   FROM facultyX
   WHERE annualSalary > (SELECT annualSalary
                         FROM facultyX
                         WHERE facultyId = "FF09671";
   ```

   - a. The display shows the facultyIds of faculty members whose annual salaries are the same as the faculty member with facultyId "FF09671".
   - b. The display shows the facultyIds of faculty members whose annual salaries are higher than the faculty member with facultyId "FF09671".
   - c. The display shows the facultyIds of faculty members whose annual salaries are lesser than the faculty member with facultyId "FF09671".
   - d. none of the above.

4. A subquery is used to determine a value that is not known to the
   - a. user.
   - b. program.
   - c. database.
   - d. computer.

5. Which of the following is not a valid subquery type?
   - a. multiple-row subquery.
   - b. multiple-column subquery.
   - c. single-row subquery.
   - d. single-column subquery.

6. Which of the following operators used in subqueries returns a Boolean value?
    a. EXISTS operator.
    b. >ANY operator.
    c. IN operator.
    d. =ANY operator.

7. When a null value is returned by a subquery, the outer query will display
    a. several records.
    b. a single record.
    c. no record.
    d. none of the above.

8. In MS Access SQL, subqueries can be embedded inside outer subqueries through _____ clause.
    a. FROM
    b. WHERE
    c. HAVING
    d. all of the above

9. With a correlated subquery,
    a. the outer query is executed first.
    b. the inner query is executed first.
    c. both the outer and inner queries are executed at the same time.
    d. all of the above.

10. Which of the following is not true? Another name for a subquery is _____ statement.
    a. inner SELECT
    b. sub-SELECT
    c. outer SELECT
    d. nested SELECT

True or False Questions

11. A subquery is a valid SELECT statement.
    a. True
    b. False

12. A subquery must be placed on the right side of the query (comparison) operator when connected with the WHERE clause.
    a. True
    b. False

13. There are two types of subqueries.
    a. True
    b. False

14. The result of an uncorrelated subquery is used as an input for the outer query.
    a. True
    b. False

15. A single-row subquery cannot be placed in the HAVING clause of a SELECT statement.
    a. True
    b. False

16. With a correlated subquery, the outer query is executed first.
    a. True
    b. False

17. Generally, a subquery cannot be placed inside a SELECT...INTO statement.
    a. Tue
    b. False

Fill in the blank Questions

18. In a _____ subquery, the records of the outer query are processed first.

19. The result of a subquery that is embedded in the FROM clause of the outer query is called _____.

20. When a subquery contains no condition clause, the subquery is called _____ subquery.

21. Alternatively, in processing a subquery, you can substitute _____ operator for IN operator to achieve the same result.

22. Alternatively, in processing a subquery, you can use _____ operator in place of >SOME operator to achieve the same result.

23. Single-row subqueries use _____ operators.

Essay Type Questions

24. Explain the differences between correlated and uncorrelated subqueries and write a SQL statement for each?

25. Describe how a multiple-column subquery can be achieved in MS Access SQL using the WHERE clause?

26. State the differences between single-row and multiple-row subqueries?

27. What happens when a subquery is nested in the SELECT clause of a SELECT statement and what is the main reason for creating such a subquery?

28. How does a null value, if returned by a subquery, affects the result of the outer query? Explain how such a problem is corrected?

Hands-on Activities

Study the structures and the data of *AcademicX* database tables in appendix A (pages 355 through 360) and perform the following hands-on exercises.

1. Display the identification number and the last name of each faculty member whose annual salary is greater than the average salary of all faculty members.

2. Display identification numbers, first names, and last names of students whose country of origin is the United States.

3. Write a SQL statement to list the complete records of faculty members whose first names begin with the letter "J" and whose individual monthly salary is $4000 or less.

4. Write a SQL statement to show identification numbers, last names, and dates first enrolled for students from the Philippines who enrolled before the date the student with identification number "EM001254" enrolled. Use column alias **ID #** for the student identification number column, column alias **Student Lname** for the last name column, and column alias **First Enrollment** for the date of first enrolled column.

5. Write a SQL statement to display titles, selling prices, and classifications for the least expensive books in each classification. Assign column alias **retail price** to the selling price column and format the result of the column to currency.

6. Display identification numbers and last names of students who have at least earned the letter grade "A" in any course.

7. Display countries and the number of students from those countries for countries that have enrolled more than three students so far. Assign column alias **how many** to the column that

displays the number of students. Sort the result in ascending order using the number of students' column.

8. Write a SQL statement to display the identification number and the concatenation of first and last names of each faculty member who is assigned to teach fewer courses than the faculty member with the identification number "AL501828". Assign column alias *full name* to the concatenation column.

9. Using INNER JOIN...ON clause, perform similar operation as in question 8, but this time display faculty members who are assigned to teach more courses than the faculty member with the identification number "EE987654".

10. Display identification numbers and last names of students who have the highest number of courses registered for so far.

Chapter Nine

Creating and Maintaining Tables Structures

Chapter Objectives

After completing this chapter, you should be able to
- Create structures for new tables
- Understand MS Access SQL data types
- Display SQL statements Queries
- Display tables structures
- Create new tables using existing tables
- Modify tables structures
- Remove tables from a database
- Rename and display tables and columns using MS Access GUI

Creating Tables Structures

Once a relational database structure has been created, the next step is to plan and describe the layouts of the tables to be contained in the database. Planning and describing tables' structures are part of database design. Describing the layouts of tables or other database objects means defining their structures. In the case of tables, their structures are defined by the columns the tables will contain. Columns determine tables' structures. On that note, the phrase "no column, no table" can be regarded as a fair and appropriate statement.

To create tables in MS Access SQL environment, you use the CREATE TABLE command to code the CREATE TABLE statement. SQL uses statements to perform actions and the statements usually consist of sections called clauses. The CREATE TABLE statement consists of one mandatory clause, namely, the CREATE TABLE clause. The CREATE TABLE command is part of SQL subsection called data definition language (DDL).

CREATE TABLE Statements: A CREATE TABLE statement is a SQL instruction used to define the physical structure of a table.

Statements: A statement is an instruction that directs the computer to do something.

The basic syntax for the CREATE TABLE statement is

CREATE TABLE *newTableName(newColumnName dataType [constraintType], newColumnName dataType [constraintType], …);*

where

- *newTableName* is the name of the table to be created
- *newColumnName* is the name of the column to be included in the table
- *dataType* is the type of data the column will store
- *constraintType* is the type of rule that is defined for the column
- Symbols [ ] mean items are optional
- Symbols … mean more columns can be listed

Creating and Maintaining Tables Structures

Data Types: A data type is a specific kind of data values a column is expected to store.

Constraints: A constraint is a rule used to enforce restrictions to a database table so data contained in the table are accurate and have integrity.

Constraints are discussed in detail in chapter ten of this textbook.

> **Note:** The person creating the table can continue adding columns until the number of columns needed in the table is reached or until the maximum number of columns allowed by the database software is reached.

When creating tables, you can include, although optional, constraints to columns' definitions at the same time. However, constraints can be defined later when modifying or changing tables' structures. Constraints are discussed in detail in chapter ten of this textbook.

The two words CREATE TABLE are keywords or reserved words. The words are required when creating tables' structures. The keywords are the first to be written in the CREATE TABLE statement and the TABLE keyword must follow the keyword CREATE in that order.

Tables' and columns' names should be descriptive in nature as the names are used to identify them in a database. The names are given by the person creating the database and the objects and the names are identifiers. Since the names are given by the person creating the database and the objects, the names are referred to as user-defined or programmer-defined names.

Identifiers: An identifier is a non-keyword text expression used as a name to identify an item in a programming language or in an application package.

User-defined (programmer-defined) names: A user-defined name is non-keyword expression or an identifier created by a programmer or a program user in a programming language or in an application package to identify an item.

After assigning a name to the new table in the CREATE TABLE statement, the next step is to define each column that will be part of the table. A column's definition must be enclosed in a pair of parentheses. However, if more than one column is to be defined for a table, the columns definitions must be separated by commas.

Columns Definitions: A column definition is all the elements or components a column must have in order to properly describe the structure of a table.

A good column definition for a table includes, at least, a column name, a column data type, a column size where appropriate, and a column constraint(s).

Columns Sizes: A column size is the number of character positions that is reserved for a column to use to store its data values.

A column definition must begin with a column name. Following the column name is the data type for the column. A data type indicates the type of data the column must store. Any other types of data will be rejected or wrong data type – after conversion - will be stored in that column. In addition to defining the column size and constraints, a default value for the column can also be defined during the table creation. A default values, in MS Access, is initiated through MS Access graphical user interface (GUI).

The last element of a SQL statement is the semicolon (;). Typically, a SQL statement must end with semicolon. The semicolon indicates the end of one SQL statement or the beginning of another. In MS Access SQL environment, the semicolon is optional. Omitting it intentionally or by mistake would not affect the result of the statement. An error message is not generated for not including the semicolon at the end of a SQL statement in MS Access.

The following generic rules are guides that can be helpful when assigning names to tables and columns. The names

1. must be one word. That is no space between words if the name is a compound name (more than one word). MS Access allows spaces in compound names as long as the compound names are enclosed in square brackets [ ].
2. can contain letters, digits, and underscore (_).
3. must begin with letters.
4. cannot be keywords.
5. must be unique. That is tables' names cannot be duplicated within the same database and columns' names cannot be duplicated within the same table.

> **Note:** The number of characters allowed for a name varies depending on the database programming language being used, but usually not more than sixty four (64) characters long. Individual tables of different databases can be given the same table name and individual columns in different tables of the same database or in different tables of different databases can be given the same column name.

Now, let's revisit the basic syntax for the CREATE TABLE statement. The form is

CREATE TABLE *newTableName(newColumnName dataType [constraintType], newColumnName dataType [constraintType], ...);*

Let's say a student table that stores some of a college's students' data is to be created. The college decides to include six columns to define the structure of the new table. The columns will store data for student identification number, first name, middle name initial, last name, classification, and the date the student first enrolled at the college. The columns are to be created in the order listed. Since each of the columns must have its own definition, six definitions are enclosed in a pair of parentheses, and the definitions must be separated by commas from one other.

Below is the CREATE TABLE statement that creates the structure for the student table.

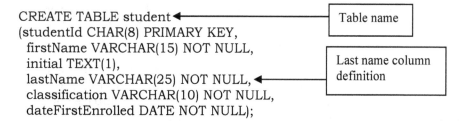

```
CREATE TABLE student                          Table name
(studentId CHAR(8) PRIMARY KEY,
  firstName VARCHAR(15) NOT NULL,
  initial TEXT(1),                            Last name column
  lastName VARCHAR(25) NOT NULL,              definition
  classification VARCHAR(10) NOT NULL,
  dateFirstEnrolled DATE NOT NULL);
```

In the above CREATE TABLE statement, each column definition includes the column name, its data type, its size except for the date data type which is assigned a default size of eight (8) bytes by the software, and the constraint type.

In the definitions, 8 character positions are reserved for students' identification numbers column, 15 character positions for first names' column, 1 character position for middle names' initials column, 25 character positions for last names' column, 10 character positions for classifications' column, and by default, 8 character positions are reserved for dates' first enrolled column.

When specifying a column size, the size must be enclosed in a pair of parentheses and must immediately follow the specified data type for that column. The column size must be written as an integer value – whole number. Example: CHAR(6).

> **Note:** The two explanation boxes that point to the table name (student) and the last name column are used only to explain table name and column definition. They are not part of the CREATE TABLE statement.

You might have noticed that the CREATE TABLE statement is written across several lines. SQL statements are format free which means you can write the statement on a single line or write the statement on several lines. The number of lines you choose to type a SQL statement is up to you. The only concern of writing a SQL statement on different lines is to know the appropriate locations in the statement where breaking the statement into multiple lines are possible. Typically, you cannot split tables' names, columns' names, and single-word keywords.

Assigning Default Values to Tables Columns

MS Access SQL does not directly support the inclusion of default (initial, beginning) values to columns when creating a table. However, it can assign initial values to a table's columns after the table has been created. This value initialization process is possible through the use of the UPDATE statement of the data manipulation language (DML) subsection of SQL. The use of the UPDATE statement to initialize columns with beginning values is successfully accomplished only after populating other columns - using the INSERT INTO statement - of the table with data. Assigning initial or beginning values to columns are optional. INSERT INTO and UPDATE statements are discussed in detail in chapter eleven of this textbook.

Default Values: A default value is a generic value of the correct data type assigned as a beginning or initial value to a column before the actual value of the column, where appropriate, is entered.

> **Note:** Oracle uses the DEFAULT clause to assign initial values to columns.
>
> Example:
> CREATE TABLE personName
> (fullName VARCHAR2(30) DEFAULT 'Ememgi Elo-Eghosa');
>
> The DEFAULT clause must be part of a column definition and usually the last element within the column definition. The above example creates one-column table with an initial value assign to the column.

For instance, if a college instructor created a database that contains, among other things, a table to store students' test scores. The instructor can initialize the tests' columns of the table to numeric values 0.0 after populating some of the table's columns such as student identification number and name columns with data. Any time a test is given, the instructor can then enter the actual test score into the appropriate test column for each of the students.

MS Access SQL Data Types

MS Access application support several types of data, but all of them are not supported in MS Access SQL environment. There are nine main data types supported by MS Access SQL. The data type groups are:

Autonumber

This data type is of numeric type and it is used to automate columns' values in incrementing order starting from value 1. The automatic increment is by 1 whenever a new record is entered into the table that contains the column defined with this data type. This data type is used to create a surrogate key and the keyword used to implement it in MS Access SQL is COUNTER. Example: studentId COUNTER. You can define the number of digit positions (size) when using this data type. Example: studentId COUNTER(6). 4 bytes of computer memory are reserved for this data type.

Character

The generic character data type in MS Access has seven (7) subtypes. The subtypes are CHAR, ALPHANUMERIC, STRING, LONGCHAR, VARCHAR, TEXT, and LONGTEXT, and they can be used in MS Access SQL. Typically, one byte is reserved for each character of this data type. Example: firstName STRING. Except for LONGCHAR and LONGTEXT subtypes, you can, in addition, define sizes (number of character positions) for the other subtypes. Example: firstName STRING(9). Except for the CHAR subtype that defines columns with fixed-length sizes other subtypes within this group define columns to be of variable-length sizes.

Data Type Subtypes: A data type subtype is a category or a unit, such as integer, of a data type, such as numeric, that can be used to specifically define the data type in that category.

Fixed-Length Columns: A fixed-length column is a field defined to store data using the exact number of character positions specified for the field by CHAR subtype data type. If data entered into the column is less than the number of character positions specified for that column, the computer will pad space(s) to the right of the column to fill the column size as defined.

Variable-Length Columns: A variable-length column is a field defined to store data with varying length. A variable-length column is defined using other subtypes of the generic character data type except for the CHAR subtype. If data entered into the column is less than the number of character positions specified for that column, the computer will remove (drop) the excess character position(s) and add the position(s) to the free memory space. In a variable-length column, the space assigned to data is calculated based on the data size. There is no padding to fill the extra space(s) not occupied by the data rather the extra space(s) are released to increase the available memory space.

> ***Note:*** If the size of a data value that is entered into a column is more than the size defined for the column, for both fixed- and variable-length columns, the computer will truncate from right side of the data value the excess character(s).

Currency

The CURRENCY data type is used to define columns that will store monetary values. In MS Access the default monetary symbol is the dollar sign ($) and two decimal places are display by default when viewing the column. Example: salary CURRENCY. 8 bytes are reserved in the computer memory for this data type.

Date

The DATE data type is used to define columns to store dates. MS Access recognizes and accepts several date formats, but the default date format in which dates are stored is mm/dd/yyyy. mm stands for the two digit of the month, dd stands for the two digits of the day, and yyyy stands for the four digits of the year. The format can be changed to

Creating and Maintaining Tables Structures

any other date format that is recognizable and can be processed by MS Access. Example: dateFirstEnrolled DATE. The computer system reserves 8 bytes of computer memory by default for this data type.

Logical

The LOGICAL (YESNO) data type is used to define columns that will contain Boolean values – True (Yes) or False (No). -1 represents True and 0 represents False. One byte is reserved in the computer memory for this data type. Example: fulltime LOGICAL.

Memo

The MEMO (NOTE) data type is used to define columns that will be used as remark, comment, or note columns. Such columns are used to give detailed descriptions of records in tables. Sometimes, columns defined with memo data type are referred to as records' documentary columns as they are used to give extensive remarks to records. Since comments are of different sizes in terms of how much text was entered, the number of bytes reserved for this data type varies. Example: noteColumn MEMO.

Number

The NUMBER (NUMERIC) data type has several subtypes. The data type and its subtypes are used to define columns that will store numeric values such as real and integer values. You can use the subtypes rather than using the generic NUMBER or NUMERIC keyword. Using NUMBER or NUMERIC keyword to define numeric data type behaves as either integer data type or floating-point data type. Example: numColumn NUMERIC. The subtype Integer is used specifically to define columns with whole numbers and the subtype Floating-point is used specifically to define columns with numbers with decimal parts.

Integer Subtype

The integer (whole number) subtype includes three additional subtypes of BYTE (INTEGER1), SMALLINT (SHORT, INTEGER2) and INT (LONG, INTEGER4).

The BYTE subtype is used to store numbers 0 through 255 and one byte is reserved for this subtype in the computer memory. Example: numColumn INTEGER1. The SMALLINT subtype stores numeric values in the range of -32767 through +32767 and 2 bytes are reserved for this subtype in the computer memory. Example: numColum SMALLINT. The INT subtype stores numeric values in the range of -2,147,483,647 through +2,147,483,647 and 4 bytes are reserved for this subtype in the computer memory. Example: numColumn INT.

Floating-Point Subtype

The floating-point subtype has two subtypes. One of the subtypes is the SINGLE (FLOAT4, IEEESINGLE) data type and it is used to define columns that will store single-precision values. In MS Access, the scale or decimal positions is set to AUTO by default which means you can enter the number of decimal positions you want using the subtype, but not to exceed seven (7) decimal positions. If you enter the value without the decimal part, MS Access will record the value without a decimal part and the value will be displayed as integer value. Example: numColumn SINGLE. This subtype occupies 4 bytes of computer memory.

Single-Precision Values: A single-precision value is a floating-point number with the decimal part not to exceed seven (7) digits.

The other floating-point subtype is the DOUBLE (FLOAT8, IEEEDOUBLE) data type and it is used to define columns that will store double-precision values. Also the scale (decimal positions) is set to AUTO by default and the AUTO behaves exactly the same way as with the single-precision subtype. This subtype occupies 8 bytes of computer memory. Example: numColumn DOUBLE.

Double-Precision Values: A double-precision value is a floating-point number with the decimal part exceeding seven (7) digits but not to exceed fourteen (14) digits.

Oleobject

The OLEOBJECT (GENERAL, LONGBINARY) data type is used to define columns that will store images, graphics, sounds, and other types of files or objects that can be linked to MS Access tables or embedded in the tables. Example: imageColumn OLEOBJECT. Up to one gigabyte is reserved for this data type in the computer memory.

Time

The TIME data type is used to define columns that will store time. Times are displayed in hours, minutes, and seconds. In MS Access, the default format for TIME data type is hh:mm:ss am/pm. hh stand for hours, mm stand for minutes, ss stand for seconds, and am/pm stand for morning and evening respectively. The colon (:) that separate the elements of the TIME data type must be included when entering time into a column. To enter time into a column, you must, at the minimum, enter values for hour and minute for the entry to be valid. 8 bytes are reserved for this data type in the computer memory.

Note: All data types, including their subtypes that are mentioned in this chapter can be used to define columns' data types.

The AUTO setting for integer, floating-point, date, and time data type values can be changed. These settings are done through the **Design** command for tables in the **Objects** window of the GUI environment. The values can be set when creating tables or when tables are being modified. MS Access SQL also provides ways for changing the formats of some data types, such as the date data type. To accomplish formats' alterations, the FORMAT keyword is used. The FORMAT function is discussed in chapter six.

Now, start MS Access and create a database called **Academics**. Then, navigate to open the SQL window. To refresh your memory, you can revisit the steps discussed in chapter one on how to activate the SQL window in MS Access 2007. You are to create the student table using the following CREATE TABLE statement.

```
CREATE TABLE student
(studentId CHAR(8) PRIMARY KEY,
  firstName VARCHAR(15) NOT NULL,
  initial TEXT(1),
  lastName VARCHAR(25) NOT NULL,
  classification VARCHAR(10) NOT NULL,
  dateFirstEnrolled DATE NOT NULL);
```

After opening the SQL window, type and run the CREATE TABLE statement listed above. See figure 9.1

Creating and Maintaining Tables Structures

Figure 9.1

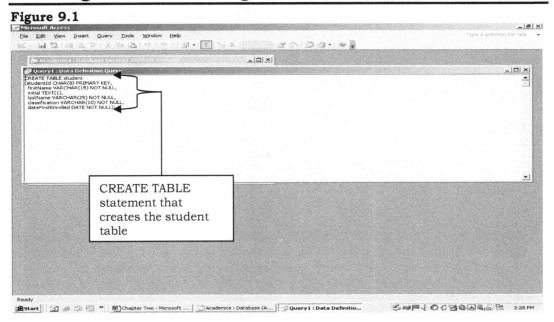

CREATE TABLE statement that creates the student table

Remember that to run SQL statements, either click on the **Run** button (! - exclamation symbol) on the standard toolbar or click on **Query** menu and then click the **Run** command. MS Access does not display confirmation messages when tables are successfully created. So when no message is displayed after running the CREATE TABLE statement means that the table is successfully created. If not, a message is displayed.

The message is either an error message indicating that a syntax error has occurred in the CREATE TABLE statement or that a table with the same name as the one you are creating has previously been created. If the message indicates a syntax error, you have to correct the CREATE TABLE statement and run it again. If the table name has been used previously, you will have to change the name of the table in the CREATE TABLE statement and run the statement again.

Syntax Errors: A syntax error is an error that occurs in a programming statement when the rule (syntax) of the programming language is not obeyed or followed.

Displaying SQL Statements Queries

To view SQL statements that are contained in queries or to modify such queries, you use the Object pane of the Object window. Click the QUERIES button of the Object pane to display the names of the existing SQL statements' queries on the right pane. Then select the name of the query you want to view or to modify its content. The content, in this case, is the SQL statement stored in the query. Click the **Design** command of the Object window to reveal the content of the selected query.

If you are making changes to the SQL statement contained in the query, you must save the query after the modification to keep the new changes made to the statement. See figure 9.2.

Figure 9.2

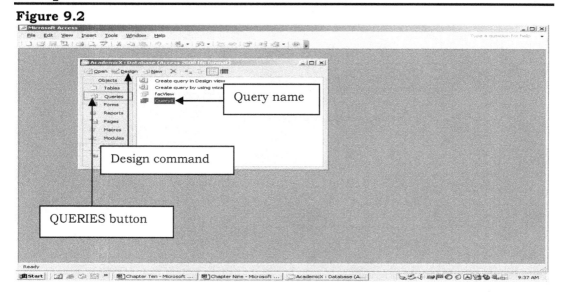

Displaying Tables Structures

The SQL environment of MS Access does not directly support the display of tables' structures. Instead, in MS Access, the graphical user interface (GUI) approach is used to display tables' structures.

To view the columns that make up a table's structure, use the **Documenter** command of the **Tools** menu of the MS Access window. To view a table's structure, click the **Tools** menu, point to the **Analyze** submenu to display commands of the submenu, and then click the **Documenter** command. Clicking on the **Documenter** command will display the **Documenter** dialog box. Make sure the **tables** tab is selected on the dialog box, check the box beside the table name you want the structure displayed, and then click the **Ok** button. See figures 9.3 and 9.4

> **Note:** Refer to chapter two on how to open a database. Besides using different hyperlinks to create and open databases, every other steps discussed in chapter one on how to activate and use the SQL window of MS Access are the same.

Figure 9.3

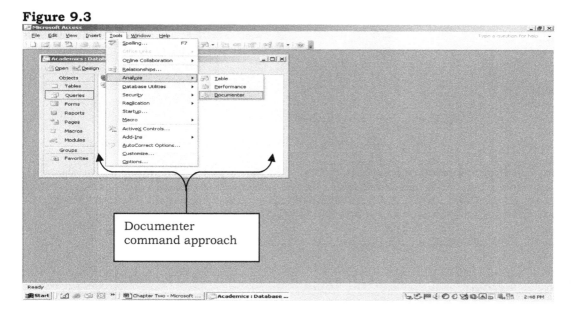

Creating and Maintaining Tables Structures

Figure 9.4

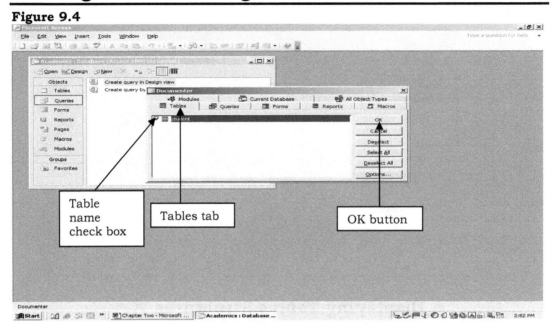

Table name check box

Tables tab

OK button

Figure 9.5 shows a portion of the structure of the student table.

Figure 9.5

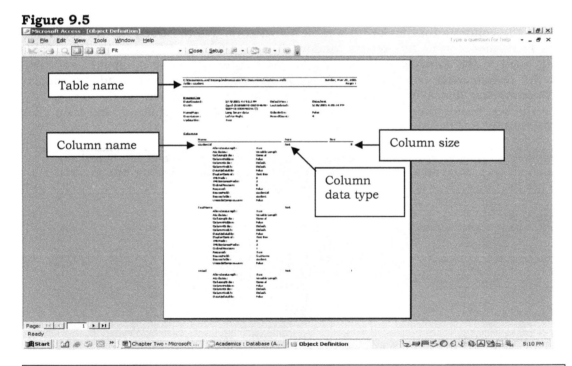

Table name

Column name

Column size

Column data type

Note: The ***Documenter*** command does not only display a table's structure, it also shows table's relationships, defined constraints for the table's columns, the table's indexes, users' permissions, and other structural facts about the table. In MS Access, the ***Documenter*** is a database's data dictionary or system catalog.

Oracle uses the DESCRIBE command to display the structure of a table.

Example:
DESCRIBE student

Creating New Tables Using Existing Tables

An alternative way of creating new tables in MS Access SQL is using the SELECT...INTO statement. This statement uses an INTO clause. The SELECT...INTO statement is a special SELECT statement. The statement can be used to copy the structures of existing tables or copy the structures and contents of existing tables and uses the structures or the structures and the contents to create new tables. This special SELECT statement displays a confirmation message, just as data manipulation language (DML) statements do, before completing its task.

The statement can produce the exact replica of existing single tables if so desired. In other words, the statement can be used to clone existing single tables if you want the new tables to maintain identical structures and contain the same contents as the tables being copied. However, the SELECT...INTO statement does not transfer constraints defined for the existing tables to the new tables. You have to redefine the constraints, if so desired, for the new tables after creating them.

You can also use this special SELECT statement to create a new table by combining the structures or structures and data from two or more existing tables. To do so, list the existing tables in the FROM clause of the statement and separate them by commas.

The basic syntax for the SELECT...INTO statement is

SELECT [predicate] {[ALL] * | *existingColumnName*, ... | *columnExpression*, ...}
INTO *newTableName*
FROM *existingTableName*
[WHERE *condition*];

where

- predicate is a condition keyword, such as DISTINCT, used to restrict records
- Symbol * is to include all columns in the new table
- *existingColumnName* is the column to be copied from the existing table to the new table
- *columnExpression* is the expression formed by the combination of column(s) and data value(s). The column(s) and the data used in a column expression must be of the same data type.
- *newTableName* is the name of the table to be created
- *existingTableName* is the table that is being copied
- *condition* is a restriction on records to be copied from the existing table if the table contains data.
- Symbols [ ] mean items are optional
- Symbol | symbolizes **Or** Boolean operator. You can also list both *existingColumnName* and *columnExpression* in the SELECT clause of the statement
- Symbols ... mean more columns and/or columns' expressions can be listed

There are three required clauses for this special SELECT statement. The mandatory clauses are the SELECT clause, the INTO clause, and the FROM clause. The fourth clause, the WHERE clause, is a condition clause and it is optional. The column list and the columns' expressions of the SELECT clause are also optional. You may list the columns you want to include from the existing table or you may list acceptable columns' expressions as the columns of the new table.

Creating and Maintaining Tables Structures

Alternatively, you may want to copy the entire columns of the existing table in the same order to the new table. Following the INTO keyword is the name of the new table you are creating. Following the FROM keyword is the name of the existing table you are copying. SELECT statements are discussed in detail in chapter two of this textbook.

For the purpose of demonstration, the complete structure of the student table in the **Academics** database will be copied to a new table called studentMod. That is studentMod table is created using the structural definition of the student table. The MS Access SQL statement to accomplish the operation is

SELECT *
INTO studentMod
FROM student;

The asterisk symbol (*) in the SELECT clause is used to include all columns with identical names from the existing table to the new table.

Now, open the **Academics** database and type and run the SELECT...INTO statement to create the new table called studentMod. In MS Access 2007, a confirmation message dialog box is displayed when this special SELECT statement is run. The table, after its creation, will be identical in structure to the student table.

Note: Oracle uses an approach that includes a subquery to create new tables using existing tables. The columns' lists of the existing tables are optional just as in MS Access SQL environment. The asterisk symbol (*) can be included in the SELECT clause of the subquery to copy the entire structure and the contents (if any) of an existing table to a new table.

Example:
CREATE TABLE studentMod
AS (SELECT *
FROM student);

Modifying Tables Structures

Situations may arise when you might want to change the structures of tables. MS Access SQL provides ways of performing such structural alterations. To make structural changes, you use the ALTER TABLE command to code the ALTER TABLE statement. The statement is used in MS Access SQL to (i) add new columns to tables, (ii) change the data types and sizes of columns, (iii) remove columns from tables, (iv) define constraints for columns, and (v) remove constraints from columns. The ALTER TABLE statement is written in different forms depending on the type of structural modification that is to be performed.

ALTER TABLE Statements: An ALTER TABLE statement is a SQL instruction used to modify the structure of a table and the properties that are associated with the structure.

The ALTER TABLE command is part of SQL subsection called data definition language (DDL). Like the CREATE TABLE statement, the ALTER TABLE statement and other data definition language statements do not display confirmation messages. In MS Access SQL, when a DDL statement is executed and no message is displayed, that is an indication that the operation is successful.

Chapter Nine

Adding Columns to Tables

The ALTER TABLE...ADD statement is used to add new columns to tables. The basic syntax for the ALTER TABLE...ADD statement used to add columns to a table is

ALTER TABLE *existingTableName*
ADD *newColumnName dataType* [*constraintType*], *newColumnName dataType* [*constraintType*], ...;

where

- *existingTableName* is the table where the column is to be added
- *newColumName* is the name of the column to be included in the table
- *dataType* is the type of data the column will store
- *constraintType* is the type of rule that is defined for the column
- Symbols [ ] mean items are optional
- Symbols ... mean more columns can be listed

This statement consists of two mandatory clauses, namely, the ALTER TABLE clause and the ADD clause. The ALTER TABLE clause is used to specify the existing table and the ADD clause is used to list new columns to be added to the table. Following the ALTER TABLE keywords is the existing table. Following the ADD keyword are the new columns' definitions.

You can use the statement to add one column or more columns to a table. When adding more than one column, use commas to separate one column definition from the other in the ADD clause of the statement. Using this statement, the new columns are appended as the last columns of the table. In SQL environment, columns that are added to a table after the table has being created are listed as the last columns in the table's structure.

> **Note:** You can also include constraints' definitions when adding new columns to tables. The only exception is the primary key constraint. The primary key constraint can only be defined after adding the column(s) to the table, populate the column(s) with unique data and that there is no primary key defined previously for the table.

To change the structure of the student table in the ***Academics*** database by adding a new column called userId to it, type and run the following ALTER TABLE...ADD statement.

ALTER TABLE student
ADD userId VARCHAR(8) NOT NULL;

The ALTER TABLE...ADD statement, after its execution, adds the userId column defined with not null constraint to the student table.

It is assumed that the new userId column stores students' logon user identification data. Now, let's add two more columns (state and gpa) using one ALTER TABLE...ADD statement. Type and run the following ALTER TABLE...ADD statement.

ALTER TABLE student
ADD state VARCHAR(15), gpa SINGLE;

The state column with fifteen character positions and the gpa column are added with no constraints. Constraints can be defined later for the two columns.

Creating and Maintaining Tables Structures

> **Note:** Oracle allows the use of parentheses to enclose the columns in the ADD clause of the ALTER TABLE statement. Oracle also allows the use of DEFAULT clause in the ADD clause to assign a beginning value to a column.
>
> Example:
> ALTER TABLE student
> ADD (firstName VARCHAR2(15) DEFAULT 'Ememgi Elo-Eghosa');

To set beginning values to columns that are added to tables in MS Access SQL, use the UPDATE statement.

Changing Columns Data Types and Sizes

MS Access SQL allows you to change of columns' data types and sizes where applicable. You can change a column's data type from integer to floating or adjust the size of the column. The ALTER TABLE...ALTER [COLUMN] statement is used to modify columns' data types and sizes. The basic syntax for the statement is

ALTER TABLE *existingTableName*
ALTER [COLUMN] *existingColumnName dataType [constraintType]*;

where

- *existingTableName* is the table that contains the column which data type and/or size is to be changed
- *existingColumName* is the column which data type and/or size is to be changed
- *dataType* is the new type of data the column will store
- *constraintType* is the type of rule that is defined for the column
- Symbols [ ] mean items are optional

This statement consists of two mandatory clauses, namely, the ALTER TABLE clause and the ALTER [COLUMN] clause. The COLUMN keyword in the ALTER [COLUMN] clause is an optional keyword. The ALTER TABLE clause is used to specify the table and the ALTER [COLUMN] clause is used to list the column which data type and/or size is to be modified. Following the ALTER TABLE keywords is the existing table. Following the ALTER [COLUMN] keyword is the column to be modified. In MS Access SQL, the statement is used to change only one column at a time.

> **Note:** In MS Access SQL, except for the primary key constraint, you can modify columns' data types and sizes regardless of whether the columns contain data or not. In other words, the columns, in terms of their data types and sizes, can be changed at any time. A warning message may be displayed if you try to change the data type of a table's primary key from one type to another once the primary key contains data. The warning message will appear when converting a primary key column with character data type to numeric data type if the column is filled with text rather than digits. The warning message may also be an indication that the primary key column cannot contain null values, so the data type modification cannot be performed. Sometimes, a data type conversion will delete the previous content of a non primary key column.

You can also include constraint definitions when modifying the data type and/or size of an existing column. Again, the only exception is the primary key constraint. The primary key constraint can only be defined if the column that is being altered contains no null values, the values are unique, and there is no primary key defined for the table previously.

Chapter Nine

When the statement is used to change the data type of a non-key column that is already filled with data to a different data type, the column data are either deleted to accept the new data type or the data are converted to agree with the new data type.

To change the data types of both state and gpa columns of the student table in the **Academics** database to CHAR and DOUBLE respectively, type and run the following two ALTER TABLE...ALTER [COLUMN] statements. Each of the statement is executed independently as MS Access SQL window allows the execution of one SQL statement at a time.

ALTER TABLE student
ALTER COLUMN state CHAR(10);

ALTER TABLE student
ALTER COLUMN gpa DOUBLE;

The first ALTER TABLE...ALTER [COLUMN] statement changes the state column to the CHAR subtype data type with the size of the column to 10 character positions from the previous size of 15. The second ALTER TABLE...ALTER [COLUMN] statement modifies the gpa column from the SINGLE subtype data type to DOUBLE subtype data type.

Changing Data Types and Sizes of Foreign Keys Columns
To modify the data types and/or sizes of columns already defined with the foreign key constraint, the constraint must first be removed from the columns. It is only then that the data types and/or sizes can be changed. Once the foreign key constraint has been removed and the changes to the columns have been made, the columns can remain either as non-key columns or used again as foreign key columns.

The following basic syntax is used to redefine a column again as a foreign key once the constraint has been dropped and the data type and/or size has been changed.

ALTER TABLE existingTableName
ALTER [COLUMN] existingColumnName dataType [CONSTRAINT constraintName]
REFERENCES parentTableName(referencedColumnName, ...);
where

- existingTableName is the table where the column exists
- existingColumName is the column to be defined with the foreign key constraint type
- dataType is the type of data the column will store
- constraintName is the name to be assigned to the constraint
- parentTableName is the parent table that is being referenced
- referencedColumnName is the column that is being referenced in the parent table
- Symbols [ ] mean items are optional
- Symbols ... mean more columns can be listed

The REFERENCES clause consists of the REFERENCES keyword, the parent table that is being referenced by the foreign key, and the column that is being referenced in the parent table by the foreign key. A foreign key can consist of more than one column and in such situation the foreign key columns must be separated by commas in the REFERENCES clause. The constraint type FOREIGN KEY keywords are not included or written as part of the REFERENCES clause.

Creating and Maintaining Tables Structures

The CONSTRAINT keyword is used to assign a descriptive name to a constraint and it must precede the constraint name. Likewise, the REFERENCES keyword is used to indicate the parent table and the column(s) that are being referenced and the keyword must precede the parent table and the referenced column(s). The column(s) that are being referenced in the parent table must be enclosed in parentheses.

Assume, for example, that a table called fac2 exists and one of its columns named studentId serves as a foreign key. Let's assume that the name of the constraint is studId_fk. We want the constraint to be dropped, change the column size from eight to six character positions, and then use the column as a foreign key to reference the departmentCode column of the department table. The following ALTER TABLE...DROP statement and the ALTER TABLE...ALTER [COLUMN] statement accomplish the operation.

ALTER TABLE fac2
DROP CONSTRAINT studId_fk;

ALTER TABLE fac2
ALTER COLUMN studentId CHAR(6) CONSTRAINT dept_fk REFERENCES department(departmentCode);

> **Note:** The MODIFY clause is used to change the data types of a table's columns in Oracle. Oracle also allows the changing of several columns' data types and sizes using one ALTER TABLE statement. The use of parentheses to enclose the columns in the MODIFY clause of the statement are allowed. In Oracle, it is easier to modify columns' data types when the table contains no data. If the columns contain data, there are certain rules to observe especially with numeric columns. These rules are also observed when adjusting the sizes of character data type columns that already contain data. Oracle also allows the DEFAULT clause in the MODIFY clause to assign a beginning value to a column.
>
> Example:
> ALTER TABLE student
> MODIFY (firstName VARCHAR2(15) DEFAULT 'Ememgi Elo-Eghosa');

Removing Columns from Tables

There are times when tables may contain columns that are no longer needed. The data in those columns may be obsolete or the columns may no longer serve vital purposes. In such situations, you may want to delete or remove the columns permanently from the tables. The ALTER TABLE...DROP [COLUMN] statement is used to remove columns from tables. The basic syntax for the statement is

ALTER TABLE existingTableName
DROP [COLUMN] existingColumnName, existingColumnName, ...;

where

- *existingTableName* is the table that contains the column to be removed
- *existingColumName* is the column to be removed
- Symbols [ ] mean item is optional
- Symbols ... mean more columns can be listed

The ALTER TABLE...DROP [COLUMN] statement that is used to remove columns from tables in MS Access SQL allows the listing of more than one column in one DROP [COLUMN] clause. In MS Access SQL, the COLUMN keyword in the DROP [COLUMN] clause of the statement is optional. The DROP keyword can be used alone in that clause when removing columns from a table. If you are listing more than one column to be removed in the DROP [COLUMN] clause of the statement, you must separate the columns with commas.

This statement consists of two mandatory clauses, namely, the ALTER TABLE clause and the DROP [COLUMN] clause. The ALTER TABLE clause is used to specify the table and the DROP [COLUMN] clause is used to list the column(s) to be removed from the table. Following the ALTER TABLE keywords is the table. Following the DROP [COLUMN] keywords is/are the column(s) to be removed.

To remove both state and gpa columns from the student table in one statement, the following ALTER TABLE statement, after its execution, accomplishes the operation. Type and run the ALTER TABLE...DROP [COLUMN] statement to remove the columns from the student table.

ALTER TABLE student
DROP COLUMN state, gpa;

Once columns are dropped, they cannot be recovered. You have to create the columns again if you want them to again be part of the table they are deleted from.

> **Note:** To remove or delete primary key and foreign key columns, you must first drop the keys' constraints from the columns before deleting them.
>
> Oracle allows only one column to be removed at a time. For example, to drop five columns from a table in Oracle, you have to type and run the statement five times, one for each column to be removed. Example:
>
> ALTER TABLE student
> DROP COLUMN state;

Truncating Tables

Truncating is the process of deleting all data from tables but leaving the tables' structures intact. To truncate is to keep a table's structure without data. In MS Access SQL, the DELETE statement is used to truncate tables. The DELETE statement is discussed in detail in chapter eleven of this textbook.

The basic syntax for the DELETE statement is

DELETE [[ALL] * | *existingColumnName*, ...]
FROM *existingTableName*
[WHERE *condition*];

where

- Symbol * means to include all columns
- *existingColumnName* is the column in the table to be truncated
- *existingTableName* is the table that contains the data to be deleted
- *condition* is a restriction on data to be deleted from the existing table
- Symbols [ ] mean items are optional
- Symbol | symbolizes **Or** Boolean operator
- Symbols ... mean more columns can be listed

The DELETE statement has only two mandatory clauses, namely, the DELETE clause and the FROM clause. The WHERE clause and the column list of the DELETE clause

Creating and Maintaining Tables Structures

are optional. To truncate a table in MS Access SQL, you must not include the optional WHERE clause. Following the DELETE keyword of the statement, you can list the optional (i) columns, (ii) combination of the ALL keyword and the asterisk symbol, or (iii) asterisk symbol. Following the FROM keyword, you list the table to be truncated.

To truncate the studentMod table in the *Academics* database, type and run the following DELETE statement.

```
DELETE
FROM studentMod;
```

When the statement is run, a confirmation message is displayed informing you that a certain number of records will be deleted from the table. You click the **Ok** button of the message box if you want to truncate the table.

> **Note:** In MS Access SQL, the execution of all data manipulation language (DML) statements displays confirmation messages. Oracle uses the TRUNCATE command to code the TRUNCATE statement that removes all data from a table.
>
> Example:
> TRUNCATE TABLE studentMod;

Renaming and Displaying Tables and Columns

MS Access SQL does not directly support the renaming of tables or displaying the tables. Rather those actions are achieved through MS Access graphic user interface (GUI) environment. To change or display the name of a table, you must display the database Object window. Review chapter one on how to activate MS Access SQL window until the database Object window is displayed. See figure 9.6.

Figure 9.6

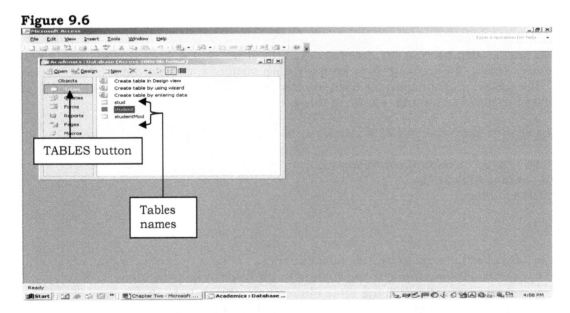

Make sure the TABLES button is clicked to display the names of the tables in the current database. In the *Academics* database, there are three tables currently in the database as shown in figure 9.6. To rename a table right-click (click the right button of the mouse) the table's name and then click the **Rename** command on the shortcut menu. See figure 9.7.

Figure 9.7

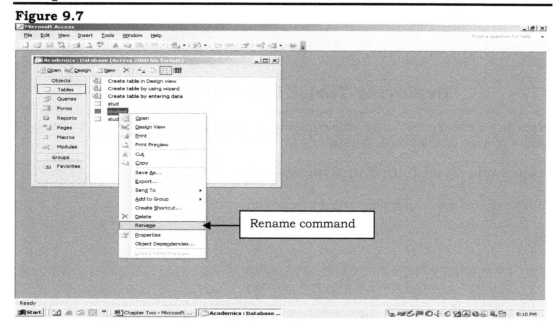

Rename command

Once you have clicked the **Rename** command, a small rectangular box is placed around the table's name. Delete the old name in the rectangular box and type the new name you want to assign to the table. When you have finished typing the new name, click any where outside the rectangular box but within the Object window of MS Access to register the new name.

To change or display the name of a table's column, you must display the database object window. Review figure 9.6. To rename a column double-click the table's name to display the table's column(s). Alternatively, you can right-click the table's name to display the shortcut menu for the table. Then click the **Open** command on the shortcut menu to display the table's column(s).

Right-click the column you want to rename to display the column's shortcut menu. Then click the **Rename Column** command of the menu to highlight the column's name. Delete the name and type the new name you want to assign to the column. When you have finished typing the new name, press the ENTER key to register the new name for the column. See figure 9.8.

Figure 9.8

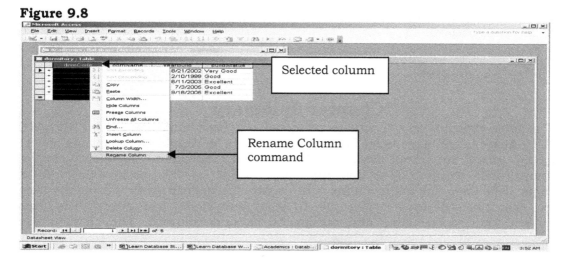

Selected column

Rename Column command

> **Note:** Oracle uses the RENAME...TO statement to assign a new name to a table.
>
> Example:
> RENAME studentMod TO studentModOne;

Removing Tables from Databases

Tables are removed from a database when they are no longer needed. Dropping tables becomes an excellent option when their uses have expired. The DROP TABLE statement is used to remove tables from a database.

The basic syntax for the DROP TABLE statement is.

DROP TABLE *existingTableName*, *existingTableName*, ...;

where

- *existingTableName* is the table to be removed
- Symbols ... mean more tables can be listed

DROP TABLE Statement: A DROP TABLE statement is a SQL instruction used to remove a table permanently from a database.

The DROP TABLE statement has only one mandatory clause, namely, the DROP TABLE clause. The statement can be used in MS Access SQL to remove more than one table at the same time. If you are removing more than one table using one DROP TABLE statement, you must separate the tables with commas.

Following the keywords DROP TABLE is the table(s) to be removed. The DROP TABLE statement removes tables permanently from the databases. In addition, all other database objects, such as indexes, created for the deleted tables are also removed permanently. To have deleted tables exist again in their previous databases, the tables must be created again in their respective databases.

To remove the studentMod table from the *Academics* database, type and run the following DROP TABLE statement.

DROP TABLE studentMod;

> **Note:** Oracle allows only one existing table to be removed at a time. For example, to drop five tables from a database in Oracle, you have to type and run the statement five times, one for each table to be removed.
>
> Example
> DROP TABLE studentMod;

Chapter Summary

This chapter explains how to create relational database tables using the CREATE TABLE statement and the special SELECT statement. The chapter also explains how to (i) modify tables' structures using the ALTER TABLE command, (ii) display tables' structures and view the SQL statements stored in queries, (iii) specify data types in columns' definitions, (iv) add columns with constraints defined (v) drop columns from tables, (vi) truncate tables using the DELETE statement, (vii) drop tables from databases, and (viii) rename and display tables and columns. The chapter also indicates, where SQL statements differ, how their syntax and statements are written in both MS Access and Oracle.

Tables Structures Syntax and Statements Summary

The table below presents the tables' structures syntax and statements' examples discussed in this chapter for creating, modifying, and removing tables.

Statement Type	Statement Syntax	Statement Example
CREATE TABLE statement is used to create the structure for a new table	CREATE TABLE *newTableName(newColumnName dataType [constrainTtype], newColumnName dataType [constraintType], …);*	CREATE TABLE student (studentId CHAR(8) PRIMARY KEY, firstName VARCHAR(15) NOT NULL, initial TEXT(1), lastName VARCHAR(25) NOT NULL, classification VARCHAR(10) NOT NULL, dateFirstEnrolled DATE NOT NULL);
SELECT…INTO…FROM statement is used to create the structure or the structure and content for a new table using an existing table	SELECT [predicate] {[ALL]* | *existingColumnName*, *columnExpression*, …} INTO *newTableName* FROM *existingTableName* [WHERE *condition*];	SELECT TOP 60 PERCENT * INTO studentMod FROM student;
ALTER TABLE…ADD statement is used to add new columns to a table	ALTER TABLE *existingTableName* ADD *newColumnName dataType* [constraintType], *newColumnName dataType* [constraintType], …;	ALTER TABLE student ADD userId VARCHAR(8) NOT NULL;
ALTER TABLE…ALTER [COLUMN] statement is used to change a column's data type and size	ALTER TABLE *existingTableName* ALTER [COLUMN] *existingColumnName dataType* [constraintType];	ALTER TABLE student ALTER COLUMN state CHAR(10);
ALTER TABLE…DROP [COLUMN] statement is used to remove columns from a table	ALTER TABLE *existingTableName* DROP [COLUMN] *existingColumnName*, *existingColumnName*, …;	ALTER TABLE student DROP COLUMN state;
DELETE statement is used to truncate a table	DELETE [[ALL]* | *existingColumnName*, …] FROM *existingTableName*;	DELETE FROM studentMod;
DROP TABLE statement is used to remove tables from a database	DROP TABLE *existingTableName*, *existingTableName*, …;	DROP TABLE studentMod;

Key Terms

ALTER TABLE
Character
Column specifications
Constraints
CREATE TABLE
Data types
Double-precision
DROP TABLE
Fixed-length columns
Identifiers

Integer
Keywords
MS Access SQL
Oracle
SELECT
Single-precision
Table structures
Truncate
User-defined names
Variable-length columns

Chapter Review Questions

Multiple Choice Questions

1. Creating a table's structure is the same as describing the table's
      a. layout.
      b. plan.
      c. frame.
      d. all of the above.

2. An instruction that direct the computer to do something is called a
      a. line.
      b. language.
      c. statement.
      d. logic.

3. Which of the following is not true? A column definition at least contains a
      a. column name.
      b. table name.
      c. data type where appropriate.
      d. constraint type.

4. A name assigned by a programmer in a programming language is called a
      _____ name.
      a. program
      b. programmer
      c. user-defined
      d. language

5. Which of the following is not a subtype of numeric data type?
      a. SHORT.
      b. LONG.
      c. FLOAT4.
      d. LONGBINARY.

6. In MS Access SQL, to truncate a table, we use the _____ statement.
      a. TRUNCATE
      b. DELETE
      c. DROP
      d. DROP FROM

7. When a column defined with variable-length size contains data with fewer
    characters than the space provided, the ____ side of the column is truncated.
      a. left
      b. middle
      c. right
      d. none of the above

8. In MS Access, Time data type occupies _____ bytes.
      a. 8
      b. 4
      c. 16
      d. 2

9. Assume that the facultyX table exists and the table contains the column called facLastName.
    Study the following SQL statement and point out the errors if any.
      ALTER TABLE facultyX,
      DROP COLUMN facLastName;

      a. The ALTER TABLE clause is written incorrectly.
      b. The DROP COLUMN clause is written incorrectly.

c. A table must not be named facultyX.

d. there is nothing wrong with the statement.

10. Assume that the facInfo table exists and that the word "facModInfo" is a valid name for a table. Study the following SQL statement and choose the best answer.

SELECT *
INTO facModInfo
FROM facInfo;

a. It creates a table called facInfo using the data from facModInfo table.

b. It creates a table called facModInfo using the data from facInfo table.

c. It displays some of the data from facInfo table.

d. It displays some of the data from facModInfo table.

True or False Questions

11. A syntax error is a runtime error.
    a. True
    b. False

12. One of the elements of a column definition is the constraint type.
    a. True
    b. False

13. In MS Access SQL, one can change the data type and size of any column at any time.
    a. True
    b. False

14. To delete a column from an existing table, we use the ALTER TABLE...DROP [COLUMN] statement.
    a. True
    b. False

15. Once a column is removed from a table, the removal of the column is permanent.
    a. True
    b. False

16. A column that exists in one table can have identical name as another column that exists in a different table.
    a. True
    b. False

17. In a CEATE TABLE statement, one column definition must be separated from another column definition by a semicolon.
    a. True
    b. False

Fill in the blank Questions

18. A _____ is an instruction that directs the computer to do something.

19. Tables' identifiers are _____ used to identify tables

20 Oracle uses the _____ clause with the ALTER TABLE clause to change the data type of a column.

21. An error that occurs when the rules of a programming language is not followed is called a _____ error.

22. A column specification is the same as a column _____.

23. To add a new column to a table we use the _____ statement.

Creating and Maintaining Tables Structures

Essay Type Questions

24. What does the acronym SQL represents?

25. What is table truncating and how is it achieved in MS Access SQL environment?

26. In designing a good relational database, what elements must be included, at least, in the columns' definitions of the tables?

27. Define a data type and give an example using a SQL statement?

28. List three functions of the ALTER TABLE clause?

Hands-on Activities

Perform the following hands-on exercises using the *Academics* database.

1. Create a new table called residentHall that contains two columns. The columns are called hallCode and hallName. The two columns' data types are character data types with the hallCode column having a fixed-length size of six and the hallName column having a variable-length size of twenty.

2. Add a new column called yearBuild with date data type to the table.

3. Modify the hallName column to have a variable-length size of twenty five.

4. Create a new table called studentInfo with four columns namely; studentId, fullName, birthDate, and birthPlace. The studentId column should be of short numeric data type, fullName column should be of variable-length size character data type, birthDate column should be of date data type, and birthPlace column should be of variable-length size character data type. Choose columns' dimensions of your choice for fullName and birthPlace columns.

5. Change the data type of the studentId column of the studentInfo table to long numeric data type.

6. Create a new table called studentCopy using the student table and the SELECT...INTO statement.

7. Drop the classification column from the studentCopy table.

8. Truncate the studentCopy table.

9. Remove the studentCopy table from the database.

10. Delete the studentInfo table from the database.

Chapter Ten

Applying Constraints to Tables Columns

Chapter Objectives
After completing this chapter, you should be able to
- Define constraints at column level for new tables
- Define constraints at table level for new tables
- Define constraints after tables have been created
- Define constraints for columns not previously defined with constraints
- Remove constraints from tables

Defining Constraints

Constraints are rules used to enforce restrictions to relational databases' tables so data contained in the tables are accurate and have integrity. Constraints make certain that valid data are entering the tables and that data fall within the validation ranges defined for the tables' columns.

Constraints are all about correctness and validity of data rather than security measures, and they assist databases to be in consistent or error-free states. Good databases must contain data that have integrity and constraints are the yardsticks for maintaining that integrity. There are six constraints that can be defined for tables' columns. They are:

Primary Key Constraint
This constraint is used to establish entity integrity. That is a column that serves as the primary key of a table cannot contain the null value and the non-null values the column stores must be unique (not duplicated). The primary key constraint implicitly establishes both the unique constraint and the not null constraint for the column that serves as the primary key of a table. However, a composite primary key which usually consists of more than one column allow duplication of data within its columns, but there must be certain entries of the composite primary key columns that must not be duplicated for the records of the composite primary key table to be unique.

This constraint is a row-level constraint and therefore is used to make each record in a table unique. A table can only have one primary key.

Foreign Key Constraint
This constraint is used to establish referential integrity. The constraint ensures that when the foreign key of a child table contains values, those values must match some values in the primary key of the parent table the child table is referencing. The foreign key column(s) of a child table must have the same structural definitions as the primary key column(s) of the parent table they are referencing. The names of the foreign key and the primary key columns may defer, but their data types and sizes must match. A child table can have more than one foreign key if it is designed to have relationships with more than one parent table.

The foreign key constraint implicitly establishes the associations that exist between tables. The constraint is a table-level constraint and therefore is used to establish relationships between tables.

Applying Constraints to Tables Columns

Unique Constraint

This constraint is used to establish unique (no duplication) integrity. The constraint ensures that data entered into a particular column cannot be duplicated, but the column can contain the null value. The unique constraint is a column-level constraint and therefore is used to ensure that data contained in a column are not duplicated.

Not Null Constraint

This constraint is used to establish not null (a-must-value) integrity. That is a particular column must always receive data when data entry operations are performed for that column. The constraint also permits the column to accept duplicate values. This constraint is a column-level constraint and therefore is used to ensure that data values are entered into all the entries of a column.

Null Constraint

The null constraint is used to establish null (can-be-empty) integrity. This constraint is the default constraint when no other constraint is defined for a column. This constraint allows a particular column to receive no data if so desired. In addition, the constraint also allows the column to receive values if the column needs to be filled with data. In MS Access SQL, this constraint is defined for a new column by simply not defining a constraint for the column. The null constraint is a column-level constraint and therefore is used to make sure that a column has the option of storing no data.

Check Constraint

The check constraint is used to establish domain integrity. This constraint declares the permissible values and controls the legitimacy of values that must enter a particular column. For example, a column defined to accept numeric data might also be declared to accept values ranging from 10 to 25 only or to accept list of values such as 2.0, 3.25, and 7.50. Numeric values outside the specified range or list is rejected even though the values meet the requirements of the column's data type. The check constraint is a column-level constraint and therefore is used to make sure that data entering into a column fall within the permissible values for that column.

Except for the check constraint, MS Access SQL directly supports all other constraints. The check constraint is defined through MS Access graphical user interface (GUI).

The standard conventions used as suffix when assigning descriptive names to constraints are
- _pk for primary key
- _fk for foreign key
- _uk for unique
- _nn for not null
- _ck for check

> *Note:* A record's entries for a table are rejected when any column constraint for that table is violated.

Establishing Constraints

Constraints are defined either when tables are created using CREATE TABLE statement or when tables are modified using ALTER TABLE statement. You can choose to give constraints descriptive names or you can allow the database management system that is being used to assign generic names to constraints. Assigning meaningful names to constraints are optional. When constraints are given descriptive names, it is easier to identify them in the system catalog or in the data dictionary and in SQL statements.

Like tables' and columns' names, descriptive constraints' names are identifiers and created by the person creating or modifying the tables. The names are user- or programmer-defined names.

The following generic rules are guides that can be helpful when assigning descriptive names to constraints. The names

1. must be one word. That is no space between words if the name is a compound name. MS Access allows spaces in compound names as long as the compound names are enclosed in square brackets [ ].
2. can contain letters, digits, and underscore (_),
3. must begin with letters.
4. cannot be keywords.
5. must be unique. That is constraints' names cannot be duplicated within the same database.

> **Note:** The number of characters permitted for a constraint name varies depending on the database programming language that is being used.

MS Access SQL provides two methods for defining constraints for columns. The two approaches are the column-level method and the table-level method.

Column-Level Approach

In the column-level approach, constraints are defined as part of columns' definitions when a table is created using the CREATE TABLE statement. The basic syntax for this approach is

CREATE TABLE *newTableName(newColumnName dataType* [CONSTRAINT *constraintName*] *constraintType, newColumnName dataType* [CONSTRAINT *constraintName*] *constraintType, ...)*;

where

- *newTableName* is the name of the table to be created
- *newColumName* is the name of the column to be included in the table
- *dataType* is the type of data the column will store
- *constraintName* is the name to be assigned to the constraint
- *constraintType* is the type of constraint defined for the column
- Symbols [ ] mean items are optional
- Symbols ... mean more columns can be listed

> **Note:** To assign a descriptive name to a constraint, the CONSTRAINT keyword is used and the keyword must precede the name to be assigned to the constraint. Following the constraint name is the constraint type.
>
> The person creating the table can continue adding columns until the number of columns needed in the table is reached or until the maximum number of columns allowed by the database management system is reached.

You are about to create a faculty table in the **Academics** database to include constraints using the column-level approach. Start MS Access to open the SQL window. The following CREATE TABLE statement shows how constraints are defined at the column-level when creating a table using CREATE TABLE statement. Type and run the CREATE TABLE statement to create the faculty table.

Applying Constraints to Tables Columns

Note: Do not include the three explanation boxes used in the CREATE TABLE statement. The boxes explain how constraints are defined at the column level.

CREATE TABLE faculty
(facultyId CHAR(8) CONSTRAINT facultyid_pk PRIMARY KEY,
firstName VARCHAR(15) NOT NULL,
initial TEXT(1) NULL,
lastName VARCHAR(25) CONSTRAINT lastnname_nn NOT NULL);

Keyword used to assign a name to a constraint	Constraint name	Constraint type

In the CREATE TABLE statement, the first and the last columns' definitions assign meaningful names to the constraints. The constraint name given to the facultyId column constraint (PRIMARY KEY) is facukty_pk and the constraint name given to the lastName column constraint (NOT NULL) is lastname_nn. The other two columns of the faculty table are defined with constraints, but are not given descriptive names. The database management system used to create the table will, therefore, give the two columns generic constraints' names. The constraints are said to be defined using column-level approach because they appear in the columns' definitions of the table being created.

Defining Foreign Key Constraint at the Column Level

Defining the foreign key constraint at the column level for a CREATE TABLE statement uses the REFERENCES clause.

Note: The clause includes the REFERENCES keyword, the parent table the foreign key is referencing, and the column(s) from the parent table that are being referenced by the foreign key. The column(s) that are being referenced in the parent table must be enclosed in parentheses.

The constraint type FOREIGN KEY keywords are not written as part of the constraint definition.

The basic syntax for defining the foreign key constraint for one column at the column level using the CREATE TABLE statement is

CREATE TABLE *newTableName*
(*newColumnName*   *dataType*   [CONSTRAINT   *constraintName*]   REFERENCES
parentTableName(*referencedColumnName*));

where

- *newTableName* is the name of the table to be created
- *newColumName* is the name of the column to be included in the table
- *dataType* is the type of data the column will store
- *constraintName* is the name to be assigned to the constraint
- *parentTableName* is the parent table that is being referenced
- *referencedColumnName* is the column that is being referenced in the parent table
- Symbols [ ] mean item is optional

> *Note:* The REFERENCES keyword is used to indicate the parent table and the column(s) that are being referenced in the parent table of the constraint definition. The keyword must precede the parent table and the referenced column(s). The parent table column(s) that are being referenced must be enclosed in parentheses.

The following CREATE TABLE statement creates a table called dom with a student identification column named studentId to be defined with the foreign key constraint. The table associates with the student table.

CREATE   TABLE   dom(studentId   int   CONSTRAINT   stud_fk   REFERENCES student(studenId));

The dom table is the child table and the student table is the corresponding parent table. The studentId column of the student (parent) table is enclosed in parentheses. You might have noticed that the constraint type FOREIGN KEY keywords are missing.

> *Note:* The primary key of a parent table and the foreign key of the corresponding child table must have identical columns' definitions. That is if the primary key column(s) of the parent table is of numeric data type, the foreign key column(s) of the corresponding child table must also be of numeric data type. The names of the primary key column(s) and the foreign key column(s) of the relating tables may be different but their structures must be identical.

The only constraint that cannot be created at the column level is the composite primary key constraint. A composite primary key is a primary key that consists of two or more columns. When a table has a composite primary key, the only place to define the primary key constraint for such a table is by using the table-level approach.

In MS Access SQL, tables with the foreign key constraint cannot be created if their corresponding parents' tables do not exist. For tables to be defined with the foreign key constraint, their corresponding parents' tables must first be created. Remember that the values of foreign keys of childs' tables must conform to some values in the primary keys of their corresponding parents' tables.

> *Note:* In Oracle, tables with the foreign key constraint also cannot be created if their respective parents' tables do not exist. But Oracle uses two keywords to enter data into foreign key columns of childs' tables even if the corresponding primary key columns of their parents' tables contain no data. The two keywords are DISABLE and ENABLE. DISABLE is used to deactivate the foreign key constraint so that data can be loaded into the foreign key columns of childs' tables without referencing the data in the primary key columns of the corresponding parents' tables. ENBLE is used to activate or reactivate the foreign key constraint so that data entered in the foreign key columns of childs' tables match some data in the primary key columns of the corresponding parents' tables. The DISABLE keyword can be included when defining the foreign key constraint for columns at the table level using the CREATE TABLE statement. In such situation, the keyword must be written after the REFERENCES clause used to define the foreign key constraint.
>
> Example:
> CREATE TABLE dom(studentId int CONSTRAINT stud_fk
> REFERENCES student(studentId) DISABLE);
>
> In Oracle, the two keywords are also used with the ALTER TABLE statement to deactivate and reactivate constraints.
>
> Example (to activate):
> ALTER TABLE dom
> ENABLE CONSTRAINT stud_fk;

Applying Constraints to Tables Columns

> and
> Example (to deactivate):
> ALTER TABLE dom
> DISABLE CONSTRAINT stud_fk;

Table-Level Approach

The table-level method defines columns' constraints separately after all other elements of columns' definitions have been defined in the CREATE TABLE statement. At the table level, constraints' definitions are listed at the bottom part of the CREATE TABLE statement. At the table level, constraints definitions are considered as individual sections of the CREATE TABLE statement. They must be separated by commas from the columns' definitions listed at the upper part of the CREATE TABLE statement and they must also be separated by commas from one another in the statement if constraints are defined for different columns or defined for different groups of columns.

The basic syntax for defining columns' constraints at the table level using the CREATE TABLE statement is

CREATE TABLE *newTableName(newColumnName dataType, newColumnName dataType, newColumnName dataType, ...,* [CONSTRAINT *constraintName*] *constraintType(newColumnName),* [CONSTRAINT *constraintName*] *constraintType(newColumName), ...*);

where

- *newTableName* is the name of the table to be created
- *newColumName* is the name of the column to be included in the table
- *dataType* is the type of data the column will store
- *constraintName* is the name to be assigned to the constraint
- *constraintType* is the type of constraint that is defined for the column
- *newColumName* is the column to be defined with the constraint
- Symbols [ ] mean items are optional
- Symbols ... mean more columns and/or constraints can be listed

The column(s) immediately following the constraint type must be enclosed in a pair of parentheses.

The following CREATE TABLE statement creates the academic department table in the **Academics** database with constraints defined at the table level. Type and run the CREATE TABLE statement to create the department table.

CREATE TABLE department
(departmentCode CHAR(6),
departmentName VARCHAR(30),
CONSTRAINT deptCode_pk PRIMARY KEY(departmentCode),
CONSTRAINT deptNam_uk UNIQUE(departmentName));

The last two lines of the CREATE TABLE statement are constraints' definitions lines. The first of the two constraints' lines defines the departmentCode column with the primary key constraint. In other words, the column is the table's primary key. The second constraint line defines the departmentName column with the unique constraint. That is data in that column cannot be duplicated.

226

Chapter Ten

Note: Except for null and not null constraints, all other constraints can be defined at the table level. The null and not null constraints can only be defined at the column level.

The following CREATE TABLE statement creates a table called course with a composite primary key constraint that is defined at the table level. Type and run the CREATE TABLE statement to create the course table in the **Academics** database.

CREATE TABLE course
(courseCode CHAR(6), courseName VARCHAR(25) NOT NULL,
section CHAR(4), creditHours int NOT NULL,
CONSTRAINT couSec_pk PRIMARY KEY(courseCode, section));

Notice that the PRIMARY KEY keywords listed on the last line of the CREATE TABLE statement precede the two columns enclosed in a pair of parentheses. The two columns constitute the table's composite primary key.

Defining Foreign Key Constraint at the Table Level
Defining the foreign key constraint at the table level for a CREATE TABLE statement uses the REFERENCES clause.

Note: Refer to the topic titled "Defining Foreign Key Constraint at the Column Level" in this chapter to review the function of the REFERENCES clause.

The constraint type FOREIGN KEY keywords are written as part of the constraint definition.

The basic syntax for defining a foreign key constraint portion for one column when a table is created at the table level is

[CONSTRAINT *constraintName*] *constraintType*(*newColumnName*) REFRENCES *parentTableName*(*referencedColumnName*),

where

- *constraintName* is the name to be assigned to the constraint
- *constraintType* is the type of constraint that is defined for the column
- *newColumName* is the column to be defined with the constraint
- *parentTableName* is the parent table that is being referenced
- *referencedColumnName* is the column that is being referenced in the parent table
- Symbols [ ] mean item is optional

The REFERENCES keyword is used to indicate the parent table and the column(s) that are being referenced in the parent table of the constraint definition. The keyword must precede the parent table and the referenced column(s). The parent table column(s) that are being referenced must be enclosed in parentheses.

Now, let's create one more table called grade in the **Academics** database to demonstrate how the foreign key constraint is defined at the table level. Type and run the following CEATE TABLE statement to create the grade table.

Applying Constraints to Tables Columns

CREATE TABLE grade(courseCode CHAR(6), section CHAR(4), facultyId CHAR(8), studentId CHAR(8), letterGrade TEXT(2) NOT NULL, CONSTRAINT couSec_pk PRIMARY KEY(courseCode, section, facultyId, studentId), CONSTRAINT couSec_fk FOREIGN KEY(courseCode, section) REFERENCES course(courseCode, section), CONSTRAINT facId_fk FOREIGN KEY(facultyId) REFERENCES faculty(facultyId), CONSTRAINT studId_fk FOREIGN KEY(studentId) REFERENCES student(studentId));

> **Note:** The column(s) defined with any of the following three constraints - primary key, foreign key, unique - must be enclosed in parentheses and they must be listed immediately after the constraint type. The column(s) must be separated by commas if more than one column is listed for the particular constraint type.

The REFERENCES clause of the foreign key constraint definition must follow the constraint type portion of the definition before the commas that separate one constraint definition from another should the CREATE TABLE statement contains several constraints' definitions.

> **Note:** When defining the primary key constraint, the foreign key constraint, and the unique constraint at the table level, the columns being defined with these constraints must be listed more than once in the CREATE TABLE statement. The columns must be listed once in the columns' definitions' part of the CREATE TABLE statement and they must be listed again at the constraints' definitions' part of the CREATE TABLE statement. If the columns are used as both the primary key and the foreign key of a table, as in the case of the grade table just created, the columns must also appear in their respective keys' definitions in the constraint part of the CREATE TABLE statement.

Just as a primary key can be a composite primary key, a foreign key can also be a composite foreign key. The CREATE TABLE statement for the grade table includes a composite foreign key (courseCode and section columns) that references the course (parent) table.

Defining Constraints for Columns after Tables Have Been Created

You can define constraints for columns after tables have been created. To accomplish constraints' definitions after tables have been created, you use the ALTER TABLE statement. The ALTER TABLE statement is used to modify tables' structures and the statement is written in various forms. Two examples of the statement's forms are the ALTER TABLE...ADD statement and the ALTER TABLE...ALTER [COLUMN] statement. The particular form used is determined by the type of the structural modification that is to be performed.

Defining Columns Constraints Using ALTER TABLE...ADD Statement

The ALTER TABLE...ADD statement is used to add new columns to a table and define the constraints for the columns at the same time. The ADD clause of the statement is used to add the new columns and define constraints for the columns.

The basic syntax for adding new columns and defining constraints for those columns after a table has been created is

ALTER TABLE *existingTableName*
ADD *newColumnName dataType* [CONSTRAINT *constraintName*] *constraintType*, *newColumnName dataType* [CONSTRAINT *constraintName*] *constraintType*, ...;

where

- *existingTableName* is the table that will contain the column and its constraint definition
- *newColumName* is the name of the column to be added to the table
- *dataType* is the type of data the column will store
- *constraintName* is the name to be assigned to the constraint
- *constraintType* is the type of constraint that is defined for the column
- Symbols [ ] mean items are optional
- Symbols ... mean more columns can be listed

You can add more than one column with constraints to a table using one ALTER TABLE... ADD statement as long as you separate the columns with commas.

The following ALTER TABLE...ADD statement demonstrates how the office phone number column with the not null constraint is added to the faculty table. Type and run the ALTER TABLE...ADD statement to add the column with the constraint to the table in the **Academics** database.

ALTER TABLE faculty
ADD offPhone CHAR(10) CONSTRAINT offPhone_nn NOT NULL;

In the ALTER TABLLE...ADD statement, the new column is called offPhone and the column's constraint name is offPhone_nn. The not null constraint is defined for the column.

Defining Foreign Key Constraint for New Columns after Tables Have Been Created
Like the column-level approach of the CREATE TABLE statement, adding new columns to a table and defining them with the foreign key constraint at the same time using the ALTER TABLE statement uses the REFERENCES clause.

Note: Refer to the topic titled "Defining Foreign Key Constraint at the Column Level" in this chapter to review the function of the REFERENCES clause.

The constraint type FOREIGN KEY keywords are not written as part of the REFERENCES clause.

The basic syntax for adding a column to a table with the foreign key constraint using the ALTER TABLE statement is

ALTER TABLE *existingTableName*
ADD *newColumName dataType* [CONSTRAINT *constraintName*] REFERENCES *parentTableName*(*referencedColumnName*);

where

- *existingTableName* is the table that will contain the column and its constraint definition
- *newColumName* is the name of the column to be added to the table
- *dataType* is the type of data the column will store
- *constraintName* is the name to be assigned to the constraint
- *parentTableName* is the parent table that is being referenced
- *referencedColumnName* is the column that is being referenced in the parent table
- Symbols [ ] mean item is optional

Applying Constraints to Tables Columns

> **Note:** Refer to the topic titled "Defining Foreign Key Constraint at the Table Level" in this chapter to review the function of the REFERENCES keyword.

The following ALTER TABLE...ADD statement adds the departmentCode column of the department table as a foreign key to the faculty table. Type and run the ALTER TABLE...ADD statement to add the departmentCode column of the department table to the faculty table in the **Academics** database.

ALTER TABLE faculty
ADD   departmentCode   CHAR(6)   CONSTRAINT   departCode_fk   REFERENCES department(departmentCode);

In the ALTER TABLE...ADD statement, the new column is called departmentCode and it is used as a foreign key to reference the departmentCode column (primary key) of the department table.

Defining Columns Constraints Using ALTER TABLE...ALTER [COLUMN] Statement

The ALTER TABLE...ALTER [COLUMN] statement is used, except for null constraint, to define constraints for existing columns that have not been previously defined with constraints. The statement is also used to change columns' constraints from one type to another. However, you cannot convert the current constraints of the primary keys' columns and the foreign keys' columns of tables to new types if the columns are used in establishing tables' relationships. Also, you cannot change other constraints' types of existing columns to the null constraint.

The ALTER [COLUMN] clause of the statement is used to define constraints or to change constraints' types for existing columns.

The basic syntax for defining a constraint for an existing column or changing the constraint type of an existing column is

ALTER TABLE *existingTableName*
ALTER [COLUMN] *existingColumnName* *dataType* [CONSTRAINT *constraintName*] *constraintType*;

where

- *existingTableName* is the table that contains the column
- *existingColumName* is the column to be defined with the constraint
- *dataType* is the type of data the column will store
- *constraintName* is the name to be assigned to the constraint
- *constraintType* is the type of constraint that is defined for the column
- Symbols [ ] mean items are optional

The COLUMN keyword is optional in the ALTER [COLUMN] clause of the ALTER TABLE statement. Following the constraint name is the constraint type.

> **Note:** In MS Access SQL, the ALTER TABLE...ALTER [COLUMN] statement syntax is used to define constraints or change constraints' types for all types of constraints.

The following ALTER TABLE...ALTER [COLUMN] statement defines the column called initial in the faculty table to include the not null constraint. Type and run the ALTER TABLE...ALTER [COLUMN] statement to define the column with the not null constraint.

230

Chapter Ten

ALTER TABLE faculty
ALTER COLUMN initial TEXT(1) CONSTRAINT init_nn NOT NULL;

Defining Foreign Key Constraint Using ALTER TABLE...ALTER [COLUMN] Statement

The foreign key constraint can be defined for existing non-key column(s) if the column(s) can be used to establish relationships between the tables that contain the column(s) and other tables.

The basic syntax for defining a foreign key constraint for an existing non-key column using the ALTER TABLE...ALTER [COLUMN] statement is

ALTER TABLE *existingTableName*
ALTER [COLUMN] *existingColumnName dataType* [CONSTRAINT *constraintName*]
REFERENCES *parentTableName*(*referencedColumnName*);

where

- *existingTableName* is the table where the column exists
- *existingColumName* is the column to be defined with the constraint type
- *dataType* is the type of data the column will store
- *constraintName* is the name to be assigned to the constraint
- *parentTableName* is the parent table that is being referenced
- *referencedColumnName* is the column that is being referenced in the parent table
- Symbols [ ] mean items are optional

Note: Refer to the topic titled "Defining Foreign Key Constraint at the Column Level" in this chapter to review the function of the REFERENCES clause.

The constraint type FOREIGN KEY keywords are not written as part of the REFERENCES clause. The COLUMN keyword in the ALTER [COLUMN] clause of the statement is optional.

Note: Refer to the topic titled "Defining Foreign Key Constraint at the Table Level" in this chapter to review the function of the REFERENCES keyword.

Let's assume that a new table called fac2 is created with a non-key column named facultyId. It is believed that the values of the facultyId column can be used to establish a relationship between the table and the faculty table. The following ALTER TABLE...ALTER [COLUMN] statement can be used to alter or change the facultyId column of the fac2 table to be defined with the foreign key constraint.

ALTER TABLE fac2
ALTER COLUMN facultyId CHAR(8) CONSTRAINT fac2_fk REFERENCES faculty(facultyId);

Note: With the exception of the not null constraint, Oracle uses the ALTER TABLE...ADD statement to define constraints for existing columns. For the not null constraint, Oracle uses the MODIFY clause of the ALTER TABLE statement to assign the constraint to existing columns.

Example:
ALTER TABLE faculty
MODIFY (initial CONSTRAINT init_nn NOT NULL);

Applying Constraints to Tables Columns

In addition to the ALTER TABLE...ALTER [COLUMN] statement, MS Access SQL provides an alternative and a better way of defining the primary key constraint and the unique constraint for existing columns in tables. The alternative method uses the ALTER TABLE...ADD statement.

The basic syntax for the alternative method is

ALTER TABLE *existingTableName*
ADD [CONSTRAINT *constraintName*] *constraintType* (*existingColumnName*, *existingColumnName*, ...);

where

- *existingTableName* is the table that contains the column
- *constraintName* is the name to be assigned to the constraint
- *constraintType* is the type of constraint that is defined for the column
- *existingColumName* is the column to be defined with the constraint
- Symbols [ ] mean item is optional
- Symbols ... mean more columns can be listed

Following the constraint name is the constraint type. This syntax option allows you to include more than one column to the constraint definition. With this syntax, you can define the (i) composite primary key constraint, (ii) composite foreign key constraint, and (iii) unique constraint that consist of more than one column

To demonstrate how to define constraints for existing columns using the alternative way, a new table called courseStudent is created in the **Academics** database. The table is created without primary key and foreign key constraints at this time. Following the table's creation, constraints are defined for both the primary key and the foreign key columns using the alternative method. Type and run the following CREATE TABLE statement to create the courseStudent table.

CREATE TABLE courseStudent
(courseCode CHAR(6), section CHAR(4),
studentId CHAR(8), semester VARCHAR(6) NOT NULL,
semYear DATE NOT NULL);

The following ALTER TABLE...ADD statement is used to define the primary key constraint for the courseStudent table. Type and run the ALTER TABLE...ADD statement to define the primary key constraint for the table.

ALTER TABLE courseStudent
ADD CONSTRAINT coSecStud_pk PRIMARY KEY(courseCode, section, studentId);

Defining Foreign Key Constraint for Existing Columns
The foreign key constraint definition can be accomplished by using the alternative approach. The REFERENCES clause must be included in the definition.

> **Note:** Refer to the topic titled "Defining Foreign Key Constraint at the Column Level" in this chapter to review the function of the REFERENCES clause

The basic syntax for defining a column with a foreign key constraint using the alternative method is

ALTER TABLE *existingTableName*
ADD   [CONSTRAINT   *constraintName*]   *constraintType*(*existingColumnName*)
REFERENCES *parentTableName*(*referencedColumnName*);

where

- *existingTableName* is the table that contains the column
- *constraintName* is the name to be assigned to the constraint
- *constraintType* is the type of constraint that is defined for the column
- *existingColumName* is the column to be defined with the constraint
- *parentTableName* is the parent table that is being referenced
- *referencedColumnName* is the column that is being referenced in the parent table
- Symbols [ ] mean item is optional

> **Note:** Refer to the topic titled "Defining Foreign Key Constraint at the Table Level" in this chapter to review the function of the REFERENCES keyword.

Following the constraint name is the constraint type. The constraint type FOREIGN KEY keywords are written and the keywords are followed immediately by the foreign key column(s) enclosed in parentheses.

> **Note:** With the exception of the ADD keyword in the ADD clause of the alternative approach, the constraint definition is identical to the constraint definition at the table level.

The following ALTER TABLE...ADD statement is used to define the foreign key constraint for the courseStudent table. Type and run the ALTER TABLE...ADD statement to define the foreign key constraints for the table.

ALTER TABLE courseStudent
ADD CONSTRAINT coSec_fk FOREIGN KEY(courseCode, section) REFERENCES course(courseCode, section), CONSTRAINT stud_fk FOREIGN KEY(studentId) REFERENCES student(studentId);

The statement defines two foreign keys for the courseStudent table. The first is a composite foreign key that consists of both courseCode and section columns that reference the course table. The second is a foreign key that consists of a single column called studentId that references the student table.

Removing Constraints from Columns

Constraints can be removed from columns once they have been defined for those columns. To remove or drop constraints from columns, the ALTER TABLE...DROP statement is used. The basic syntax is

ALTER TABLE *existingTableName*
DROP CONSTRAINT *existingConstraintName*, CONSTRAINT *existingConstraintName*, ...;

where

- *existingTableName* is the table that contains the column which constraint is to be dropped
- *existingConstraintName* is the name assigned to the constraint
- Symbols ... mean more columns can be listed

Applying Constraints to Tables Columns

The CONSTRAINT keyword must precede the constraint name in the DROP clause of the statement.

In MS Access SQL, the syntax is used to drop all types of constraints supported by MS Access. In addition, one ALTER TABLE...DROP statement can be used to remove more than one constraint at the same time.

The following ALTER TABLE...DROP statement will remove the primary key constraint from the courseStudent table. Type and run the ALTER TABLE...DROP statement to drop the primary key constraint from the courseStudent table created in the **Academics** database.

ALTER TABLE courseStudent
DROP CONSTRAINT coSecStud_pk;

Note: To drop the primary key constraint of a table, Oracle uses the keywords PRIMARY KEY. To drop a unique constraint, Oracle uses the keyword UNIQUE followed by the column defined with the unique constraint in parentheses.

Example (to drop primary key constraint):
ALTER TABLE courseStudent
DROP PRIMARY KEY;
     or
Example (to drop unique constraint);
ALTER TABLE house
DROP UNIQUE(houseName);

Redefine the primary key constraint for the courseStudent table. To re-establish the constraint, type and run the following ALTER TABLE...ADD statement.

ALTER TABLE courseStudent
ADD CONSTRAINT coSecStud_pk PRIMARY KEY(courseCode, section, studentId);

Defining Check Constraint Using MS Access GUI

MS Access SQL does not directly support the check constraint. The constraint is defined through MS Access graphical user interface (GUI). The following demonstrates how to define the constraint for columns.

Start MS Access application to open the database that has the table that contains the columns to be defined with the check constraint. Go through the steps discussed in chapter two on how to open a database until figure 10.1 is displayed.

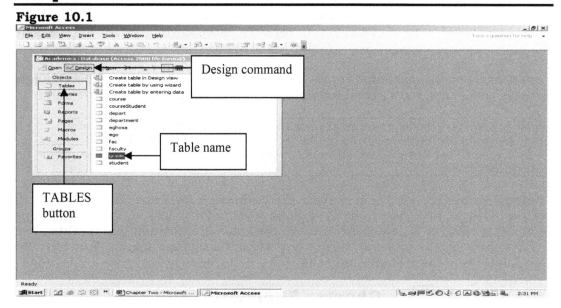

Chapter Ten

Figure 10.1

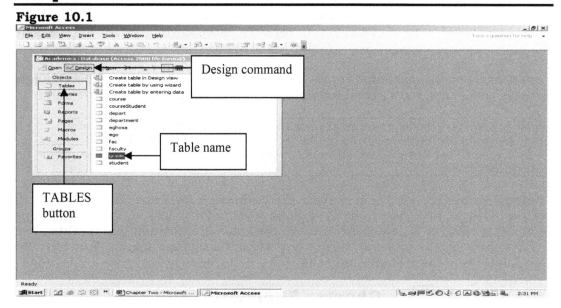

The TABLES button on the left pane must be clicked to display all tables in the database. For the purpose of demonstration, the grade table of the **Academics** database is used. The intent is to list the valid data values that must be accepted by the table's column called letterGrade. The acceptable list of data values for the column are "A", "B", "C", "D", "F", "I", "WP", and "WF".

With the displayed tables showing on the right pane, select the table that contains the column(s) to be defined with the check constraint. Click the **Design** command on the toolbar of figure 10.1 to open the table's design window. See figure 10.2.

Figure 10.2

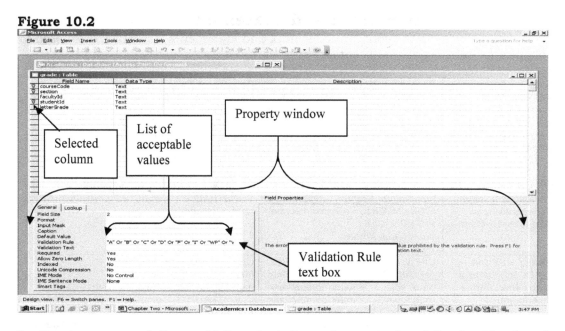

In the top pane of figure 10.2, select the column to be defined with the check constraint. In the column property window (bottom pane), click the **Validation Rule** text box. Type the list or the range of values to be accepted by the column. If the list or the range of values are of text data type or date data type, they must be enclosed in quotation marks. In MS Access, date data can also be enclosed using number signs (#).

235

Applying Constraints to Tables Columns

However, if the list or the range of values is of numeric data type, the values must not be quoted and must not be enclosed in number signs. Save the table when you are done to make the necessary changes to the table.

You can define a check constraint for any number of columns by selecting the columns individually and setting the acceptable values before saving the changes to the table.

> **Note:** When specifying the list or range of values to use for defining a check constraint for a column, you must use Boolean operators (Not, And, Or) or comparison operators (>, >=, <, <=, =, <>) or combinations of both operators depending on how you plan to set up the acceptable list or range.

The **Default Value** text box which is above the **Validation Rule** text box in the column property window can be used to set a beginning value for a column. If the beginning value is a text value or a date value, enclose the value in quotation marks. Otherwise write the value, usually numeric, in the box without quotation marks. You can also enclose a date value using number signs (#).

Chapter Summary

This chapter discusses constraints and how to define them for columns. In addition, the chapter discusses and demonstrates how to assign constraints to columns when tables are created using two approaches, namely, the column-level method and the table-level method. The chapter also explains and demonstrates how to use the ALTER TABLE statement to construct the appropriate SQL statements used to (i) add new columns to tables with constraints defined for those columns at the same time, (ii) define constraints for existing columns, (iii) change constraints of existing columns, and (iv) remove constraints from existing columns. In conclusion, the chapter demonstrates how to define the check constraint using MS Access GUI approach.

Constraints Syntax and Statements Summary

The table below presents the constraints' syntax and statements' examples discussed in this chapter for defining columns' constraints.

Constraint Type	Constraint Syntax	Constraint Example
PRIMARY KEY, UNIQUE, NOT NULL, and NULL definitions at the column level during table creation	CREATE TABLE newTableName(newColumnName datatType [CONSTRAINT constraintName] constraintType, newColumnName dataType [CONSTRAINT constraintName] constraintType, ...);	CREATE TABLE faculty (facultyId CHAR(8) CONSTRAINT facultyid_pk PRIMARY KEY, firstName VARCHAR(15) NOT NULL, initial TEXT(1) NULL, lastName VARCHAR(25) CONSTRAINT lastnname_nn NOT NULL);
FOREIGN KEY definition for a column at the column level during table creation	CREATE TABLE newTableName (newColumnName dataType [CONSTRAINT constraintName] REFERENCES parentTableName(referencedColumnName));	CREATE TABLE dom(studentId int CONSTRAINT stud_fk REFERENCES student(studentId));
PRIMARY KEY and UNIQUE definitions at the table level during table creation	CREATE TABLE newTableName(newColumnName dataType, newColumnName dataType, newColumnName dataType, ..., [CONSTRAINT constraintName] constraintType(newColumnName) , [CONSTRAINT constraintName] constraintType(newColumName), ...);	CREATE TABLE department (departmentCode CHAR(6), departmentName VARCHAR(30), CONSTRAINT deptCode_pk PRIMARY KEY(departmentCode), CONSTRAINT deptNam_uk UNIQUE(departmentName));

FOREIGN KEY definition for a column at the table level during table creation	CREATE TABLE *newTableName(newColumnName dataType,* [CONSTRAINT *constraintName*] *constraintType(newColumnName)* REFERENCES *parentTableName(referencedColumnName*));	CREATE TABLE facStudId(facultyId CHAR(8), studentId CHAR(8), CONSTRAINT facstud_pk PRIMARY KEY(facultyId, studentId), CONSTRAINT facId_fk FOREIGN KEY(facultyId) REFERENCES faculty(facultyId), CONSTRAINT studId_fk FOREIGN KEY(studentId) REFERENCES student(studentId));
PRIMARY KEY, UNIQUE, NOT NULL, and NULL definitions for new columns after table creation	ALTER TABLE *existingTableName* ADD *newColumnName dataType* [CONSTRAINT *constraintName*] *constraintType,* *newColumnName dataType* [CONSTRAINT *constraintName*] *constraintType, ...;*	ALTER TABLE faculty ADD offPhone CHAR(10) CONSTRAINT offPhone_nn NOT NULL;
FOREIGN KEY definition for new a column after table creation	ALTER TABLE *existingTableName* ADD *newColumnName dataType* [CONSTRAINT *constraintName*] REFERENCES *parentTableName(referencedColumnName*);	ALTER TABLE faculty ADD departmentCode CHAR(6) CONSTRAINT departCode_fk REFERENCES department(departmentCode);
PRIMARY KEY, UNIQUE, NOT NULL, and NULL definitions for an existing column or change constraint type of an existing column	ALTER TABLE *existingTableName* ALTER [COLUMN] *existingColumnName dataType* [CONSTRAINT *constraintName*] *constraintType;*	ALTER TABLE faculty ALTER initial TEXT(1) CONSTRAINT init_nn NOT NULL;
FOREIGN KEY definition for an existing column or change constraint type of an existing column	ALTER TABLE *existingTableName* ALTER [COLUMN] *existingColumnName dataType* [CONSTRAINT *constraintName*] REFERENCES *parentTableName(referencedColumnName*);	ALTER TABLE fac2 ALTER facultyId CHAR(8) CONSTRAINT fac2_fk REFERENCES faculty(facultyId);
PRIMARY KEY and UNIQUE definitions for existing columns	ALTER TABLE *existingTableName* ADD [CONSTRAINT *constraintName*] *constraintType (existingColumnName, existingColumnName, ...);*	ALTER TABLE courseStudent ADD CONSTRAINT coSecStud_pk PRIMARY KEY(courseCode, section, studentId);
FOREIGN KEY definition for an existing column	ALTER TABLE *existingTableName* ADD [CONSTRAINT *constraintName*] *constraintType(existingColumnName)* REFERENCES *parentTableName(referencedColumnName*);	ALTER TABLE courseStudent ADD CONSTRAINT stud_fk FOREIGN KEY(studentId) REFERENCES student(studentId);
Dropping constraints from columns contained in a table	ALTER TABLE *existingTableName* DROP CONSTRAINT *existingConstraintName,* CONSTRAINT *existingConstraintName, ...;*	ALTER TABLE courseStudent DROP CONSTRAINT coSecStud_pk;

Key Terms

ADD clause
ALTER clause

ALTER TABLE clause
Check

Applying Constraints to Tables Columns

Column   Foreign Key
Column Level   Not Null
Constraint Names   Null
Constraint Types   Primary Key
Data Types   Table
Defining Constraints   Table Level
DROP CONSTRAINT clause   Unique

Chapter Review Questions

Multiple Choice Questions

1. Which of the following is not what constraints are about?
   - a. correctness of data.
   - b. validity of data.
   - c. consistency of data.
   - d. security of data.

2. Which of the following is not a constraint type?
   - a. foreign key constraint.
   - b. unique constrain.
   - c. distinct constraint.
   - d. null constraint.

3. _____ is a table-level constraint.
   - a. Primary key constraint
   - b. Foreign key constraint
   - c. Unique constraint
   - d. not null constraint

4. Not null constraint is a _____ constraint.
   - a. column-level
   - b. row-level
   - c. table-level
   - d. database-level

5. _____ constraint is used to establish domain integrity.
   - a. Unique
   - b. Primary key
   - c. Check
   - d. Foreign key

6. To assign a descriptive name to a constraint, the _____ keyword is used.
   - a. CON
   - b. CONST
   - c. RESERVE
   - d. CONSTRAINT

7. Which of the following constraints cannot be defined at the table-level?
   - a. Unique constraint.
   - b. Not null constraint.
   - c. Primary key constraint.
   - d. none of the above.

8. A table that contains a foreign key can be referred to as a _____ table.
   - a. parent
   - b. composite
   - c. system
   - d. child

9. The _____statement is used to remove a constraint from a column.
   a. ALTER TABLE...DROP CONSTRAINT
   b. ALTER TABLE...REMOVE CONSTRAINT
   c. ALTER TABLE...DELETE CONSTRAINT
   d. ALTER TABLE...ERASE CONSTRAINT

10. Check constraint is a _____ constraint.
   a. table-level
   b. row-level
   c. column-level
   d. database-level

True or False Questions
11. Constraints are rules used to enforce restrictions on tables.
   a. True
   b. False

12. Constraints are about security measures.
   a. True
   b. False

13. Constraints are only defined at the time tables are created.
   a. True
   b. False

14. Using the table-level approach, constraints are defined as part of columns' definitions during tables' creations.
   a. True
   b. False

15. The not null constraint is only defined at the column-level.
   a. True
   b. False

16. A table's foreign key can be a composite foreign key.
   a. True
   b. False

17. Defining a foreign key constraint at the column-level in a CREATE TABLE statement requires the REFERENCES clause.
   a. Tue
   b. False

Fill in the blank Questions
18. Constraints are all about _____ and _____ of data.

19. Defining the foreign key constraint at the column level does not require the _____.

20. To change a constraint from one type to another, you use the _____ statement.

21. To assign a descriptive name to a constraint, you use the _____ keyword.

22. To remove a constraint from a column, you use the _____ clause.

23. The not null constraint can only be defined at the _____ level

24. The composite primary key constraint can only be defined at the _____ level.

Applying Constraints to Tables Columns

Essay Type Questions

25. State the two functions of the ALTER TABLE...ALTER statement.

26. How is adding a not null constraint to a column in MS Access SQL environment differs from doing the same in Oracle?

27. Describe the function of the primary key constraint.

28. How is the unique constrain differs from the primary key constraint?

29. When is the table-level constraint definition method required for defining the primary key constraint, the foreign key constraint, and the unique constraint?

Hands-on Activities

Perform the following hands-on exercises using the *Academics* database.

1. Create a new table called dormitory that contains two columns. The columns are called domCode and domName. The domCode column should be of byte data type and should be defined with the primary key constraint. The domName column should be of variable-length size character data type and should be defined with the unique constraint. Both constraints should be defined at the column level.

2. Add a new column called yearBuild with date data type to the dormitory table and define the column with the not null constraint.

3. Add a new column called buildStatus with character data type to the dormitory table and define the column with the null constraint.

4. Redefine the constraint established for the buildStatus column to the not null constraint.

5. Create a new table called studentInfo with three columns namely; studentId, fullName, and domCode. The studentId column should be of integer data type and is the table's primary key. The primary key constraint should be defined at the table level. The fullName column should be defined with the not null constraint at the column level, and the domCode column should be defined with the foreign key constraint at the table level. The foreign key is used to establish a relationship with the dormitory table.

6. Drop the Primary key constraint from the studentId column of the studentInfo table.

7. Define the primary key constraint for the studentId column of the studentInfo table.

8. Drop the foreign key constraint from the domCode column of the studentInfo table.

9. Using the better way of defining a foreign key constraint, as discussed in this book, add the foreign key constraint back to the domCode column.

10. Create a new table called dormMod that contains two columns. The columns are called domCode and domName. The domCode column should be of byte data type and should be defined with primary key and foreign key constraints. The domName column should be of variable-length size character data type and should be defined with the not null constraint. Both the primary key constraint and the foreign key constraint should be defined at the table level. The domCode column is used to establish a relationship with the dormitory table.

Chapter Eleven

Manipulating Data in Tables

Chapter Objectives
After completing this chapter, you should be able to
- Define DML statements
- Populate tables with data
- Update data in tables
- Delete data from tables
- Use IN clause
- Use PARAMETERS declaration statement
- Use PROCEDURE clause statement
- Understand COMMIT and ROLLBACK commands

Data Manipulation Language (DML) Statements
Data Manipulation Language (DML) statements are used to (i) load data into tables, (ii) change data contained in tables, and (iii) remove data from tables. DML is one of the main components that constitute Structured Query Language (SQL). In MS Access environment, DML statements display confirmation messages before completing their tasks.

Populating Tables with Data
One of the functions of DML is to load data into rows of a table. Populating a table row with data is achieved through the INSERT INTO command. The command is used to create the INSERT INTO statement. Typically, the statement loads data into one row of a table at any given time. However, the INSERT INTO statement can be altered to allow the loading of data into multiple rows of a table at the same time.

INSERT INTO Statements: An INSERT INTO statement is a SQL instruction used to populate a table with data.

The basic syntax for the INSERT INTO statement is

INSERT INTO *existingTableName* [(*existingColumnName, existingColumnName, …*)]
VALUES(*columnValue, columnValue, …*);

where

- *existingTableName* is the table that contains the column that will receive data
- *existingColumnName* is the column in the table that is being used
- *columnValue* is the data value that is assigned to the column
- Symbols [ ] mean items are optional.
- Symbols … mean more columns' names and/or columns' values can be listed

The INSERT INTO statement has two mandatory clauses, namely, the INSERT INTO clause and the VALUES clause. The INSERT INTO clause is used to list the table that is to receive data and the optional column list. The VALUES clause is used to specify the required values that are to be loaded into columns of the table.

Manipulating Data in Tables

The following facts about the INSERT INTO statement should be noted.

- If the INSERT INTO clause contains columns, the columns must be enclosed in a pair of parentheses
- Whenever the INSERT INTO clause contains more than one column, the columns must be separated by commas
- The values in the VALUES clause must be enclosed in a pair of parentheses
- Whenever the VALUES clause contains more than one value, the values must be separated by commas.
- If no column is listed in the INSERT INTO clause, the values listed in the VALUES clause must match the table's columns both in data types and in positions of the columns in the table.
- If no column is listed in the INSERT INTO clause, the number of values listed in the VALUES clause must correspond to the number of columns in the table
- If columns are listed in the INSERT INTO clause, the values listed in the VALUES clause must match the listed columns of the INSERT INTO clause both in data types and in positions
- In the VALUES clause, numeric values are not enclosed in quotation marks or in a pair of number signs, but text values are enclosed in quotation marks and date values are enclosed in a pair of number signs.

Inserting Records into Tables without Using Columns Lists

Usually, data are loaded into a table without specifying the columns to receive data in the INSERT INTO clause of the INSERT INTO statement. The traditional approach is to fill all columns' entries of the intending new record with data.

Columns Lists: A column list is a collection of columns listed in a SQL clause.

The basic syntax for this version of INSERT INTO statement is

INSERT INTO *existingTableName*
VALUES(*columnValue* [, *columnValue*, ...]);

where

- *existingTableName* is the table that contains the column that will receive data
- *columnValue* is the data value that is assigned to the column
- Symbols [ ] mean item is optional
- Symbols ... mean more columns' values can be listed

Figure 11.1 shows a SQL window with an INSERT INTO statement that adds one new faculty member's record to the facultyX table. Figure 11.1 also shows the associated dialog box with a confirmation message. In MS Access, this type of dialog box is a common occurrence with DML statements. Anytime a DML statement is run, a dialog box with a confirmation message is displayed before the statement can complete its task. The dialog box displays two answer option buttons (Yes and No). If you click the **Yes** button or press the ENTER key when the **Yes** button is selected, the statement performs the operation. However, if the **No** button is clicked or selected and the ENTER key is pressed, the operation is aborted.

Figure 11.1

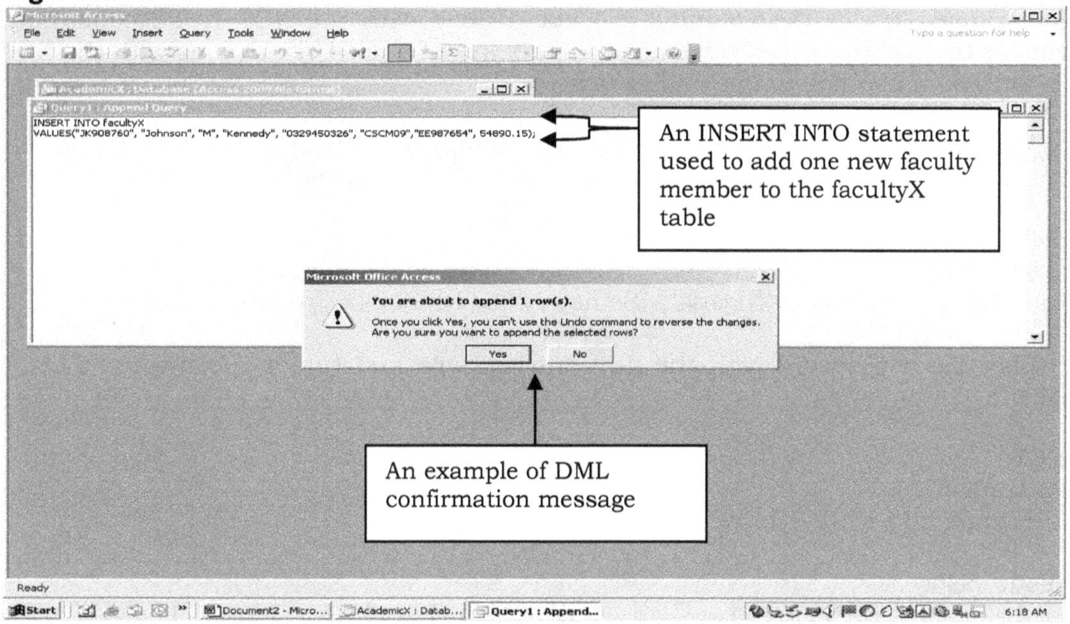

Figure 11.1 is used to demonstrate how an INSERT INTO statement is written in MS Access SQL window and how the confirmation message dialog box is displayed. From this point on, INSERT INTO statements will be typed and their results will be displayed without showing MS Access SQL window. Start MS Access and open the **AcademicX** database

To load the data of the faculty member shown in figure 11.1, type and run the following INSERT INTO statement.

INSERT INTO facultyX
VALUES("JK908760", "Johnson", "M", "Kennedy", "0329450326", "CSCM09", "EE987654", 54890.15);

To display the result of the INSERT INTO statement, type and run the following SELECT statement.

SELECT *
FROM facultyX
WHERE facultyId = "JK908760";

See result below.

faculty Id	first Name	initial	last Name	offPhone	department Code	chairId	annual Salary
JK908760	Johnson	M	Kennedy	0329450326	CSCM09	EE987654	54890.15

Notice that the new record is added to the facultyX table and all columns' entries for the new record are filled with data.

Inserting Records into Tables Using Null Values
Although, you can fill all columns' entries of a record in a table with known data values when populating the table with data, however, there are times when you want some columns' entries of the record to contain null values. MS Access SQL allows the

Manipulating Data in Tables

entering of null values to columns of a table as long as the columns are not part of the table's primary key or the columns are not defined with the NOT NULL constraint. Remember that columns that serve as a primary key of a table or columns with the NOT NULL constraint can not accept null values.

To add Johnson Paulson as a new student along with the necessary data into the studentX table, type and run the following INSERT INTO statement.

INSERT INTO studentX
VALUES("JP401169", "Johnson", NULL, "Paulson", "675 Paulson Lane", "Ukpor","Anambra", NULL, "Nigeria", "Senior", #06/12/2004#, "jp1169");

To display the new record with the null entries, type and run the following SELECT statement.

SELECT *
FROM studentX
WHERE studentId = "JP401169";

See result below.

student Id	first Name	initial	last Name	address	city	state	zip Code	country	classifi cation	date First Enrolled	user Id
JP401169	Johnson		Paulson	675 Paulson Lane	Ukpor	Anambra		Nigeria	Senior	6/12/2004	jp1169

Notice that both initial and zipCode columns (third and eighth positions in the VALUES clause) contain null values. This is because the INSERT INTO statement loads the new record with null values into those columns.

> **Note:** Columns that participate as part of a table's primary key or columns defined with the NOT NULL constraint cannot contain null values, and as such, assigning null values to those columns generate error messages.

There are two other methods used to instruct columns to receive null values using the INSERT INTO statement. One method is to use a pair of quotation marks with no data value between the quotation marks, and the other method is to list only the columns that are to receive known values as part of the INSERT INTO clause.

The following INSERT INTO statement loads the same record as the last INSERT INTO statement. The statement uses a pair of double quotation marks to substitute for the NULL keyword for columns that will receive null values in the VALUES clause.

INSERT INTO studentX
VALUES("JP401169", "Johnson", "", "Paulson", "675 Paulson Lane", "Ukpor","Anambra", "", "Nigeria", "Senior", #06/12/2004#, "jp1169");

Again, both the initial column and the zipCode column (third and eighth positions in the VALUES clause) contain null values. This is due to the fact that each of both positions has a pair of double quotation marks which also indicates a null value.

Inserting Records into Tables Using Columns Lists
The use of a column list in the INSERT INTO clause of an INSERT INTO statement has three main advantages. The column list of the INSERT INTO clause (i) is used to avoid

entering actual data to columns that will contain null values, (ii) allows the listing of columns to indicate which columns can receive actual values, and (iii) gives you the flexibility of entering columns' values in whatever order you desire in the VALUES clause. However, the order in which the values are arranged in the VALUES clause is controlled by the order of the arrangement of the columns in the INSERT INTO clause.

The basic syntax for this form of the INSERT INTO statement is

INSERT INTO *existingTableName* (*existingColumnName* [, *existingColumnName*, ...])
VALUES(*columnValue* [, *columnValue*, ...]);

where

- *existingTableName* is the table that contains the column that will receive data
- *existingColumnName* is the column in the table that is being used
- *columnValue* is the data values that is assigned to the column
- Symbols [ ] mean items are optional
- Symbols ... mean more columns' names and columns' values can be listed

Using Columns Lists to Enter Null Values to Columns
The last section shows and demonstrates two methods of entering null values into columns of a table when populating a table with data. The two methods use NULL keyword and a pair of double quotation marks respectively. Using a column list in the INSERT INTO clause of an INSERT INTO statement is the third method of entering null values into columns when loading data into a table.

The column list approach can be used to insert null values into a table's columns. Johnson Paulson's data, as in the last section, is used again in the following INSERT INTO statement to demonstrate how the approach is accomplished.

INSERT INTO studentX (studentId, firstName, lastName, address, city, state, country, classification, dateFirstEnrolled, userId)
VALUES("JP401169", "Johnson", "Paulson", "675 Paulson Lane", "Ukpor","Anambra", "Nigeria", "Senior", #06/12/2004#, "jp1169");

Notice that two columns (initial and zipCode) from the studentX table are not part of the column list in the INSERT INTO clause. As a result, the values for the two columns are also not listed in the VALUES clause. Because the two columns and their values are omitted in the INSERT INTO statement, null values are assigned to the columns once the insertion operation is run.

Using Columns Lists to Indicate Columns that will Receive Data
Another main function of a column list is to identify the columns of a table that will receive actual data during a data entry operation. Although, you can list columns in the INSERT INTO clause and still assign null values to those columns in the VALUES clause, but the underlying reason for using a column list is to eliminate the time spent in entering null values to columns of a table.

To add a new textbook titled "Business Ethics" along with the isbn and the classification using the bookX table, type and run the following INSERT INTO statement.

INSERT INTO bookX (isbn, bookTitle, classification)
VALUES("08739512", "Business Ethics", "Business Administration");

Manipulating Data in Tables

To display the record of the newly entered textbook, type and run the following SELECT statement.

SELECT *
FROM bookX
WHERE isbn = "08739512";

See result below.

isbn	bookTitle	costPrice	sellingPrice	classification
08739512	Business Ethics	0	0	Business Administration

You might have noticed, from the result, that the bookX table contains five columns. However, the INSERT INTO statement performed the task of entering three values for the three columns listed in the INSERT INTO clause. In the INSERT INTO statement, the three columns listed in the INSERT INTO clause can only be provided with actual values in the VALUES clause. In MS Access SQL, supplying values for all the columns' entries for the new record in the bookX table generates an error.

Using Columns Lists to Enter Columns Data in Specified Order

The column list of an INSERT INTO statement is also used to enter columns' values in whatever arrangement you specified. You do not have to load data into a table according to the original column arrangement of the table. You can list the columns in a table, using the INSERT INTO clause, in any order that is different from the original physical arrangement of the columns. However, you must supply the data in the VALUES clause to the columns in the same order (arrangement) as the column list in the INSERT INTO clause. In addition, the values supplied must match the data types of the columns.

To add a new textbook titled "IT for Dummies" with the desired data and in the desired order of columns' arrangement using the bookX table, type and run the following INSERT INTO statement.

INSERT INTO bookX (bookTitle, classification, isbn, costPrice)
VALUES ("IT for Dummies", "Computer Science", "09876453", 38.95);

To display the record of the newly entered textbook, type and run the following SELECT statement.

SELECT *
FROM bookX
WHERE isbn = "09876453";

See result below.

isbn	bookTitle	costPrice	sellingPrice	Classification
09876453	IT for Dummies	38.95	0	Computer Science

The result of the SELECT statement shows the original columns' arrangement of bookX table. You might have noticed that the arrangement is different from the arrangement of columns in the INSERT INTO clause of the INSERT INTO statement. However, when the INSERT INTO statement is executed, as long as the values in the VALUES clause of the statement are arranged correctly, the values are entered into their corresponding columns as originally arranged in the table.

Chapter Eleven

Using Functions in VALUES Clause of INSERT INTO Statement

MS Access SQL allows the use of certain single-row functions in the VALUES clause of an INSERT INTO statement. The following two INSERT INTO statements demonstrate how single-row functions are used in the VALUES clause.

To add a new textbook titled "Biology for Dummies" with the cost and selling prices rounded to zero decimal position, and the book's classification stored in mixed cases using the bookX table, type and run the following INSERT INTO statement.

```
INSERT INTO bookX
VALUES ("08793876", "Biology for Dummies", ROUND(23.95), ROUND(34.65),
STRCONV( "NATURAL SCIENCE", 3));
```

To display the record of the newly entered textbook, type and run the following SELECT statement.

```
SELECT *
FROM bookX
WHERE isbn = "08793876";
```

See result below.

isbn	bookTitle	costPrice	sellingPrice	classification
08793876	Biology for Dummies	24	35	Natural Science

Notice the ROUND function and the STRCONV function and how they are used in the VALUES clause of the INSERT INTO statement. The ROUND function rounds the values (actual arguments) to the nearest whole numbers before storing the values in the costPrice and sellingPrice columns. Similarly, the STRCONV function converts the value of the classification column which is in uppercases to mixed cases before storing the value.

To add a new student with first and last names of "John Felly" along with the necessary data using the studentX table, type and run the following INSERT INTO statement.

```
INSERT INTO studentX
VALUES("JF407463", "John", NULL, "Felly", "115 Back Road", "Tortola",NULL, NULL,
"British Virgin Islands", "Sophomore", DATE(), LCASE("JF7463"));
```

To display the newly entered record, type and run the following SELECT statement.

```
SELECT *
FROM studentX
WHERE studentId = "JF407463";
```

See result below.

student Id	first Name	initial	last Name	address	City	state	zip Code	country	classifi cation	date First Enrolled	user Id
JF407463	John		Felly	115 Back Road	Tortola			British Virgin Islands	Sophomore	9/8/2005	jf7463

In the last INSERT INTO statement, the date is entered using the DATE function and the letters in the userId column entry is converted to lowercases using LCASE function.

Manipulating Data in Tables

Inserting Records into Tables Using Columns as Formal Parameters in VALUES Clause

MS Access SQL supports the use of columns or user-defined names in the VALUES clause. When names rather than actual values are listed in the VALUES clause of an INSERT INTO statement, the names behave like formal parameters. In such situation, the names become memory locations and are used to receive data values that, in turn, are stored in the corresponding columns of the table that the values are intended for. The main advantage of using formal parameters is that the parameters give the user the flexibility of entering the appropriate data whenever the INSERT INTO statement is run. The data values are not physically written or hard-coded into the VALUES clause of the INSERT INTO statement, rather the values are supplied at run-time.

Formal Parameters: A formal parameter, in MS Access, is a memory location used to store a data value that is passed to a column or a function.

When columns or user-defined names are used in the VALUES clause of an INSERT INTO statement, a Parameter Value box is displayed for each name listed in the VALUES clause. A Parameter Value box is a dialog box telling you to enter a value for the specified column. Figure 11.2 shows a Parameter Value box.

Figure 11.2

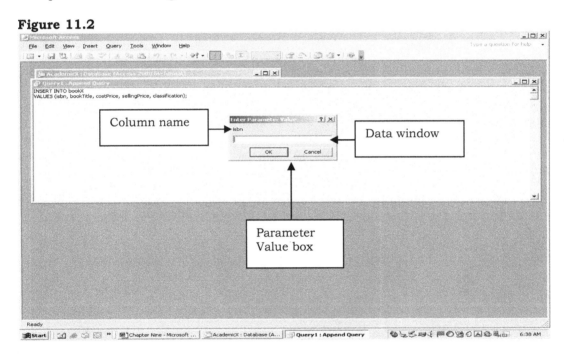

Once the Parameter Value box for a particular column is displayed, the column name or the user-defined name for that column is shown as part of the information displayed by the box. Usually, the name appears beneath the title bar of the Parameter Value box. The white rectangular data window of the box is used to supply the needed data value to the column. The box has two buttons namely, the **OK** button and the **Cancel** button. The **OK** button is clicked if the value entered is correct and to store the value in the column. The **Cancel** button is clicked if the data value entered in the window is incorrect. This button cancels or aborts the value.

Alternatively, you can use the TAB key of the computer keyboard to select any of the buttons before pressing the ENTER key on the computer keyboard. Using this approach

Chapter Eleven

is identical to clicking with the mouse. Typically, the TAB key is used to select any of the buttons and the white rectangular data window of the Parameter Value box.

The following INSERT NTO statement demonstrates the use of columns as formal parameters in the VALUES clause of the statement. To add a new textbook to the bookX table using formal parameters, type and run the INSERT INTO statement.

INSERT INTO bookX
VALUES (isbn, bookTitle, costPrice, sellingPrice, classification);

In the VALUES clause, the columns of the bookX table are used as formal parameters.

> **Note:** In MS Access SQL, names that are used in the VALUES clause of an INSERT INTO statement as formal parameters must not be enclosed in quotation marks. In programming environment, valid made-up names are called identifiers and are sometimes referred to as user- or programmer-defined names.

When a table's column list is omitted from the INSERT INTO clause of an INSERT INTO statement, you must enter data according to the columns' positions and data types of the columns in the table when using formal parameters of the VALUES clause. If you use a column list in the INSERT INTO clause of an INSERT INTO statement, you must arrange the formal parameters and enter the correct values in the VALUES clause in the same order as the column list.

MS Access SQL also allows the use of functions with formal parameters in the VALUES clause of an INSERT INTO statement.

> **Note:** Oracle uses a substitution variable in place of a formal parameter. The substitution variable uses both the ampersand symbol (&) and a name to serve as the formal parameter. The name can be any valid name including columns' names of the table that is receiving the data, as long as the name is not a keyword. The substitution variable for numeric data must not be enclosed in single quotation marks. The Substitution variables for text and date data are usually enclosed in single quotation marks.
>
> Example:
> INSERT INTO bookX
> VALUES ('&isbn', '&bookTitle', &costPrice, &sellingPrice, '&classification');

Inserting Records into Tables Using Data from Other Tables

In MS Access SQL, you can insert new records into a table by copying the records of another table that exists in a database. The INSERT INTO statement that performs this type of loading operation uses a subquery. The subquery is substituted for the VALUES clause. When populating a table using data of another table, the VALUES clause of the INSERT INTO statement is replaced with a SELECT statement (subquery). Typically, the INSERT INTO statement adds one record to a table whenever the statement is executed. However, by using a subquery, several records can be inserted into a table at the same time.

The basic syntax for this approach is

INSERT INTO *existingTableName* [(*existingColumnName, exisingColumnName, …*)]
subquery;

where

- *existingTableName* is the table that contains the column that will receive data

- *existingColumnName* is the optional column that exists in the table that is being used
- *subquery* is the SELECT statement used to generate the data to be copied to the table
- Symbols [ ] mean items are optional
- Symbols ... mean more columns can be listed

Note: A SELECT statement is the subquery, and depending on your data requirement, the SELECT statement can be written to contain all the statement's clauses.

When populating a table with data that are from another table, the receiving table column structures must match some or all of the column structures of the table supplying the data. In other words, the columns' definitions of the receiving table must be identical to some or all of the columns' definitions of the table providing the data.

For demonstration purposes, a table called "bookCopyX" exists in the **AcademicX** database. The table is to be used to store some records of the bookX table. Type and run the following SELECT statement to display the content of the bookCopyX table.

SELECT *
FROM bookCopyX;

See result below.

isbn	bookTitle	costPrice	sellingPrice	classification

The table's structure, along with its columns, is displayed instead. This is because the table contains no data. Let's populate the table with Computer Science textbooks using the bookX table. Type and run the following INSERT INTO statement.

INSERT INTO bookCopyX
SELECT *
FROM bookX
WHERE classification = "Computer Science";

To display the records in the bookCopyX table, type and run the following SELECT statement.

SELECT *
FROM bookCopyX;

See result below.

isbn	bookTitle	costPrice	sellingPrice	classification
01133887	Programming with Java	49.45	56.9	Computer Science
05683420	SQL Programming	44	50.25	Computer Science
06142546	Database Design	25.95	36.9	Computer Science
07452771	Principles of Programming	31.95	39.9	Computer Science

The table contains four records as the result of running the INSERT INTO statement. Alternatively, you can insert data to few columns of a table when loading the table with data from another table. To accomplish such operation, you use the column list of the INSERT INTO clause. Refer to **Inserting Data Records into Tables Using Columns Lists** section of this chapter for a quick review. If the column list method is used, the

SELECT clause of the SELECT statement (subquery) must also list the corresponding columns from the table supplying the data. Otherwise, the records that are being copied from the supplying table will be duplicated in the receiving table.

The following INSERT INTO statement, after its execution, copies three columns (isbn, bookTitle, classification) of Natural Science textbook records from the bookX table to the bookCopyX table.

```
INSERT INTO bookCopyX (isbn, bookTitle, classification)
SELECT isbn, bookTitle, classification
FROM bookX
WHERE classification = "Natural Science";
```

Updating Tables Data

There are times when you no longer need certain data contained in a table. The reason probably might be that the data are providing inadequate information or the data are no longer needed. For example, a faculty member's annual salary might change due to promotion. In such situation, the faculty member's record must be updated to reflect the change in salary.

To keep records up-to-date, the tables that contain the records should be updated from time to time or when the need arises to make the records current. MS Access SQL provides the UPDATE command that is used to construct the UPDATE statement. The statement is used to change records in tables. The UPDATE statement can be used to change one record, several records, or all records contained in a table. The statement is used to assign new values to columns, and as a result, the UPDATE statement can be considered as an assignment statement.

UPDATE Statements: An UPDATE statement is a SQL instruction used to modify data records that are contained in a table.

The basic syntax for the statement is

UPDATE *existingTableName*
SET *existingColumnName* = *columnValue* [, *existingColumName* = *columnValue*, ...]
[WHERE *condition*];

where

- *existingTableName* is the table that contains the column to be updated
- *existingColumnName* is the column that contains the value to be updated
- *columnValue* is the new data value – including the NULL keyword - that is assigned to the column
- *condition* is the restriction that indicates the records to be updated
- Symbols [ ] mean items are optional
- Symbols ... mean more columns to be updated can be listed

Note: *columnValue* can be any combination of valid values, columns, user-defined names, functions, and operators that will evaluate to a single value.

The UPDATE statement consists of two mandatory clauses, namely, the UPDATE clause and the SET clause. As with the INSERT INTO statement, the UPDATE statement also displays a confirmation dialog box that allow you to accept and store the new value in the appropriate column or cancel (abort) the operation.

Manipulating Data in Tables

The UPDATE clause is used to list the table that contains the records to be updated. The SET clause is used to list the columns that contain the values to be updated. The WHERE clause is used to retrieve the records which columns' values are to be updated. If the WHERE clause is omitted, the values of the columns listed in the SET clause for all records in the table will be changed. In that case, the values for each of the column listed in the SET clause will be the same for the affected records.

Changing the Value of One Column of a Record

To change the value of one column for one record and if the table contains several records, the WHERE condition clause must be included in the UPDATE statement to hold back other records in the table from being updated.

Before updating the textbook titled "Programming with Java" in the bookCopyX table, let's display the book's record. To display the textbook's information, type and run the following SELECT statement.

SELECT *
FROM bookCopyX
WHERE isbn = "01133887";

See result below.

Isbn	bookTitle	costPrice	sellingPrice	classification
01133887	Programming with Java	49.45	56.9	Computer Science

Figure 11.3 shows a SQL window with the UPDATE statement that changes the cost price of the textbook. Figure 11.3 also shows the associated dialog box with a confirmation message.

Figure 11.3

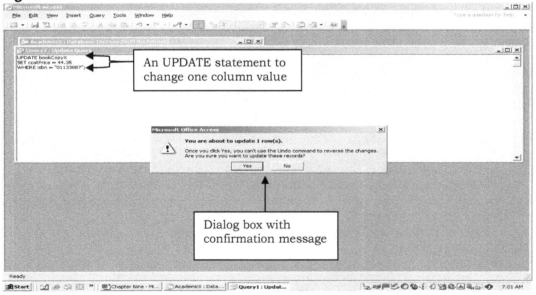

Figure 11.3 is used to demonstrate how an UPDATE statement is written in MS Access SQL window and how the confirmation message dialog box is displayed. From this point on, UPDATE statements will be typed and their results will be displayed without showing MS Access SQL window. Type and run the following UPDATE statement.

```
UPDATE bookCopyX
SET costPrice = 44.35
WHERE isbn = "01133887";
```

The new value for the costPrice column is recorded to the bookCopyX table after running the UPDATE statement. Type and run the following SELECT statement to display the complete record, including the new cost price, for the textbook.

```
SELECT *
FROM bookCopyX
WHERE isbn = "01133887";
```

See result below.

Isbn	bookTitle	costPrice	sellingPrice	classification
01133887	Programming with Java	44.35	56.9	Computer Science

The cost price of the book is changed from is original cost price of 49.45 to the new cost price of 44.35.

Changing the Values of One Column of Multiple Records

With MS Access SQL, it is possible to change several values' entries of one column for several records at the same time if the specified column contains the same data values. Again, if the table contains more records than the ones which columns' values are to be modified, the WHERE clause must be included in the UPDATE statement.

To change the classification "Computer Science" to "Computing Studies" using the bookCopyX table, type and run the following UPDATE statement.

```
UPDATE bookCopyX
SET classification = "Computing Studies"
WHERE classification = "Computer Science";
```

To display the updated records, type and run the following SELECT statement.

```
SELECT *
FROM bookCopyX
WHERE classification = "Computing Studies";
```

See result below.

isbn	bookTitle	costPrice	sellingPrice	classification
06142546	Database Design	25.95	36.9	Computing Studies
07452771	Principles of Programming	31.95	39.9	Computing Studies
05683420	SQL Programming	44	50.25	Computing Studies
01133887	Programming with Java	44.35	56.9	Computing Studies

Notice that all textbooks that are once classified as Computer Science textbooks are now grouped as Computing Studies textbooks.

Changing the Values of Multiple Columns of a Record

An occasion may arise when you want to update values of several columns' entries for one record in a table. In MS Access SQL, you list the columns and their new values in the SET clause of the UPDATE statement. However, when several columns and their

Manipulating Data in Tables

assigned values are listed in the SET clause, each column with its new value entry must be separated from one another by a comma.

To update the values entries of both costPrice and sellingPrice columns for the textbook with the isbn of "08739512", type and run the following UPDATE statement.

UPDATE bookX
SET costPrice = 43.25, sellingPrice = 51.10
WHERE isbn = "08739512";

To display the newly updated record, type and run the following SELECT statement.

SELECT *
FROM bookX
WHERE isbn = "08739512";

See result below.

isbn	bookTitle	costPrice	sellingPrice	classification
08739512	Business Ethics	43.25	51.1	Business Administration

Notice that the cost price and selling price columns of the updated record have the new prices. The two columns' values are changed using one UPDATE statement.

> **Note:** It is also possible to change values of several columns' entries of several records at the same time using one UPDATE statement. This operation is possible if each one of the specified column of the records contains the same data value. Again, if the table contains more records than the ones which columns' values are to be updated, the WHERE clause must be included in the UPDATE statement.

Using Functions in SET Clause of UPDATE Statement

MS Access SQL allows the use of certain single-row functions in the SET clause of an UPDATE statement. The following two UPDATE statements demonstrate how single-row functions are used in the SET clause.

UPDATE bookX
SET sellingPrice = ROUND(51.1)
WHERE isbn = "08739512";

UPDATE studentX
SET dateFirstEnrolled = DATE()
WHERE studentId = "JF407463";

The first UPDATE statement rounds the sellingPrice column value for the textbook with an isbn of "08739512" to 51. The second UPDATE statement uses the computer system's current date as the first enrollment date for the student with the identification number of "JF407463"

Changing Records in Tables Using Formal Parameters in SET Clause

MS Access SQL also supports the use of user-defined names in the SET clause. When such names, rather than actual values, are listed in the SET clause of an UPDATE statement, the names behave like formal parameters. Unlike the VALUES clause of the INSERT INTO statement, the names must not be columns' names if the update operation is to be successful.

Like the VALUES clause of an INSERT INTO statement, when user-defined names are used in the SET clause of an UPDATE statement, a Parameter Value box is displayed for each user-defined name listed in the SET clause. A Parameter Value box is a dialog box telling you to enter a value for the specified column. Refer to figure 11.2 of the INSERT INTO statement section of this chapter to review the Parameter Value box.

The following UPDATE statement, after its execution, uses two formal parameters to assign new values to dateFirstEnrolled and userId columns for the student with identification number "JF407463". In the SET clause of the statement, the user-defined names "Enrolled" and "uid" are the formal parameters.

```
UPDATE studentX
SET dateFirstEnrolled = Enrolled, userId = LCASE(uid)
WHERE studentId = "JF407463";
```

In MS Access SQL, names that are used in the SET clause of an UPDATE statement as formal parameters must not be enclosed in quotation marks.

> **Note:** MS Access SQL does not support using a subquery in the value part of the SET clause of an UPDATE statement. In Oracle, such a construct where a subquery is used in the value portion of an UPDATE statement is possible.
>
> Example:
> UPDATE facultyXOne
> SET annualSalary = (SELECT annualSalary
>   FROM facultyX
>   WHERE facultyId = "EE987654")
> WHERE facultyId = "ZM567123";

Changing the Values of Columns to Null Values for Records

MS Access SQL allows the updating of actual data values of columns' entries to null values. This type of data alteration is possible as long as the columns which values are to be changed to null are defined with the null constraint or the unique constraint. If the columns are defined with other types of constraints, the update operations generate error messages.

To change the selling price of the textbook titled "Programming with Java" to null value using the bookCopyX table, type and run the following UPDATE statement.

```
UPDATE bookCopyX
SET sellingPrice = NULL
WHERE isbn = "01133887";
```

Notice that the NULL keyword is used to assign the null value. This is the standard method of assigning null values to columns entries in the UPDATE statement.

To display the newly updated record, type and run the following SELECT statement.

```
SELECT *
FROM bookCopyX
WHERE isbn = "01133887";
```

See result below.

isbn	bookTitle	costPrice	sellingPrice	classification
01133887	Programming with Java	44.35		Computer Science

Manipulating Data in Tables

The selling price column entry for the book now contains a null value.

Deleting Tables Data

Removing obsolete records or records that are no longer needed from tables is another way of keeping a database current or up-to-date. For example, a faculty member might resign from his or her position and leaves the academic institution. In such situation, the faculty member's record can be removed from the active database and archived somewhere for future reference. MS Access SQL provides the DELETE command that is used to construct the DELETE statement. The DELETE statement removes records permanently from tables.

DELETE Statements: A DELETE statement is a SQL instruction used to remove data records permanently from a table.

The DELETE statement can be used to remove one record, few records, or all records contained in a table. The basic syntax for the statement is

DELETE [[ALL] * | *existingColumnName, ...*]
FROM *existingTableName*
[WHERE *condition*];

where

- Symbol * is to include all columns
- *existingTableName* is the table that contains the record to be deleted
- *existingColumnName* is the column in the table
- *condition* is the restriction that indicates the record to be deleted
- Symbols [ ] mean items are optional
- Symbol | symbolizes **Or** Boolean operator.
- Symbols ... mean more columns can be listed

The DELETE statement consists of two mandatory clause, namely, the DELETE clause and the FROM clause. As with the INSERT INTO statement and the UPDATE statement, the DELETE statement also displays a confirmation message dialog box that allows you to accept and remove the specified record(s) or cancel (abort) the operation.

The DELETE clause is used to list the optional column(s) that are associated with the record(s) to be removed from the table. The FROM clause is used to list the table that contains the record(s) to be removed and the optional WHERE clause is used to retrieve the record(s) to be removed.

Deleting One Record

To remove one record from a table and if the table contains several records, the WHERE condition clause must be included in the DELETE statement to avoid deleting other records in the table.

For demonstration purposes, a table called facultyXMod that contains faculty members whose academic positions have the title "instructor" exists in the **AcademicX** database. Type and run the following SELECT statement to display the records of the table.

SELECT *
FROM facultyXMod;

See result below.

faculty Id	first Name	initial	last Name	offPhone	department Code	chairId	annual Salary
JS994450	John		Semina	0327859031	BUSA02	EM001254	45876.25
ZM567123	Zenat	J	Miller	0323751906	EDUD05	DM674543	49980.95
JH682508	Jenny		Hendix	0323458096	SOCC06	ES509264	48000

Three records are displayed from the facultyXMod. In other words, three faculty members hold instructor positions.

Figure 11.4 shows a SQL window with a DELETE statement that deletes one record from the facultyXMod table. Figure 11.4 also shows the associated dialog box with a confirmation message.

Figure 11.4

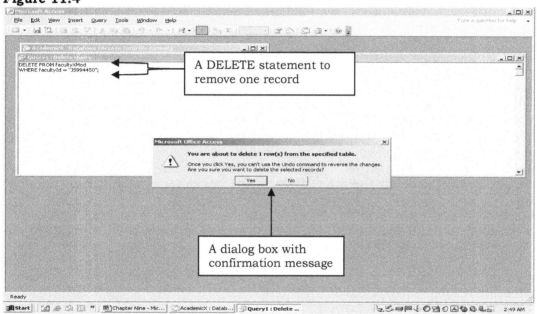

Figure 11.4 is used to demonstrate how a DELETE statement is written in MS Access SQL window and how the confirmation message dialog box is displayed. From this point on, DELETE statements will be typed and their results will be displayed without showing MS Access SQL window. Type and run the following DELETE statement.

DELETE
FROM facultyXMod
WHERE facultyId = "JS994450";

Alternatively, the following DELETE statement, after its execution, could have performed the same delete operation.

DELETE facultyXMod.annualSalary
FROM facultyXMod
WHERE facultyId = "JS994450";

The faculty member whose identification number is "JS994450" is removed permanently from the facultyXMod table.

Manipulating Data in Tables

To display the records in the table, type and run the following SELECT statement.

SELECT *
FROM facultyXMod;

See result below.

faculty Id	first Name	initial	last Name	offPhone	department Code	chairId	annual Salary
ZM567123	Zenat	J	Miller	0323751906	EDUD05	DM674543	49980.95
JH682508	Jenny		Hendix	0323458096	SOCC06	ES509264	48000

After the delete operation, the record with the identification number "JS994450" is removed.

> **Note:** It is also possible to delete several records at the same time using one DELETE statement. This type of operation is possible if the condition specified in the WHERE clause of the DELETE statement contains data value(s) that are common to more than one record.

Deleting All Records

A situation may arise when you want to delete all records that are contained in a table. MS Access SQL supports such an operation. You can remove all records permanently from a table either by including the WHERE condition clause or by omitting the clause from the DELETE statement. The logic of removing all records from a table permanently, if the WHERE clause is included in the DELETE statement, is to specify a column from the table that does not contain null values or a column that has null values in all entries of the column. If you are using a column that contains non-null values, one method is to use the primary key of the table in which all records are to be deleted.

To delete all records in the facultyXMod table without including the WHERE clause, type and run the following DELETE statement.

DELETE
FROM facultyXMod;

Alternatively, you could have type and run the following DELETE statement with the WHERE clause included to perform the same operation as the last DELETE statement.

DELETE
FROM facultyXMod
WHERE facultyId IS NOT NULL;

To display the content of facultyXMod table after the delete operation, type and run the following SELECT statement.

SELECT *
FROM facultyXMod;

See result below.

faculty Id	first Name	initial	last Name	offPhone	department Code	chairId	annualSalary

The result of the display shows only the table's structure as all records are removed from the table. The table can again be populated with data if so desired.

Using Functions in WHERE Clause of DELETE Statement
MS Access SQL allows the use of certain single-row functions in the WHERE clause of a DELETE statement. The following statement demonstrates how a single-row function is used in the WHERE clause.

Let's populated the facultyXMod table again with the same set of record the table contained previously. Type and run the following INSERT INTO statement.

```
INSERT INTO facultyXMod
SELECT *
FROM facultyX
WHERE annualSalary BETWEEN 45000 AND 50000;
```

To display the records of the facultyXMod table after the insertion operation, type and run the following SELECT statement.

```
SELECT *
FROM facultyXMod;
```

See result below.

faculty Id	first Name	initial	last Name	offPhone	department Code	chairId	annual Salary
JS994450	John		Semina	0327859031	BUSA02	EM001254	45876.25
ZM567123	Zenat	J	Miller	0323751906	EDUD05	DM674543	49980.95
JH682508	Jenny		Hendix	0323458096	SOCC06	ES509264	48000

To delete the faculty member whose identification number is "JH682508" using a single-row function in the DELETE statement, type and run the following DELETE statement.

```
DELETE
FROM facultyXMod
WHERE LCASE(facultyId) = "jh682508";
```

The WHERE clause of the DELETE statement first converts the letters in the facultyId column to lowercases before searching for the faculty member whose identification number is "jh682508". The record is then removed if found.

To display the records of the table, type and run the following SELECT statement.

```
SELECT *
FROM facultyXMod;
```

See result below.

faculty Id	first Name	initial	last Name	offPhone	department Code	chairId	annual Salary
JS994450	John		Semina	0327859031	BUSA02	EM001254	45876.25
ZM567123	Zenat	J	Miller	0323751906	EDUD05	DM674543	49980.95

Manipulating Data in Tables

Deleting Records from Tables Using Formal Parameters in WHERE Clause

MS Access SQL also supports the use of user-defined names in the WHERE clause of a DELETE statement. When names, rather than actual values, are listed in the WHERE clause, the names behave like formal parameters. Unlike the VALUES clause of the INSERT INTO statement, the names must not be columns' names if the delete operation is to be successful.

Like the VALUES clause of an INSERT INTO statement, when user-defined names, rather than actual data values, are used in the WHERE clause of a DELETE statement, a Parameter Value box is displayed for each user-defined name listed in the WHERE clause. A Parameter Value box is a dialog box telling you to enter a value for the specified column. Refer to figure 11.2 of the INSERT INTO statement section of this chapter to review the Parameter Value box.

The following DELETE statement uses a formal parameter to delete a faculty member's record whose identification number is "JS994450" from the facultyXMod table. Type and run the DELETE statement.

```
DELETE
FROM facultyXMod
WHERE facultyId = fId;
```

When the Parameter dialog box appears, enter the facultyId "JS994450" and press the ENTER key.

To display the records of the facultyXMod table, type and run the following SELECT statement.

```
SELECT *
FROM facultyXMod;
```

See result below.

faculty Id	first Name	initial	last Name	offPhone	department Code	chairId	annual Salary
ZM567123	Zenat	J	Miller	0323751906	EDUD05	DM674543	49980.95

In MS Access SQL, names that are used in the WHERE clause of a DELETE statement as formal parameters must not be enclosed in quotation marks.

Deleting Records from Tables Using Data from Other Tables

In MS Access SQL, you can delete records from a table by using values of another table that exists in a database. This type of delete operation uses a subquery. The subquery is part of the WHERE clause of the DELETE statement. The basic syntax for this version of the DELETE statement is

```
DELETE [[ALL] * | existingColumnName, ...]
FROM existingTableName
WHERE existingColumnName subqueryOperator (subquery);
```

where

- Symbol * is to include all columns
- *existingTableName* is the table that contains the record to be deleted
- *existingColumnName* is the column in the table

- *subqueryOperator* is the comparison operator that is used to connect the subquery
- *subquery* is the SELECT statement used to generate the data to be deleted
- Symbols [ ] mean items are optional
- Symbol | symbolizes **Or** Boolean operator
- Symbols ... mean more columns can be listed

For demonstration purposes, let's delete the present content of facultyXMod table and then copy the needed records from the facultyX table to the facultyXMod table. Type and run the following two DML statements in the order they are written. The statements must be run independently.

DELETE
FROM facultyXMod
WHERE facultyId IS NOT NULL;

INSERT INTO facultyXMod
SELECT *
FROM facultyX
WHERE chairId IS NULL;

To display the records of facultyXMod table, type and run the following SELECT statement.

SELECT *
FROM facultyXMod;

See result below.

Faculty Id	first Name	initial	last Name	offPhone	department Code	chairId	annual Salary
EM001254	Eghosa		Maklasi	0327854090	BUSA02		74563.55
RU123098	Rischi	B	Ugboma	0327555491	NASC08		70760.89
ES509264	Euhan	S	Stevenson	0329773782	SOCC06		69852.25
DM674543	Doris	V	Mea	0324569132	EDUD05		62980.25
EE987654	Ememgini	M	Erochi	0327840108	CSCM09		68261.39

The table now contains five records after the DELETE statement and the INSERT INTO statement are run.

To delete faculty members who are also students from the facultyXMod table using both facultyXMod and studentX tables and a subquery, type and run the following DELETE statement.

DELETE *
FROM facultyXMod
WHERE facultyId IN (SELECT studentId
                    FROM studentX, facultyXMod
                    WHERE studentId = facultyId);

The DELETE statement uses a subquery and the subquery is connected to the WHERE clause of the statement.

To display the records in the facultyXMod table after the delete operation, type and run the following SELECT statement.

SELECT *
FROM facultyXMod;

See result below.

Faculty Id	first Name	initial	last Name	offPhone	department Code	chairId	annual Salary
RU123098	Rischi	B	Ugboma	0327555491	NASC08		70760.89
ES509264	Euhan	S	Stevenson	0329773782	SOCC06		69852.25
EE987654	Ememgini	M	Erochi	0327840108	CSCM09		68261.39

Notice that two faculty members are removed from the table. Faculty members with identification numbers "EM001254" and "DM674543" are deleted from the table. The deleted faculty members are also students.

> **Note:** If the WHERE clause of a DELETE statement contains a compound condition, each of the simple conditions of the compound condition can be a subquery.

IN Clause

Typically, the IN clause is used to connect to an external database that contains the tables to be queried by another database that is currently running without physically opening the external database. However, the clause can also be used to manipulate the tables of a database that is opened and active (running). A database that is opened and active is called an internal database. In other words, the IN clause can be used to manipulate the tables in an internal database as well as the tables in an external database. In this scenario, an internal database is the database a user has currently opened and using. An external database is a database that contains the tables that are to be queried by the database a user is currently using. These external tables can be manipulated from a different database. You can use the IN clause to query data stored in the tables of a database and the clause works with databases created using MS Access software and databases created with other database software programs that are compatible with MS Access.

Internal Databases: An internal database, in this situation, is an existing database application that is currently opened and used by a user and the database resides in the location the user is currently using.

External Databases: An external database, in this situation, is an existing database application that may not physically be opened and resides in a location that is different from the location a user with an opened database is currently using.

The IN clause can be used with the (i) FROM clause of a SQL statement that uses the FROM clause, (ii) INTO clause of the SELECT...INTO statement, (iii) INSERT INTO clause of the INSERT INTO statement, and (iv) UPDATE clause of the UPDATE statement. The SQL statements that usually use the FROM clause include the SELECT statement, the SELECT...INTO statement, and the DELETE statement.

You might have noticed that the clauses that work with the IN clause are those clauses that typically require the names of the tables that are being queried. Therefore, the IN clause must operate in conjunction with such SQL clauses. The following shows the different syntax forms for the IN clause based on the different SQL statements' clauses that work with the clause.

The basic syntax for the IN clause using the FROM clause of the SELECT statement and the DELETE statement is

FROM   *existingTableName,*   ...   IN   [*"existingInternalDatabaseName"*] |
"existingExternalDatabaseName"

The basic syntax for the IN clause using the INTO clause of the SELECT...INTO statement is

INTO   *newTableName*   IN   [*"existingInternalDatabaseName"*] |
"existingExternalDatabaseName"

The basic syntax for the IN clause using the INSERT INTO clause of the INSERT INTO statement is

INSERT INTO *existingTableName* [(*existingColumnName, existingColumnName, ...*)] IN [*"existingInternalDatabaseName"*] | *"existingExternalDatabaseName"*

The basic syntax for the IN clause using the UPDATE clause of the UPDATE statement is

UPDATE   *existingTableName*   IN   [*"existingInternalDatabaseName"*] |
"existingExternalDatabaseName"

where

- *existingInternalDatabaseName* is the pathname of the database currently opened and used by a user and the pathname must be enclosed in quotation marks
- *existingExternalDatabaseName* is the pathname of the database that contains the tables that are being imported, linked, queried, or manipulated by the database currently opened and used by a user and the pathname must be enclosed in quotation marks
- Symbols [ ] mean items are optional
- Symbol | symbolizes **Or** Boolean operator

Pathnames: A pathname is, usually, a list that consists of a drive name, the root directory, subdirectories' or folders' names if any, and the name and the extension of the item being sought in a computer system – be it a database or a file.

A pathname can be written in full or in part (partial). A full pathname consists of all the elements mentioned in the definition above. A partial pathname typically has its drive name missing and probably folder(s) missing from the pathname. The way a partial pathname is written depends on a user's current location in a computer system. Example: "\SURGE\sqldatabase.mdb".

> ***Note:*** Both *existingInternalDatabaseName* and *existingExternalDatabaseName* must include the locations and names of the databases and the quotation marks used to enclose pathnames can either be double quotation marks or single quotation marks. Again, a pathname is a road map used in a computer system to locate an item at a designated storage location. A pathname must be written in the order presented in the definition and from left to right when searching to locate an item in a computer system. Pathnames are non-case sensitive. They can be written in uppercases, in lowercases, or in mixed cases.

Let's assume, for example, that a database called **AcademicX** with the extension **.mdb** exists in a folder called SURGE that is created in the root directory of the E: drive. The

Manipulating Data in Tables

full pathname for the database and written according to the IN clause syntax is as follows.

"E:\SURGE\AcademicX.mdb"

Except for the leftmost backslash symbol in a pathname, other backslash symbols used in a pathname are separators. They are used to separate one element from the next element. The leftmost backslash symbol represents the root directory. However, if the intended storage location is the root directory of a drive, the backslash symbol can be omitted. Example: "E:AcademicX.mdb".

> **Note:** The general extension for databases created using MS Access 2003, MS Access 2002, and MS Access 2000 is *.mdb*. The general extension for the MS Access 2007 database is *.accdb*

Let's say you are currently using a database that is stored in the C: drive of your computer system and you want to update both costPrice and sellingPrice columns with appropriate valid values for the textbook with the isbn of "08739512" stored in the bookX table of the **AcademicX** database. The database has the extension *.mdb* and it resides in the root directory of the F: drive. If you are to use the IN clause for the update operation, the following UPDATE statement performs the update.

```
UPDATE bookX IN "F:\AcademicX.mdb"
SET costPrice = 49.99, sellingPrice =58.25
WHERE isbn = "08739512";
```

PARAMETERS Declaration and PROCEDURE Clause

The previous sections of this chapter demonstrate how to use columns and user-defined names as formal parameters. In this section you are shown how to formally use formal parameters in MS Access SQL environment. The PARAMETERS declaration and the PROCEDURE clause are used particularly for DML operations that are performed very frequently or regularly. Instead of writing queries that contained data values, you can use either a PARAMETERS declaration statement or a PROCEDURE clause statement to supply data to the queries.

You use both methods to automate the manipulation of data in tables. Both the PARAMETERS declaration and the PROCEDURE clause use formal parameters, and they must be used in conjunction with an acceptable SQL statement. When using any one of the two methods, you must separate the method's portion from the SQL statement that is associated to it with a semicolon. In other words, both the PARAMETERS declaration portion and the PROCEDURE clause portion of the statements must end with semicolons. In MS Access SQL, a semicolon can be used to end the SQL statement that is associated to any of the two methods or the semicolon can be omitted.

The formal parameter names can be columns, user-defined names, or user-defined text expressions. The text expressions can be message prompts and if the text expressions contain spaces, you must enclose them in square brackets. When using both methods to run queries, you must supply data to the formal parameters to successfully complete the specified operation.

When the PARAMETERS declaration or the PROCEDURE clause is used with an acceptable SQL statement, a Parameter Value box is displayed for each user-defined name listed. A Parameter Value box is a dialog box telling you to enter a value for the specified column. Refer to figure 11.2 of INSERT INTO statement section of this chapter to review the Parameter Value box.

> **Note:** If the PARAMETERS declaration or the PROCEDURE clause is using more than one formal parameter, you must separate the parameters with commas. In addition, you can use the formal parameters in the WHERE clause, the HAVING clause, or the VALUES clause of an INSERT INTO statement.

Using PARAMETERS Declaration Statement

The basic syntax for the PARAMETERS declaration is

PARAMETERS *parameterName* *parameterDataType* [, *parameterName* *parameteDataType* , ...]; *acceptableSqlStatement*;

where

- *parameterName* is a column or user-defined name
- *parameterDataType* is the type of data the *parameterName* must stored
- *acceptableSqlStatement* is a data manipulation language statement or a SELECT statement
- Symbols [ ] mean items are optional
- Symbols ... mean more parameter declarations can be listed

The PARAMETERS declaration has only one mandatory clause, namely, the PARAMETERS clause. The clause is used to list the formal parameters and their data types. However, the clause must associate or connect to an acceptable SQL statement in order to obtain a valid PARAMETERS declaration statement.

To display the first name, the last name, and the annual salary of the faculty member whose identification number is "EE987654" from the facultyX table by using the identification number column (facultyId) value entry as the value passed to the formal parameter, type and run the following PARAMETERS declaration statement.

```
PARAMETERS [Enter Faculty ID#] VARCHAR;
SELECT firstName AS [Faculty First Name], lastName AS [Faculty Last Name],
FORMATCURRENCY(annualSalary) AS [Annual Salary]
FROM facultyX
WHERE facultyId = [Enter Faculty ID#];
```

Enter the faculty member identification number when the parameter dialog box appears in the SQL window and press the ENTER key. You can also complete the operation by clicking the **Yes** button of the dialog box.

See result below.

Faculty First Name	Faculty Last Name	Annual Salary
Ememgini	Erochi	$68,261.39

You might have noticed that the formal parameter is a text expression enclosed in a pair of square brackets. The parameter is used also in the WHERE clause of the SELECT statement that is associated to the PARAMETERS declaration. This is acceptable in MS Access SQL programming.

Using PROCEDURE Clause Statement

The basic syntax for the PROCEDURE clause is

PROCEDURE *procedureName* [*parameterName parameterDataType, parameterName parameterDataType, ...*]; *acceptableSqlStatement*;

where

- *procedureName* is the name of the procedure
- *parameterName* is the optional user-defined name
- *parameterDataType* is the type of data the *parameterName* must stored
- *acceptableSqlStatement* is a data manipulation language statement or a SELECT statement
- Symbols [ ] mean items are optional
- Symbols ... mean more parameter declarations and their data types can be listed

The PROCEDURE clause has one mandatory clause, namely, the PROCEDURE clause. The clause is used to specify the procedure name and to declare the optional formal parameters if needed. However, the clause must associate or connect to an acceptable SQL statement in order to obtain a valid PROCEDURE clause statement.

> **Note:** Columns cannot be used as formal parameters in the PROCEDURE clause statement. However, you can use user- or programmer-defined names.

To update the annual salary range of between 50,000 and 55,500 for the instructor position in the positionX table using the numericNumbering column, type and run the following PROCEDURE clause statement.

PROCEDURE [Enter Position Number Code] INTEGER, [Enter Minimum Annual Salary] SINGLE, [Enter Maximum Annual Salary] SINGLE;
UPDATE positionX
SET minAnnualSalary = [Enter Minimum Annual Salary], maxAnnualSalary = [Enter Maximum Annual Salary]
WHERE numericNumbering = [Enter Position Number Code];

When the parameter dialog box appears to enter position code, enter the value 4 and press the ENTER key. Use the dialog box to complete the remaining data entries' operations.

You might have noticed that the PROCEDURE clause name is missing from the statement. This type of approach is allowed in MS Access SQL if the PROCEDURE clause statement is written using formal parameters. The first parameter then serves as both the PROCEDURE clause name and a formal parameter. However, if no parameter is used when writing the statement, the PROCEDURE clause must be given a name.

To display the updated record in the positionX table, type and run the following SELECT statement.

SELECT *
FROM positionX
WHERE numericNumbering = 4;

See result below.

numericNumbering	academicPosition	minAnnualSalary	maxAnnualSalary
4	Instructor	50000	55500

The annual salary range for the position of Instructor is updated to reflect the new values of the range.

COMMIT and ROLLBACK Commands

In most high-end SQL platforms, such as Oracle, COMMIT and ROLLBACK commands are used to affect the status of transaction control statements. The COMMIT command permanently records the changes made to columns' data while the ROLLBACK command undo the changes and makes the specified columns to keep their previous values intact.

Transaction Control Statements: A transaction control statement is a data manipulation language statement used to populate a table with data, change data in a table, and delete data from a table.

In MS Access SQL, columns that receive data, columns which data are updated, or columns which data are deleted are committed automatically when the appropriate DML statement is executed. In MS Access SQL, you do not need to issue the COMMIT command for the appropriate DML operation to be successful. MS Access supports and performs the implicit COMMIT command operation. Once the implicit COMMIT command is executed, the data values recorded in the specified columns or deleted from the specified columns cannot be reversed.

In MS Access SQL, the ROLLBACK command cannot reverse or undo DML operations once the operations are performed. One common way of reversing the implicit COMMIT command function of MS Access is to update the columns in question to again contain their last values before the implicit COMMIT command was executed. Another way to restore the columns' values is to always keep at least one back-up copy of a database before the DML statements are run for the tables of the database.

> *Note:* In Oracle, a COMMIT command must be issued after a DML statement is run if the changes made by the statement are to be permanent. Similarly, a ROLLBACK command must also be issued after a DML statement is run if the changes made by the statement are to be reversed.
>
> Example:
> UPDATE studentX
> SET dateFirstEnrolled = '10-Jan-05', userId = 'jf7463'
> WHERE studentId = "JF407463";
>
> COMMIT;

Chapter Summary

This chapter teaches Data Manipulation Language (DML) statements. The INSERT INTO, UPDATE, and DELETE statements and their functions, and how they are used in MS Access SQL are outlined and demonstrated. In addition, the chapter discusses PARAMETERS declaration and PROCEDURE clause statements and how they are used to manipulate data in MS Access SQL. In conclusion, the chapter explains how MS Access SQL uses the implicit COMMIT command to achieve transaction control statement operations, and why the ROLLBACK command is not productive in MS Access SQL.

DML Syntax and Statements Summary

The table below presents DML syntax discussed in this chapter and the SQL statements' examples for manipulating data in tables.

Statement Type	Basic Statement Syntax	Statement Example
INSERT INTO statement is used to load data into tables	INSERT INTO *existingTableName* [(*existingColumnName*, *existingColumnName*, ...)] VALUES(*columnValue*, *columnValue*, ...);	INSERT INTO facultyId(facultyId, firstName, lastName) VALUES("SM098761", "Steven", "Mathew");
This version of INSERT INTO statement is used to populate tables with data using data from other tables	INSERT INTO *existingTableName* [(*existingColumnName*, *exisingColumnName*, ...)] *subquery*;	INSERT INTO bookCopyX (isbn, bookTitle, classification) SELECT isbn, bookTitle, classification FROM bookX WHERE classification = "Natural Science";
UPDATE statement is used to change or modify data contained in tables	UPDATE *existingTableName* SET *existingColumnName* = *columnValue* [, *existingColumName* = *columnValue*, ...] [WHERE *condition*];	UPDATE bookCopyX SET classification = "Computing Studies" WHERE classification = "Computer Science";
DELETE statement is used to remove data from tables	DELETE [[ALL]* | *exisingColumnName*, ...] FROM *existingTableName* [WHERE *condition*];	DELETE FROM facultyXMod WHERE facultyId = "JS994450";
This version of DELETE statement is used to remove data from tables using data from other tables	DELETE [[ALL]* | *exisingColumnName*, ...] FROM *existingTableName* WHERE *existingColumnName* *subqueryOperator* (*subquery*);	DELETE * FROM facultyXMod WHERE facultyId IN (SELECT studentId FROM studentX, facultyXMod WHERE studentId = facultyId);
IN clause is typically used to connect an external database to a database that is opened and in use	FROM existingTableName, ... IN ["existingInternalDatabaseName"] | "existingExternalDatabaseName"	SELECT ALL * FROM bookX IN "D:\SURGE\AcademicX.mdb" WHERE costPrice >= 42.99;
PARAMETERS declaration statement is used to automate the manipulation of data in tables	PARAMETERS *parameterName parameterDataType* [, *parameterName parameteDataType* , ...]; *sqlStatement*;	PARAMETERS [Enter Faculty ID#] VARCHAR; SELECT firstName AS [Faculty First Name], lastName AS [Faculty Last Name], FORMATCURRENCY(annualSalary) AS [Annual Salary] FROM facultyX WHERE facultyId = [Enter Faculty ID#];
PROCEDURE clause statement is also used to automate the manipulation of data in tables	PROCEDURE *procedureName* [*parameterName parameterDataType*, *parameterName parameterDataType*, ...]; *sqlStatement*;	PROCEDURE [Enter Position Number Code] INTEGER, [Enter Minimum Annual Salary] SINGLE, [Enter Maximum Annual Salary] SINGLE; UPDATE positionX SET minAnnualSalary = [Enter Minimum Annual Salary], maxAnnualSalary = [Enter Maximum Annual Salary] WHERE numericNumbering = [Enter Position Number Code];

Key Terms

COMMIT

DELETE FROM clause

Formal Parameters

INSERT INTO clause

PARAMETERS declaration

PROCEDURE clause

ROLLBACK

SET clause

Transaction Control statements

UPDATE clause

User-defined names

VALUES clause

Chapter Review Questions

Multiple Choice Questions

1. Which of the following is not true? DML statements are used to
   a. create data tables.
   b. load data into tables.
   c. modify data contained in tables.
   d. remove data contained in tables.

2. The _____ statement is used to populate a table with data.
   a. UPDATE
   b. SELECT INTO
   c. INSERT INTO
   d. CREATE TABLE

3. The column list of the INERT INTO clause
   a. is used to avoid entering data to columns that will contain null values.
   b. allows the listing of columns' names.
   c. allows you to enter columns' values in whatever order you desire in the VALUES clause.
   d. all of the above.

4. Which of the following is not true? The UPDATE statement can be used to modify
   a. one record in a table.
   b. several records in a table.
   c. all records in a table.
   d. none of the above.

5. The UPDATE statement consists of _____ clause(s)
   a. four
   b. three
   c. two
   d. one

6. To remove a record from a table, you use the _____ statement.
   a. REMOVE
   b. DELETE
   c. FROM
   d. all of the above

7. In MS Access SQL, the DML statements use certain _____ functions.
   a. multiple-column
   b. multiple-row
   c. single-row
   d. single-column

8. Which of the following is not used with DML operations?
   a. The UPDATE statement.
   b. The PARAMETERS declaration statement.
   c. The PROCEDURE clause statement.
   d. none of the above.

9. A transaction control statement is a _____ statement.
   a. DML
   b. DDL
   c. DCL
   d. DTL

10. MS Access SQL performs the _____ COMMIT command.
    a. explicit
    b. implicit
    c. all of the above
    d. none of the above

True or False Questions

11. In MS Access SQL, DML statements display confirmation messages.
    a. True
    b. False

12. A column list is only allowed in a SELECT clause.
    a. True
    b. False

13. Whenever the values listed in the VALUES clause of the statement used to populate a table with data is more than one, the values must be separated by commas.
    a. True
    b. False

14. In MS Access SQL, The UPDATE statement allows the use of certain multiple-row functions.
    a. True
    b. False

15. In MS Access SQL, it is possible to remove records from one table by using the values of another table.
    a. True
    b. False

16. In Oracle, the COMMIT command is used to affect the status of transaction control statements.
    a. True
    b. False

17. In Oracle, the ROLLBACK command is used to affect the status of transaction control statements.
    a. Tue
    b. False

Fill in the blank Questions

18. To modify a table's data, you use the _____ statement.

19. The clause that is used to list columns' data for a record when loading a table with data is called the _____ clause.

20. The function of the INSERT INTO clause is to indicate the optional column list and the _____.

21. In MS Access SQL, to delete all records from a table, you can use the DELETE clause and the _____ clause.

22. _____ names must be used in the PROCEDURE clause portion of a PROCEDURE clause statement.

23. A reserved location of the main memory that is used to store a data value passed to a function is called _____.

Manipulating Data in Tables

Essay Type Questions

24. How does the PARAMETERS declaration statement differ from the PROCEDURE clause statement and what are their functions?

25. When and where, in MS Access SQL, are subqueries used in DML operations?

26. Define a transaction control statement and write a SQL statement that corresponds to the statement?

27. What is the gain of using formal parameters and write a SQL statement that uses a formal parameter?

28. Besides using the NULL keyword and the null indicator (double quotation marks with no values in between) in the VALUES clause of an INSERT INTO statement, describe another alternative method of entering null values to columns when populating a table with data?

Hands-on Activities

Perform the following hands-on exercises using the *Academics* database.

1. Use the INSERT INTO statement, without the optional column list and without formal parameters, to populate the table called dormitory with one record. The record should contain numeric data 11 for the first column, text data "East Beach" for the second column, date data #08/21/2002# for the third column, and text data "Good" for the fourth column.

2. Using formal parameters, insert four more unique records of your choice into the dormitory table. The entries (cells) of the fourth column should contain text data value "Excellent", "Very Good", "Good", or "Poor". Display the records of the dormitory table.

3. Run the appropriate INSERT INTO statement once to populate the domMod table to contain the same number of records as the dormitory table using the first two columns of the dormitory table. Display the records of the domMod table.

4. Update the "East Beach" record's buildStatus column of the dormitory table to "Very Good".

5. Using formal parameters, insert seven records of your choice into the studentInfo table. One of the records must contain numeric data 204 for the first column, text data "Paul Stedam" for the second column, and numeric data 11 for the third column. The domCode column is the table's foreign key and is used to establish a relationship with the dormitory table. Enter null values, when prompted, to the domCode column for any three of the records.

6. Using a single UPDATE statement, change the records in the studentInfo table that have null values in their domCode column to numeric data 11. Display the records of the studentInfo table.

7. Delete the record that has numeric data 11 in its domCode column of the domMod table.

8. Using the dormitory table in a subquery, delete all remaining records from the domMod table.

9. Using the PARAMETERS declaration statement and the domCode column of the studentInfo table, display all records that are related to records with the dormitory code number 11 in the dormitory table.

10. Using a single UPDATE statement, change the values of the domCode column for all records in the studentInfo table that have the value 11 in their domCode column to null values. Display the records of the studentInfo table.

Chapter Twelve

Views and Indexes

Chapter Objectives
After completing this chapter, you should be able to
- Define views
- Create simple and complex views
- Use simple and complex views
- Modify view structures
- Delete views
- Define indexes
- Create unique and nonunique indexes
- Use indexes
- Modify indexes
- Delete indexes

Views
Views are virtual structures or virtual tables used to represent how an individual, an organization, or an application sees the data in tables. Typically, views display subsets, portions, or segments of tables' data. Views show less or fewer data values than physical tables.

Views are not physical tables and as such, they do not store data or take up memory spaces. However, like tables, views can be used to create new views and one or several views can be created for one table. Views are logical windows through which data in tables are displayed. Data displayed through views are derived from tables used to create them hence views are sometimes called derived tables. Views remain in a database until the tables used to create them are removed from the database.

The following are some of the benefits of a view.

- A view makes the user to think that he/she is using all data from a table
- Because a view displays a portion of a table's data, it is used to simplify DML operations for the table
- A view provides a measure of security because sensitive (critical) data values can be hidden from being displayed by not including the sensitive data columns in the view
- With a view the user can display the same data from a table in different ways

Creating Views in MS Access SQL
MS Access SQL has no defined standard command or statement for creating a view, rather it allows you to create a view by using the SELECT statement and then save the result of the SELECT statement as a view. Because a view is created in MS Access SQL through a SELECT statement, a view is also called a saved query. A view created from a SELECT statement behaves the same way as any view created by other versions of SQL. A view can be manipulated in the same way a table is manipulated. A view can be categorized either as a simple view or as a complex view.

To create a view in MS Access SQL, you must first type and run a SELECT statement to display the required records from a table or joined tables. When the result of the query is displayed, you then save the result with a new name. The saved result becomes the view. To save the query result as a view, use the **Save As** command of the **File** menu of the MS Access window.

Figure 12.1 shows MS Access SQL window with a SELECT statement that when run, the result can be saved as a view.

Figure 12.1

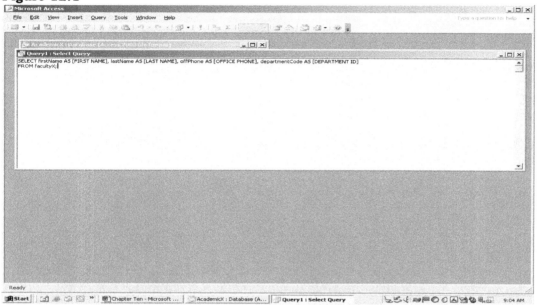

Figure 12.2 shows the result of the query in figure 12.1, the **File** menu, and the **Save As** dialog box used to create a view in MS Access environment.

Figure 12.2

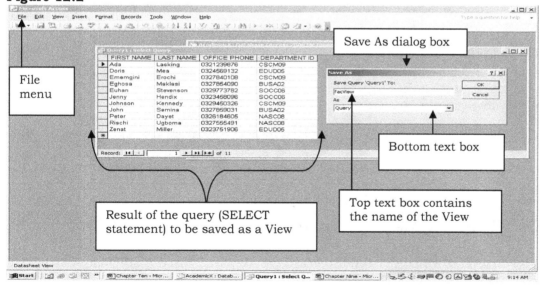

The bottom text box following the word "As" in the **Save As** dialog box must contain the QUERY keyword. Once the result of the query is saved as a view, the view becomes a physical table. Figures 12.1 and 12.2 are used to demonstrate how a view is created in

273

Chapter Twelve

MS Access SQL. From this point on, SQL statements used to create and manipulate views will be typed and their results will be displayed without showing MS Access SQL window.

> **Note:** The CREATE VIEW statement is used to create views in Oracle. The statement uses a subquery to create views.
>
> Example:
> CREATE VIEW facView
> AS SELECT firstName, lastName, offPhone, departmentCode
> FROM facultyX;

Creating Simple Views

A view created from a single table with certain specifications is called a simple view. The SELECT statement used to create such a view will list only one table in the FROM clause of the statement. The basic syntax for creating a simple view is

SELECT [ALL] * | existingColumnName, ...
FROM existingTableName
[WHERE rowCondition]
[ORDER BY existingColumnName, ...];

where

- Symbol * is to include all columns
- existingColumnName is the column in the table listed in the FROM clause
- existingTableName is the table that contains the column for the view
- rowCondition is the restriction that is applied to each record in the table
- Symbols [ ] mean items are optional
- Symbol | symbolizes **Or** Boolean operator.
- Symbols ... mean more columns can be listed

Below are the qualifications that make a view to be referred to as a simple view. A simple view is a virtual table that has the following.

- Retrieves and displays data from a single table
- Can perform DML operations – INSERT INTO, UPDATE, and DELETE
- Cannot contain the DISTINCT keyword
- Cannot contain functions
- Cannot contain grouped data - data values derived from a GROUP BY clause
- Cannot contain expressions - such as mathematical expressions

Start MS Access, open the **AcademicX** database, and activate MS Access SQL window.

To create a simple view called facViewX that is used to display first names, last names, office phone numbers, and department codes for faculty members using the facultyX table, type and run the following SELECT statement.

SELECT firstName AS [FIRST NAME], lastName AS [LAST NAME], offPhone AS [OFFICE PHONE], departmentCode AS [DEPARTMENT ID]
FROM facultyX;

274

Views and Indexes

See partial result below.

FIRST NAME	LAST NAME	OFFICE PHONE	DEPARTMENT ID
Ada	Lasking	0321239876	CSCM09
Doris	Mea	0324569132	EDUD05
⋮	⋮	⋮	⋮
⋮	⋮	⋮	⋮
Euhan	Stevenson	0329773782	SOCC06
Jenny	Hendix	0323458096	SOCC06

Save the result of the SELECT statement with the view name facViewX. Once saved, the saved query becomes a view. You can manipulate this simple view by using its name in DML statements - including the SELECT statement, just as you would with other simple views created in other versions of SQL. You might have noticed that the view is created using column aliases.

Displaying Data Using Simple Views

A table's data can be displayed using a simple view. A view uses the SELECT statement to display data stored in a table. Like querying a table, a view's SELECT statement can contain all SELECT statement clauses. The WHERE clause of the view's SELECT statement can be used to display records that meet the specified conditions either by listing data values or by using formal parameters as part of the WHERE condition clause.

The following SELECT statement is used to create a view called depViewX that displays faculty records of a specified department code using a formal parameter. The view is created using the facultyX table. Type and run the SELECT statement.

SELECT *
FROM facultyX
WHERE departmentCode = [Please Enter Department ID];

When the formal parameter dialog box appears, enter a data value that represents a department code from the facultyX table to display a result for the query. Save the result of the query as depViewX. You can use the view to display faculty records of other departments stored in the facultyX table.

Populating Tables with Data Using Simple Views

If a simple view contains the primary key and other non-null constraint columns of the table used to create the view, then the view can be used to populate the table with the necessary data. However, if any of the non-null columns, including the primary key, are not part of the view, it is impossible to insert data into the table using the view. An error message occurs if such situation arises.

Let's create a new view called facViewXMod that contains all columns from the facultyX table. The view is used to enter a new faculty member's record whose full name is "Joseph Irubor". To create the view, type and run the following SELECT statement.

SELECT *
FROM facultyX;

Save the result of the query with the view name facViewXMod.

To enter the new faculty member's record using the facViewXMod view, type and run the following INSERT INTO statement.

INSERT INTO facViewXMod
VALUES("JI907821", "Joseph", NULL, "Irubor", "0327786120", "CSCM09", "EE987654", 51500.26);

Although the faculty member's information is entered in the facViewXMod view, the corresponding record is actually registered in the facultyX table.

To make sure the new faculty member's record is entered into the facultyX table, type and run the following SELECT statement.

SELECT *
FROM facultyX
WHERE facultyId = "JI907821";

See result below.

faculty Id	first Name	initial	last Name	offPhone	department Code	chairId	annual Salary
JI907821	Joseph		Irubor	0327786120	CSCM09	EE987654	51500.26

> **Note:** You can also use formal parameters in the VALUES clause of the INSERT INTO statement. In MS Access SQL, you cannot populate a table with data through a view created with a WHERE clause that contains formal parameters. However, you can load data into a table through a view created with a WHERE clause that contains data values.

Changing Tables Data Using Simple Views

Like populating a table with data through a simple view, it is also possible to update a table's data values using a simple view. However, updating a table through a simple view is much easier if the view contains the primary key and other non-null constraint columns of the table used to create the view. In MS Access SQL, you can use a simple view created with or without the WHERE clause to update data values in the table used to create the view.

The update the first name of the newly entered faculty member "Joseph Irubor" to "Jos" using the facViewXMod view, type and run the following UPDATE statement.

UPDATE facViewXMod
SET firstName = "Jos"
WHERE facultyId = "JI907821";

To display the updated faculty member's record using the facultyX table, type and run the following SELECT statement.

SELECT *
FROM facultyX
WHERE facultyId = "JI907821";

See result below.

faculty Id	first Name	initial	last Name	offPhone	department Code	chairId	annual Salary
JI907821	Jos		Irubor	0327786120	CSCM09	EE987654	51500.26

Deleting Tables Data Using Simple Views

As with INSERT INTO and UPDATE statements, it is also possible to delete data values from a table through a simple view that is created using the table. Again, it is much

Views and Indexes

easier to delete data values from a table using a simple view if the view contains the primary key and other non-null constraint columns of the table used to create the view.

To delete the newly updated faculty member's record from the facultyX table using the facViewXMod view, type and run the following DELETE statement.

DELETE FROM facViewXMod
WHERE facultyId ="JI907821";

To make sure the faculty member's record is removed from the facultyX table, type and run the following SELECT statement.

SELECT *
FROM facultyX
WHERE facultyId ="JI907821";

See result below.

faculty Id	first Name	initial	last Name	offPhone	department Code	chairId	annual Salary

Notice that null record (record with no data) is displayed. This is an indication that the faculty member with faculty identification number of "JI907821" no longer exists in the facultyX table.

> **Note:** When DML statements are used with a view created from a single table, the DML operations actually affect the table. In addition, records displayed through a view may not necessary be arranged in the table in the same form they are displayed by the view.

Creating Complex Views

A complex view can be created in MS Access SQL using one, two, or more tables. A view containing functions, grouped data, or both created from a single table or created from more than one table is called a complex view. The method used to create a complex view is similar to the one used to create a simple view. The only difference is that a complex view might be created using more than one table and certain DML operations cannot be performed on such a view.

The basic syntax for creating a complex view is

SELECT [predicate] {[ALL] * | *existingColumnName, ...* | *columnExpression, ...*}
FROM *existingTableName, ...*
[WHERE *rowCondition*]
[GROUP BY *existingColumnName, ...*]
[HAVING *groupCondition*]
[ORDER BY *existingColumnName, ...*];

where

- Predicate is a condition keyword, such as DISTINCT, used to restrict records
- Symbol * is to include all columns
- *existingColumnName* is the column in the table listed in the FROM clause
- *columnExpression* is the expression formed by the combination of column(s) and data value(s). The column(s) and the data used in a column expression must be of the same data type

- *existingTableName* is the table that contains the column for the view
- *rowCondition* is the restriction that is applied to each record in the table
- *groupCondition* is a restriction on groups of records contained in the table
- Symbols [ ] mean items are optional
- Symbol | symbolizes *Or* Boolean operator. You can also list both *existingColumnName* and *columnExpression* or both * and *columnExpression* in the SELECT clause of the statement
- Symbols ... mean more columns and/or columns' expressions, or more tables can be listed

A complex view is a virtual table that has the following characteristics.

- Retrieves and displays data from one or multiple tables
- Cannot perform DML operations – INSERT INTO, UPDATE, and DELETE
- Can contain predicate keywords such as DISTINCT
- Can contain functions
- Can contain grouped data - data values derived from a GROUP BY clause
- Can contain expressions - such as mathematical expressions

Creating Complex Views Using Single Tables

In SQL programming, it is permissible to create a complex view using a single table. A complex view created from a single table must either use DISTINCT keyword, function(s), grouped data, expression(s), or any combination of the four.

The following SELECT statement creates a complex view using a single table. Type and run the SELECT statement.

SELECT classification, FORMATCURRENCY(MAX(costPrice)) AS [High Cost Price], FORMATCURRENCY(MAX(sellingPrice)) AS [High Selling Price]
FROM bookX
GROUP BY classification;

See result below.

classification	High Cost Price	High Selling Price
Business Administration	$43.25	$51.20
Computer Science	$49.45	$56.90
Natural Science	$49.00	$54.65
Social Science	$38.45	$44.95

Save the result of the query with the view name bookViewX.

Notice that the SELECT statement uses FORMATCURRENCY and MAX functions and the GROUP BY clause to create the view. Although, the view is created from a single table, however, by including the functions and the GROUP BY clause in the SELECT statement used to create the view makes it a complex view.

> *Note:* When an expression or expressions, such as numeric and text expressions, are included in the SELECT clause of the SELECT statement used to create a view from a single table, the view is also considered as a complex view.

The following SELECT statement contains mathematical expressions that calculate the profit gained in cash and in percent from selling computer science textbooks. Once the

Views and Indexes

SELECT statement is run and the result saved, it becomes a complex view. Type and run the SELECT statement.

SELECT bookTitle AS [Title of Book], FORMATCURRENCY(costPrice) AS [Cost Price], FORMATCURRENCY(sellingPrice) AS [Selling Price], FORMATCURRENCY(sellingPrice - costPrice) AS [Profit in Cash], ROUND((sellingPrice - costPrice) / costPrice * 100, 0) & "%" AS [Profit in Percent]
FROM bookX
WHERE classification = "Computer Science";

See result below.

Title of Book	Cost Price	Selling Price	Profit in Cash	Profit in Percent
Database Design	$25.95	$36.90	$10.95	42%
Principles of Programming	$31.95	$39.90	$7.95	25%
SQL Programming	$44.00	$50.25	$6.25	14%
Programming with Java	$49.45	$56.90	$7.45	15%

Save the result of the query with the view name bookXViewX.

The fourth column and the fifth column listed in the SELECT clause of the SELECT statement are expressions. Column aliases "Profit in Cash" and "Profit in Percent" are assigned to the expressions respectively to reveal the type of data they store.

Creating Complex Views Using Multiple Tables

A complex view can also be created from two or more tables. To create such a view, the FROM clause of the SELECT statement must contain two or more tables. If the same table is used more than once in the FROM clause, as in the case of a self join operation, the table must be given different aliases.

The following SELECT statement creates a complex view that can be used to display names and sections of courses taught by any faculty member. The SELECT statement uses a formal parameter in its WHERE clause. Type and run the SELECT statement.

SELECT courseName AS [Name of Course Taught], section AS [Course Section]
FROM courseX C INNER JOIN facultyX F
ON C.facultyId = F.facultyId
WHERE F.facultyId = [Please Enter Faculty ID];

When the Parameter Value box appears, enter the faculty identification number "EM001254".

See result below.

Name of Course Taught	Course Section
Fundamentals of Business II	2010
Principles of Programming	2020

Save the result of the query with the view name courSecViewX.

Performing DML operations using the courSecViewX view is not as easy as performing the operations using a simple view.

Alternatively, the following SELECT statement generates the same result as the last SELECT statement.

SELECT courseName AS [Name of Course Taught], section AS [Course Section]
FROM courseX C, facultyX F
WHERE C.facultyId = F.facultyId
AND F.facultyId = [Please Enter Faculty ID];

Populating Tables with Data Using Complex Views

Typically, a complex view is not used to perform DML operations. This is due to the fact that the view contains data that are generated from (a) columns' expressions, (b) functions such as SUM, (c) a single table that uses certain specifications like the DISTINCT keyword, or (d) several tables. However, when a complex view is created from several tables, the view can be used to perform the load operation to only one table. The table that the load operation can be used on is the table which primary key and non-null columns are included in the view. That table is called the primary or key-preserved table. The primary key of the key-preserved table also functions as the primary key of the view.

Key-Preserved Tables: A key-preserved table is a table which primary key functions as the primary key of a complex view, and the only table which data can be inserted using the view.

In MS Access SQL, to create a complex view that can be used to perform certain DML operations, you write a SELECT statement that must include the INNER JOIN...ON clause. To specify that the primary key of the key-preserved table is also the primary key of the view, you must include the primary key of the table in the condition of the ON portion of the INNER JOIN...ON clause.

The following SELECT statement can serve as a complex view that contain data from both facultyX and courseX tables. The key-preserved table is the facultyX table because the primary key (F.facultyId) column of the table is used in the condition of the ON portion of the INNER JOIN...ON clause. The C.facultyId column is a foreign key from the courseX table and although it appears in the condition cannot be used to perform the insertion operation. Type and run the SELECT statement.

SELECT F.facultyId, firstName, initial, lastName, courseCode, courseName, section
FROM courseX AS C INNER JOIN facultyX AS F
ON C.facultyId = F.facultyId;

Save the result of the query with the view name complexV.

Although, the primary key (courseCode and section columns) of the courseX table is listed in the SELECT clause of the SELECT statement, since the primary key columns of the courseX table are not listed as part of the condition, that table is regarded as a non key-preserved table. An insertion operation cannot be performed on the table using the complex view.

Non Key-Preserved Tables: A non key-preserved table is a table that cannot receive data by using a complex view, even if the table's primary key column(s) are listed in the SELECT clause of the SELECT statement used to create the view.

However, once a complex view is created, you can use it to populate a key-preserved table with data and update data in a non key-preserved table. You cannot delete records from tables using a complex view.

Views and Indexes

> **Note:** DML operations are possible through the use of complex views if there are no constraints' violations.

To add a new faculty member to the facultyX table using the complexV view and based on the columns from the facultyX table that are contained in the view, type and run the following INSERT INTO statement.

INSERT INTO complexV (F.facultyId, firstName, initial, lastName)
Values ("OM671192", "Ogie", NULL, "Minista");

To display the newly entered record, type and run the following SELECT statement.

SELECT facultyId AS ID, firstName AS [FIRST NAME], lastName AS [LAST NAME]
FROM facultyX
WHERE facultyId = "OM671192";

See result below.

ID	FIRST NAME	LAST NAME
OM671192	Ogie	Minista

The result of the SELECT statement is an indication that the insertion of the new faculty member to the facultyX table using the complexV complex view is successful.

Changing Tables Data Using Complex Views

A complex view can be used to change data values in a non key-preserved table. Let's create another complex view called complexVMod that includes, among other columns, the primary key of the facultyX table and the foreign key of the courseX table. Type and run the following SELECT statement.

SELECT F.facultyId, firstName, initial, lastName, courseCode, courseName, section, C.facultyId
FROM courseX C INNER JOIN facultyX F
ON C.facultyId = F.facultyId;

Save the result of the query with the view name complexVMod.

The following UPDATE statement changes a faculty member's identification number of "EE987654" to "OM671192" in the courseX table. Type and run the UPDATE statement.

UPDATE complexVMod
SET C.facultyId = "OM671192"
WHERE C.facultyId = "EE987654";

Note that the faculty identification number column in the courseX table is the table's foreign key.

To display the newly changed record in the courseX table, type and run the following SELECT statement.

SELECT *
FROM courseX
WHERE facultyId = "OM671192";

See result below.

courseCode	courseName	section	creditHours	facultyId
CSC445	Database Concepts and Design	2010	3	OM671192

In the displayed result, the facultyId column reveals the new faculty identification number.

To reverse the identification number to its previous value using the complex view, type and run the following UPDATE statement.

UPDATE complexVMod
SET C.facultyId = "EE987654"
WHERE C.facultyId = "OM671192";

> **Note:** In MS Access SQL environment, it is not possible to permanently remove records from tables by using complex views. The delete operation results to nothing being deleted.

Modifying Views Structures

MS Access does not directly support the SQL statement used to change the structure of a simple view or a complex view. Instead, to modify a view's structure, you open the view using the QUERIES button of the Object pane of the Object window. You then select the name of the view you want the structure modified and click the **Design** command of the Object window.

The command displays the SELECT statement used to create the view in MS Access SQL window. You can then modify the SELECT statement either by adding or removing (a) columns, (b) tables, (c) optional clauses of the SELECT statement, or (d) any possible combinations of the three. However, adding or removing optional clauses depends on the type of view that is being modified. When the structural changes to the view has been completed, save the view again. Figure 12.3 shows the window of the **AcademicX** database used to modify a view.

Figure 12.3

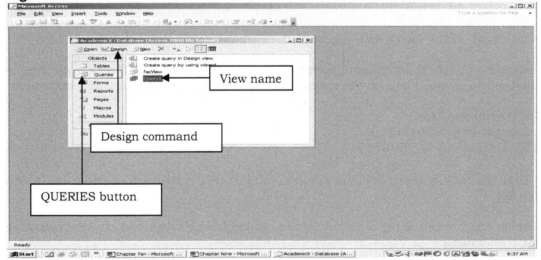

Views and Indexes

> **Note:** In Oracle, the structure of a view is modified using the CREATE OR REPLACE VIEW statement.
>
> Example:
> CRERATE OR REPLACE VIEW complexV
> AS SELECT F.facultyId, lastName, courseCode, section
> FROM courseX C, facultyX F
> WHERE C.facultyId = F.facultyId;

Deleting Views from Databases

Removing a simple view or a complex view using a SQL statement is not supported directly by MS Access SQL. Rather the QUERIES button of the Object pane of the Object window is used to delete the view. Click the QUERIES button to display the views in the database. Then select the name of the view you want to delete and right-click the mouse to display the view's shortcut command menu. Figure 12.4 shows a highlighted view and the shortcut command menu.

Figure 12.4

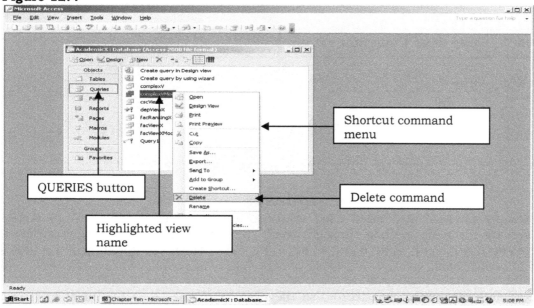

Click the **Delete** command on the shortcut command menu to remove the view from the database.

> **Note:** In Oracle, a view is removed by using the DROP VIEW statement.
>
> Example:
> DROP VIEW complexV;

Creating Inline Views

An inline view is a special type of view that is created using the FROM clause of a SELECT statement. Data displayed from such a view tend to behave as if they are generated from a physical table hence an inline view is called a temporary table. An inline view is assigned an alias to represent its name and an inline view can only be referenced by other clauses, such as the SELECT clause, in the SELECT statement that contains it. Subsequent SELECT statements cannot reference the inline view. The main distinction between a normal view and an inline view is that a normal view is a virtual

283

table with a structure that exists in a database, whereby an inline view exists temporarily only when the SELECT statement that contains it is run.

Using the same example as in chapter eight of this textbook, to display identification numbers, last names, and monthly salaries for faculty members whose individual monthly salary is greater than the average monthly salary of their department using both the facultyX table and an inline view, type and run the following SELECT statement.

SELECT F.facultyId AS ID, F.lastName AS LAST_NAME, ROUND(F.annualSalary / 12, 2) AS MONTHLY_SALARY, ROUND(G.MONTHLY_AVERAGE_BY_DEPARTMENT, 2) AS MONTHLY_AVERAGE_BY_DEPARTMENT
FROM facultyX F, (SELECT departmentCode, AVG(annualSalary / 12) AS
        MONTHLY_AVERAGE_BY_DEPARTMENT
        FROM facultyX
        GROUP BY departmentCode) G
WHERE F.departmentCode = G.departmentCode
AND F.annualSalary /12 > G.MONTHLY_AVERAGE_BY_DEPARTMENT;

See result below.

ID	LAST_NAME	MONTHLY_SALARY	MONTHLY_AVERAGE_BY_DEPARTMENT
EM001254	Maklasi	6213.63	5018.32
RU123098	Ugboma	5896.74	5319.37
ES509264	Stevenson	5821.02	4910.51
DM674543	Mea	5248.35	4706.72
EE987654	Erochi	5688.45	5108.98

In the SELECT statement, the inline view is given a table alias G.

Indexes

Indexes are physical structures used to speed up the retrieval of data from tables. Indexes are the main method through which records in tables are quickly retrieved. Indexes occupy memory spaces and as such, they slow down the updating of the tables used to create them.

Indexes are independent structures, so they can be created or removed at any time without affecting the tables used to create them. Although they are independent of the tables they index, indexes are automatically updated when the tables used to create them are updated. They are automatically deleted from a database when the tables used to create them are removed from the database. In MS Access, an index can contain up to ten columns. These columns are often referred to as index keys.

Index Keys: An index key is the column used to create an index for a table.

An index can be created implicitly or explicitly for a table. An index that is created implicitly is automatic and such index is created when a primary key or a unique constraint is defined for a table when the table is created or after the table's structure is modified. This type of index is called a unique index and it is created by the database management system, such as MS Access. MS Access also allows the creation of a unique index manually.

Views and Indexes

An index can also be created manually by explicitly specifying the columns in a statement used to create the index. This type of index is referred to as a nonunique index.

Unique Indexes: A unique index is an index created automatically for a table by a database management system using columns defined with primary key or unique constraints.

Nonunique Indexes: A nonunique index is an index that is manually created by a database user using columns that are listed in a statement used to create it.
The following are some advantages of creating an index for a table.

- The table is large and queries are very often performed to retrieve a very small percentage of records from the table
- A column contains a large range of data values in a table
- A large number of null values exists in a column of a table
- The frequent use of column(s) in a condition clause of a table or a join condition of join tables
- The table is not updated very often
- The indexed column(s) are not listed as part of an expression

The reasons for not creating an index are the opposite of the advantages for creating an index. The basic syntax for creating an index is

CREATE [UNIQUE] INDEX *newIndexName*
ON *existingTableName* (*existingColumnName* [ASC | DESC] [, *existingColumnName* [ASC | DESC] [, ...])
[WITH {PRIMARY | DISALLOW NULL | IGNORE NULL}];

where

- *newIndexName* is the name assigned to the new index
- *existingTableName* is the table that contains the column used to create the index
- *existingColumnName* is the column used to create the index
- Symbols [ ] mean items are optional
- Symbol | symbolizes **Or** Boolean operator
- Symbols ... mean more columns can be listed
- Symbols { } indicate to include an option in the WITH clause

The CREATE INDEX statement has two mandatory clauses, namely, the CREATE INDEX clause and the ON clause. The primary function of the CREATE INDEX clause is to assign a name to the index. The main function of the ON clause is to list the table that contains the column(s) to be used to create the index and to list the column(s).

Creating Indexes Using Single Columns
An index can be created using a single column. To create a single-column index, list the column in the pair of parentheses following the table. The following CREATE INDEX statement creates a one-column index called facLastIndX using the facultyX table. Type and run the CREATE INDEX statement.

CREATE INDEX facLastIndX
ON facultyX (lastName);

After the index is created, retrieving records from the facultyX table using the last name column is automatic. The database management system automatically uses the facLastIndX index to search, locate, and display records once a search in the facultyX table is based on the last name column.

Creating Indexes Using Optional UNIQUE Keyword

You can create an index that will not allow duplicate records' values to be displayed as part of the retrieval operation. To avoid the duplications of values in the indexed column(s) of records, use the UNIQUE keyword.

The following CREATE INDEX statement creates an index called bookUnIndX that retrieves records from the bookX table without duplicating the indexed columns' values. Type and run the CREATE INDEX statement.

CREATE UNIQUE INDEX bookUnIndX
ON bookX(costPrice);

After the index is created, retrieving records from the bookX table using the cost Price column is fast and there is no duplication in the indexed column for the displayed records.

Creating Indexes Using Multiple Columns

An index can also be created using two or more columns of a table. To create a multiple-column index, list each column to be included in the index in the pair of parentheses following the table. The columns must be separated by commas.

The following CREATE INDEX statement creates an index called studNameIndX that retrieves students' records from the studentX table based on both their first and last names. Type and run the CREATE INDEX statement.

CREATE INDEX studNameIndX
ON studentX(firstName, lastName);

After creating the studNameIndX index, whenever MS Access refers to the index to retrieve students' records, it searches the studentX table using the combination of the data values contained in both first name and last name columns.

Creating Indexes Using ASC and DESC Optional Keywords

By default, indexes are created using the ascending order approach. That is the data values in the column(s) used to create indexes are arranged in ascending order. To create indexes whereby the indexes' column values are arranged in descending order, use the DESC keyword with the column(s) when the indexes are created.

The following CREATE INDEX statement creates an index called studLFIndX using descending order approach to retrieve students' records from the studentX table based on both their last and first names. Type and run the CREATE INDEX statement.

CREATE INDEX studLFIndX
ON studentX(lastName DESC, firstName DESC);

After the studLFIndX index is created, whenever a search to retrieve students' records in descending order using the combination of last name and first name columns' values, MS Access references the index automatically to retrieve the needed students' records.

Views and Indexes

> **Note:** Although indexes are created by default in ascending order, you can optionally include the ascending order ASC keyword with columns to explicitly instruct the CREATE INDEX statement to create the indexes in the ascending order.
>
> MS Access SQL does not support the creating of function-based indexes. Function-based indexes are those created from expressions or by including functions to their indexed columns. However, Oracle supports function-based indexes. The following example shows a function-based index in Oracle environment.
>
> Example:
> CREATE INDEX bookGainIndX
> ON bookCopyX(sellingPrice - costPrice);

Creating Indexes Using WITH Optional Clause

An index can be created using one of the options of the WITH optional clause when the clause is listed in the CREATE INDEX statement. The optional WITH clause can be used to enforce rules that affect data in a table.

The DISALLOW NULL option of the clause denies null entries in the indexed column(s) for new records. The IGNORE NULL option prevents records with null values in the indexed column(s) from being included in the display. This option eliminates records that have null values in the indexed column(s) when the index is used to retrieve records.

The PRIMARY option specifies the indexed column(s) as the primary key of the table that is being indexed. The use of the PRIMARY option in the WITH optional clause implies that the column is unique, therefore the UNIQUE keyword in the CREATE INDEX clause of the CREATE INDEX statement can be omitted.

> **Note:** Do not use the PRIMARY option of the WITH optional clause to create a new index for a table that is created with a primary key, otherwise an error will occur. The PRIMARY option is used when a table to be indexed is created without a primary key.

Creating Indexes Using DISALLOW NULL Option

To demonstrate how an index with the DISALLOW NULL option is created, a table called bookCopyX that exists in the *AcademicX* database is used. The following CREATE INDEX statement creates an index called bookDNIndX using the cost price column of the table as the indexed column. Type and run the CREATE INDEX statement.

CREATE INDEX bookDNIndX
ON bookCopyX (costPrice)
WITH DISALLOW NULL;

After the index is created, null values can no longer be allowed in the cost price column for any new record that is inserted into the table.

> **Note:** In MS Access SQL, using the DISALLOW NULL option for columns that already contain null values to create indexes is not allowed. A clarification message is displayed if such columns are used.

Creating Indexes Using IGNORE NULL Option

With the IGNORE NULL option of the WITH optional clause, you can create an index to quickly display data records that only contain actual values in the column(s) used to create the index. If the indexed column(s) contain entries that are of null values, the records associated with the null entries are not displayed.

The following CREATE INDEX statement creates an index called bookINIndX using the selling price column of the bookCopyX table as the indexed column. Type and run the CREATE INDEX statement.

```
CREATE INDEX bookINIndX
ON bookCopyX (sellingPrice DESC)
WITH IGNORE NULL;
```

Retrieving records from the bookCopyX table that are based on the selling price column will automatically use the bookINIndX index. As a result, the index prevents all records that have null values in the selling price column from being displayed.

Creating Indexes Using PRIMARY Option

Let's create a new table called bookXMod from the bookX table. In MS Access SQL, the SELECT...INTO statement is an alternative method of creating a new table using the structure and/or data of an existing table. Usually, when a new table is created using the SELECT...INTO statement, the constraints defined for the table used to create the new table are removed from the new table's columns' definitions. Therefore, required constraints must be redefined for the new table.

To create the bookXMod table, type and run the following SELECT...INTO statement.

```
SELECT *
INTO bookXMod
FROM bookX
WHERE classification = STRCONV("computer science", 3);
```

The new table is used to demonstrate the creation of an index that includes the PRIMARY option of the WITH optional clause. Let's create a new index called bookIndX for the bookXMod table using the isbn column as both the indexed column and the primary key column for the table. Type and run the following CREATE INDEX statement.

```
CREATE INDEX bookIndX
ON bookXMod (isbn)
WITH PRIMARY;
```

Using Indexes to Retrieve Records from Tables

An index is the main mechanism with which records are quickly retrieved and displayed from tables. Unique indexes created with the primary key column(s) or with column(s) defined with the unique constraint are used automatically or implicitly by a database management system to retrieve records from tables.

However, to use non unique indexes - those created with non primary key column(s) or non unique constraint column(s) - to speed up the retrieving of records from tables, the indexed columns must be listed in the appropriate clauses, such as the WHERE condition clause, of a SELECT statement.

Verifying and Modifying Indexes

In MS Access environment, indexes created for a table can be viewed. The indexes' names, columns, or the order in which data are arranged can also be changed. To verify indexes created for a table, open the Object window of MS Access window. Select the TABLES button from the Object pane of the Object window. Then select the table's name from the list of names displayed in the right pane of the Object window. Click the

Views and Indexes

Design command button to open the table's Design window. Figure 12.5 shows how to display the indexes created for a table.

Figure 12.5

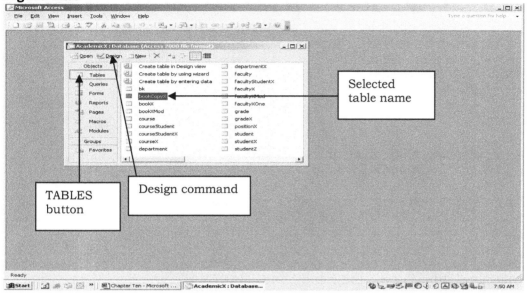

Figure 12.6 shows the Design and Index windows of the selected table. The Design window appears when the **Design** command is clicked.

Figure 12.6

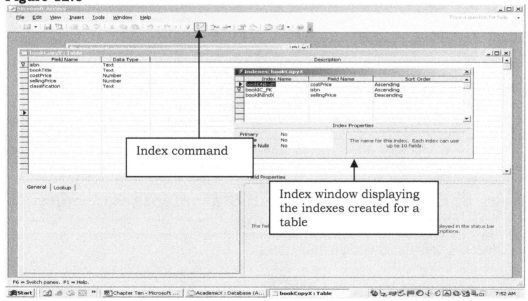

To open the Index window that contains the indexes created for the selected table, click the **Indexes** command on the MS Access window. The Index window displays the indexes created for the table. With the Index window opened, you can rename the index, change the indexed column(s), and/or change the order of the indexes' arrangement. The window also displays the property of the selected index.

Alternatively, after opening a table's Design window, you can display the Index window of the table by clicking the **Indexes** command in the **View** menu of MS Access window.

Deleting Indexes from Databases

There are situations when indexes created for a table are no longer needed or are no more useful. Deleting obsolete or non-useful indexes speeds up the updating of the table used to create the indexes. The basic syntax for deleting an index is

DROP INDEX *existingIndexName*
ON *existingTableName*;

where

- *existingIndexName* is the index
- *existingTableName* is the table used to create the index

The DROP INDEX statement consists of two mandatory clauses, namely, the DROP INDEX clause and the ON clause. The DROP INDEX clause is used to specify the index and the ON clause is used to list the table used to create the index.

The following DROP INDEX statement removes permanently from the database the index called bookINIndX. Type and run the DROP INDEX statement.

DROP INDEX bookINIndX
ON bookCopyX;

> **Note:** Oracle does not use the ON clause for the DROP INDEX statement.
>
> Example:
> DROP INDEX bookINIndX;

Chapter Summary

This chapter explains views and indexes that can be created for tables. The chapter outlines the main distinction between simple views and complex views and how they are created and used in MS Access SQL. The chapter also explains indexes which are the main method of retrieving data fast from tables. How index structures are created - with or without options, modified, and deleted from a database are explained. In addition, the chapter discusses how to use non unique indexes to retrieve records from tables.

Views and Indexes Syntax and Statements Summary

The table below presents the views' and indexes' syntax, special symbols, and keywords discussed in this chapter and the SQL statements' examples for creating and using views and indexes, and deleting them from tables.

Views		
Statement Type	**Basic Statement Syntax**	**Statement Example**
SELECT statement with limited optional clauses is used to create a simple view	SELECT [ALL] * | *existingColumnName*, ... FROM *existingTableName* [WHERE *rowCondition*] [ORDER BY *existingColumnName*, ...];	SELECT facultyId, lastName, offPhone, departmentCode FROM facultyX;

SELECT statement with more optional clauses is used to create a complex view	SELECT [DISTINCT] ([ALL] * | existingColumnName, ... | columnExpression, ...) FROM existingTableName, ... [WHERE rowCondition] [GROUP BY existingColumnName, ...] [HAVING groupCondition] [ORDER BY existingColumnName, ...];	SELECT classification, FORMATCURRENCY(MAX(costPrice)) AS [High Cost Price], FORMATCURRENCY(MAX(sellingPrice)) AS [High Selling Price] FROM bookX GROUP BY classification;

Indexes

Statement Type	Basic Statement Syntax	Statement Example
CREATE INDEX statement is used to create an index	CREATE [UNIQUE] INDEX newIndexName ON existingTableName (existingColumnName [ASC | DESC] [, existingColumnName [ASC | DESC], ...]) [WITH { PRIMARY | DISALLOW NULL | IGNORE NULL }];	CREATE INDEX facLastIndX ON facultyX (lastName); Or CREATE UNIQUE INDEX bookUnIndX ON bookX(costPrice);
DROP INDEX statement is used to remove an index	DROP INDEX existingIndexName ON existingTableName;	DROP INDEX bookINIndX ON bookCopyX;

Clause Type	Clause Syntax	Clause Example
WITH clause is an optional clause used to enforce rules for an index	WITH { PRIMARY | DISALLOW NULL | IGNORE NULL };	WITH DISALLOW NULL;

Special Symbol and Keyword	Description	Statement Example
, (comma)	Used to separate columns listed in the ON clause of the CEATE INDEX statement	CREATE INDEX studNameIndX ON studentX(firstName, lastName);
ASC	Used in the ON clause to arrange indexed columns' values in ascending order	CREATE INDEX studLFIndX ON studentX(lastName ASC, firstName ASC);
DESC	Used in the ON clause to arrange indexed columns' values in descending order	CREATE INDEX studLFIndX ON studentX(lastName DESC, firstName DESC);

Key Terms

ASC
Complex view
CREATE INDEX
DESC
DISALLOW NULL
DROP INDEX
IGNORE NULL
Key-preserved table
Multiple-column index

Non key-preserved table
Nonunique index
PRIMARY
Simple view
Single-column index
UNIQUE
Unique index
WITH clause

Chapter Review Questions

Multiple Choice Questions

1. Which of the following is not true? A view represents how a(n)_____ sees the data in a database.
   a. individual
   b. organization

c. application
d. table

2. Views
   a. are physical tables.
   b. are non physical tables.
   c. take up memory spaces.
   d. none of the above.

3. In MS Access SQL, views are created using the _____ statement.
   a. CREATE VIEW
   b. INSERT INTO
   c. SELECT
   d. ALTER VIEW

4. A simple view
   a. retrieves data from a single table.
   b. can contain the DISTINCT keyword.
   c. can contain functions.
   d. all of the above.

5. Which of the following is not true? A complex view
   a. can contain the DISTINCT keyword.
   b. can contain functions.
   c. can contain grouped data.
   d. is not a virtual table.

6. The key-preserved table is a table which primary key functions as the primary key of a _____ view.
   a. simple
   b. complex
   c. projected
   d. selected

7. An inline view is created using the _____ clause of a SELECT statement.
   a. SELECT
   b. GROUP BY
   c. FROM
   d. HAVING

8. Which of the following is not true? Indexes
   a. are physical structures.
   b. are virtual structures.
   c. speed up databases' data retrieval operations.
   d. all of the above.

9. An index that is manually created by the user is called a _____ index.
   a. nonunique
   b. unique
   c. frequently used
   d. large record

10. Which of the following is not a valid create index clause?
    a. CREATE INDEX clause.
    b. ON clause.
    c. WITH clause.
    d. IGNORE NULL clause.

Views and Indexes

True or False Questions

11. Views show less data values than tables.
    - a. True
    - b. False

12. Data displayed through views are derived from the views.
    - a. True
    - b. False

13. With views, users can display the same data from tables in different ways.
    - a. True
    - b. False

14. A view is called a saved query.
    - a. True
    - b. False

15. In MS Access SQL, indexes can only be created explicitly.
    - a. True
    - b. False

16. You can create an index with the WITH clause.
    - a. True
    - b. False

17. To remove an index from a database, you use the DELETE INDEX statement.
    - a. Tue
    - b. False

Fill in the blank Questions

18. A structure that represents how an individual sees the data in a database is called a _____.

19. When a view uses the DISTINCT keyword during its creation, that view is called a _____.

20. An index is the main method through which data in a table are _____.

21. An index that is created implicitly by the database software is called a _____.

22. The PRIMARY option can be included in a CREATE INDEX statement through the _____ clause.

23. Columns used to create indexes are often referred to as _____.

Essay Type Questions

24. Explain the differences between key-preserved table and non key-preserved table?

25. Describe the functions of both DISALLOW NULL and IGNORE NULL options of the WITH clause?

26. What is the main function of the WITH clause and write a valid SQL statement that includes the clause?

27. Define a complex view and explain how it differs from a simple view?

28. What is a nonunique index and write a SQL statement that depicts an example of this type of index?

Hands-on Activities

Perform the following hands-on exercises using the ***Academics*** database.

1. Create a simple view called studentDomView that displays students' identification numbers and the dormitory codes.

2. Create a simple view called insertDisplayView that can be used to add and show records of students' identification numbers, students' full names, and dormitory codes.

3. Write a INSERT INTO statement that uses the view created in question 2 to add a new record to the studentInfo table. Use appropriate data of your choice, but the new record must contain dormitory code 11.

4. Create a complex view called countStuDomView that can be used to display the number of students in each dormitory. Assign column alias of your choice to the column that contains the number of students in each dormitory.

5. Create a nonunique index called domNameIndex using the domName column of the dormitory table.

6. Create an index called domCodeIndex using the domCode column of the studentInfo table. The index file, when activated, retrieves data based on the indexed column's values in descending order.

7. Delete the index called domCodeIndex that was created earlier for the studentInfo table.

8. Using the WITH optional clause, create an index called domCodeIndx using the domCode column of the studentInfo table. This index file, when activated, retrieves records that contain non-null values in the indexed column.

9. Create an index called fullCodeIndex using fullName and domCode columns of the studentInfo table. The indexed columns' values should be arranged in descending order.

10. Delete the index file created in question 9.

Chapter Thirteen

Using VBA Procedures to Manipulate SQL Statements

Chapter Objectives

After completing this chapter, you should be able to

- Define VBA procedures
- Use VBA procedures to run DDL statements
- Use VBA procedures to run DML statements
- Use VBA procedures to run SELECT statements
- Use VBA format features to display records
- Use VBA procedures to group and summarize tables data
- Use VBA procedures to send queries results to sequential output files

Procedures

A procedure is a subprogram or a portion of a program that performs a given or a specific task. One can write a program in MS Access environment by using a programming language called Visual Basic for Application (VBA). The main method of running several MS Access SQL statements at the same time is to include the statements in a VBA procedure. Unfortunately, VBA programming language does not allow the writing of SQL statements in its code in the same way the statements are written in SQL environment. However, the language provides a mean through which SQL statements can be included in its code. This inclusion extends the capabilities of SQL.

Visual Basic for Applications (VBA)

VBA is a special programming language that is incorporated into MS Office Suite and the language is made available to the software packages that are part of the Suite. In other words, this programming language is built-in into or is a component of MS Office Suite and it is open for use by any of the MS application packages in the Suite.

The intent of this textbook is not to teach VBA programming language, rather this chapter's concern is to demonstrate how MS Access SQL statements can be run in VBA environment. The main aim of the chapter is to strengthen the capabilities of MS Access SQL statements through VBA programming environment. Teaching VBA language is outside the scope of this textbook. To learn about VBA procedures and programming, it is highly suggested that you refer to textbooks specifically written for the programming language.

Typically, MS Access SQL window allows only one SQL statement to be run at any given time. Running more than one SQL statement at the same time using the window causes an error message to be generated. But with a single VBA procedure, you can run several SQL statements either for the same table or for different tables. In addition to running several SQL statements in one VBA procedure, using VBA procedures to support MS Access SQL activities provide the following additional benefits.

- Displaying query results without the usual MS Access grid
- Displaying query results in formatted table form
- Displaying query results in formatted column form

Using VBA Procedures to Manipulate SQL Statements

- Permitting actual arguments for SQL statements
- Permitting formal parameters for SQL statements

Including SQL statements in VBA Procedures

To include SQL statements in a VBA procedure, you declare and assign the statements to string variables or type the statements directly into the procedure as string data or text data. The object commands **DoCmd.RunSQL** and **Debug.Print** and the IMMEDIATE window that are provided within VBA programming language are used in this chapter to demonstrate how SQL statements are run using VBA procedures. These commands and the window assist in running the statements, and in storing and displaying the results of SQL statements that are part of the procedures.

String Variables: A string variable is a memory location that is reserved to store zero, one, or more character symbols.

The basic syntax for declaring a string variable for a SQL statement in VBA is

Dim *sqlVariableName*, *sqlVariableName*, ... As String

where

- *sqlVariableName* is the name of the string variable
- Symbols ... mean more string variables can be listed

Example: Dim UpSQL As String.

The basic syntax for assigning a SQL statement to a string variable in VBA is

sqlVariableName = "*sqlStatement*"

where

- *sqlVariableName* is the string variable
- *sqlStatement* is a SQL statement enclosed in double quotation marks

Example: UpSQL = "DELETE FROM bk" & ";"

Note: Oracle uses a programming language called PL/SQL to create procedures. Each of the procedures can be used to run several SQL statements at the same time. However, the structural layouts of Oracle procedures are different from that of MS Access VBA. In Oracle, SQL statements are not written as strings in PL/SQL procedures, rather the statements are written exactly the same way as they are normally typed in Oracle SQL environment.

```
Example:
DECLARE
  facFN   VARCHAR2(15);
  facLN   VARCHAR2(30);
  facAS   NUMBER(7,2);
BEGIN
  SELECT firstName, lastName, annualSalary
  INTO facFN, facLN, facAS
  FROM facultyX
  WHERE facultyId = 'JH682508';
```

SELECT statement

```
DBMS_OUTPUT.PUT_LINE ('The Annual Salary for Dr. ' || facLN || ', ' ||
facFN || 'is ' || facAS);
END;
```

To learn more about Oracle PL/SQL procedures, refer to Oracle SQL textbooks.

For easy understanding, the Function Procedure of VBA is used to demonstrate how SQL statements are run. In VBA environment, procedures are stored in containers called modules. The standard module is used to demonstrate how SQL statements are embedded into VBA procedures. A standard module can contain one or several procedures.

One way to write a procedure in MS Access is to use the MODULES button on the left pane of the Object window. Figure 13.1 shows one way of creating or inserting VBA modules. The figure uses the **AcademicX** database as an example.

Figure 13.1

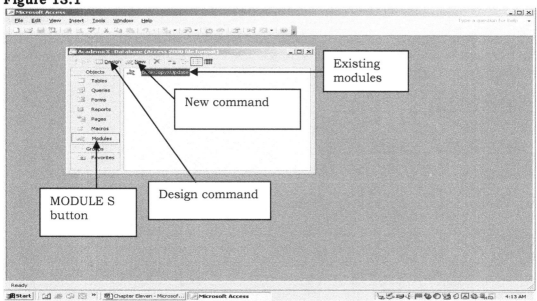

To create a new module, click the MODULES button and then click the **New** command. These actions open the new module window which is also the MS Access VBA window. Click the **Insert** menu of the VBA window and select the **Procedure** command to add the type of procedure to be created. Figure 13.2 shows the MS Access VBA window and how the **Procedure** command is selected.

Using VBA Procedures to Manipulate SQL Statements

Figure 13.2

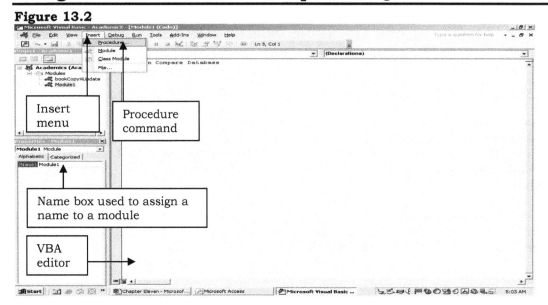

Clicking the **_Procedure_** command displays the Add Procedure dialog box. With the dialog box, you assign a name to the procedure, and choose the procedure type, property, and scope. Figure 13.3 shows the Add Procedure dialog box.

Figure 13.3

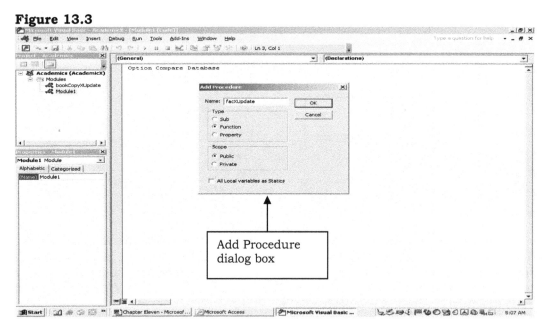

After you have given a name to the procedure and have chosen the type and scope of the procedure, click the **_OK_** button to create the procedure. You can save the module that stores the procedure (i) either before or after the procedure is created, (ii) after running the procedure, or (iii) before exiting the VBA window. If the save operation is not performed, both the module and the procedure are lost when you exit the VBA widow. Figure 13.4 shows the VBA editor and the frame for a procedure named facXUpdate.

Figure 13.4

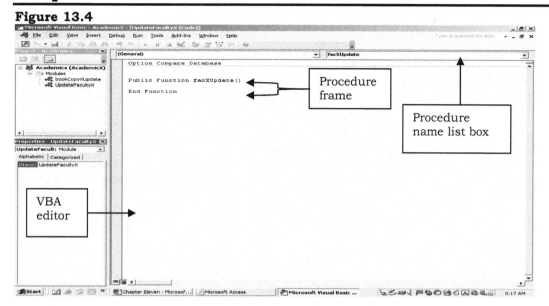

The VBA editor is the right pane of figure 13.4. The editor is used to enter the SQL statements and the associated VBA statements. SQL statements and VBA statements for a procedure – be it a Function procedure or any other type of procedure – are entered within the procedure's frame in the VBA editor. An empty procedure frame consists initially of the procedure's header and the end of the procedure's delimiter. The Procedure Name list box displays the name of the activated procedure or the names of the procedures that are associated with an object.

Again for easy understanding, VBA Function procedures are used in this chapter and they are created using the standard module. Procedures that are stored in the standard module are procedures that can be called by other procedures in the same project. The **AcademicX** database created for this textbook as the practice database is the project. This chapter uses the IMMEDIATE window to run individual Function procedures that contain SQL statements.

Figure 13.5 shows a sample of VBA editor containing a Function procedure called updi(). The procedure contains two SQL statements. In addition, the figure also shows the IMMEDIATE window.

Using VBA Procedures to Manipulate SQL Statements

Figure 13.5

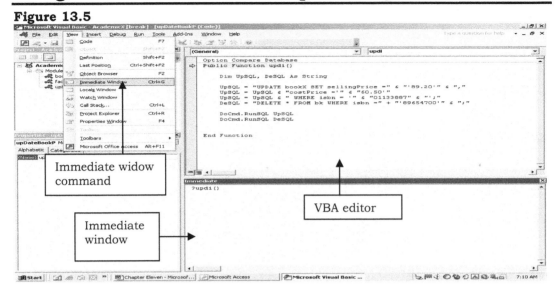

To use the IMMEDIATE window to run and debug VBA code, open the window by clicking the **View** menu on the VBA window and then select the **Immediate Window** command from the menu. The command displays the IMMEDIATE window beneath the VBA editor. To run and debug the program procedure using the IMMEDIATE window, click the IMMEDIATE window to select it, then type either the question mark symbol (?) or the PRINT keyword, followed by the name of the procedure, and a pair of parentheses. Press the ENTER key to run the procedure. See the IMMEDIATE window of figure 13.5.

The intended result, if the program is syntactically and logically correct, is displayed in the IMMEDIATE window. The pair of parentheses that follows the procedure name in the IMMEDIATE window is used to supply the procedure with values if the procedure is created using formal parameters. To include a module as part of a MS Access database, you must save the module. To perform the save operation, click the **File** menu on the VBA window and click the **Save** command. Usually, the **Save** command of the **File** menu shows also the name of the project that contains the module.

> **Note:** There are other ways of accessing the VBA window, inserting modules, and creating procedures. Again, it should be noted that this textbook teaches SQL using MS Access and not VBA programming. The aim here is to strengthen the capabilities of MS Access SQL through VBA. As a result, teaching VBA programming language is outside the scope of this textbook.

Writing SQL Statements in VBA Procedures
Writing SQL statements as part of VBA code is similar to writing the statements in MS Access SQL window. In VBA you can write a SQL statement in a single line or write the statement in multiple lines. The following two topics discuss and demonstrate how to type SQL statements in VBA procedures using single and multiple line formats.

Writing One SQL statement in One Line
To use the one-line approach, each SQL statement must be enclosed in double quotation marks and assigned to a string variable in a VBA procedure. Text data values (strings and characters) in the SQL statement must be enclosed in single quotation marks. Similarly, date values in the SQL statement must be enclosed within a pair of number signs (#). If formal parameters are used in place of data values, the parameters are not enclosed either in quotation marks or number signs.

Chapter Thirteen

The following example demonstrates how a SQL statement containing text and date values is entered in a VBA program. It is assumed that the string variable called studentUpDate has been declared, and a table called studentZ that contains the columns' names listed in the UPDATE statement is the one that is being updated.

studentUpDate = "UPDATE studentZ SET lastName = 'Steveson' ,dateFirstEnrolled = #1/20/2005# WHERE studentId = 'KZ934582';"

Alternatively, a SQL statement can be embedded as a string or text in the procedure without assigning it to a string variable. To use this approach, the statement must be written as part of a VBA statement.

The following example, using the last UPDATE statement, demonstrates how the statement is typed directly into a VBA procedure. In the example, the statement is embedded as part of a VBA ***DoCmd.RunSQL*** statement.

DoCmd.RunSQL "UPDATE studentZ " & "SET lastName = 'Paul'" & ", " _
& "lastName = 'Steveson' " & "WHERE dateFirstEnrolled = " _
& "#1/20/2005#" & ";"

Writing One SQL statement in Multiple Lines

Each SQL statement can be broken into several lines if so desired. To use the several-line method to include a SQL statement in a VBA procedure, you must concatenate the statement's segments' lines using concatenating operators. The concatenating operators for both SQL and VBA are the ampersand symbol (&) and the plus symbol (+).

One way to write a SQL multiple-line statement in VBA code is to place an underscore symbol (_) at the end of a segment line - except for the last segment line - and continue the next segment line with a concatenation operator. With this method, the string variable assigned to store the SQL statement only appears once in the assignment statement.

The following example uses the UPDATE statement in the previous section to demonstrate how the multiple-line approach is written in a VBA procedure using the underscore symbol and the ampersand concatenating operator.

studentUpDate = "UPDATE studentZ " _ ◄——— [Underscore symbol]
& "SET lastName = 'Steveson'" _
& "," & "dateFirstEnrolled = " _
& "#1/20/2005#" ◄——————————— [Value segment]
& " WHERE studentId = 'KZ934582'" & ";"

You can split a SQL statement to any number of segments' lines of your choice. The only concern is that you must enclose each SQL segment in double quotation marks when writing the segment in its own line and when concatenating it to another SQL segment line. Data values, if broken into their own segments' lines, must also be enclosed in double quotation marks. This is in addition to the single quotation marks used for text values and numeric values (although the single quotation marks are optional for numeric values), the number signs used for date values, and the actual arguments in the SQL statement. You can equally use the plus symbol (+) in place of the ampersand symbol (&) to perform the concatenation operation.

Alternatively, the multiple-line statement can be written in a way that the string variable assigned to store the statement appears in all the segments' lines that

Using VBA Procedures to Manipulate SQL Statements

constitute the statement. Using this method, the string variable, beginning with the second segment line up to the last segment line, is written as part of the expressions of the multiple-line assignment statements. The string variable also appears on the left side of the assignment operator (=) in the assignment statements of all the segments' lines.

> **Note:** An expression, in this case, is the data item or data items written on the right side of the assignment operator (=).

The following example uses the UPDATE statement in the previous section to demonstrate how the multiple-line statement is written in VBA code using the alternative method.

```
studentUpDate = "UPDATE studentZ "
studentUpDate = studentUpDate & "SET lastName = 'Steveson'"
studentUpDate = studentUpDate & "," & "dateFirstEnrolled = "
studentUpDate = studentUpDate & "#1/20/2005#"
studentUpDate = studentUpDate & " WHERE studentId = 'KZ934582'" & ";"
```

The logic behind splitting a SQL statement into segments' lines in VBA program is that you must understand how the statement is written in SQL environment. In a SQL statement, at least one blank space is required between (i) two clauses, (ii) two adjacent keywords, (iii) a keyword and a column, or (iv) a keyword and an expression. Embedding spaces in other areas of the statement is for readability purposes. The required space can be part of the segment line or attached to the segment line using a concatenating operator.

> **Note:** To type and run VBA procedures written in this chapter, you must open the **AcademicX** database and activate the VBA editor window.

Embedding DDL and DML Statements in VBA Procedures

It is practically easy to run data definition language (DDL) and data manipulation language (DML) statements in VBA code. To run the statements in VBA environment, you use the **DoCmd.RunSQL** command. The special SELECT...INTO statement is also considered a DDL statement since it is used to create a new database table by copying the structure and/or the content of an existing table, and as such, the statement can be run using the **DoCmd.RunSQL** command.

The basic syntax for the **DoCmd.RunSQL** statement is

DoCmd.RunSQL *sqlVariableName* | *"sqlStatement"*

where

- *sqlVariableName* is the string variable containing the DDL or DML statement
- *sqlStatement* is the DDL or DML statement enclosed in double quotation marks
- Symbol | symbolizes **Or** Boolean operator.

The following two Function procedures demonstrate how the CREATE TABLE and SELECT...INTO statements, and the UPDATE and DELETE statements can be embedded and run in VBA code. The ctMod() Function procedure creates two new tables. The first table called employee is created using the CREATE TABLE statement and the second table called bkCopyX is created from the existing bookX table using the

SELECT...INTO statement. The updi() Function procedure updates the bookX table and delete a record from a table called bk.

```
Public Function ctMod()

    Rem Declaring a string variables called UpSQL and CrSQL
    Dim UpSQL, CrSQL As String
    Rem Assigning a CREATE TABLE statement to the UpSQL string variable
    UpSQL = "CREATE TABLE employee " _
    + "(empId VARCHAR(8), empFName VARCHAR(20), empLName VARCHAR(25) " _
    + "basicMonSalary CURRENCY, commission CURRENCY, bonusRate SINGLE, " _
    + "CONSTRAINT empPK PRIMARY KEY(empId))" _
    + ";"
    Rem Assigning a SELECT...INTO statement to the CrSQL string variable
    CrSQL = "SELECT * INTO bkCopyX FROM bookX;"
    Rem Running the contents of the two string variables
    DoCmd.RunSQL UpSQL
    DoCmd.RunSQL CrSQL

End Function

Public Function updi()

    Rem Declaring string variables called UpSQL and DeSQL
    Dim UpSQL, DeSQL As String
    Rem Assigning an UPDATE statement to the UpSQL string variable
    UpSQL = "UPDATE bookX SET sellingPrice =" & "'89.20'" & ","
    UpSQL = UpSQL & "costPrice ='" & "60.50'"
    UpSQL = UpSQL & " WHERE isbn = '" & "01133887" & "';"
    Rem Assigning a DELETE statement to the DeSQL string variable
    DeSQL = "DELETE * FROM bk WHERE isbn =" + "'89654700'" & ";"
    Rem Running the contents of the two string variables
    DoCmd.RunSQL UpSQL
    DoCmd.RunSQL DeSQL

End Function
```

You might have noticed that each of the Function procedure is used to perform SQL operations on two different tables. VBA allows the inclusion of SQL statements for a single table or for several tables in a single procedure. Also, both CREATE TABLE and UPDATE statements are each written in segments across several lines while both SELECT...INTO and DELETE statements are each written on a single line.

Using Formal Parameters to Supply Data to SQL Statements in VBA Procedures

You can include a SQL statement containing formal parameters in a VBA procedure. When the VBA procedure is run, you pass data values called actual arguments to the SQL statement through the formal parameters. To use the parameter-driven method, you must list the formal parameters as part of the procedure's header declaration. The parameters are listed within the pair of parentheses following the Function procedure's name in the procedure header.

The SQL statement must also contain the formal parameters and if you are using the IMMEDIATE window to run the program, the parameters must also be listed in the pair of parentheses after the procedure's name in the IMMEDIATE window. The following VBA code contains a SQL INSERT INTO statement that uses formal parameters for its operation.

Using VBA Procedures to Manipulate SQL Statements

Public Function updMod(Enter_isbn, Entrer_book_Title, Enter_cost_Price,
Enter_selling_Price, Enter_classification) *'Formal parameters included*

```
Dim UpSQL As String
UpSQL = "INSERT INTO bookCopyX"
UpSQL = UpSQL + " VALUES(Enter_isbn, Entrer_book_Title,
Enter_cost_Price, Enter_selling_Price, Enter_classification)"
UpSQL = UpSQL + ";"
DoCmd.RunSQL UpSQL
```

End Function

Figure 13.6 shows how a VBA procedure containing a SQL statement with formal parameters is run using the VBA IMMEDIATE window.

Figure 13.6

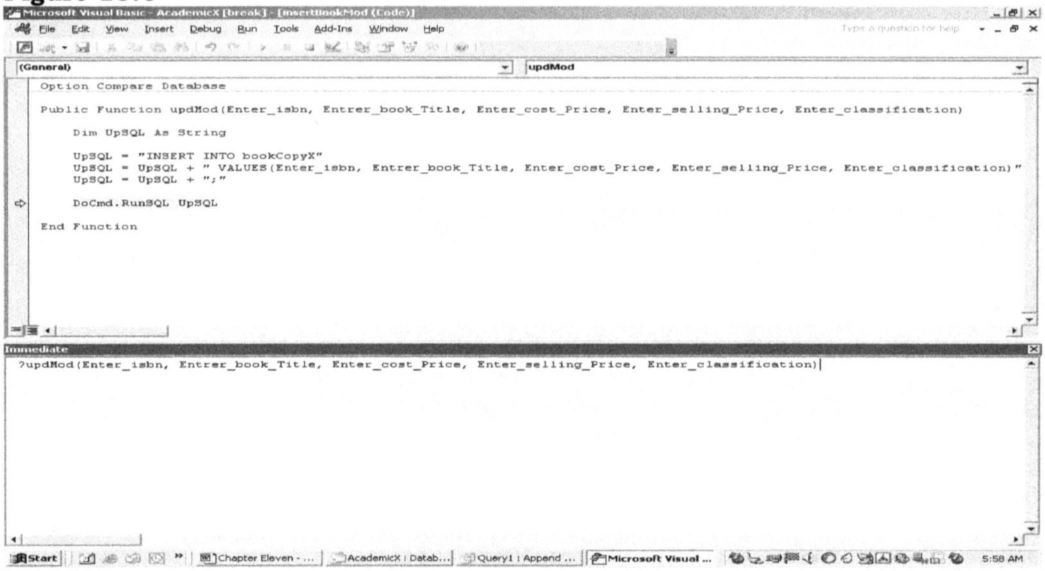

When the procedure is run, a Parameter dialog box for each formal parameter appears allowing you to enter a value for the column represented by the parameter in the SQL statement.

Embedding SELECT Statements in VBA Procedures

Except for the special SELECT...INTO statement that is considered a data definition language (DDL) statement, using ***DoCmd.RunSQL*** command to run a SELECT statement in a VBA procedure creates a problem. The cause of the problem is due to the fact that a SELECT statement reads from tables and could display more than one record as its output. One way to include a SELECT statement in VBA code is to use the ActiveX Data Objects (ADO) architecture. In addition to declaring the string variable for the statement, you must define three identifiers as objects for the SELECT statement that is being run. The objects are CONNECTION, RECORDSET, and COMMAND. The CONNECTION object is used to connect to the database that is being queried. The RECORDSET object is used to establish the result (records' set) for the SELECT statement and the COMMAND object is used to associate the result (records' set) created for the SELECT statement with the ***Open*** command statement.

The basic syntax for the CONNECTION object is

```
Dim connectionObjectName As ADODB.Connection
Set connectionObjectName = CurrentProject.Connection
```

where

- *connectionObjectName* is the name of the object that specifies the default database for the connection

The basic syntax for the RECORDSET object is

```
Dim recordsetObjectName As ADODB.Recordset
Set recordsetObjectName = New ADODB.Recordset
```

where

- *recordsetObjectName* is the name of the object that contains the results' set of the SELECT statement

The basic syntax for the COMMAND object and the associated **Open** command statement is

```
recordsetObjectName.Open sqlVariableName | "sqlStatement", connectionObjectName [, cursorType, lockType]
```

where

- *recordsetObjectName* is the object that contains the results' set of the SELECT statement
- *sqlVariableName* is the string variable that contains the SELECT statement
- *sqlStatement* is the SELECT statement enclosed in double quotation marks
- *connectionObjectName* is the object that specifies the default database for the connection
- *cursorType* is the optional cursor type property used to identify the type of the records' set to be created
- *lockType* is the optional lock type property used to avoid updating problems when more than one user is trying to update the same set of a data table records
- Symbols [ ] mean items are optional
- Symbol | symbolizes **Or** Boolean operator.

The following procedure demonstrates how a SELECT statement that displays only one record as its output is run in VBA language environment.

```
Public Function displayRecOne()

    Rem Defining a connection object
    Dim AcademicX As ADODB.Connection
    Set AcademicX = CurrentProject.Connection
     Rem Defining a recordset object
    Dim op As ADODB.Recordset
    Set op = New ADODB.Recordset
    Dim SeSQL As String
    SeSQL = "SELECT * FROM bookX" + " WHERE isbn ='" + "01133887" + "';"
    Rem Defining an open statement to read the content of the strng variable
    op.Open SeSQL, AcademicX, adOpenDynamic, adLockReadOnly
     Rem Displaying the result of the SELECT statement
```

Using VBA Procedures to Manipulate SQL Statements

Debug.Print (op!bookTitle), (op!costPrice), (op!sellingPrice), (op!classification)

End Function

After the code is run, the procedure displays the result below.

Programming with Java   49.45   56.9   Computer Science

In the procedure, the RECORDSET object is defined as "op". The CONNECTION object is the **AcademicX** database. The COMMAND object is part of the **Open** command statement. Alternatively, you can declare and activate the RECORDSET object in one statement by using the NEW keyword.

The following statement defines and activates the RECORDSET object at the same time. The statement corresponds and performs the same task as the two statements used to declare and set the RECORDSET object in the last procedure.

Dim op As New ADODB.Recordset

You might have noticed that the **Open** command statement in the last procedure is linked to the SQL statement and not the table. However, the SQL statement contains the name of the table. Also notice how the data values of each column of the bookX table are displayed using the **Debug.Print** statement.

The basic syntax for displaying a table's data values or text data using VBA **Debug.Print** statement is

Debug.Print *existingColumnName* | *"textData"*, ...

where

- *existingColumnName* is the column in the table
- *textData* is the text data enclosed in double quotation marks
- Symbol | symbolizes **Or** Boolean operator.
- Symbols ... mean more columns or text data can be listed

The last two attributes (adOpenDynamic and adLockReadOnly) of the **Open** command statement represent one aspect of the CURSOR type and the LOCK type properties of the RECORDSET object respectively. Both the CURSOR type and the LOCK type properties are optional.

Figure 13.7 below shows all aspects of both CURSOR type and LOCK type properties.

Figure 13.7

Specification	Meaning
CURSOR Type	
AdOpenDynamic	Allows forward and backward movement through the record set, as well as, allows the user to perform DML operations and view the results of the DML operations performed by other users.
AdOpenKeyset	Similar to AdOpenDynamic property, except that the user can not view the results of the DML operations performed by other users.
AdOpenStatic	Allows forward and backward movement through the record set. However, the user cannot perform DML operations on the record set and cannot view the results of the DML operations performed by other users.

Specification	Meaning
	CURSOR Type
AdOpenForwardOnly	Similar to AdOpenStatic property, except that this property allows movement through the record set in forward direction only.
	LOCK Type
AdLockReadOnly	Allows read-only records' set to be created. No DML operations are allowed with the records' set.
AdLockPessimistic	Allows the locking of records when the user begins to edit the records.
AdLockOptimistic	Allows the locking of records when the user attempts to update the records by activating the UPDATE method.
AdLockBatchOptimistic	Allows the execution of more than one SQL statements using one single command.

Note: When AdLockReadOnly property is used as the LOCK type in a VBA procedure that contains DML statements, warming messages are displayed informing the user the DML tasks failed due to the LOCK type property. The AdLockReadOnly property is used only to view or display a records' set.

The last VBA procedure can also be used to run a SELECT statement that retrieves and displays several records at the same time. The main difference between the SELECT statement that shows one-record result and the one that displays several records is that the **_Debug.Print_** statement that contains the required columns of the several-record SELECT statement is embedded in a loop.

The basic syntax for using a loop for a SELECT statement is

Do While Not *recordsetObjectName*.Eof
  loopStatement
  ...
Loop
         or
Do Until *recordsetObjectName*.Eof
  loopStatement
  ...
Loop

where

- *recordsetObjectName* is the object that is defined for the recordset
- *loopStatement* is a VBA statement that contains data attributed to the SELECT statement
- Symbols ... mean more VBA statements can be listed

The following VBA procedure shows how a SELECT statement that displays several records is written.

```
Public Function displayRec()

    Dim AcademicX As ADODB.Connection
    Set AcademicX = CurrentProject.Connection
    Dim op As ADODB.Recordset
    Set op = New ADODB.Recordset
    Dim SeSQL As String
    SeSQL = "SELECT * FROM bookX" + " WHERE classification ='" + "Computer Science" + "';"
```

Using VBA Procedures to Manipulate SQL Statements

```
   op.Open SeSQL, AcademicX, adOpenDynamic, adLockReadOnly
   Rem Defining a While loop to display the result of the SELECT statement
   Do While Not (op.Eof)
     Debug.Print (op!isbn), (op!bookTitle), (op!costPrice), (op!sellingPrice)
     op.MoveNext 'Move the pointer to the next record in the data table
   Loop

End Function
```

The following result is displayed when the procedure is run.

06142546	Database Design	25.95	36.9
07452771	Principles of Programming	31.95	39.9
05683420	SQL Programming	44	50.25
01133887	Programming with Java	49.45	56.9

In the last procedure, the Do While loop statement is used to display all records that met the set criteria for the table listed in the SELECT statement. The end-of-file expression (op.Eof) that follows the multiple keywords - Do While Not - in the Do While clause of the Do While Loop statement is enclosed in a pair of parentheses for readability purposes. The pair of parentheses is not required. You might have also noticed the **op.MoveNext** statement in the loop. This statement which consists of the RECORDSET object and the **MoveNext** command is used to move the pointer to the next record in the table. You can also use the DO UNTIL loop to achieve the same result.

Using VBA Formatting Features to Display Records
Visual Basic for Application language provides a set of formatting features that can be used to change the alignments of output values when displaying data records retrieved by a SELECT statement.

The formatting features discussed in this section are the two separators (commas and semicolon), the two functions (TAB and SPC), the Predefined formatting features, and the **RSet** statement.

Comma and Semicolon Separators
If you look at the VBA procedure in the last section, you might have noticed that the columns in the **Debug.Print** statements are separated by commas. In VBA programming arena, comma separators are used to display data values in print zones. A print zone is approximately fourteen print positions of a horizontal line and a computer display screen, normally, can contain five print zones per line. The results of the SELECT statements in the last section are displayed in print zones using the comma separators.

The following **Debug.Print** statement example displays the data values in print zones.

Debug.Print (op!isbn), (op!bookTitle), (op!costPrice), (op!sellingPrice)

The semicolon formatting separator behaves slightly different from the comma separator. Semicolon separators are used to display data values closely together. In other words, the subsequent data value is displayed immediately after the preceding data value without separation spaces. The following **Debug.Print** statement example displays the data values closely together.

Debug.Print (op!isbn); (op!bookTitle); (op!costPrice); (op!sellingPrice)

Chapter Thirteen

TAB and SPC Functions

You may, sometimes, want your data values to be displayed beginning at particular or specified print positions on a print line. In such environment, the formatting features that are more appropriate for that type of display are the TAB and SPC functions. The TAB function directs the computer to display a value following it starting at the print position indicated by a numeric digit enclosed in the pair of parentheses of the function.

The basic syntax for the TAB function is

Tab(*tabNumericDigit*)

where

- *tabNumericDigit* represents an integer value

The following **Debug.Print** statement example displays the data values beginning at print positions as specified by the TAB function.

Debug.Print Tab(10); (op!isbn); Tab(45); (op!bookTitle); Tab(55); (op!costPrice); Tab(65); (op!sellingPrice)

The above statement lists the isbn column values beginning at print position 10, the bookTitle column values beginning at print position 45, the costPrice column values beginning at print position 55, and the sellingPrice column values beginning at print position 65.

The SPC function's action is similar to that of the TAB function. The main difference is that the SPC function inserts a specified number of print positions before displaying a data value. Like the TAB function, you enter a numeric digit that represents the number of print positions to be skipped in the pair of parentheses of the function. The basic syntax for the SPC function is

Spc(*spcNumericDigit*)

where

- *spcNumericDigit* represents an integer value

The following **Debug.Print** statement example displays the data values after skipping numbers of print positions as specified by the SPC function.

Debug.Print Spc(10); (op!isbn); Spc(15); (op!bookTitle); Spc(10); (op!costPrice); Spc(10); (op!sellingPrice)

The above statement lists the isbn column values after skipping 10 print positions, and then skipped 15 print positions to display the values of the bookTitle column. The costPrice column values are then listed after skipping 10 print positions, and the sellingPrice column values are displayed after skipping another 10 print positions.

Formatting Numeric Data

VBA language provides four basic formatting features that can be applied to numeric data values. These formatting features can also be applied to numeric data displayed through SELECT statements that are embedded in VBA procedures. The formatting features are Currency, Fixed, Percent, and Standard. It should be noted however that

Using VBA Procedures to Manipulate SQL Statements

numeric data values not initially assigned specific numeric data subtypes, such as SMALLINT and SINGLE subtypes, in a database are converted to text values when formatted with any of the four basic formatting features.

The basic syntax for formatting a numeric value listed in a SELECT statement that is contained in VBA code using the formatting features is

Format(*existingColumnName* | *numericExpression*, "*formattingFeature*")

where

- *exisingColumnName* is the column of numeric data type in the table listed in the FROM clause
- *numericExpression* is a numeric value or a numeric expression
- *formattingFeature* is the desired formatting feature enclosed in double quotation marks
- Symbol | symbolizes **Or** Boolean operator

The following **Debug.Print** statement example shows how the formatting features are used in a VBA program.

Debug.Print (op!isbn), (op!bookTitle), Format(op!costPrice, "Currency"), Format(op!sellingPrice, "Currency")

The above statement formats both costPrice and sellingPrice columns to currency.

Spacing Out Records with Blank Lines

The **Debug.Print** statement is mainly used to debug and display results on the computer screen. However, the statement can also be used to space out displayed records on the computer screen. To include blank lines to space out displayed data records of a SELECT statement in a VBA procedure, you write the **Debug.Print** statement without actual arguments.

Example: *Debug.Print*

The actual arguments are the list of items that are usually listed as part of the statement.

Using RSet Statements to Align Numeric Columns Data

A SELECT statement is embedded into a VBA procedure as a string and as such, any column in the SELECT statement that is defined with a numeric data type is treated as a text column and therefore the values for that column are left-aligned. Remember that numeric data values, by default, are aligned to the right within the columns that contain them. To right-align data values of numeric columns that are part of a SELECT statement in a VBA procedure, you use the **RSet** statement.

To use the **RSet** statement to right-align values of numeric columns in a SELECT statement, the **RSet** statement's string variables to be used to align the columns' values must be defined as fixed-length variables. However, the maximum number of characters the string variables are defined for must be sufficient to store and right-align the numeric columns' values.

The basic syntax for the **RSet** statement used for a SELECT statement is

RSet *fixedLenghtStringVariable* = *existingColumnName*

where

- *fixedLengthStringVariable* is the name of the fixed-length string variable
- *exisingColumnName* is the column of numeric data type in the table

The following VBA code example shows how the **RSet** statement is used to align values to the right within a column.

```
Dim cost As String * 14
Dim selling As String * 14
RSet cost = (op!costPrice)
RSet selling = (op!sellingPrice)
Debug.Print (op!isbn), (op!bookTitle), cost, selling
```

The above statement shows how the **RSet** statement string variables - cost and selling - are declared and used in VBA environment. The two variables are declared to hold values consisting of up to fourteen (14) character positions.

The following procedure include some of the formatting features discussed so far to show how they are used to improve the appearance and the readability of the resulting records of a SELECT statement. Columns' headings are also included to describe the columns of the records. The output of this procedure is displayed in a browse form.

Browse Forms: A browse form is an arrangement of data values that consists of more than one column and may contain one or several rows.

```
Public Function ShowRec()

    Dim AcademicX As ADODB.Connection
    Set AcademicX = CurrentProject.Connection
    Dim op As ADODB.Recordset
    Set op = New ADODB.Recordset
    Dim SeSQL As String
    Rem Declaring a fixed-length string variables called CostP and SellingP
    Dim CostP As String * 10
    Dim SellingP As String * 13
    SeSQL = "SELECT * FROM bookX" + " WHERE classification ='" + "Computer Science" + "';"
    op.Open SeSQL, AcademicX, adOpenDynamic, adLockReadOnly
    Rem Using Tab function in a Debug.Print statement
  Debug.Print Tab(10); "ISBN"; Tab(25); "Book Title"; Tab(55); "Cost Price"; Tab(70); "Selling Price"
 Do While Not (op.Eof)
    Debug.Print 'Displaying a blank line
    Rem Formatting and aligning value to the right using the RSet statement
    RSet CostP = Format(op!costPrice, "Currency")
    RSet SellingP = Format(op!sellingPrice, "Currency")
    Rem Using Tab function in a Debug.Print statement
    Debug.Print Tab(10); (op!isbn); Tab(25); (op!bookTitle); Tab(55); CostP; Tab(70);
    SellingP
    op.MoveNext
 Loop
Debug.Print

End Function
```

Using VBA Procedures to Manipulate SQL Statements

The output of the procedure, after running it, is shown below in a browse form.

ISBN	Book Title	Cost Price	Selling Price
06142546	Database Design	$25.95	$36.90
07452771	Principles of Programming	$31.95	$39.90
05683420	SQL Programming	$44.00	$50.25
01133887	Programming with Java	$49.45	$56.90

Carriage Return and Newline Codes

A situation may arise when you want the displayed records of a SELECT statement that is embedded in a VBA procedure to be in an edit form rather than in a browse form. To achieve such arrangements, you include a new line code Chr(10) after each SQL column display statement in the VBA procedure. To use blank rows to space out the query result, you can use the carriage return code Chr(13). These two codes are primarily used in output statements such as the **Debug.Print** statement. The carriage return code Chr(13) behaves in a similar fashion as a **Debug.Print** statement with no actual arguments.

Edit Forms: An edit form is an arrangement of data values that consists of one column and may contain one or several rows.

The following procedure, using Chr(13) and Chr(10) codes, displays the result of a SELECT statement in an edit form. The Chr(13) code is used to insert a single blank row between records while the Chr(10) code is used to display each column data value of a record in its own separate line. Row titles are also included to describe the columns of each record.

```
Public Function displayRec()

    Dim AcademicX As ADODB.Connection
    Set AcademicX = CurrentProject.Connection
    Dim op As ADODB.Recordset
    Set op = New ADODB.Recordset
    Dim SeSQL As String
    op.Open SeSQL, AcademicX, adOpenDynamic, adLockReadOnly
    Rem Defining a Do Until loop to display records in edit form
    Do Until op.Eof
       Debug.Print Chr(13); "ISBN Number: "; (op!isbn); Chr(10); "Book Name: ";
       (op!bookTitle); Chr(10);
       Debug.Print "Cost Price: "; Format(op!costPrice, "Currency"); Chr(10);
       Debug.Print "Selling Price: "; Format(op!sellingPrice, "Currency")
       op.MoveNext
    Loop

End Function
```

The output of the above procedure, after running it, is shown below in an edit form.

ISBN Number: 06142546
Book Name: Database Design
Cost Price: $25.95
Selling Price: $36.90

ISBN Number: 07452771
Book Name: Principles of Programming
Cost Price: $31.95
Selling Price: $39.90

ISBN Number: 05683420
Book Name: SQL Programming
Cost Price: $44.00
Selling Price: $50.25

ISBN Number: 01133887
Book Name: Programming with Java
Cost Price: $49.45
Selling Price: $56.90

Using Comments on SQL statements in VBA Procedures

By now you might have noticed certain lines in the VBA procedures that begin with the REM keyword or certain VBA statements that have the apostrophe symbol (') and a note to the right of the symbol. Those lines or the apostrophe symbols and notes are referred to as comments. Comments are remarks or explanatory notes that help programmers or program users to clearly understand the functions of programs. Comments are referred to as non-executing statements and they can be used to describe the purpose of an entire program, a program's procedures, individual statement in a program, or different segments of a program. When remarks are included as part of a program's statements, they are referred to as internal documentation. The apostrophe symbol is also known as single quotation mark.

Traditionally, it is not possible to add comments to SQL statements in MS Access SQL window. However, such remarks can be made on SQL statements when the statements are embedded in VBA code. To include comments in a VBA procedure, you use either the REM keyword or an apostrophe symbol ('). An apostrophe symbol is also called a single quotation mark.

The basic syntax for including comments to SQL statements in VBA code is

Rem *sqlRemark*   Or   '*sqlRemark*

where

- *sqlRemark* is the explanatory note, comment, or remark

The following procedure includes remarks that indicate the purpose of the embedded SQL statement.

Public Function updMod(Enter_isbn, Entrer_book_Title, Enter_cost_Price, Enter_selling_Price, Enter_classification)

```
Rem    The INSERT statement embedded in this VBA code uses formal
Rem    parameters to add new record to the bookCopyX table each time this
Rem    program is run.
   Dim UpSQL As String        'The string variable stores the INSERT statement
   UpSQL = "INSERT INTO bookCopyX"
   UpSQL = UpSQL + " VALUES(Enter_isbn, Entrer_book_Title, " _
   + "Enter_cost_Price, Enter_selling_Price, Enter_classification)"
   UpSQL = UpSQL + ";"
```

Using VBA Procedures to Manipulate SQL Statements

DoCmd.RunSQL UpSQL 'The VBA command used to run the SQL statement

End Function

In the above procedure, the three lines of text that begin with the REM keyword are comments. Also the text to the right of the declaration statement that defined the string variable UpSQL and the text to the right of the **DoCmd.RunSQL** statement are remarks.

Grouping and Summarizing Tables Data in VBA

Chapter seven of this textbook discusses grouping and summarizing (aggregating) tables' data using UNION or UNION ALL statements of SQL. The peculiar facts about grouping and summarizing tables' data using UNION or UNION ALL statements require the utilization of multiple-row functions and the GROUP BY clause. Another abnormal fact about using the UNION or UNION ALL statements to achieve grouping and summarizing tables' data is determining the number of SELECT statements required in each type of grouping and aggregating. The number can represent a considerable amount of SELECT statements needed to achieve such activities.

This section explains and demonstrates alternative ways of grouping and aggregating tables' data using VBA procedures. In this section, grouping and summarizing records are achieved through sorting, selection (decision) statement, and repetition (loop) statement. To group and/or summarize tables' records using VBA procedures, the records of the tables must first be sorted, preferably in ascending order. However, tables' data can also be re-organized in descending order. The selection (decision) statement is used to test whether a new grouping is to be initiated. This test is performed for each record that is read by the repetition (loop) statement. The repetition statement is used to read records to be grouped from tables.

Usually, in SQL environment, tables' data, when displayed and if the sort clause is not exclusively listed in the SELECT statement, are arranged implicitly in ascending order using the primary keys' columns of the tables as the sort keys. Nonetheless, tables' data can also be sorted using the appropriate SQL statements, such as a SELECT statement that includes the ORDER BY clause or the data can be sorted in VBA procedures. However, it is easier and less complicated to sort tables' data in SQL environment. Another easy approach to rearranging tables' data is to include SQL statements that sort the data in VBA procedures. For the purpose of simplifying grouping and aggregating, this textbook re-organizes tables' data in SQL environment before manipulating the tables in VBA procedures.

The following VBA procedure, using the bookX table of the **AcademicX** database, displays selected columns of books' records in groups based on the table's classification (category) column in ascending order. Within each group, the records are sorted by the table's title column also in ascending order and the total number (grand total) of books in all categories is displayed as the last information in the result. The SELECT statement that sorts the bookX table's data is listed in the VBA procedure.

Public Function GroupBook()

```
Dim op As New ADODB.Recordset
Dim AcademicX As ADODB.Connection
Dim GroupSQL As String
Dim BookGroup As String
Dim GroupCounter As Integer
Dim TotalBook As Integer
Dim CostP As String * 6
```

314

```
Dim SellingP As String * 6
Set AcademicX = CurrentProject.Connection
GroupSQL = "SELECT * FROM bookX ORDER BY classification, bookTitle;" 'SELECT statement
that   rearranges the data
op.Open GroupSQL, AcademicX, adOpenDynamic, adLockReadOnly
Debug.Print 'Displaying one blank lines
Rem Printing main report title
Debug.Print Tab(32); "GROUPING BOOKS BY CATEGORY"
Debug.Print
BookGroup = op!classification 'initializing testing variable BookGroup with the first value of
classification column
GroupCounter = 0
TotalBook = 0
Rem Printing Books' Category Titles
Debug.Print Tab(32); op!classification; " Books"
Rem Printing columns' headings for Books
Debug.Print Tab(18); "ISB NUMBER"; Tab(30); "BOOK TITLE"; Tab(58); "COST PRICE"; Tab(75);
"SELLING PRICE"
 Do While Not (op.EOF)
  If (op!classification = BookGroup) Then
  RSet CostP = Format(op!costPrice, "Currency")
  RSet SellingP = Format(op!sellingPrice, "Currency")
  Debug.Print Tab(18); (op!isbn); Tab(30); (op!bookTitle); Tab(61); CostP; Tab(81); SellingP
'displaying table's data
  GroupCounter = GroupCounter + 1
  TotalBook = TotalBook + 1
  Else
  GroupCounter = 0
  Debug.Print
  BookGroup = op!classification
  Debug.Print Tab(32); op!classification; " Books"
  Debug.Print Tab(18); "ISB NUMBER"; Tab(30); "BOOK TITLE"; Tab(58); "COST PRICE"; Tab(75);
"SELLING PRICE"
  RSet CostP = Format(op!costPrice, "Currency")
  RSet SellingP = Format(op!sellingPrice, "Currency")
  Debug.Print Tab(18); (op!isbn); Tab(30); (op!bookTitle); Tab(61); CostP; Tab(81); SellingP
  GroupCounter = GroupCounter + 1
  TotalBook = TotalBook + 1
  End If
  op.MoveNext
 Loop
 Debug.Print
 Debug.Print Tab(20); "Total Number (Grand Total) of books in all Categories is "; TotalBook
'Displaying grand total
 Debug.Print

End Function
```

The output of the grouping and summarizing procedure, after running it, is shown below.

GROUPING BOOKS BY CATEGORY

Business Administration Books

ISB NUMBER	BOOK TITLE	COST PRICE	SELLING PRICE
05621458	Business Ethics	$42.50	$49.95
06739214	Business Law	$42.85	$51.20
09978423	Introduction to Marketing	$29.95	$37.45

Computer Science Books

ISB NUMBER	BOOK TITLE	COST PRICE	SELLING PRICE
06142546	Database Design	$25.95	$36.90
07452771	Principles of Programming	$31.95	$39.90
01133887	Programming with Java	$49.45	$56.90
05683420	SQL Programming	$44.00	$50.25

Natural Science Books

ISB NUMBER	BOOK TITLE	COST PRICE	SELLING PRICE
08720982	Advanced Biology	$49.00	$54.65
03821069	Basic Physics	$38.90	$46.70
03451105	Beginning Chemistry	$39.65	$42.80

Social Science Books

ISB NUMBER	BOOK TITLE	COST PRICE	SELLING PRICE
05588332	Basic Criminology	$31.60	$39.80
07225360	Elements of Sociology	$38.45	$44.95

Total Number (Grand Total) of books in all Categories is 12

Rather than including SELECT statements to sort tables' data in VBA code before grouping and/or summarizing the data, you can rearrange the data first in SQL environment and then list the sorted tables in VBA procedures. MS Access and VBA allow the grouping and/or summarizing of data from individual tables or joined tables.

Sending Queries Results to Sequential Output Files

In MS Access SQL, you cannot send SQL statements or the results of SELECT statements directly to the printer. Instead, what MS Access SQL programmers and users do is to copy the statements and results to a text editor, such as Note Pad, and then send the content of the text editor to the printer.

In a VBA procedure, you can create a sequential output file that can contain SQL statements and/or the results of SELECT statements, and later sent the file to the printer. The sequential output file must be created with an **Open** statement and closed with a **Close** # statement. The basic syntax for the **Open** statement is

Open "*outputFilePathName*" For *outputMode* As # *outputFileNumber*

where

- *outputFilePathName* is the location and the name of the output file to be opened or created. The location must include the drive name and folders (if any) and the *outputFilePathName* must be enclosed in double quotation marks
- *outputMode* is the type of open operation mode for the output file. The open mode can be Output or Append
- *outputFileNumber* is an integer value assigned to the output file. The combination of both the number sign (#) and the value forms the channel through which communication is established with the output file

By reviewing the following Function procedure called ShowRec(), you might have noticed some statements in the procedure that contain, among other facts, the number sign (#) and the integer value 1. These statements are used to communicate with the output file. One such statement is the Close #1 statement.

> **Note:** You can open a sequential output file in Output mode or you can open the file in Append mode. If the file is opened in Output mode, VBA creates a new file if the file does not exist and writes data values to it. If the file already exists, VBA erases the content of the file

Chapter Thirteen

> and writes data values to it. If the file is opened in Append mode, VBA adds data values to the end of the file if the file exists, otherwise VBA creates a new file and writes data values to it.

The two main methods for writing data values to a sequential output file are **Print #** and **Write #** statements. The basic syntax for **Close #, Print #**, and **Write #** statements is

Close # *outputFileNumber* | Print # *outputFileNumber* | Write # *outputFileNumber*

where

- *outputFileNumber* is an integer value assigned to the output file. The value is the channel through which communication is established with the output file
- Symbol | symbolizes **Or** Boolean operator.

The following procedure creates a sequential output file that stores the result of a SELECT statement. The output file is called bCopyX.dat and it is created in the root directory of the C: drive. The file will contain the result of the SELECT statement embedded in the VBA procedure after it is run. The procedure also displays the result of the SELECT statement in the IMMEDIATE window.

```
Public Function ShowRec()

Dim op As New ADODB.Recordset
Dim AcademicX As ADODB.Connection
Dim SeSQL As String
Dim CostP As String * 10
Dim SellingP As String * 13
Set AcademicX = CurrentProject.Connection
SeSQL = "SELECT * FROM bookX" + " WHERE classification ='" + "Computer Science" + "';"
op.Open SeSQL, AcademicX, adOpenDynamic, adLockReadOnly
Rem Creating a sequential output file called bCopyX.dat in the root directory
Rem of C: hard drive and assigning output file number ( logical channel) 1 to it
Open "C:\bCoyX.dat" For Output As #1
Debug.Print: Debug.Print 'Displaying two blank lines
Rem Printing report title and columns' headings on the computer screen
Debug.Print Tab(38); "COMPUTER TEXTBOKS"
Debug.Print: Debug.Print
Debug.Print Tab(10); "ISBN"; Tab(25); "Book Title"; Tab(55); "Cost Price"; Tab(70); "Selling Price"
Rem Inserting two blank lines before title heading are printed in the output file
Print #1,: Print #1,
Rem Printing report title and columns' headings in the output file
Print #1, Tab(38); "COMPUTER TEXTBOOKS"
Print #1,: Print #1,
Print #1, Tab(10); "ISBN"; Tab(25); "Book Title"; Tab(55); "Cost Price"; Tab(70); "Selling Price"
Do While Not (op.Eof)
  Debug.Print
  Print #1,   'Inserting a blank line in the output  file
  RSet CostP = Format(op!costPrice, "Currency")
  RSet SellingP = Format(op!sellingPrice, "Currency")
  Debug.Print Tab(10); (op!isbn); Tab(25); (op!bookTitle); Tab(55); CostP; Tab(70);
  SellingP
  Rem Writing data values to the output file
  Print #1, Tab(10); (op!isbn); Tab(25); (op!bookTitle); Tab(55); CostP; Tab(70);
  SellingP
  op.MoveNext
Loop
```

Using VBA Procedures to Manipulate SQL Statements

Print #1,
Close #1   'Closing the output file
Debug.Print

End Function

Figure 13.8 shows the sequential output file opened in Note Pad with the content of the file displayed after the VBA procedure is run.

Figure 13.8

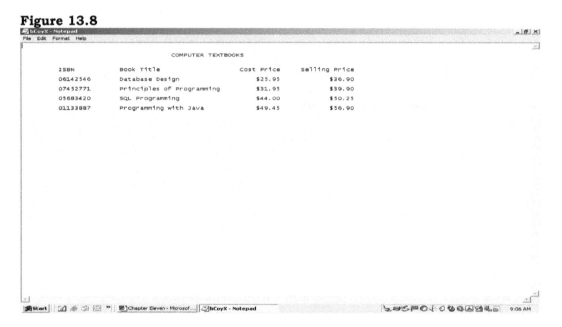

Displaying VBA Modules created for Databases

To view the VBA modules and procedures created for a specific database, select the MODULES button of the Object window of the MS Access window. Figure 13.9 displays the VBA modules created in this chapter for the *AcademicX* database.

Figure 13.9

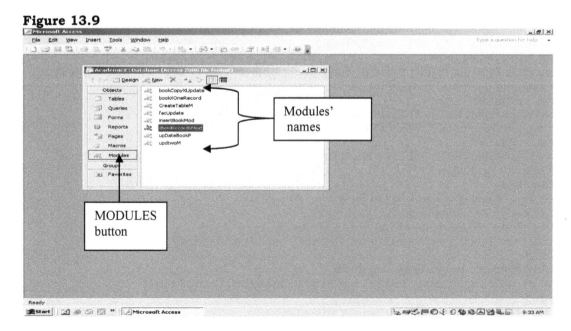

Viewing and Modifying Procedures Code, and Renaming and Deleting Modules

To view or modify a module's procedure code, either double-click the module in the right pane of the Object window or select the module in the right pane and click the **Design** command of the Object window. To rename or delete a module, right-click the module in the right pane of the Object window and select the appropriate command. Right-clicking the module displays the shortcut menu commands for that module. Figure 13.10 shows a shortcut menu commands for one of the **AcademicX** database modules.

Figure 13.10

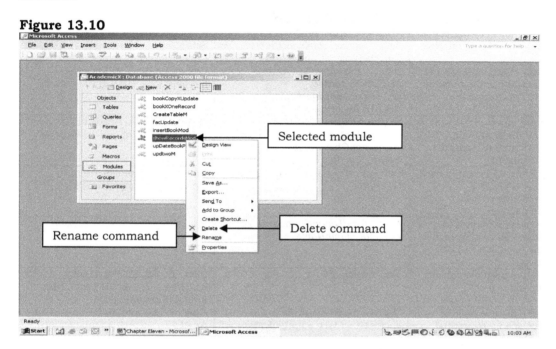

Alternatively, you can remove a module by using the **Delete** command (**X**) of the Object window.

Chapter Summary

This chapter explains Visual Basic for Applications procedures and how they are used to run several SQL statements at the same time. The chapter demonstrates how to (a) include DDL and DML statements, as well as, SELECT statements in VBA procedures, (b) display queries' results using the IMMEDIATE window, (c) use formal parameters to supply data values to SQL statements in VBA procedures, (d) use VBA formatting features to display SELECT statements' results, (e) group and summarize tables' data, and (f) create sequential output files to store the results of SELECT statements. This chapter also explains how to display modules, view and modify procedures' code, and rename and delete modules.

VBA Syntax and Statements Summary

The table below presents the VBA statement' syntax, procedures' syntax, special symbols, and the keywords discussed in this chapter and the VBA statements' examples for manipulating SQL statements.

Using VBA Procedures to Manipulate SQL Statements

Statement Type	Basic Statement Syntax	Statement Example
Dim statement is used to declare string variables to hold SQL statements	Dim *sqlVariableName, sqlVariableName, ...* As String	Dim UpSQL As String
SQL assignment statement is used to assign a SQL statement to a string variable	*sqlVariableName = sqlStatement*	UpSQL = "DELETE FROM bk" & ";"
DoCmd.RunSQL command statement is used to run DDL and DML statements	DoCmd.RunSQL *sqlVariableName* | *sqlStatement*	DoCmd.RunSQL UpSQL Or DoCmd.RunSQL "DELETE FROM bk" & ";"
Connection object statement is used to establish a connection to the database being queried	Dim *connectionObjectName* As ADODB.Connection Set *connectionObjectName* = CurrentProject.Connection	Dim AcademicX As ADODB.Connection Set AcademicX = CurrentProject.Connection
Recordset object statement is used to establish the result for a SELECT statement	Dim *recordsetObjectName* As ADODB.Recordset Set *recordsetObjectName* = New ADODB.Recordset	Dim op As ADODB.Recordset Set op = New ADODB.Recordset
Command object is used to associate the result of a SELECT statement with the Open statement	*recordsetObjectName*.Open *sqlVariableName* | *sqlStatement, connectionObjectName* [, *cursorType, lockType*]	op.Open SeSQL, AcademicX, adOpenDynamic, adLockReadOnly
Debug.Print statement is used to display a SELECT statement's result on a computer screen	Debug.Print *existingColumnName* | *textData, ...*	Debug.Print (op!bookTitle), (op!costPrice), (op!sellingPrice)
RSet statement is used to right-align values of numeric columns used in a SELECT statement	RSet *fixedLenghtStringVariable* = *existingColumnName*	RSet selling = (op!sellingPrice)
Comment is used to explain the function of a SQL statement in a VBA procedure	Rem *sqlRemark*	Rem The SELECT statement embedded in this VBA code uses formal parameters
Open statement is used to create or open a sequential output file	Open *outputFilePathName* For *outputMode* As # *outputFileNumber*	Open "c:\bCopyX.dat" For Output As #1
Close # statement is used to close an opened sequential file	Close # *outputFileNumber*	Close #1
Print # and Write # statements are used to write data to an opened output sequential file	Print # *outputFileNumber* | Write # *outputFileNumber*	Print #1 or Write #1
Function Type	**Function Syntax**	**Function Example**
Tab function directs the computer to display the value following it starting at a particular print position	Tab(*tabNumericDigit*)	Tab(10)
Spc function inserts a specified number of spaces before displaying a data value	Spc(*spcNumericDigit*)	Spc(15)
Format Feature	**Format Syntax**	**Statement Example**
Format features (Currency, Fixed, Percent, Standard) are used to format numeric data in a SELECT statement	Format(*existingColumnName* | *numericExpression, formattingFeature*)	Debug.Print (op!isbn), (op!bookTitle), Format(op!costPrice, "Currency"), Format(op!sellingPrice, "Currency")
Special Symbol	**Description**	**Statement Example**
, (comma)	Comma separator is used to display data values in print zones	Debug.Print (op!bookTitle), (op!costPrice), (op!sellingPrice)
; (semicolon)	Semicolon separator is used to display data values closely together	Debug.Print (op!bookTitle); (op!costPrice); (op!sellingPrice)

Key Terms

Browse form
Close # statement
Connection object
Connection open statement
Debug.Print command
DoCmd.RunSQL command
Edit form
IMMEDIATE window
OBJECT window

Print # statement
Procedures
Recordset object
RSet statement
Sequential file open statement
Sequential output file
Spc() function
Tab() function

Chapter Review Questions

Multiple Choice Questions

1. _____ is a component of MS Office Suite.
   - a. UBA
   - b. VBA
   - c. ABV
   - d. all of the above

2. Typically, MS Access SQL window only allows _____ SQL statement(s) to run at any given time.
   - a. 1
   - b. 2
   - c. 3
   - d. several

3. Which of the following is not a benefit for using a VBA procedure in MS Access SQL environment?
   - a. Permitting formal parameters for SQL statements.
   - b. Permitting actual arguments for SQL statements.
   - c. Displaying queries' results without the usual MS Access grid.
   - d. Permitting structure-level security.

4. In VBA, to debug a program during run time, you use the _____ window.
   - a. MODULE
   - b. IMMEDIATE
   - c. OBJECT
   - d. STANDARD

5. To write a text value for a SQL statement in VBA environment, you enclose the value in
   - a. single quotation marks.
   - b. double quotation marks.
   - c. square brackets.
   - d. parentheses.

6. Assume the statement is a valid statement, study the following SQL statement that is embedded in VBA code and point out the errors if any.
   stUp = "UPDATE senior SET firstName = 'Cecilia', enroll = #5/9/2005# WHERE studId = 'SE90564';"

   - a. The date value should be enclosed in single quotation marks.
   - b. The date value should be enclosed in double quotation marks.
   - c. The SQL statement should not be enclosed in double quotation marks.
   - d. The statement is written correctly.

7. In VBA, values are passed to SQL statement through
   a. the header of a procedure.
   b. formal parameters.
   c. all of the above.
   d. none of the above.

8. Which of the following objects is used to associate the records' set created for a SELECT statement with the OPEN command statement in VBA code?
   a. FILE.
   b. RECORDSET.
   c. CONNECTION.
   d. COMMAND.

9. When the Tab function is included in a VBA display statement, it displays records
   a. beginning at the specified print positions.
   b. after inserting a specified number of spaces.
   c. closely together.
   d. in print zones.

10. The edit form is an arrangement of data values that consists of _____ column(s) only.
   a. one
   b. two
   c. three
   d. four

True or False Questions

11. Using a VBA procedure in MS Access SQL environment allows you to display queries' results in formatted column forms.
   a. True
   b. False

12. A VBA procedure is stored in a module.
   a. True
   b. False

13. The COMMAND object is used to connect to the database that is being queried when using the ActiveX Data Objects (ADO) architecture.
   a. True
   b. False

14. Including commas in a VBA display statement will display records closely together.
   a. True
   b. False

15. Since the SELECT...INTO statement is a special type of a SELECT statement, you cannot run the statement in a VBA procedure using the DoCmd.RunSQL command.
   a. True
   b. False

16. In Oracle, SQL statements are written as strings in PL/SQL procedures.
   a. Tue
   b. False

17. In VBA environment, standard modules contain procedures that can be accessed by other procedures in an application.
  a. True
  b. False

Fill in the blank Questions

18. An arrangement of data values that consists of more than one column and may contain one or several rows is called a _____.

19. The _____ is used to align columns' values to right.

20. A _____ is used to run one or several SQL statements in a single operation.

21. The _____ is used to run and debug VBA code or VBA procedures.

22. The function that directs the computer to skip a certain number of spaces before displaying a data value is called the _____ function.

23. To join multiple lines' segments that constitute a single SQL statement, you use the _____ and a _____ operator.

Essay Type Questions

24. How is the manipulation of DML statements and SELECT statements differ in VBA environment?

25. What are the functions of the numeric data formatting features discussed in this chapter? Write a VBA print statement using two of the formatting features of your choice to illustrate how they affect numeric outputs?

26. Describe a procedure?

27. Explain the differences between a carriage return code and a new line code? Write a VBA print statement to illustrate how the codes are used?

28. Explain the differences between the comma symbol and the semicolon symbol in a VBA print statement? Write a VBA print statement to illustrate how the symbols are used?

Hands-on Activities

Perform the following hands-on exercises using the ***Academics*** database. Write and run a VBA Function procedure to

1. Create a new table called studCopyMod using the student table and the SELECT...INTO statement.

2. Define the studentId column as the studCopyMod table's primary key and drop the classification column from the table.

3. Create a new table called studentHall that contains two columns. The columns' names are hallCode and hallName. The two columns' data types are character data types with the hallCode column having a fixed-length size of six and the hallName column having a variable-length size of twenty. The hallCode column is the table's primary key and it should be defined at the table level. After creating the table, add a new column called yearBuild with date data type and define the column with the null constraint.

4. Populate the studentHall table, using formal parameters in the VALUES clause of the INSERT INTO statement, with six records. Enter three records with primary key values of 11, 13, and 20.

5. Display the records in the studentHall table. The result should include all columns' data of the table.

6. Populate the studCopyMod table with two records of your choice using actual data values in the VALUES clause of the INSERT INTO statement.

7. Change the hall name of the record with the hall code 11 to "Central Beach" and the hall name of the record with the hall code 13 to "Premiere".

8. Display only hallCode and hallName columns of records with primary key values of 11 or 13.

9. Truncate the studCopyMod table and then remove the table permanently from the database.

10. Send the records, including all columns' data, in the studentHall table to a sequential output file called studentHall.dat. The file should be saved in the root directory of a storage medium of your choice.

Chapter Fourteen

Using VBA Procedures to Establish Database Security

Chapter Objectives
After completing this chapter, you should be able to
- Use VBA procedures to establish database access security
- Use VBA procedures to create users and groups
- Use VBA procedures to add users to groups
- Use VBA procedures to grant permissions to users and groups
- Use VBA procedures to revoke permissions from users and groups

Database Security
Database security is an established measure that is used to deny or prevent an unauthorized user from accessing a database. Two types of security measures can be established for a database. One type called the application- or database-level security is used to control the opening of the database itself and the other type called the user-level security is used to control how a user manipulates the tables and other objects of the database. To establish security measures for a database at both the database-level and the user-level, the database must be opened in exclusive mode.

Security Measures: A security measure is a way of disallowing a user who has not been given the appropriate permissions to use a database.

Exclusive Modes: An exclusive mode, in a database, is an environment where a database is opened for one user only at any given time.

In MS Access, setting up security for a database is usually done through graphical user interface (GUI). The GUI method is very often used by MS Access textbooks to demonstrate how security can be established for a database. In addition to the GUI method, this chapter shows an alternative approach of establishing security for a database. The alternative method uses MS Visual Basic for Applications (VBA) procedures.

Workgroup Information File
Whenever MS Access is launched, a special system file called Workgroup Information File is also activated. The file is activated at MS Access startup time. The file is used to register users, their passwords, their personal identifiers (PID), workgroups, workgroups' identifiers (WID), and the workgroups to which users belong when the user-level security measure is established. Using the Workgroup Information File, different users' and workgroups' access permissions to a database are controlled. This file has the name **system.mdw** and it is very often located in the SYSTEM folder of the COMMON FILES folder of the PROGRAM FILES folder. The PROGRAM FILES folder is usually located, by default, in the C: hard drive.

If the special system file is not located in the SYSTEM folder on your computer, use the search feature of MS Windows to locate it. Generally, when you set up the user-level security, users are prompted to enter their logon credentials, such as their names, that give them access to the database. This special file controls all databases created with

Using VBA Procedures to Establish Database Security

MS Access and establishes the user-level security for a particular database. However, it is always a good practice to create a Workgroup Information File exclusively for a particular database.

To create the system file for a particular database, simply copy the original system file and assign a new name to the copied version. The copied version of the file is then associated with the database. Using this method keeps the original Workgroup Information File unchanged.

Figure 14.1 demonstrates how to begin creating a copy of the Workgroup Information File for a particular database.

Figure 14.1

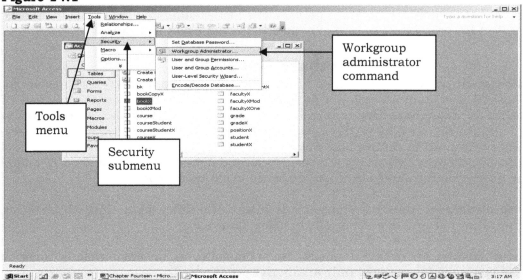

Once a database is opened in exclusive mode, click the **Tools** menu of MS Access window, point to the **Security** submenu and then click the **Workgroup Administrator** command to open the dialog box. Figure 14.2 shows how to create the file.

Figure 14.2

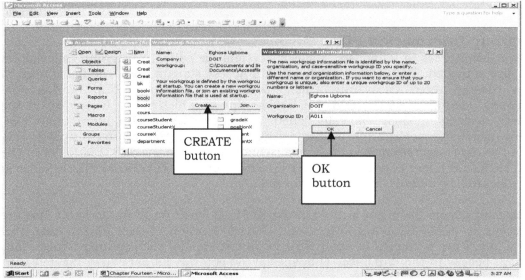

On the Workgroup Administrator dialog box, click the CREATE button. This action opens the Workgroup Owner Information dialog box. Enter the necessary information in each of the text box that appears in the Workgroup Owner Information dialog box and then click the OK button. Clicking the OK button displays the Workgroup Information File dialog box. See figure 14.3.

Figure 14.3

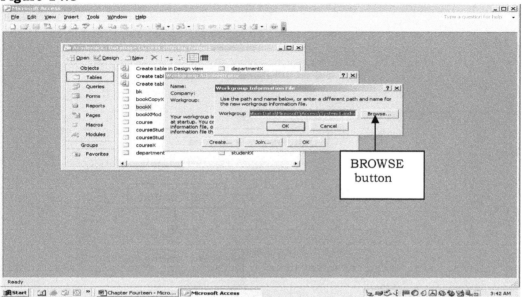

Click the BROWSE button to open the location where you want to store the copied version of the file. Type a name for the copied version without a file extension and then click the OPEN button. Click the OK button and then click the button again when it shows up. At this point you see a message confirming that you have created a copy of the Workgroup Information File successfully. Click the OK button to complete the operation. Finally, click the OK button again to leave the Workgroup Information File environment.

The copied version of the Workgroup Information File of the **AcademicX** database used for demonstration in this textbook is called **AcademicX.mdw**. The following section shows how MS Access is informed to use the **AcademicX.mdw** file when the database is launched through the COMMAND PROMPT window. The last part of the COMMAND PROMPT statement contains the Workgroup Information File and that part also includes the pathname where the file is located in the computer system.

Database-Level Security

Establishing a database-level security for a database application is easier than establishing the user-level security. The database-level security denies an unauthorized user from viewing the content of a database. The unauthorized user can not see the database objects. This type of security measure does not differentiate one user from another user, and as such, users access to the database objects are not controlled once they have successfully passed the database-level security test - logged on to the database.

The database-level security involves creating a password for the database. However, if the database is to be replicated, it should not be opened with a password. To assign a password to a database, the database must be opened in exclusive mode.

Using VBA Procedures to Establish Database Security

Databases Passwords: A database password is a coded word or secret code used as a means of denying an unauthorized user from viewing the content of a database.

Databases Replications: A database replication is a process of copying a database in order to exchange updated data among the copies of the database.

Figure 14.4 shows how to open a database in exclusive mode using the graphic user interface (GUI) approach.

Figure 14.4

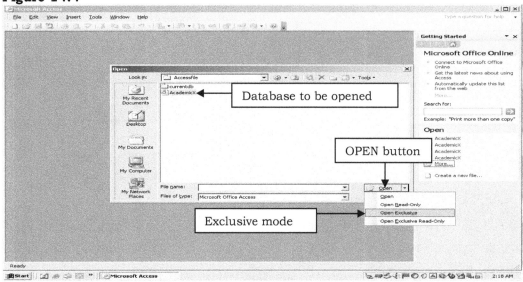

With the GUI method, you start MS Access and then select the database from the appropriate storage location. Click the list arrow of the OPEN button to display the available open modes and then click on the text expression "Open Exclusive". This action opens the database exclusively for the user.

To practice with the VBA procedures listed in this chapter, you must start MS Access, open ***AcademicX*** database, and activate the VBA editor window.

Creating, Changing, and Deleting Passwords for Databases

Once a database is open in exclusive mode, the database can then be assigned a password to prevent an unauthorized user from accessing and viewing the content of the database. The password security measure can, as an alternative method, be established through a VBA procedure. Once a password is created for a database, any future access to the database must supply the password, otherwise access to the database objects is denied.

To create a password for a database through VBA, refer to the steps discussed in chapter thirteen of this textbook on VBA procedures. However, to run a Sub procedure using the IMMEDIATE window, type the Sub procedure name only. Unlike running a Function procedure, the name of a Sub procedure must not be preceded by the PRINT keyword or the question mark print symbol (?). The name of the Sub procedure must also not be followed by the pair of parentheses that usually ends the name of a procedure.

Chapter Fourteen

The following example shows how to run a Sub procedure named SetDBPassWord()
using the IMMEDIATE window.

SetDBPassWord

After typing the name of the Sub procedure in the IMMEDIATE window, Press the
ENTER key to run the procedure.

In VBA, the NewPassword method is used to create a password for a database. The
method requires two actual arguments and each argument must be enclosed in a pair
of double quotation marks. The first argument (the leftmost one) represents the current
or the old password for the database, and the second argument (the rightmost one)
represents the new password. The arguments must be separated by a comma. The
method can equally be used to change the password for a database.

The basic syntax for the NewPassword method is

databaseObject.NewPassword "*databaseOldPassword*", "*databaseNewPassword*"

where

- *databaseObject* is the name of the object that is defined for the database
- *databaseOldPassword* represents the expression used as the old password
- *databaseNewPassword* represents the expression used as the new password

> **Note:** Each of the actual arguments (*databaseOldPassword, databaseNewPassword*) of the
> method can be a null value. In such a case, the null value is represented using a pair of
> double quotation marks. Alternatively, the password for a database can also be created
> through the graphic user interface (GUI) approach. However, the emphasis of this textbook
> is on programming and as a result, the use of the GUI method for demonstrations is
> minimized.

The following VBA Sub procedure code creates a password for the **AcademicX**
database.

```
Public Sub SetDBPassWord()

Rem Creates a database object called DBpass
Dim DBpass As Database
Rem Assigns the current database to the database object
Set DBpass = CurrentDb()
Rem Assigns a password to the database
DBpass.NewPassword "", "AcademicX"

End Sub
```

The first statement in the procedure defines an object for the database. The second
statement assigns the current database - the database that is currently opened - to the
object, and the third statement creates a password for the database. In the procedure,
the new password for the **AcademicX** database is "AcademicX".

Notice that the first actual argument in the third statement is null - a pair of double
quotation marks. This means that the database has not been previously assigned a
password or the database has no password.

Using VBA Procedures to Establish Database Security

Once a password has been established for a database, the next time the database is launched, the user must supply the password for the database to gain access to the objects of the database. Figure 14.5 shows a Password Required dialog box used to enter a password for a database.

Figure 14.5

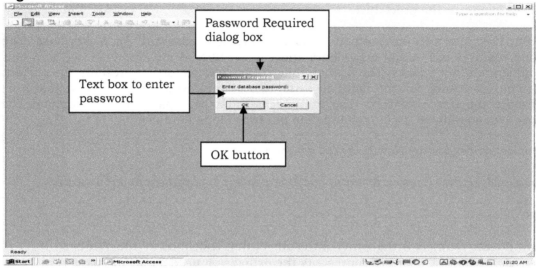

To change the database password to "Ac", modify the third statement of the Sub procedure to

DBpass.NewPassword "AcademicX", "Ac"

Alternatively, you can use the ChangePassword method in place of the NewPassword method to change the password of a database. The ChangePassword method syntax is similar to that of the NewPassword method. Substitute the ChangePassword keyword for the NewPassword keyword in the NewPassword method syntax to obtain the syntax for the ChangePassword method.

To delete the password "Ac" from the database so that the database can be accessed without password security modify the third statement of the Sub procedure to

DBpass.NewPassword "Ac", ""

The second actual argument in the third statement is now a null value (a pair of double quotation marks). This means that the password for the database has been deleted, so any user can access the database without restrictions.

User-Level Security

There are two main user categories when establishing the user-level security measure for a database. The two categories are the ADMINS account group and the USERS account group. The ADMINS account group contains users who are database administrators and members of this group have full rights (permissions) to view and manipulate all available objects within a database. This group also has the authority to grant (assign), change (modify), and revoke (deny) access permissions to other users of a database. The default database user when an unsecured database is launched is the ADMIN. The ADMIN is a user who is a member of the ADMINS account group.

Therefore, any user who accesses an unsecured database logs on as an ADMIN and he or she has the full permission (all privileges) to manipulate the database.

The USERS account group contains users who simply access a database and manipulate the database objects according to the access permissions granted to them by the ADMINS account group. Sometimes, members of the USERS account group are referred to as the "other users". They are users without full rights to a database. However, members of the USERS account group can also be assigned as members of the ADMINS account group.

Two types of accounts can further be created within the USERS account group. The two types are Individual Users' accounts and Workgroup Users' accounts. Just as a member of the USERS account group can become a member of the ADMINS account group, an individual user can also be part of a workgroup. The Workgroup Information File is fully activated when the user-level security is created for a database. The file then uses the information stored in it to control who accesses the database.

Creating Users Accounts

The first step in establishing the user-level security is to create new users' accounts. These individual users can later be assigned as members of the ADMINS account group, members of the Workgroup accounts' groups within the USERS account group, or simply let the new users be individual users in the USERS account group. The new users can also be members of the three groups. The CreateUser method is used to create new users' accounts for a database.

The basic syntax for the CreateUser method is

workSpaceObject.CreateUser("*username*")

where

- *workSpaceObject* is the name of the workspace object that is defined for the database
- *userName* is the name of the user whose account is being created and the name must be enclosed in double quotation marks

The following VBA Sub procedure code shows how to create a new individual user for a database.

```
Public Sub NewUser()

Dim WSpace As WorkSpace 'Defines a current workspace object called WSpace
Dim UserName As User  'Defines a user object called UserName
Set WSpace = DBEngine(0)  'Assigns current database to the workspace object
Set UserName = WSpace.CreateUser("Doris")  'Creates a new user called Doris
UserName.Password = "dor"  'Assigns the password "dor" to the new user
UserName.PID = "6667"  'Assigns the personal identifier "6667" to the new user
WSpace.Users.Append UserName  'Adds the new user to the USERS account group

End Sub
```

The Sub procedure is used to create a new user called "Doris". Each instruction in the procedure has a comment written in italics and placed beside the instruction to describe its function. To create a new user, the CreateUser method is used within the Workspace object.

Using VBA Procedures to Establish Database Security

The Sub procedure contains the actual user information, and as such, the procedure only creates one user whose name is Doris. To use the procedure to create another user, you must replace user Doris information with the new user information and that can be a time consuming effort.

You can create a new user without initially assigning a password for the user. To create a new user without a password, do not include the UserName.Password statement in the VBA code that is used to create the new user. The user can log on to the database without a password and then create his or her password. If a user was created with a password, the user can also change the password once he or she logs on to the database.

> **Note:** Oracle uses the CREATE USER statement to create a new user and to assign a password to the user. The CREATE USER clause of the statement is used to assign a name to the new user and the IDENTIFIED BY clause of the statement is used to assign a password to the user.
>
> Example:
> CREATE USER Doris
> IDENTIFIED BY dor;

Creating Users Accounts Using Formal Parameters

To use VBA code to create a new user without physically entering the user's information as part of the code, include formal parameters in the procedure. Using formal parameters in the procedure allows you to create several new users without modifying the code each time you want to add a new user to the database. Whenever the procedure is run, you simply pass the new user's information through the formal parameters. However, for the parameter-driven method to be successful, you must use a Function procedure.

The following Function procedure demonstrates the use of formal parameters to create users for a database.

```
Public Function CreateUsers(UName, UserPassWord, UserPID)   'Uses three formal parameters

Dim WSpace As WorkSpace 'Defines a current workspace object called WSpace
Dim UserName As User    'Defines a user object called UserName

Set WSpace = DBEngine(0)   'Assigns  current database to the workspace object
Rem Creates a new user through the formal parameter called UName
Set UserName = WSpace.CreateUser(UName)
Rem Assigns a password to the new user through the formal parameter called UserPassWord
UserName.Password = UserPassWord
Rem Assigns a personal identifier to the user through the formal parameter called UserPID
UserName.PID = UserPID
Rem Adds the new user to the USERS account group
WSpace.Users.Append UserName


End Function
```

Chapter Fourteen

Figure 14.6 shows how the Function procedure is run using the IMMEDIATE window.

Figure 14.6

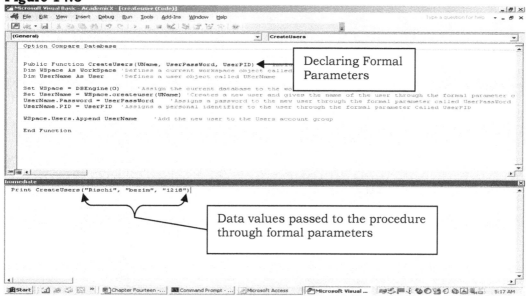

Three formal parameters are declared as part of the header of the Function procedure. The parameters are named UName, UserPassWord, and UserPID, and they are used to enter a new user's name, his or her password, and his or her personal identifier respectively. An example of the data values that can be passed to the parameters are shown in the IMMEDIATE window. Reading the supplied data values - values enclosed in a pair of parentheses - in the window from left to right, the first value represents the user's name, the second represents the user's password, and the third value represents the user's personal identifier. Each data value must be enclosed in double quotation marks.

Changing Users Passwords

To change the password of a user, you use either the NewPassword method or the ChangePassword method. To be able to change a user's password, you must log on as the user, as an ADMIN, or as a member of the ADMINS workgroup.

The basic syntax for changing a user's password using the NewPassword method is

workSpaceObject.Users("*username*").NewPassword   "*databaseOldPassword*", "*databaseNewPassword*"

where

- *workSpaceObject* is the name of the workspace object that is defined for the database
- *userName* is the user whose password is being changed and the name must be enclosed in double quotation marks
- *databaseOldPassword* represents the expression used as the old password and must be enclosed in double quotation marks
- *databaseNewPassword* represents the expression used as the new password and must be enclosed in double quotation marks

Using VBA Procedures to Establish Database Security

The following Sub procedure shows how to change the password of a user called Doris. The code changes the password from "dor" to "ris" using the NewPassword method.

```
Public Sub ChangePassWord()

Dim WSpace As WorkSpace
Set WSpace = DBEngine(0)
Rem Changes user Doris password from dor to ris
WSpace.Users("Doris").NewPassword "dor", "ris"

End Sub
```

The NewPassword method requires two actual arguments, the old or the current password and the new password. The old password must be separated from the new password using a comma. The old password is written first followed by the new password and both passwords can be null. For example, to clear or remove the password of a user, you enter a null value (a pair of double quotation marks) as the new password in the procedure statement that contains NewPassword method.

To use the ChangePassword method to change users' passwords, substitute the ChangePassword keyword for the NewPassword keyword in the NewPassword method syntax to obtain the syntax for the ChangePassword method.

Creating Workgroups Accounts

A situation may arise when several users are assigned the same types of permissions to access a database. Giving the same types of permissions individually to each user can be a time consuming and sometime a tiresome effort. To simplify such permission-granting activities, you can create a Workgroup User account, add the users who are to be assigned the same types of permissions to the account, and then assign the permissions to the workgroup once.

The steps used to create a new workgroup's account are very similar to the steps used to create a new individual user's account. To create a new workgroup, the CreateGroup method is used within the Workspace object.

The basic syntax for the CreateGroup method is

workSpaceObject.CreateGroup("*groupName*")

where

- *workSpaceObject* is the name of the workspace object that is defined for the database
- *groupName* is the name of the group whose account is being created and the name must be enclosed in double quotation marks

The following Sub procedure creates a new workgroup called "FacGroup" that will contain, as users, faculty members.

```
Public Sub CreateNewGroup()

Dim WSpace As WorkSpace
Dim GroupName As Group     'Defines a Group object called GroupName
Set WSpace = DBEngine(0)
Rem Creates a group called FacGroup
```

```
Set GroupName = WSpace.CreateGroup("FacGroup")
Rem Assigns the group personal identifier "0123" to the new group
GroupName.PID = "0123"
Rem Adds the new group to the GROUPS account group
WSpace.Groups.Append GroupName

End Sub
```

You might have noticed, by reviewing the procedure's statements, that the Password attribute is omitted. The only two attributes required when creating a workgroup are the Name attribute that is used to give the new workgroup a name, and the group identifier (WID) attribute that is used to uniquely identify the workgroup.

> **Note:** A role in Oracle is similar to a workgroup in MS Access. The CREATE ROLE statement is used to create a workgroup in Oracle. The statement has one clause - CREATE ROLE clause – and the clause is used to assign a name to a workgroup that is being created.
>
> Example:
> CREATE ROLE FacGroup;
>
> Oracle database administrator can add a password to a role once the role is created. The ALTER ROLE statement is used to assign a password to a role. This statement has two clauses. The ALTER ROLE clause of the statement is used to identify the role name and the IDENTIFIED BY clause of the statement is used to assign a password to the role.
>
> Example:
> ALTER ROLE FacGroup
> IDENTIFIED BY fac;

Creating Workgroups Accounts Using Formal Parameters

You can also create a new workgroup without physically entering the group's information as part of the VBA code. You do this by including formal parameters in the procedure. Using this method allows you to create several new workgroups without modifying the code each time you want to add a new workgroup to the database. Whenever the procedure is run, you simply pass the new workgroup's information through the formal parameters. This method is similar to creating a new user with formal parameters, and as a result, you must use a Function procedure.

The following Function procedure demonstrates how formal parameters are used to create new workgroups for a database.

```
Public Function CreateGroups(GName, GroupPID)   'includes two formal parameters

Dim WSpace As WorkSpace
Dim GroupName As Group
Set WSpace = DBEngine(0)
Rem Creates a new group and gives the name of the group through the formal parameter called GName
Set GroupName = WSpace.CreateGroup(GName)
Rem Assigns a group personal identifier to the group through the formal parameter Called GroupPID
GroupName.PID = GroupPID
Rem Adds the new group to the GROUPS account group
WSpace.Groups.Append GroupName

End Function
```

Using VBA Procedures to Establish Database Security

Running the Function procedure using the IMMEDIATE window is performed exactly the same way as described in the "Creating Users Accounts using Formal Parameters" section of this chapter.

Adding Users to the USERS Group and Other Workgroups

Users can be added to the USERS group and/or to other workgroups. Once a workgroup is created and for the workgroup to function as intended, a user or users must be added to the workgroup. To add a user to the USERS group or to a workgroup, the User object and the USERS group object or the User object and the Workgroup object must be defined in the procedure that is used to perform the operation. The user is appended to the USERS account collection which, in turn, is appended to the GROUPS account collection. The basic syntax for adding a user to a workgroup is

workSpaceObject.Groups("*groupName*").Users.Append *userObject*

where

- *workSpaceObject* is the name of the workspace object that is defined for the database
- *groupName* is the workgroup in which a user is to be added and the group name must be enclosed in double quotation marks
- *userObject* is the object that contains the user to be added to the workgroup

The following procedure demonstrates how to add a user called Doris that was created earlier to a workgroup called FacGroup that was also created earlier.

```
Public Sub AddIndUserToGroup()

Dim WSpace As WorkSpace
Dim UserName As User
Dim GroupName As Group
Set WSpace = DBEngine(0)
Rem Identifies a user called Doris that was created earlier to be added to the workgroup account
Set UserName = WSpace.CreateUser("Doris")
Rem Adds the user to the FacGroup workgroup that was created earlier
WSpace.Groups("FacGroup").Users.Append UserName

End Sub
```

Notice that the user's name (Doris) is also enclosed in double quotation marks in the Set UserName statement in the procedure. You can substitute the word "Users" for the FacGroup workgroup in the last statement of the procedure to add the user to the USERS group. Alternatively, rather than identifying the user in the procedure, you can identify a workgroup that was created earlier and append the workgroup to the user.

The basic syntax for using the alternative method to add a user to a workgroup is

workSpaceObject.Users("*username*").Groups.Append *groupObject*

where

- *workSpaceObject* is the name of the workspace object that is defined for the database
- *userName* is the user to be added to the workgroup and the user name must be enclosed in double quotation marks

336

Chapter Fourteen

- *groupObject* is the object that contains the workgroup name the user is to be added to

The following Sub procedure shows the alternative method of adding a user to a workgroup.

```
Public Sub AddIndUserToGroup()

Dim WSpace As WorkSpace
Dim UserName As User
Dim GroupName As Group
Set WSpace = DBEngine(0)
Rem Identifies a workgroup called FacGroup that was created earlier to add a user account to it
Set GroupName = WSpace.CreateGroup("FacGroup")
Rem Adds the user called Doris that was created earlier to the FacGroup workgroup
WSpace.Users("Doris").Groups.Append GroupName

End Sub
```

Again, notice that the workgroup's name (FacGroup) is enclosed in double quotation marks in the Set GroupName statement in the procedure. The workgroup is appended to the GROUPS account collection which, in turn, is appended to user Doris in the USERS account collection.

> **Note:** In Oracle, The GRANT statement is used to make a user a member of a workgroup (role). The statement has two clauses. The GRANT clause of the statement is used to identify the workgroup name and the TO clause of the statement is used to assign the user to the workgroup.
>
> Example:
> GRANT FacGroup
> TO Rischi;

Adding Users to the ADMINS Group

You may, sometimes, want certain users who do not previously have administrative privileges to perform duties as the administrators of a database. In other words, you want these users to be able to manage the database and other users. One way of assigning other users all the authority a database administrator has is to add them to the ADMINS group. The steps used to add a user to the ADMINS group are very similar to the steps used to add a user to the USERS workgroup.

The following procedure demonstrates how a user called Rischi is added to the ADMINS group to give him all the privileges as a database administrator.

```
Public Sub AddUserToAdmins()

Dim WSpace As WorkSpace
Dim UserName As User
Dim GroupName As Group
Set WSpace = DBEngine(0)
Rem Identifies a user called Rischi that was created earlier to be added to the ADMINS group account
Set UserName = WSpace.CreateUser("Rischi")
Rem Adds the user to the Admins workgroup that was created earlier
WSpace.Groups("Admins").Users.Append UserName

End Sub
```

Using VBA Procedures to Establish Database Security

> **Note:** A user who is added as a member of the ADMINS group must also, at least, be a member of the USERS group. This avoids database conversion errors.

Adding Users to Workgroups Using Formal Parameters

Like creating users and workgroups using formal parameters, you can also add a user to a workgroup by supplying the user's and the workgroup's information through formal parameters. Using this method, the procedure's code does not have to be modified each time you want to add a user to a workgroup. Simply supply the user's and the workgroup's information using the formal parameters whenever the procedure is run. Again, like creating users and workgroups using formal parameters, the procedure should be written as a Function procedure and run as described in the "Creating Users Accounts using Formal Parameters" section of this chapter.

The following procedure demonstrates how to add a user to a workgroup by using formal parameters.

Public Function AddUToGParameter(UName, GName)

Dim WSpace As WorkSpace
Dim UserName As User
Dim GroupName As Group
Set WSpace = DBEngine(0)
Rem *Identifies a user that was created earlier by supplying the user's name through a formal parameter called UName*
Set UserName = WSpace.createuser(UName)
Rem *Adds the user to a workgroup that was created earlier by supplying the group name through a formal parameter called GName*
WSpace.Groups(GName).Users.Append UserName

End Function

Viewing Users and Workgroups Accounts Information

To view users' and workgroups' accounts created for a database, you display the information through the **Tools** menu of MS Access window. Figure 14.7 shows how to view users' and workgroups' accounts that are created for a database using the GUI approach.

Figure 14.7

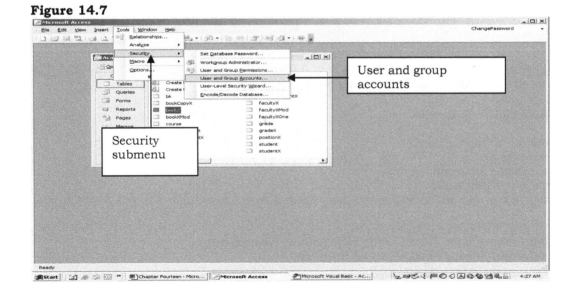

Chapter Fourteen

Click the **Tools** menu of MS Access window. Point to the **Security** submenu and then click the **User and Group Accounts** command. The action opens the User and Group Accounts dialog box. Figure 14.8 shows the dialog box.

Figure 14.8

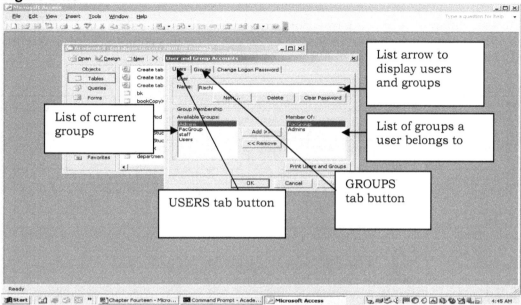

To view a particular user and the workgroup(s) the user belongs to, if any, click the USERS tab button and then click the list arrow to select the user. The workgroup or workgroups the user belongs to is listed in the bottom right text box of the User and Group Accounts dialog box. For example, as displayed in figure 14.8, user Rischi is a member of the ADMINS group and the FACGROUP workgroup. You can also view workgroups by clicking the GROUPS tab button.

Granting Permissions to Users and Workgroups

For an individual user or a workgroup to effectively use a secured database, the user or the workgroup must be giving permissions to access and manipulate the database. Typically, the permissions granted to a user or a workgroup to access and manipulate a particular database object are stored or contained within that database object. However to grant a user or a workgroup different types of access permissions in MS Access application through VBA procedures, you have to understand the concepts of CONTAINERS and DOCUMENTS objects. These two objects are the primary means of granting permissions in MS Access databases.

Containers: A container is an object structure that contains all the necessary information about the objects that exist in a MS Access database.

Documents: A document is an object structure that contains all the necessary information about a particular object that exists in a MS Access database.

Each database application that is created in MS Access usually has eight containers, namely, DATABASES, FORMS, MODULES, RELATIONSHIPS, REPORTS, SCRIPTS, SYSREL, and TABLES. For example, the TABLES container contains within it all the necessary information about the tables and queries created for a specific database. Each table or query in a TABLES container has its own unique DOCUMENT that contains all the information about the table or the query. A container is a collection of objects' documents where each document uniquely describes the characteristics of one object, the owner of the object, and the permissions to access the object exclusively.

Databases Permissions: Database permission is a privilege granted to a database user or a database workgroup to use a particular database object.

In MS Access, different types of permissions can be granted to a user or to a workgroup through VBA procedures. Figure 14.9 shows the list of permissions that are frequently granted to a user or a workgroup in MS Access database.

Figure 14.9

Permission	Meaning
dbSecCreate	Grants permission to create a specific object type within a database
dbSecDBAdmin	Grants a user or a workgroup a database administrator's privileges
dbSecDBCreate	Grants permission to create different database object types within a database
dbSecDBExclusive	Grants permission to open a database in exclusive mode
dbSecDBOpen	Grants permission to open a database in nonexclusive or in shared mode
dbSecDelete	Grants permission to delete a database object
dbSecDeleteData	Grants permission to delete data from a database table or a query object
dbSecFullAccess	Grants a user or workgroup full access permission to a database object
dbSecInsertData	Grants permission to insert or add data to a database table or a query object
dbSecNoAcess	Denies a user or a workgroup all access permission to a database object
dbSecReadDef	Grants permission to display or view a database object structure
dbSecReadSec	Grants permission to read security information of a database object
dbSecReplaceData	Grants permission to update or modify data in a database table or a query object
dbSecRetrieveData	Grants permission to display or view data from a database table or a query object
dbSecWriteDef	Grants permission to change or modify a database object structure
dbSecWriteSec	Grants permission to modify or alter access permissions of a database object
dbSecWriteOwner	Grants permission to modify or alter owner's property setting for a database object

To grant permission on an object to a user or a workgroup, use the Permissions property of the document created for the object. The basic syntax for granting permissions to users using the Permissions property approach is

documentObject.Permissions = *typeOfPermission*

where

- *documentObject* is the name of the object that is defined for the current document
- *typeOfPermission* is the type of permission that is granted to the user or to the workgroup

The following procedure demonstrates how to grant the Read permission to user Doris to enable her display or view the content of the bookX table.

Chapter Fourteen

```
Public Sub GrantReadPerm()

Rem Defines a current database object called Dbase
Dim Dbase As Database
Rem Defines a current document called Ddoc
Dim Ddoc As Document
Rem Assigns the current database to the object Dbase
Set Dbase = CurrentDb()
Rem Assigns the bookX table document from the TABLES container of the current database to the
object Ddoc
Set Ddoc = Dbase.Containers("Tables").Documents("bookX")
Rem Specifies the user name to be granted the permission
Ddoc.UserName = "Doris"
Rem Grants the permission by specifying permission type
Ddoc.Permissions = dbSecRetrieveData

End Sub
```

Notice that the container's name, the document's name, and the user's name are enclosed in double quotations in their respective statements in the procedure. Granting permissions to a workgroup is performed in the same fashion as setting permissions for a user. To grant permissions to a workgroup, simply substitute the workgroup's name for the user's name in the UserName property statement of the code.

The following procedure demonstrates how to grant Read permission on the bookX table to the FacGroup workgroup.

```
Public Sub ReadDPermGroup()

Dim Dbase As Database
Dim Ddoc As Document
Set Dbase = CurrentDb()
Set Ddoc = Dbase.Containers("Tables").Documents("bookX")
Rem Specifies the group name to be granted the permission
Ddoc.UserName = "FacGroup"
Rem Grants the permission by specifying permission type
Ddoc.Permissions = dbSecRetrieveData

End Sub
```

Again, notice that the container's name, the document's name, and the workgroup's name are enclosed in double quotation marks in their respective statements in the procedure.

Note: The GRANT statement is used in Oracle to assign database tables' permissions to a user or a workgroup (role). The GRANT statement consists of three clauses. The GRANT clause of the statement is used to specify the type of permissions to be granted to a user. The ON clause of the statement is used to identify the table the user will have access to, and the TO clause of the statement is used to identify the user who is being granted the permissions.

Example:
GRANT SELECT
ON bookX
TO Doris;

The method used to grant permissions to a workgroup or a role is similar to the method used to grant permissions to a user. To grant permissions to a role, substitute the role name

---

for the user name in the TO clause of the GRANT statement.

Alternatively, you can use formal parameters to supply a user's name or a workgroup's name when granting permissions to a user or a workgroup. The following Function procedure demonstrates how to use a formal parameter in the UserName property statement of the procedure to grant the display permission to a user.

```
Public Function GrantPwithParameter(UName)

Dim Dbase As Database
Dim Ddoc As Document
Set Dbase = CurrentDb()
Set Ddoc = Dbase.Containers("Tables").Documents("bookX")
Rem Specifies the user or the workgroup name to be granted the permission through a formal
parameter called UName
Ddoc.UserName = UName
Rem Grants the permission by specifying permission type
Ddoc.Permissions = dbSecRetrieveData

End Function
```

Like creating users and workgroups using formal parameters, the procedure should be written as a Function procedure and run as described in the "Creating Users Accounts using Formal Parameters" section of this chapter.

Using AND, OR, and NOT Logical Operators to Grant Permissions

There are times when more than one type of permission or individual permissions on an object is to be granted to a user or a workgroup. In VBA environment, the OR logical operator is usually used to grant multiple permissions on an object to a user or a workgroup.

The following Sub procedure demonstrates how to grant Read, Update, and Insert permissions to user Doris to enable her view, make changes, and add records to the bookX table.

```
Public Sub GrantUserRUIPerm()

Dim Dbase As Database
Dim Ddoc As Document
Set Dbase = CurrentDb()
Set Ddoc = Dbase.Containers("Tables").Documents("bookX")
Ddoc.UserName = "Doris"
Rem Grants Read, Update, and Insert permissions using the OR logical operator
Ddoc.Permissions = dbSecRetrieveData Or dbSecReplaceData Or dbSecInsertData

End Sub
```

You might have noticed that in the Permissions property line - the last statement in the procedure's code, the three permissions are connected with the OR logical operator. The connection indicates that the user (Doris in this case) has the privilege to view the content of the bookX table, update data in the table, and add new records to the table.

Similarly, the same approach is used to assign multiple permissions to a workgroup. Simply replace the user's name with the workgroup's name in the UserName property statement of the procedure.

The AND and the NOT logical operators can also be used to grant multiple permissions on an object to a user or a workgroup. The following Sub procedure demonstrates how to grant full (all) permission on the bookX table to the FacGroup workgroup except for the permission to update the table.

```
Public Sub GrantPermGroup()

Dim Dbase As Database
Dim Ddoc As Document
Set Dbase = CurrentDb()
Set Ddoc = Dbase.Containers("Tables").Documents("bookX")
Ddoc.UserName = "FacGroup"
Rem Grants full access permission, but revoke Update permission using both the AND and NOT
logical operators
Ddoc.Permissions = dbSecFullAccess And Not dbSecReplaceData

End Sub
```

Reviewing the Permissions property statement (last statement) in the procedure's code, you might have noticed the combined use of the AND and the NOT logical operators. The two operators are used jointly to revoke one set of permissions on an object to a user or a workgroup while granting another set of permissions on the object to the user or the workgroup. In the procedure, the FacGroup workgroup is granted full permission on the bookX table, but at the same time the workgroup is denied the permission to update data in the table.

Launching Databases Using Users Accounts

Once a database is created and users are assigned logon credentials and access permissions to the database and its objects, the database becomes a secured database. However, for users to be able to access the database and its objects, they must log on to the database. This section shows how to set and display the user-level security dialog box for users to be able to log on to a secured database.

In MS Access, the ADMIN user is a default database user who is initially not assigned a password, and the ADMIN user has all the privileges to administer a database. To avoid other users from logging on to a database without passwords, the first step is to assign the ADMIN user a password to the database.

To change the password of the ADMIN user for a database, you go through the **Tools** menu of MS Access window. Figure 14.10 shows how to change the ADMIN user's password for a database using the GUI approach.

Using VBA Procedures to Establish Database Security

Figure 14.10

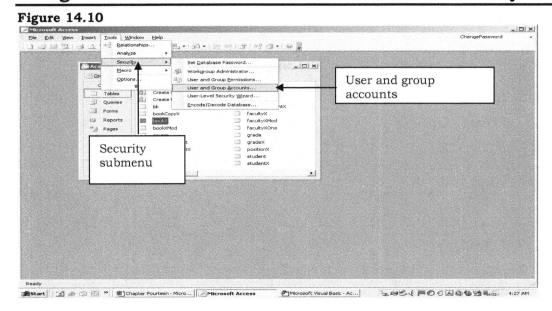

Click the **Tools** menu of MS Access window. Point to the **Security** submenu and then click the **User and Group Accounts** command. The action opens the User and Group Accounts dialog box. Figure 14.11 shows the dialog box.

Figure 14.11

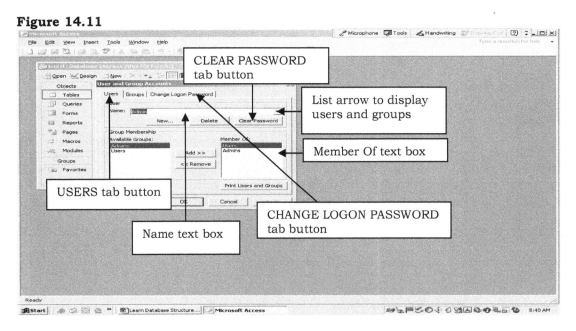

Click the USERS tab button and make sure the ADMIN (the user name) appears in the Name text box. If the name does not appear in the Name text box, click the list arrow of the Name text box and select the name - ADMIN. The Member Of text box must contain, at least, both the ADMINS group and the USERS group. Click the CHANGE LOGON PASSWORD tab button to display the Change Password dialog box. See figure 14.12.

Note: The CLEAR PASSWORD tab button is used to remove (clear) and set a user's password to null. Alternatively, if you are to change a user's password and forgot the user's current password, you click the button to set the current password to null. In the Change Password dialog box, skip the Old Password text box and enter the new password into the other two text boxes.

Figure 14.12

The default ADMIN user is not initially assigned a password when a new MS Access database is created. For the reason, skip the Old Password text box. Leave it the way it is (blank). Do not enter data in that text box. Click the New Password text box and enter a password of your choice. Click the Verify (reconfirm password) text box to enter the password again for reconfirmation purposes. After assigning a password to the ADMIN user, click the **OK** button to register the password in the workgroup information file. Figure 14.13 shows the logon dialog box when a user launches a secured database.

Figure 14.13

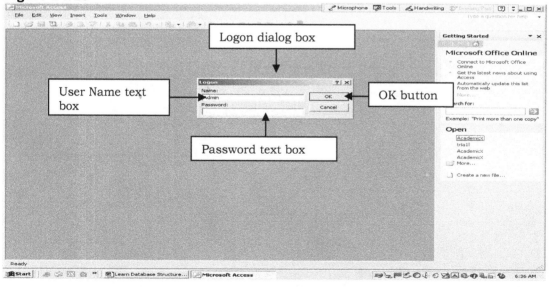

Note: Alternatively, you can use the Tab key to move from one text box to the text box. It is a good programming practice to create passwords that you can easily remember. In VBA environment, establishing user-level securiy measures for the ADMIN user can be performed before or after creating other users, assigning the users to workgroups including ADMINS and USERS groups, and/or assigning the users access permissions. This textbook chooses to demonstrate how the logon security measures' dialog box is setup and displayed at this point.

Viewing Permissions Granted to Users and Workgroups

To view the various permissions granted to a user or a workgroup, use the **Tools** menu of MS Access window. Figure 14.14 shows how to display the permissions granted to a user or a workgroup.

Figure 14.14

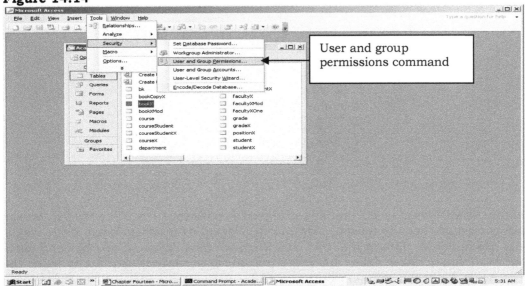

Click the **Tools** menu of MS Access window. Point to the **Security** submenu and then click the **User and Group Permissions** command. The action opens the User and Group Permissions dialog box. Figure 14.15 shows the dialog box.

Figure 14.15

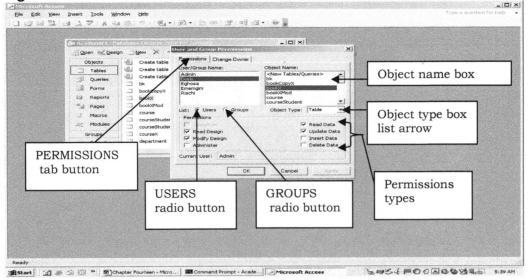

To see the permissions granted to a particular user, if any, Select the user from the User/Group Name text box and then click the USERS radio button. Click the object name in the Object Name text box and then use the list arrow to display the object type.

Click the type of object that contains the permissions you want to view. The permissions granted to the user on that object are checked in the Permissions' pane of the dialog box. For example, as displayed in figure 14.15, user Doris has the privileges of viewing (read), modifying (update) the data, and modifying the design (structure) of the bookX table. You can also view the permissions granted to a group by clicking the GROUPS radio button.

Revoking Permissions from Users and Workgroups

When a user or a workgroup no longer needs the access permissions that were once granted to the user or the workgroup, the permissions must be revoked to help maintain both the integrity of the data and the security of the objects in the database. The NOT logical operator is used to revoke permissions granted to a user or a workgroup. The permission type is usually connected to the operator in the Permissions property statement of the procedure's code to revoke the permission.

The basic syntax for revoking a permission using the Permissions property is

documentObject.Permissions = Not *typeOfPermission*

where

- *documentObject* is the name of the object that is defined for the current document
- *typeOfPermission* is the type of permission that is being revoked from the user or the workgroup

However, to maintain the denial position of any previously revoked permission or permission not previously granted on an object to a user or a workgroup, you must write the permission to be revoked and the previously revoked permission in the negative form using the NOT logical operator. The permission to be revoked and the previously revoked permission must be connected with the AND logical operator in the Permissions property statement of the procedure.

In the section titled "Granting Permissions to Users and Workgroups" of this chapter, a user named Doris is granted the permissions to view, change data, and add data to the bookX table. She is not granted the permission to delete data from the table. Let's assume that the database administrator decides to deny her the permission to add data to the table. The revoke permission operation will be successful when the appropriate procedure is run. However, the permission to delete data from the table that was not previously granted to her will automatically be granted to her. Although, user Doris can no longer insert new records to the bookX table, she can now be able to delete records from the table.

To ensure that the permission to delete data remains inactive (not granted) while revoking her permission to add data to the table, you must write both permissions individually in the negative form by preceding each permission with the NOT logical operator, and then connect the permissions with the AND logical operator in the Permissions property statement of the procedure.

The following procedure demonstrates how to revoke the Insert permission on bookX table from user Doris, while at the same time making the Delete permission that was not previously granted to her to remain inactive.

Using VBA Procedures to Establish Database Security

```
Public Sub RevokeInsertPerm()

Dim Dbase As Database
Dim Ddoc As Document
Set Dbase = CurrentDb()
Set Ddoc = Dbase.Containers("Tables").Documents("bookX")
Ddoc.UserName = "Doris"
Rem Revokes Insert permission while keeping Delete permission not previously granted to remain
inactive
Ddoc.Permissions = Not dbSecInsertData And Not dbSecDeleteData

End Sub
```

To revoke all permissions or to deny full (complete) access on an object from a user or a workgroup, use the dbSecNoAccess permission type in the Permissions property statement of the procedure.

The following procedure demonstrates how to revoke all access permissions on the bookX table from the FacGroup workgroup.

```
Public Sub RevokePermGroup()

Dim Dbase As Database
Dim Ddoc As Document
Set Dbase = CurrentDb()
Set Ddoc = Dbase.Containers("Tables").Documents("bookX")
Ddoc.UserName = "FacGroup"
Rem Revokes all access permissions from the workgroup
Ddoc.Permissions = dbSecNoAccess

End Sub
```

> **Note:** In Oracle, to revoke permissions from a user on a table, the REVOKE statement is used. The REVOKE statement consists of three clauses. The REVOKE clause of the statement is used to specify the type of permissions to be revoked. The ON clause of the statement is used to identify the table the user will no longer have access to, and the FROM clause of the statement is used to identify the user who is being denied access.
>
> Example:
> REVOKE SELECT
> ON bookX
> FROM Doris;
>
> The method used to revoke permissions from a workgroup or a role is similar to the method used to remove permissions from a user. To revoke a role's permissions, substitute the role name for the user name in the FROM clause of the REVOKE statement.

Removing Users and Workgroups from Databases

When a user or a workgroup is no longer needed to access a secured database, the user or the workgroup must be deleted from the database in order to maintain the security measures that are established for the database. In MS Access, to remove a user or a workgroup from a secured database, you use the **Tools** menu of the MS Access window.

Figure 14.16 shows how to remove a user account or a workgroup account that is created for a database using the GUI approach.

Figure 14.16

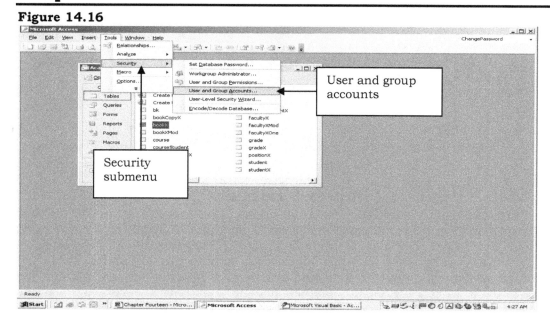

Click the **Tools** menu of MS Access window. Point to the **Security** submenu and then click the **User and Group Accounts** command. The action opens the User and Group Accounts dialog box. Figure 14.17 shows the dialog box that contains the user and the workgroup information.

Figure 14.17

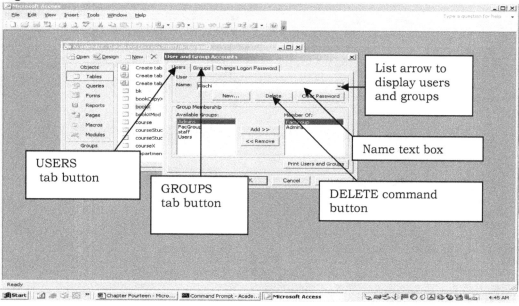

To remove a particular user or a particular workgroup, click the appropriate tab button (USERS or GROUPS) and then click the list arrow to select the user or the workgroup. Once the correct name appears in the list arrow text box, click the **Delete** command button to remove the user or the workgroup from the database. For example, as displayed in the Name text box of figure 14.17, user Rischi will be removed if the **Delete** command button is clicked.

> **Note:** In Oracle, the DROP USER statement is used to remove a user from a database while the DROP ROLE statement is used to remove a role or a workgroup from a database. The DROP USER statement or the DROP ROLE statement consists of only one clause that identifies the user or the role to be removed respectively.
>
> Example:
> DROP USER Rischi;
>
> To remove a role, substitute the ROLE keyword for the USER keyword followed by the role name.

Chapter Summary

This chapter discusses Visual Basic for Applications (VBA) procedures and how to use the procedures to secure a database and create users and workgroups for a secured database. The chapter also discusses methods for (a) changing users' passwords, (b) adding users to workgroups, (c) assigning various access permissions to users and workgroups, and (d) viewing users and workgroups including the permissions that are granted to them. In conclusion, the chapter demonstrates how to revoke permissions from users and workgroups, and how to remove users and workgroups that are no longer needed from a secured database.

VBA Syntax and Statements Summary

The table below presents the VBA methods' syntax, VBA property syntax, and special symbols discussed in this chapter and the VBA statements' examples for establishing database security.

Method Type	Basic Method Syntax	Method Statement Example
NewPassword method is used to set and change the password for a database. The method can also be used to change passwords for users	*databaseObject*.NewPassword *databaseOldPassword*, *databaseNewPassword* Or *workSpaceObject*.Users(*userName*).NewPassword *databaseOldPassword*, *databaseNewPassword*	DBpass.NewPassword "", "AcademicX" Or WSpace.Users("Doris").NewPassword "dor", "ris"
CreateUser method is used to create new users' accounts for a database	*workSpaceObject*.CreateUser(*userName*)	Set UserName = WSpace.CreateUser("Doris")
ChangePassword method is used to change the password for a database. The method is also used to change passwords for users	*databaseObject*.ChangePassword *databaseOldPassword*, *databaseNewPassword* Or *workSpaceObject*.Users(*userName*).ChangePassword *databaseOldPassword*, *databaseNewPassword*	DBpass.ChangePassword "", "AcademicX" Or WSpace.Users("Doris").ChangePassword "dor", "ris"
CreateGroup method is used to create new workgroups' accounts for a database	*workSpaceObject*.CreateGroup(*groupName*)	Set GroupName = WSpace.CreateGroup("FacGroup")
Users object in association with Append method is used to add users to workgroups	*workSpaceObject*.Groups(*groupName*).Users.Append *userObject*	WSpace.Groups("FacGroup").Users.Append UserName

Groups object in association with Append method is also used to add users to workgroups	*workSpaceObject*.Users(*userName*).Groups.Append *groupObject*	WSpace.Users("Doris").Groups.Append GroupName
Property Type	**Basic Property Syntax**	**Property Statement Example**
Permissions property is used to grant permissions on database objects to users and workgroups. The property is also used to revoke permissions on database objects from users and workgroups	*documentObject*.Permissions = *typeOfPermission* Or *documentObject*.Permissions = Not *typeOfPermission*	Ddoc.Permissions = dbSecRetrieveData Or Ddoc.Permissions = Not dbSecRetrieveData
Special Symbol	**Description**	**Statement Example**
, (comma)	Comma separator is used to separate data items such as actual arguments in a statement	DBpass.NewPassword "", "AcademicX"
" (double quotation mark)	Quotation mark is used to enclosed a data item, such as a user name, in a statement	Set GroupName = WSpace.CreateGroup("FacGroup")

Key Terms

Users accounts
Workgroups accounts
Security measure
Workgroup information file
Password
Database-level
ADMINS group
User-level

USERS group
Permissions
Containers
Documents
Revoke
Grant
Database Security
Security control

Chapter Review Questions

Multiple Choice Questions

1. Which of the following is not a valid security-level name in MS Access database?
   a. application-level security.
   b. database-level security.
   c. user-level security.
   d. none of the above.

2. The file used to register users when MS Access is launched is called
   a. user information file.
   b. workgroup information file.
   c. database information file.
   d. all of the above.

3. The file that controls MS Access database access permissions has the _____ extension.
   a. .mdb
   b. .xls
   c. .mdw
   d. .grp

4. _____ measure does not restrict access to MS Access database objects.
   a. Database-security
   b. User-level security
   c. All of the above
   d. None of the above

5. To assign a password to MS Access database, the database must be opened in
   a. read-only.
   b. exclusive read-only.
   c. share mode.
   d. exclusive mode.

6. Which of the following is not a category of the user-level security?
   a. ADMINS account group.
   b. DATABASE account group.
   c. USERS account group.
   d. none of the above.

7. In MS Access database, Individual Users' accounts and Workgroup Users' accounts are found in the _____ account group.
   a. DATABASE
   b. ADMINS
   c. USERS
   d. SYSTEM

8. The _____ is used to create new users' accounts for MS Access database.
   a. CreateUser statement
   b. CreateUser method
   c. CreateUser procedure
   d. CreateUser workspace

9. In MS Access database, a user can be added to
   a. a workgroup.
   b. an ADMINS group.
   c. all of the above.
   d. none of the above.

10. In VBA, to grant permissions on an object to a user use the _____ of the document created for the object.
    a. Permissions statement
    b. Permissions clause
    c. Permissions code
    d. Permissions property

True or False Questions

11. An exclusive mode in MS Access database is an environment where the database is opened for one user only at any given time.
    a. True
    b. False

12. Three types of security measures can be implemented for MS Access database.
    a. True
    b. False

13. The database-level security denies an unauthorized user from viewing the contents of MS Access database.
    a. True
    b. False

14. The database-level security does not differentiate one user from another.
   a. True
   b. False

15. The ChangeNewPassword method is used to create a password for MS Access database.
   a. True
   b. False

16. The workgroup information file is fully activated when a user-level security is created for MS Access database.
   a. True
   b. False

17. In MS Access database, a user cannot change his or her password.
   a. True
   b. False

Fill in the blank Questions

18. A way of disallowing a user who has not been given permissions to use a database is called _____.

19. _____ is the default name of the workgroup information file.

20. To create a password for a database, the database must be opened in _____ mode.

21. The _____ method is used to create a new user in VBA environment.

22. To change the password of a database, you use the _____ method.

23. To revoke permissions on an object from a user, you use the _____ property.

Essay Type Questions

24. Describe the functions of the workgroup information file?

25. Explain the differences between a container and a document?

26. What is the major drawback of database-level security? Use an example to illustrate your answer.

27. Define database permissions? List the permission type used to open a database in shared mode and the permission type used to deny a workgroup all access permission to a database object?

28. What is the ADMINS account group and how does the group differ from the ADMIN?

Hands-on Activities

Perform the following hands-on exercises using the **Academics** database. Write and run a VBA procedure to

1. Create a new password called **acadpass** for the database.

2. Open the database without a password.

3. Create a new user called James. User James must be assigned a password that consist of **ja012** and a personal identifier that consists of **0001**

4. Change the password of user James from **ja012** to **james012**

5. Add user James to the ADMINS account group.

6. Create a new workgroup called **StudManager** with a group identifier that consists of **group001**.

7. Grant the **StudManager** workgroup the permission to populate the studentHall table with data.

8. Add user James to the **StudManager** workgroup.

9. Grant user James full access permission on studentInfo table except the permission to delete data from the table.

10. Revoke the permission to modify data on the studentInfo table from user James while keeping the delete permission that was not previously granted to him inactive.

Appendix A

The **AcademicX** database is created as a practice database for this textbook. The following are the tables and their records used for hands-on demonstrations and activities during the course of using the textbook and the tables are contained in the **AcademicX** database. The primary keys of the tables are underlined.

bk, bookCopyX, bookX, bookXMod tables

These tables' structures are identical but used for different demonstrations' activities. The data describing academic books are stored in these tables. Each table's primary key is the **isbn** column.

Bk

isbn	bookTitle	costPrice	sellingPrice	classification
03451105	Beginning Chemistry			Natural Science
03821069	Basic Physics			Natural Science
05683420	SQL Programming	44	50.25	Computing Studies
06142546	Database Design	25.95	36.9	Computing Studies
07452771	Principles of Programming	31.95	39.9	Computing Studies
08720982	Advanced Biology			Natural Science
08793876	Biology for Dummies			Natural Science
09876544	Programming For Dummies	23.9	32.5	Computer Science

bookCopyX

isbn	bookTitle	costPrice	sellingPrice	classification
01133887	Programming with Java	60.5		Computing Studies
03451105	Beginning Chemistry	39.65	77.22	Natural Science
03821069	Basic Physics	38.9		Natural Science
05683420	SQL Programming	44	50.25	Computing Studies
06142546	Database Design	25.95	36.9	Computing Studies
07452771	Principles of Programming	31.95	39.9	Computing Studies
08720982	Advanced Biology	49		Natural Science
08793876	Biology for Dummies	24		Natural Science
09987773	Maths for Dummies	38.6	45.9	Computer science
89765434	Jungle Man	12.5	23	Social Science
89876234	Johnny Be Good	10.78	18.5	Social Science

bookX

isbn	bookTitle	costPrice	sellingPrice	classification
01133887	Programming with Java	49.45	56.9	Computer Science
03451105	Beginning Chemistry	39.65	42.8	Natural Science
03821069	Basic Physics	38.9	46.7	Natural Science
05588332	Basic Criminology	31.6	39.8	Social Science
05621458	Business Ethics	42.5	49.95	Business Administration
05683420	SQL Programming	44	50.25	Computer Science
06142546	Database Design	25.95	36.9	Computer Science
06739214	Business Law	42.85	51.2	Business Administration
07225360	Elements of Sociology	38.45	44.95	Social Science
07452771	Principles of Programming	31.95	39.9	Computer Science

bookX				
isbn	**bookTitle**	**costPrice**	**sellingPrice**	**classification**
08720982	Advanced Biology	49	54.65	Natural Science
08739512	Business Ethics	43.25	51	Business Administration
08793876	Biology for Dummies	24	35	Natural Science
09978423	Introduction to Marketing	29.95	37.45	Business Administration

bookXMod				
isbn	**bookTitle**	**costPrice**	**sellingPrice**	**classification**
01133887	Programming with Java	49.45	56.9	Computer Science
05683420	SQL Programming	44	50.25	Computer Science
06142546	Database Design	25.95	36.9	Computer Science
07452771	Principles of Programming	31.95	39.9	Computer Science

courseX table

The data describing academic courses are stored in this table. The table's (composite) primary key consists of **courseCode**, **section**, **facultyId**, and **studentId** columns.

courseX					
courseCode	**courseName**	**section**	**creditHours**	**facultyId**	**studentId**
BUS101	Fundamentals of Business I	2010	3	JS994450	DM674543
BUS101	Fundamentals of Business I	2010	3	JS994450	EA486741
BUS101	Fundamentals of Business I	2010	3	JS994450	EJ890321
BUS101	Fundamentals of Business I	2020	3	JS994450	AM609128
BUS101	Fundamentals of Business I	2020	3	JS994450	CJ684975
BUS101	Fundamentals of Business I	2020	3	JS994450	FK576381
BUS110	Fundamentals of Business II	2010	3	EM001254	AB778204
BUS110	Fundamentals of Business II	2010	3	EM001254	BB118945
BUS110	Fundamentals of Business II	2010	3	EM001254	CS664452
CSC220	Principles of Programming	2010	3	AL501828	CJ684975
CSC220	Principles of Programming	2010	3	AL501828	EM001254
CSC220	Principles of Programming	2010	3	AL501828	SA357864
CSC220	Principles of Programming	2020	3	EM001254	DM674543
CSC355	Database Programming	2010	3	AL501828	KZ934582
CSC355	Database Programming	2010	3	AL501828	PP886705
CSC445	Database Concepts and Design	2010	3	EE987654	AM609128
CSC445	Database Concepts and Design	2010	3	EE987654	CS664452
CSC445	Database Concepts and Design	2010	3	EE987654	EM001254
EDU101	Principles of Education	2010	3	DM674543	AU408153
EDU101	Principles of Education	2010	3	DM674543	EJ890321
EDU101	Principles of Education	2010	3	DM674543	SA357864
EDU260	Classroom Management	2010	3	ZM567123	CC396710
EDU400	Senior Project	2010	3	ZM567123	PP886705
EDU400	Senior Project	2010	3	ZM567123	SA357864
NAS101	Introduction to Chemistry	2010	3	RU123098	EA486741
NAS101	Introduction to Chemistry	2010	3	RU123098	EJ890321
NAS101	Introduction to Chemistry	2010	3	RU123098	FA213595
NAS101	Introduction to Chemistry	2010	3	RU123098	KZ934582
NAS250	Advanced Physics I	2010	3	PD002312	AB778204
NAS250	Advanced Physics I	2010	3	PD002312	BB118945
NAS250	Advanced Physics I	2010	3	PD002312	CS664452

Appendix A

courseCode	courseName	section	creditHours	facultyId	studentId
NAS250	Advanced Physics I	2010	3	PD002312	FA213595
NAS300	Advanced Physics II	2020	3	PD002312	BB118945
NAS300	Advanced Physics II	2020	3	PD002312	FK576381
SOC101	Introduction to Sociology	2010	3	JH682508	CC396710
SOC101	Introduction to Sociology	2010	3	JH682508	CJ684975
SOC101	Introduction to Sociology	2010	3	JH682508	DM674543
SOC450	Society and Sociology	2010	3	ES509264	AB778204
SOC450	Society and Sociology	2010	3	ES509264	FA213595
SOC450	Society and Sociology	2010	3	ES509264	KZ934582

Table title: **courseX**

departmentX table

The data describing academic departments are stored in this table. The table's primary key is the **departmentCode** column.

departmentCode	departmentName	chairId
BUSA02	Business Administration	EM001254
CSCM09	Computer Science	EE987654
EDUD05	Education	DM674543
NASC08	Natural Science	RU123098
SOCC06	Social Science	ES509264

Table title: **Department**

facultyX, facultyXMod, and facultyZ tables

These tables' structures are identical but used for different demonstrations' activities. The data describing faculty members are stored in these tables. Each table's primary key is the **facultyId** column.

facultyId	first Name	initial	last Name	offPhone	department Code	chairId	annual Salary
AL501828	Ada	P	Lasking	0321239876	CSCM09	EE987654	54354.15
DM674543	Doris	V	Mea	0324569132	EDUD05		62980.25
EE987654	Ememgini	M	Erochi	0327840108	CSCM09		68261.39
EM001254	Eghosa		Maklasi	0327854090	BUSA02		74563.55
ES509264	Euhan	S	Stevenson	0329773782	SOCC06		69852.25
JH682508	Jenny		Hendix	0323458096	SOCC06	ES509264	48000.00
JI907821	Joseph		Irubor	0327899908	CSCM09	EE987654	51500.26
JK908760	Johnson	M	Kennedy	0329450326	CSCM09	EE987654	54890.15
JS994450	John		Semina	0327859031	BUSA02	EM001254	45876.25
PD002312	Peter		Dayet	0326184605	NASC08	RU123098	56904.00
RU123098	Rischi	B	Ugboma	0327555491	NASC08		70760.89
ZM567123	Zenat	J	Miller	0323751906	EDUD05	DM674543	49980.95

Table title: **facultyX**

facultyId	first Name	initial	last Name	offPhone	department Code	chairId	annual Salary
JS994450	John		Semina	0327859031	BUSA02	EM001254	45876.25
ZM567123	Zenat	J	Miller	0323751906	EDUD05	DM674543	49980.95
JH682508	Jenny		Hendix	0323458096	SOCC06	ES509264	48000

Table title: **facultyXMod**

facultyId	first Name	initial	last Name	offPhone	department Code	chairId	annual Salary
EM001254	Eghosa		Maklasi	0327854090	BUSA02		74563.55
RU123098	Rischi	B	Ugboma	0327555491	NASC08		70760.89
ES509264	Euhan	S	Stevenson	0329773782	SOCC06		69852.25
JS994450	John		Semina	0327859031	BUSA02	EM001254	
PD002312	Peter		Dayet	0326184605	NASC08	RU123098	
ZM567123	Zenat	J	Miller	0323751906	EDUD05	DM674543	
AL501828	Ada	P	Lasking	0321239876	CSCM09	EE987654	
JH682508	Jenny		Hendix	0323458096	SOCC06	ES509264	
JK908760	Johnson	M	Kennedy	0329450326	CSCM09	EE987654	54890.15
JI907821	Joseph		Irubor	0327899908	CSCM09	EE987654	51500.26
DM674543	Doris	V	Mea	0324569132	EDUD05		62980.25
EE987654	Ememgini	M	Erochi	0327840108	CSCM09		68261.39

gradeX table

The data describing students' grades are stored in this table. The table's (composite) primary key consists of **facultyId**, **studentId**, **courseCode**, and **section** columns.

facultyId	studentId	courseCode	section	letterGrade
AL501828	CJ684975	CSC220	2010	C
AL501828	EM001254	CSC220	2010	AU
AL501828	KZ934582	CSC355	2010	C
AL501828	PP886705	CSC355	2010	WP
AL501828	SA357864	CSC220	2010	A
DM674543	AU408153	EDU101	2010	B
DM674543	EJ890321	EDU101	2010	B
DM674543	SA357864	EDU101	2010	B
EE987654	AM609128	CSC445	2010	I
EE987654	CS664452	CSC445	2010	B
EE987654	EM001254	CSC445	2010	AU
EM001254	AB778204	BUS110	2010	A
EM001254	BB118945	BUS110	2010	C
EM001254	CS664452	BUS110	2010	C
ES509264	AB778204	SOC450	2010	D
ES509264	FA213595	SOC450	2010	A
ES509264	KZ934582	SOC450	2010	D
JH682508	CC396710	SOC101	2010	F
JH682508	CJ684975	SOC101	2010	F
JH682508	DM674543	SOC101	2010	AU
JS994450	AM609128	BUS101	2020	C
JS994450	CJ684975	BUS101	2020	D
JS994450	DM674543	BUS101	2010	AU
JS994450	EA486741	BUS101	2010	B
JS994450	EJ890321	BUS101	2010	F
JS994450	FK576381	BUS101	2020	C
PD002312	AB778204	NAS250	2010	C
PD002312	BB118945	NAS250	2010	B
PD002312	BB118945	NAS300	2020	F

gradeX				
facultyId	**studentId**	**courseCode**	**section**	**letterGrade**
PD002312	CS664452	NAS250	2010	A
PD002312	FA213595	NAS250	2010	I
PD002312	FK576381	NAS300	2020	B
RU123098	EA486741	NAS101	2010	A
RU123098	EJ890321	NAS101	2010	C
RU123098	FA213595	NAS101	2010	WP
RU123098	KZ934582	NAS101	2010	B
ZM567123	CC396710	EDU260	2010	WF
ZM567123	PP886705	EDU400	2010	C
ZM567123	SA357864	EDU400	2010	B

positionX table

The data describing academic rankings are stored in this table. The table's primary key is the **numericNumbering** column.

positionX			
numericNumbering	**academicPosition**	**minAnnualSalary**	**maxAnnualSalary**
1	Full Professor	68100	75000
2	Associate Professor	61500	68000
3	Assistant Professor	51000	60000
4	Instructor	44000	50500

studentX and studentZ tables

These tables' structures are identical but used for different demonstrations' activities. The data describing students are stored in these tables. Each table's primary key is the **studentId** column.

StudentX											
student Id	**first Name**	**ini tial**	**last Name**	**Address**	**city**	**state**	**zip Code**	**country**	**classifi cation**	**date First Enrolled**	**user Id**
AB778204	Abel	A	Bomor	123 Main Street	Cebu	Cebu	6039	Philippines	Sophomore	6/5/2005	ab8204
AM609128	Adora	U	Manny	P. O. Box 675	London		1H6 Y8P	United Kingdom	Freshmen	6/10/2005	am9128
AU408153	Andy	C	Uzueg	856 Flamingo Avenue	Austin	Texas	75765	United States	Sophomore	8/20/2004	au8153
BB118945	Benjamin	C	Benado	21 Stadium Road	Benin	Edo		Nigeria	Junior	8/15/2004	bb8945
CC396710	Celestine		Chap	P. O. Box 874	Tortola			British Virgin Islands	Freshman	8/20/2005	cc6710
CJ684975	Cecilia		Jeffer	P. O. Box 1020	Ukpor	Anambra		Nigeria	Freshman	1/18/2006	cj4975
CS664452	Christoph er		Salat	P.M.B. 9080	Edwardville	Ontario	6W4 K1R	Canada	Junior	1/10/2004	cs4452
DM674543	Doris	V	Mea	Villarmea Compound	Tuyan-Naga	Cebu	6037	Philippines	Auditing	1/8/2005	dm4543
EA486741	Erasto		Actionbarrel	51 Palmer Way	Victoria Island	Lagos		Nigeria	Freshman	8/25/2005	ea6741
EJ890321	Efosa	J	Johnson	67 Mary John Street	Hollywood	Florida	33078	United States	Freshman	1/20/2006	ej0321
EM001254	Eghosa		Maklasi	P. O. Box 6753	Miramar	Florida	33033	United States	Auditing	6/10/2005	em1254
FA213595	Fredrica	B	Anthony	6341 Ugboma Avenue	Accra	Accra		Ghana	Sophomore	1/10/2005	fa3595
FK576381	Florence	E	Kolly	947 Emegi Way	Langtan	Plateau		Nigeria	Sophomore	1/20/2005	fk6381
JF407463	John		Felly	115 Back Road	Tortola			British Virgin Islands	Sophomore	9/11/2005	jf7463

StudentX											
student Id	first Name	ini tial	last Name	Address	city	state	zip Code	country	classifi cation	date First Enrolled	user Id
JP401169	Johnson		Paulson	675 Paulson Lane	Ukpor	Anambra		Nigeria	Senior	6/12/2004	jp1169
KZ934582	Kamaria	D	Zeberia	P. O. Box 2008	San Antonio	Texas	75098	United States	Junior	1/20/2005	kz4582
PP886705	Phil		Portiskum	750 Mans Street	Birmingham		6P4 M2Q	United Kingdom	Senior	8/15/2004	pp6705
SA357864	Suzy	M	Afik	P.M.B. 6732	Pasig	Metro Manila	3098	Philippines	Senior	1/25/2004	sa7864

studentZ						
studentId	firstName	initial	lastName	classification	dateFirstEnrolled	userId
KZ934582	Pitaqua	D	Paul	Junior	1/20/2005	kz4582
BB118945	Benjamin	C	Benado	Junior	8/15/2004	bb8945
FK576381	Florence	E	Kolly	Sophomore	2/20/2005	fk6381

Appendix B

Answers to Chapters Questions

This addendum contains the answers to the odd-numbered review questions, except for the essay type questions, at the end of each chapter. The even-numbered questions and the essay type questions are provided as tests' questions.

Chapter One

Multiple Choice Questions
1. c
3. b
5. c
7. c
9. c

True or False Questions
11. a (True)
13. a (True)
15. a (True)
17. b (False)

Fill in the blank Questions
19. Fields, columns, or attributes
21. Normalization process or Normalization
23. Primary key

Chapter Two

Multiple Choice Questions
1. a
3. d
5. a
7. a
9. c

True or False Questions
11. b (False)
13. a (True)
15. b (False)
17. b (False)

Fill in the blank Questions
19. Clause
21. Column alias or alias
23. Comma

Chapter Three

Multiple Choice Questions
1. b
3. d
5. d
7. b
9. d

True or False Questions
11. a (True)
13. b (False)
15. b (False)
17. b (False)

Fill in the blank Questions
19. ORDER BY clause
21. comparison operator or relational operator
23. IS NULL

Chapter Four

Multiple Choice Questions
1. d
3. a
5. c
7. a
9. d

True or False Questions
11. a (True)
13. a (True)
15. a (True)
17. a (True)

Fill in the blank Questions
19. equijoin or simple join or inner join
21. Cartesian join
23. Right outer

Chapter Five

Multiple Choice Questions
1. d
3. a
5. d
7. c
9. c

True or False Questions
11. a (True)
13. b (False)
15. b (False)
17. a (True)

Fill in the blank Questions
19. MID function
21. LTRIM
23. FORMATNUMBER

Chapter Six

Multiple Choice Questions
1. b
3. a
5. a
7. c
9. a

True or False Questions
11. b (False)
13. a (True)
15. a (True)
17. a (True)

Fill in the blank Questions
19. NOW function or NOW()
21. abbreviated
23. ISNULL

Chapter Seven

Multiple Choice Questions
1. d
3. b
5. b
7. a
9. d

True or False Questions
11. a (True)
13. b (False)
15. b (False)
17. b (False)

Fill in the blank Questions
19. COUNT(*)
21. VAR or VARP
23. aggregate or statistics or summary or group

Chapter Eight

Multiple Choice Questions
1. c
3. b
5. d
7. c
9. a

True or False Questions
11. a (True)
13. b (False)
15. b (False)
17. b (False)

Fill in the blank Questions
19. inline view
21. =ANY
23. single-row (comparison)

Chapter Nine

Multiple Choice Questions
1. a
3. b
5. d
7. d
9. a

True or False Questions
11. b (False)
13. b (False)
15. a (True)
17. b (False)

Fill in the blank Questions
19. names
21. syntax
23. ALTER TABLE...ADD or ALTER TABLE

Appendix B

Chapter Ten

Multiple Choice Questions
1. d
3. b
5. c
7. b
9. a

True or False Questions
11. a (True)
13. b (False)
15. a (True)
17. a (True)

Fill in the blank Questions
19. constraint type
21. CONSTRAINT
23. column

Chapter Eleven

Multiple Choice Questions
1. a
3. d
5. c
7. c
9. a

True or False Questions
11. a (True)
13. a (True)
15. a (True)
17. a (True)

Fill in the blank Questions
19. VALUES
21. WHERE
23. formal parameter

Chapter Twelve

Multiple Choice Questions
1. d
3. c
5. d
7. c
9. a

True or False Questions
11. a (True)
13. a (True)
15. b (False)
17. b (False)

Fill in the blank Questions
19. complex view
21. unique index
23. index keys

Chapter Thirteen

Multiple Choice Questions
1. b
3. d
5. a
7. b
9. a

True or False Questions
11. a (True)
13. b (False)
15. b (False)
17. a (True)

Fill in the blank Questions
19. RSet statement
21. IMMEDIATE window
23. underscore, concatenating

Chapter Fourteen

Multiple Choice Questions
1. d
3. c
5. d
7. c
9. c

True or False Questions
11. a (True)
13. a (True)
15. b (False)
17. b (False)

Fill in the blank Questions
19. System.mdw
21. CreateUser
23. Permissions

Appendix C

Solutions to Chapters Hands-on Activities

The following are the solutions to the selected odd-numbered hands-on questions from chapter two through chapter fourteen. The solutions are just one approach for solving the problems as there are other ways of writing the SQL statements that provide the solutions to some or most of the hands-on questions. The author has decided to provide one solution for each of the selected odd-numbered hands-on questions. This one-solution-for-one-question approach is intended to motivate learners and students to find alternative ways of writing the solutions to the problems.

Learners can challenge themselves to finding alternative methods of writing the SQL statements that generate the same results as the SQL statements' solutions given here. Likewise, instructors can challenge their students by instructing them to find other ways of writing the SQL statements that yield the same results as the SQL statements' solutions given here.

The even-numbered and other odd-numbered hands-on questions which solutions are not given in this appendix are projects' questions. The results of your SQL statements' solutions for these questions will reveal whether the solutions are correct or not. So check the displayed result of the solution you have written for a question against the question to determine whether the displayed result meets the question's specifications.

Solutions to Selected Questions in Chapter Two

1.	SELECT studentId, country FROM studentX;
3.	SELECT DISTINCT courseCode, courseName FROM courseX;
7.	SELECT DISTINCT "Course Code and Name Description:" & " " & courseCode & " " & courseName AS [Course Full Name] FROM courseX;

Solutions to Selected Questions in Chapter Three

1.	SELECT facultyId, lastName FROM facultyX WHERE annualSalary <= 50500;
3.	SELECT * FROM facultyX WHERE firstName LIKE "J*" AND annualSalary / 12 <= 4000;
7.	SELECT courseCode, section, courseName, facultyId FROM courseX WHERE courseCode LIKE "C*";

Solutions to Selected Questions in Chapter Four

1.	SELECT facultyId, F.departmentCode FROM facultyX F INNER JOIN departmentX D ON F.departmentCode = D.departmentCode;
3.	SELECT departmentCode, academicPosition FROM departmentX, positionX ORDER BY departmentCode;

5.	SELECT academicPosition, firstName + " " + lastName AS [Full Name] FROM facultyX, positionX WHERE annualSalary BETWEEN minAnnualSalary AND maxAnnualSalary AND annualSalary < 50000;

Solutions to Selected Questions in Chapter Five

1.	SELECT DISTINCT STRCONV(firstName, 1), STRCONV(lastName, 1) FROM facultyX WHERE firstname LIKE "E*" AND lastName LIKE "E*";
5.	SELECT DISTINCT LEFT(firstName, 1) AS FNAME_INI, LEFT(lastName, 1) AS LNAME_INI, ASC(LEFT(firstName, 1)) AS FNAME_INI_VALUE, ASC(LEFT(lastName,1)) AS LNAME_INI_VALUE FROM facultyX WHERE chairId IS NULL;
9.	SELECT STRREVERSE(F.facultyId) AS facultyId, STRREVERSE(F.lastName) AS lastName FROM facultyX F INNER JOIN studentX S ON S.studentId = F.facultyId;

Solutions to Selected Questions in Chapter Six

1.	SELECT studentId, DATEDIFF('yyyy', dateFirstEnrolled, DATE(), 1, 3) AS [Number Of Years Gone By] FROM studentX WHERE country = "United Kingdom";
3.	SELECT TIME() AS CURRENT_TIME FROM facultyX WHERE facultyId = "DM674543";
7.	SELECT facultyId, NZ(initial, "None") AS Middle_Name_Initial FROM facultyX WHERE initial IS NULL;

Solutions to Selected Questions in Chapter Seven

1.	SELECT COUNT(academicPosition) AS NumberOfAcademicPositions FROM positionX;
3.	SELECT FORMATCURRENCY(SUM(costPrice)) AS Total_Cost, FORMATCURRENCY(SUM(sellingPrice)) AS Total_Retail FROM bookX;
5.	SELECT FORMATCURRENCY(SUM(sellingPrice) * 0.20, 0) AS 20_Percent FROM bookX GROUP BY classification ORDER BY SUM(sellingPrice);

Solutions to Selected Questions in Chapter Eight

1.	SELECT facultyId, lastName FROM facultyX WHERE annualSalary > (SELECT AVG(annualSalary) FROM facultyX);
5.	SELECT bookTitle, FORMATCURRENCY(sellingPrice) AS [retail price], classification FROM bookX WHERE sellingPrice IN (SELECT MIN(sellingPrice) FROM bookX GROUP BY classification);

Appendix C

| 7. | SELECT country, COUNT(country) AS [how many]
FROM studentX
GROUP BY country
HAVING COUNT(country) =ANY (SELECT COUNT(country)
              FROM studentX
              GROUP BY country
              HAVING COUNT(country) > 3) ORDER BY 2; |

Solutions to Selected Questions in Chapter Nine

1.	CREATE TABLE residentHall (hallCode CHAR(6), hallName VARCHAR(20));
7.	ALTER TABLE studentCopy DROP classification;
9.	DROP TABLE studentCopy;

Solutions to Selected Questions in Chapter Ten

1.	CREATE TABLE dormitory (domCode BYTE CONSTRAINT dorm_pk PRIMARY KEY, domName VARCHAR(20) CONSTRAINT dorm_uk UNIQUE);
3.	ALTER TABLE dormitory ADD buildStatus VARCHAR(10);
7.	ALTER TABLE studentInfo ALTER studentId SHORT CONSTRAINT st_pk PRIMARY KEY;

Solutions to Selected Questions in Chapter Eleven

1.	INSERT INTO dormitory VALUES(11, "East Beach", #08/21/2002#, "Good");
5.	INSERT INTO studentInfo VALUES(studentId, fullName, domCode); **Note**: Run this INSERT INTO statement for each of the seven records. Enter null values in the domCode column of any three records
7.	DELETE FROM domMod WHERE domCode = 11;

Solutions to Selected Questions in Chapter Twelve

1.	SELECT studentId, domCode FROM studentInfo; (Save the result as studentDomView)
5.	CREATE INDEX domNameIndex ON dormitory(domName);
7.	DROP INDEX domCodeIndex ON studentInfo;

Solutions to Selected Questions in Chapter Thirteen

| 1. | Public Function studMod()
  Dim CreateSQL As String
  CreateSQL = "SELECT * INTO studCopyMod FROM student;"
  DoCmd.RunSQL CreateSQL
End Function |

366

Learn Database Programming Using SQL of MS Access

7.	Public Function createAddSHall()
	Dim UpSQL As String
	UpSQL = "UPDATE studentHall SET hallName = 'Central Beach' " _
	    + "WHERE hallCode = '11';"
	DoCmd.RunSQL UpSQL
	DoCmd.RunSQL "UPDATE studentHall SET hallName = 'Premiere'" _
	    & " WHERE hallCode = '13';"
	End Function

9.	Public Function DelDropStud() Dim DeleteSQL As String DeleteSQL = "DELETE FROM studCopyMod;" DoCmd.RunSQL DeleteSQL DoCmd.RunSQL "DROP TABLE studCopyMod" & ";" End Function

Solutions to Selected Questions in Chapter Fourteen

1.	Public Sub CreateDBPass() Dim AcDBPass As Database Set AcDBPass = CurrentDb() AcDBPass.NewPassword "", "acadpass" End Sub
5.	Public Sub AddIndUserToGroup() Dim WSpace As Workspace Dim Username As User Dim GroupName As Group Set WSpace = DBEngine(0) Set Username = WSpace.CreateUser("James") WSpace.Groups("ADMINS").Users.Append Username End Sub
7.	Public Sub GrantPermGroup() Dim Dbase As Database Dim Ddoc As Document Set Dbase = CurrentDb() Set Ddoc = Dbase.Containers("Tables").Documents("studentHall") Ddoc.Username = "StudManager" Ddoc.Permissions = dbSecInsertData End Sub

Appendix D

Tables Relationships and MS Windows 2000 Screen Display

The following diagram shows the primary tables of **AcademicX** database, their structures, and their relationships.

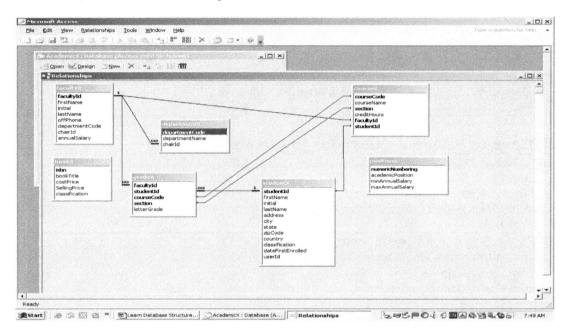

The screen display listed below shows how to launch MS Access using MS Windows 2000 operating system.

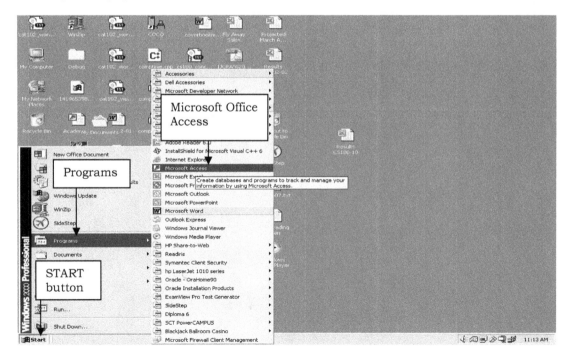

Glossary of Terms

Actual Argument: A data item supplied to a function to use to perform its assigned task.

ADMIN: The default database user when an unsecured database is launched and a member of the ADMINS account group.

ADMINS Account Group: A group with full rights, usually database administrators, to view and manipulate available objects within a database and the authority to grant, change, and revoke access permissions to other users to the database.

Aggregate Function: *See Multiple-Row Function.*

ALTER TABLE Statement: A SQL instruction used to modify the structure of a table and the properties associated with the structure.

Alternate Key: A column that has all the properties of a primary key but not chosen to be the primary key of a table.

American National Standards Institute-SQL (ANSI-SQL): The most recognizable standard in the world of SQL programming.

Application-Level Security: An established measure used to create a password for a database.

Argument-Based Function: A block of programming instructions that requires actual arguments to perform its assigned task.

Arithmetic Expression: An arithmetic form where numeric columns, date columns, numeric values, date values, and/or numeric functions, date functions are connected by numeric operators.

Attribute: *See Column.*

Autonumber Data Type: A numeric type used to automate columns' values in incrementing order starting from value 1.

Boyce-Codd Normal Form (BCNF): A normalization process yardstick used to remove special transitive dependencies from a table where the table's primary key depends on a non-key column.

Bridge Entity: A composite table used to physically implement many-to-many relationship.

Browse Form: An arrangement of data values that consists of more than one column and may contain one or several rows.

Built-In Function: A block of programming instructions that is incorporated into the programming language before the language is distributed for use.

Calculated Field: A column that contains the result of a mathematical computation and the column never existed in the table that is being queried.

Candidate Key: A column that has all the properties of a primary key and qualifies to be the primary key of a table.

Cardinality: A number of occurrences of one relation that will have an association with one occurrence of the other relation in a relationship.

Cartesian Product: A query result where each record from one table concatenates with every record in the other table.

Case Conversion Function: A block of programming instructions used to convert or change text data from one case to another.

Character Data Type: A generic nonnumeric type used to define a text value for a column.

Character Function: *See String Function.*

Character Manipulation Function: A block of programming instructions used to alter the forms of text data besides converting text data to upper, lower, and mixed cases.

Character: Any printable symbol such as **&**. A character is the smallest, usable, and meaningful piece (unit) of data that can be stored on a storage medium.

Check Constraint: A rule used to establish domain integrity that declares and controls the permissible values that must enter a specific or particular column of a table during data entry operation.

Child Table: A table that contains a foreign key in which the foreign key values reference some values in the primary key of the parent table.

Clause: A portion of a SQL statement used to perform an action and usually begins with a keyword.

Column: A field or an attribute used to describe one characteristic of a table's data.

Column Alias: A temporary secondary name given to a column and used as a column heading in the result of a query.

Column Definition: All the elements or components a column must have in order to properly describe the structure of a table

Column List: The columns listed in a SQL clause.

Column Name: A meaningful label used to identify a column

Column Position: A physical location of a column, numbered from left to right, in the SELECT clause of a SELECT statement.

Column Qualifier: A special column name that is formed by preceding the column name with a table name and a period.

Column Size: The number of character positions that is reserved for a column to use to store its data values.

Column Value: A data value that is assigned to be stored in a column of a table.

Column-Level Approach: An approach where constraints are defined as part of columns' definitions during table creation using the CREATE TABLE statement.

COMMAND Object: An object, in ActiveX Data Objects (ADO) architecture, used to associate the result (record set) created for a SELECT statement with the Open command statement.

Command-line Interface: An operating system's environment where commands are typed rather than being selected from command menus or command toolbars.

Comment: A remark or an explanatory note that help programmers or programs' users to clearly understand the functions of programs.

Commit: A command used to permanently register changes made to columns' data

Comparison Operator: A connecting symbol used to compare the degree of relationship between two data items.

Complex Condition: *See Compound Condition.*

Complex View: A virtual table that contains functions, grouped data, or both and is created from a single table or created from more than one table.

Composite Column: A collection or group of columns that are treated as a unit.

Composite Foreign Key: A foreign key of a table that consists of more than one column.

Composite Primary Key: A key that is made up of more than one column that serves as a table's primary key and the columns collectively identify each row of the table uniquely.

Compound Condition: A restriction in a condition clause of a SQL statement that contains more than one simple condition and/or more than one logical (Boolean) operator.

Computed Field: *See Calculated Field.*

Concatenation: A process of combining two or more text columns' data or one or more text columns' data with text literals to produce the data for a single column.

Conceptual Design Phase: A process that involves the mental picture or the perception of how the data are to be arranged in tables. This phase involves the conceptual discussion of planning and designing the blue prints of relational database.

Condition: A requirement in SQL environment that records of a table must satisfy to be displayed as part of the result of a query.

Glossary of Terms

Conditional Retrieval: A situation where only the rows that meet certain established criteria in a SELECT statement are included in the result of a query.

CONNECTION Object: An object, in ActiveX Data Objects (ADO) architecture, used to connect to the database that is being queried.

Constraint: A rule used to enforce restrictions to relational database tables so data contained in the tables are accurate and have integrity.

Constraint Name: A meaningful label used to identify a constraint.

Constraint Type: A type of constraint to be applied to a table column.

Container: An object structure that contains all the necessary information about all the objects that exist in a MS Access database.

Correlated Subquery: An outer query that is executed first and execution is done for each record stored in table of the outer query.

CREATE TABLE Statement: A SQL instruction used to define the physical structure of a table.

Cross-Tabulation: A results' set that is gotten by the possible combinations of columns listed in the GROUP BY clause of the first SELECT statement of aggregate operation.

Currency Data Type: A special numeric type used to define a monetary value for a column.

Data Independence: A situation where changes made to the structures of tables might not affect the data contained in the tables.

Data Consistency: A measure that assures that data are free from errors.

Data Control Language (DCL): A subsection of SQL that contains commands for establishing controls and privileges to users.

Data Definition Language (DDL): A subsection of SQL that contains commands for creating and modifying objects such as tables and views.

Data Duplication: A situation in SQL environment where the same piece of data is displayed more than once in a query result.

Data Manipulation Language (DML): A subsection of SQL that contains the commands used for entering, retrieving, updating, and deleting tables' data.

Data Redundancy: The replication or duplication of the same piece of data in several or different locations.

Data Suppression: A process of eliminating duplicated data, where possible, in a query before displaying the result.

Data Type Conversion Function: A block of programming instructions used to convert data from one type to another.

Data Type Subtype: A category or a unit (such as integer) of a data type (such as numeric) that can be used to specifically define the data type in that category.

Data Type: A specific kind of data values a column is expected to store.

Database: *See Relational Database.*

Database Password: A coded word or a secret code used as a means of denying an unauthorized user from viewing the content of a database.

Database Permission: A privilege granted to a database user or a database workgroup to use a particular database object.

Database Replication: A process of copying a database in order to exchange updated data among the copies of the database.

Database Security: An established measure used to deny or prevent an unauthorized user from accessing a database.

Database-Level Security: *See Application-Level Security.*

Data-Modeling Tool: A particular style of presenting relationships and cardinalities in entity-relationship diagrams.

Learn Database Programming Using SQL of MS Access

Date Data Type: A nonnumeric type used to define a date value for a column.

Date Function: A block of programming instructions used to determine current and future dates and how much time has elapsed between dates.

Date Interval: A time period on which a date function bases its calculations on.

Default Value: A generic value assigned as a beginning or initial value to a column.

DELETE Statement: A SQL instruction used to remove data records permanently from a table.

Derived Table: *See View.*

DIFFERENCE Statement: A SQL instruction used to display records contained in the table listed in one SELECT statement of the DIFFERENCE operation but those records are not found in the table listed in the other SELECT statement of the DIFFERENCE operation.

DIVIDE Statement: A SQL instruction used to display data from the table that is being divided listed in the SELECT statement of the DIVIDE operation, and those data are common to all records in the dividing table listed in the SELECT statement of the DIVIDE operation.

Document: An object structure that contains all the necessary information about a particular object that exists in a MS Access database.

Documenter: A command used to display the content of MS Access system catalog (data dictionary)

Double-Precision Value: A floating-point number with number of decimal places exceeding seven (7) but not more than fourteen (14) decimal places.

DROP TABLE Statement: A SQL instruction used to remove a table permanently from a database.

Edit Form: An arrangement of data values that consists of one column and may contain one or several rows.

Entity Integrity: A database rule that says the values of a primary key of a table cannot be null and cannot be duplicated, and that duplication is only allowed when the primary key is a composite primary key.

Entity-Relationship Model: A model used during a database design process to give a somewhat complete representation of data to be stored in the tables of relational databases.

Exclusive Mode: An environment where a database is opened for one user only at any given time.

External Database: An existing database application that may not physically be opened and resides in a location that is different from the location a user with an opened database is currently using.

Field: *See Column.*

Field Name: *See Column Name.*

First Normal Form (1NF): A normalization process yardstick used to eliminate repeating groups that exist within the rows of tables and to identify the primary keys' columns for the tables.

Fixed-Length Column: A field defined to store data using the exact number of character positions.

Floating-Point Subtype: A numeric type used exclusively to define a numeric value with decimal places (real value) for a column.

Foreign Key Constraint: A rule used to establish referential integrity and implicitly establishes the links (relationships) that exist between databases tables.

Foreign Key: A single column or a collection of columns of a table where the values stored in those column(s) must match some values in the primary key column(s) of the associated table.

Formal Parameter: A reserved location of the main memory used to store a data value that is passed to a column or a function.

Function: A block or collection of programming instructions which task is pre-known.

Glossary of Terms

Grand Total: A collection of subtotals.

Grant: A means of assigning users and workgroups access permissions to the objects of a database.

Group Function: *See Multiple-Row Function.*

Identifier: A non-keyword text expression used as a name to identify an item in a programming language or in an application package.

IMMEDIATE Window: A window-like structure used to monitor and view the results of a program's variables and expressions, and to debug a program during run time.

Index Key: A column used to create an index for a table.

Index: A physical structure used to speed up database data retrieval operations.

Individual User Account: A user who accesses and manipulates the objects of a database according to the access permissions granted by the ADMINS account group.

Information-Level Design Phase: *See Conceptual Design Phase.*

Inline View: A short-term table that is created when a query is embedded into the FROM clause of a SELECT statement.

INSERT INTO Statement: A SQL instruction used to populate a table with data.

Integer Subtype: A numeric type used exclusively to define a numeric value without decimal places (whole number) for a column.

Integrity Constraint: A restriction that guarantees that data in the database are valid.

Internal Database: An existing database application that is currently opened and used by a user and the database resides in the location the user is currently using.

Internal Documentation: Comments or remarks that are part of a program's code.

INTERSECT Statement: A SQL instruction used to display the records that are common to the tables listed in the SELECT statements of the INTERSECT operation.

Key Column: An attribute that serves as the primary key or as part of the attributes that serve as the primary key of a table.

Key-Preserved Table: A table which primary key is the primary key of a complex view.

Keyword: A keyword is a reserved word or a reserved expression that has a special meaning in a programming language or in an application package.

Logical Data Type: A nonnumeric type used to define a Boolean value for a column.

Logical Design Phase: *See Conceptual Design Phase.*

Many-to-Many Relationship (M:N): A relationship where no, one, or many records of one table, say table A, establish relationship with no, one, or many records of the other table, say table B and vice versa.

Memo Data Type: A nonnumeric type used to define a column that will contain a remark or a comment.

Microsoft Access: A graphical user interface (GUI) relational database management system developed by Microsoft Corporation to create databases in PC environment.

Multiple Column Sort Keys: A situation where more than three column or three columns' positions are used to reorganize data from tables.

Multiple-Column Subquery: An inner query that returns more than one column value to the outer query. The outer query uses the columns values as its input to determine the final output.

Multiple-Row Function: A block of programming instructions that works across groups of rows to return one record for each group processed in a table.

Multiple-Row Subquery: An inner query that can return more than one record that will be used as the input to the outer query when the result of the outer query is based on unknown values.

Nested Function: A block of programming instructions that is entirely placed inside another block of programming instructions.
Nested Query: *See Subquery.*

Nested Subquery: An inner query that is entirely written inside another inner query.

Non Key-Preserved Table: A table which primary key is not the primary key of a complex view.

Nonargument-Based Function: A block of programming instructions that requires no actual arguments to perform its assigned task.

Non-Categorized Single-Row Functions: A block of programming instructions that is used to return one record for each row processed in a table, but do not belong to any of the defined groups.

Non-Key Column: An attribute that is not part of a table's primary key.

Nonunique Index: An index created manually or explicitly by a database user using a CREATE INDEX statement.

Normalization Process: A course of actions used to identify and remove databases' problems called anomalies from tables in order for data in the resulting tables to have integrity.

Not Null Constraint: A rule used to establish not null (a-must-value) integrity that ensures that a specific or particular column must always receive data when data entry operation is performed for that column.

Null Constraint: A rule used to establish null (can-be-empty) integrity that allows a specific or particular column to receive no data if so desired during data entry operation. The default constraint when no other constraint is defined for a column.

Null Value: An unknown data in a column when the column receives no known value during data entry operation for the table where the column exists.

Number Data Type: A numeric type that is used to define a numeric value for a column.

Numeric Function: A block of programming instructions that is used to perform mathematical computations and alter the appearance of numeric values.

Oleobject Data Type: A nonnumeric type used to define columns that will store an image, a graphic, sound, or any other type of object that can be linked to a table or embedded in the table.

One-to-Many Relationship (1:M): A relationship where one record of a table, say table A, can establish an association with no, one, or many records of a second table, say table B, where each of the said records of table B relates to that one record of table A.

One-to-One Relationship (1:1): A relationship where one record of one table, say table A, can establish an association with only one record in the other table, say table B, and said record in table B can only relate to that particular record of table A.

Outer Join: A join created to include records that failed to meet the requirements set by theta join conditions in a query result.

Parameter Name: A column name or user-defined name for a memory space that contains the value to be entered into the specified table column.

PARAMETERS Declaration: A SQL instruction that is used to automate the manipulation of data in a table, particularly for a DML operation that is performed regularly.

Parent Table: A table with a primary key in which the primary key values are being referenced by the foreign key values of the child table.

Partial Dependency: A problem (anomaly) that exists in a table when a non-key column depends on a portion of the table's primary key.

Glossary of Terms

Pathname: Usually a list that consists of a drive name, the root directory, subdirectories' or folders' names if any, and the name and the extension of the item being sought in a computer system – be it a database or a file.

Physical Design Phase: A process of physically creating a database and its objects, and establishing appropriate tables' relationships and cardinalities on storage media using a particular relational database management system.

Planned Data Redundancy: Controlled or allowed replication or duplication of the same piece of data to uniquely identify records in tables with composite primary keys or to establish referential integrity among tables.

Planning Sheet: A database design tool used mainly to define columns for a table.

Predicate: An optional keyword used as a condition in the SELECT clause of a SELECT statement to restrict the number of records to be displayed.

Primary Key Constraint: A rule used to establish entity integrity and implicitly establishes both the unique constraint and the not null constraint.

Primary Key: A single column or a collection of columns that uniquely identifies each record in a relation. A primary key's job is to distinguish rows in a table by assigning each row its own identity.

Primary Sort Key: A column or a column position that controls the final desired arrangement of the result of a query.

PROCEDURE Clause: *See PARAMETERS Declaration.*

Procedure: A subprogram or a portion of a program that performs a given or specific task.

PRODUCT Statement: A SQL instruction used to display the concatenation of records contained in the tables listed in the SELECT statement of the PRODUCT operation.

Programmer-Defined Function: A block of programming instructions written by a programmer during program development and the code is part of the program.

Programmer-Defined Name: *See User-Defined Name.*

Query: A question posed to a database in a format that the database recognizes and can respond to.

Random Access Memory (RAM): Material primarily used by the computer to keep data and programs while the computer is working. This memory is for a short period of time.

Record: A collection or block of related columns' data that uniquely identifies an entity. Here, an entity can be a person, an event, a location, an activity, or a thing.

RECORDSET Object: An object, in ActiveX Data Objects (ADO) architecture, that is used to establish the result (record set) for a SELECT statement.

Referenced Column: A column in a parent table that is being referred by the foreign key of a child table in a relationship.

Referential Integrity: A database rule that states that when a table's foreign key contains values, those values must match some values in the primary key of the other table in a relationship or the foreign key can be null.

Relation: *See Table.*

Relational Algebra Operator: A keyword command used to create a nonphysical table.

Relational Algebra: A theoretical way of creating nonphysical tables by manipulating the data in physical tables.

Relational Database Design: A process of mentally visualizing, planning, producing the structural layout, and implementing a relational database.

Relational Database Management Systems: A collection of programs or software used in implementing relational database physically on storage media.

Relational Database Model: A popular model used in designing databases and based on the concept that data can be stored in a structure that consist of rows and columns and data can be retrieved quickly.

Relational Database: An integrated structure that contains organized collection of objects (such as tables, views, indexes), the objects' data, the description of the data, the associations among the objects, and the attributes that describe the characteristics of the objects.

Relational Operator: *See Comparison Operator.*

Repeating Groups: A situation in a relational database where several records' entries are entered into a single row of a table.

Revoke: A means of denying users and workgroups access permissions to the objects of a database.

Rollback: A command used to undo the changes and makes the specified columns to keep their previous values intact.

Row: *See Record.*

Saved Query: *See View.*

Second Normal Form (2NF): A normalization process yardstick used to remove partial dependencies from tables.

Secondary Sort Key: A column or a column position that is used to resolve position conflicts when there are records that have identical (match) data in the primary sort.

Security Measure: A way of disallowing a user who has not been given the appropriate permissions to use a database.

Security: An established measure that prevents unauthorized users from accessing data from a database.

SELECT Statement: A statement (query) used mainly to retrieve and display data from tables.

Sequential Output File: A data file where data are entered and retrieved one after the other.

SET Operator: A keyword command used to perform a special type of join operation by combining the results of queries.

Simple Condition: A restriction in the condition clauses of SQL statements that has only three parts.

Simple Retrieval: A process where all the records (rows) stored in a table is displayed.

Simple View: A virtual table created from a single physical table with certain specifications.

Single-Precision Value: A floating-point number with number of decimal places not exceeding seven (7).

Single-Row Function: A block of programming instructions that returns one record for each row processed in a table.

Single-Row Subquery: An inner query used to return a single (one) record that will be used as the input to the outer query when the result of the outer query is based on a single unknown value.

Sort Key: A column name or a column position listed in the ORDER BY clause and used to reorganize the intending result of a query.

Sorting: A process of reorganizing or rearranging displayed data records in a particular order.

SQL Statement: An instruction written in Structured Query Language environment.

Standard Module: A container that contains procedures that are made available to other procedures in an application.

Statement: An instruction that directs the computer to do something.

Statistics Function: *See Multiple-Row Function.*

Storage Media: Devices primarily used to store data and programs outside of the computer for a long period of time.

String Function: A block of programming instructions that is used to manipulate text data.

String Variable: A memory location reserved to store zero, one, or more character symbols.

Structural Independence: A situation where altering data and data types stored in tables might not affect the structures of the tables.

Glossary of Terms

Structured Query Language (SQL): An industry standard query language used to create and modify relational database objects, populate objects with data, update their data, delete data from objects, and remove objects from the database.

Subquery: A SELECT statement embedded within a clause of another SQL statement.

Subtotal: A subset or a portion of a grand total.

Summary Function: *See Multiple-Row Function.*

Surrogate Key: A replacement or substitute column for a primary key when a table is created with columns that lack the properties of being candidate keys.

Syntax: In a computer programming environment, signifies the proper way of writing statements in a programming language or in an application package.

Syntax Error: An error that occurs in a programming statement when the rule (syntax) of the programming language is not obeyed or followed.

Table Alias: A temporary secondary name given to a table and can be used to reference the table in a SELECT statement.

Table: A two-dimensional structure or matrix that is made of rows and columns. Data are arranged horizontally to indicate records and arranged vertically to denote facts about the records.

Table Name: A meaningful label used to identify a table

Table-Level Approach: An approach where columns' constraints are defined at the bottom portion of a CREATE TABLE statement.

Tertiary Sort Key: A column or a column position that is used to resolve position conflicts when there are records that have identical (match) data in the secondary sort.

Theta Join: A join created when standard comparison operators and/or special comparison operators are used in the join condition of the tables that are being joined.

Third Normal Form (3NF): A normalization process yardstick used to remove transitive dependencies from data tables.

Time Data Type: A nonnumeric type used to define a time value for a column.

Time Function: A block of programming instructions used to determine current and future time and how much time has elapsed between time periods.

TOP-N Analysis: The retrieving and displaying of a specific number of data records from a table.

Transaction Control Statement: A DML statement used to populate a table with data, to change data in a table, and to delete data from a table.

Transitive Dependency: A problem (anomaly) that exists in a table when a non-key column that depends on a table's primary key depends also on another non-key column in the same table.

Uncorrelated Subquery: An inner query that is executed first and the result passed to the outer query.

UNION ALL Statement: A SQL instruction used to display, with duplicated records if they exist, the records contained in the tables listed in the SELECT statements of the UNION ALL operation.

UNION Statement: A SQL instruction used to display, without duplicating records, the records contained in the tables listed in the SELECT statements of the UNION operation.

Unique Constraint: A rule used to establish unique (no duplication) integrity that ensures that data entering into a specific or particular column are not duplicated.

Unique Index: An index that is usually created automatically or implicitly for a table by a database management system using columns that are defined with primary key or unique constraints.

UPDATE Statement: A SQL instruction used to modify data records that are contained in a table.

User-Defined Name: A non-keyword text expression or an identifier created by a programmer or a program user in a programming language or in an application package to identify an item.

User-Defined Function: *See Programmer-Defined Function.*

User-Level Security: An established measure used to control how a user accesses and manipulates the objects of a database.

USERS Account Group: A group that accesses a database and the objects of the database according to the access permissions granted by the ADMINS account group.

Variable-Length Column: A field defined to store data with varying length.

VBA: *See Visual Basic for Applications.*

View: A virtual table used to represent how an individual, an organization, or an application sees the data in a database.

Visual Basic for Applications: A special programming language that is incorporated into MS Office Suite.

Wildcard Character: A symbol used to represents characters and works with the LIKE comparison operator to search and display text data.

Workgroup Information File: A special file that has the extension *.mdw* used to record information about users and workgroups and to control their access permissions to a database and the objects of the database.

Workgroup User Account: A group that contains users who are assigned the same permissions to access the objects of a database.

Index

A

ABS Function, 118
Activating MS Access SQL window, 15
Actual argument, 100
ADD clause, 209, 210
ALTER [COLUMN] clause, 210, 231
ALTER TABLE clause, 209, 213
ALTER TABLE statement, 208, 228
Alternate key, 6
Alternative Methods, 74, 79, 80
American National Standards Institute, 15
AND logical operator, 55
ANSI-SQL, 15
Argument-based functions, 128
Arithmetic expression, 35
Arithmetic operator, 36
AS, 34, 71
ASC Function, 115
ASC keyword, 59, 286
Autonumber data type, 201
AVG function, 153

B

BETWEEN...AND comparison operator, 48
Bridge entity, 11
Browse form, 311

C

Calculated field, 35
Candidate key, 6
Cardinality, 12
Carriage return code, 312
Cartesian join, 74
Cartesian product, 74
Case conversion functions, 100
ChangePassword method, 330
Character, 3
Character data type, 201
Character manipulation functions, 103
Check constraint, 222
Child table, 9
CHOOSE Function, 140
CHR Function, 115
Clause, 25
Close # statement, 317
Column alias, 34
Column definition, 198
Column list, 242
Column position, 60
Column qualifier, 70
Column size, 198
Column-level approach, 223
Comma separator, 308

Command-line interface, 15
Comments, 313
COMMIT command, 267
Comparison operator, 46
Complex view, 277
Composite column, 167
Composite primary key, 6
Composite table, 11
Compound condition, 54
Computed field, 35
Concatenation, 38
Conceptual design phase, 4
Condition, 45
Conditional retrieval, 45
Constraint, 198
Container, 339
Correlated subquery, 188
COUNT Function, 154
COUNT(*), 154
CREATE INDEX clause, 285
CREATE INDEX statement, 285, 287
CREATE TABLE clause, 197
CREATE TABLE statement, 197
CreateGroup method, 334
CreateUser method, 331
Cross-tabulation, 165
Curency data type, 201
cursor type, 306

D

Data Control Language, 15
Data Definition Language, 15, 197
Data duplication, 33
Data Manipulation Language, 15, 241
Data suppression, 33
Data type, 198
Data types conversion functions, 136
Data type subtype, 201
Database, 1
Database password, 328
Database permission, 340
Database replication, 328
Database security, 325
Database-level security, 327
date data, 35, 48
Date data type, 201
DATE function, 126, 127
Date interval, 126
DATEADD function, 128
DATEDIFF function, 130
DAY function, 131
DCL, 15
DDL, 15

Index

Security measure, 325
SELECT clause, 25, 27
SELECT operator, 84
SELECT statement, 25, 26
Self Join, 72, 77
Semicolon separator, 308
Sequential output file, 316
SET clause, 251, 254
SET operators, 85
Simple condition, 46
Simple join, 68
Simple retrieval, 30
Simple view, 274
Single tables, 25, 45
Single-precision value, 202
Single-row functions, 100
Single-row operators, 176, 177
Single-row subquery, 176
Sort key, 61, 62
Sorting, 59
SPACE function, 110
SPC function, 309
SQL, 15
SQL statement, 21
Standard comparison operators, 46
Statement, 197
STDEV(STDEVP) function, 157
STR function, 116
STRCOMP function, 108
STRCONV function, 102
STRING function, 109
String variable, 296
STRREVERSE function, 110
Structured Query Language (SQL), 15
Substring, 104
Subtotal, 162, 164
SUM function, 153
Summarizing data, 161, 314
Surrogate key, 8
Syntax, 26
Syntax error, 204

T

TAB function, 309
Table, 2
Table Alias, 71
Table-level approach, 226
Table structure, 197
Tertiary sort key, 62
Text data, 37, 48
Text functions, 100
Theta join, 68
Third normal form (3NF), 7
Time data type, 203
TIME function, 126, 127
TIMER function, 127

TOP clause, 92
TOP-N Analysis, 92
Total, 162
Transaction Control Statement, 267
TRIM function, 111
Truncating table, 213

U

Uncorrelated subquery, 188
UNION ALL operator, 86
UNION ALL statement, 86
UNION operator, 85
UNION statement, 85
Unique constraint, 222
Unique index, 285
UNIQUE keyword, 286
UPDATE statement, 251
Uppercase conversion, 101
User-defined name, 198
User-level security, 330
User account, 331, 332
Using non-existing columns in SET operators, 91

V

VALUES clause, 241, 247
VAR(VARP) function, 158
Variable-length column, 201
VBA, 295, 296
VBA currency format feature, 309
VBA editor, 299
VBA fixed format feature, 309
VBA formatting features, 308
VBA percent format feature, 309
VBA procedure, 302, 303
VBA standard format feature, 309
View, 272
Visual Basic for Applications, 14, 295

W

WEEKDAY function, 132
WEEKDAYNAME function, 133
WHERE clause, 25, 27
WITH optional clause, 287
WITH OWNERACCESS OPTION clause, 25, 27
Workgroup information file, 325
Workgroup account, 334, 335
Write # statement, 317

Y

YEAR function, 131